Information Systems and Outsourcing

Studies in Theory and Practice

Mary C. Lacity
University of Missouri, St. Louis, USA

and

Leslie P. Willcocks
London School of Economics and Political Science, UK

palgrave
macmillan

© Selection and editorial content © Mary Lacity and Leslie Willcocks 2009
Individual Chapters © Contributors 2009

First published 2009 by
PALGRAVE MACMILLAN

Palgrave Macmillan in the UK is an imprint of Macmillan Publishers Limited,
registered in England, company number 785998, of Houndmills, Basingstoke,
Hampshire RG21 6XS.

Palgrave Macmillan in the US is a division of St Martin's Press LLC,
175 Fifth Avenue, New York, NY 10010.

Palgrave Macmillan is the global academic imprint of the above companies
and has companies and representatives throughout the world.

Palgrave® and Macmillan® are registered trademarks in the United States,
the United Kingdom, Europe and other countries.

ISBN-13: 978–0–230–20537–6   hardback
ISBN-10: 0–230–20537–2   hardback

This book is printed on paper suitable for recycling and made from fully
managed and sustained forest sources. Logging, pulping and manufacturing
processes are expected to conform to the environmental regulations of the
country of origin.

A catalogue record for this book is available from the British Library.

Library of Congress Cataloging-in-Publication Data

Information systems and outsourcing : studies in theory and practice /
   [edited by] Mary C. Lacity and Leslie P. Willcocks.
      p. cm.
   Includes bibliographical references and index.
   ISBN 978–0–230–20537–6 (alk. paper)
      1. Electronic data processing departments–Contracting out.
      2. Information technology–Management. 3. Offshore outsourcing.
   I. Willcocks, Leslie. II. Lacity, Mary Cecelia.
      HF5548.2.I4242 2008
      004.068'4–dc22   2008034900

10   9   8   7   6   5   4   3   2   1
18   17   16   15   14   13   12   11   10   09

Printed and bound in Great Britain by
CPI Antony Rowe, Chippenham and Eastbourne

Contents

List of Figures

List of Tables

List of Contributors

Dr. Mary Cecelia Lacity is Professor of Information Systems at the University of Missouri-St. Louis. Her current research focuses on global outsourcing of business and IT services, IT's contribution to business performance, innovation diffusion, and turnover among IT professionals. She has published eight books, most recently *Offshore Outsourcing of IT Work* (Palgrave, 2008; co-author Joe Rottman) and *Global Sourcing of Business and IT Services* (Palgrave, 2006; co-author Leslie Willcocks). Her 40 journal publications have appeared in the *Harvard Business Review, Sloan Management Review, MIS Quarterly, IEEE Computer, Communications of the ACM* and many other academic and practitioner outlets. Her work has been cited more than 3000 times. She is US Editor of the *Journal of Information Technology,* and Co-editor of the Palgrave Series: *Technology, Work and Globalization* and on the Editorial Boards for *MIS Quarterly Executive, Journal of Strategic Information Systems,* and *Strategic Outsourcing.*

Dr. Leslie P. Willcocks is Professor of Technology Work and Globalization at the London School of Economics and Political Science, Head of the Information Systems and Innovation group and Director of The Outsourcing Unit there. He is known for his work on global sourcing, information management, IT evaluation, e-business, organizational transformation as well as for his practitioner contributions to many corporations and government agencies. He holds visiting chairs at Erasmus, Melbourne and Sydney universities and is Associate Fellow at Templeton, University of Oxford. He has been for the last 18 years Editor-in-Chief of the *Journal of Information Technology,* and is joint series editor, with Mary Lacity, of the Palgrave book series *Technology Work and Globalization.* He has co-authored 29 books, including most recently *Major Currents in the IS Field* (Sage, London 2008), and *Global Sourcing of Business and IT Services* (Palgrave, London, 2006) He has published over 180 refereed papers in journals such as *Harvard Business Review, Sloan Management Review, MIS Quarterly, MISQ Executive, Journal of Management Studies, Communications Of The ACM, and Journal of Strategic Information Systems.*

Notes On Co-authors

Dr. Sara Cullen is the Managing Director of The Cullen Group and a Fellow at Melbourne University. She has a leading profile in Asia Pacific having consulted to over 110 private and public sector organizations, spanning 51 countries, in over 130 projects with per annum contract values up to $1.5 billion. Her research in outsourcing has been published in MISQE and the Journal of Strategic Information Systems. Previously she was a national partner at Deloitte (Australia).

David Feeny is Professor of Information Management, and Fellow at Templeton-Green College, University of Oxford. He has published widely on CIO and retained capability, strategy and the management of Information Technology, especially in Harvard Business Review and Sloan Management Review as well as many highly ranked IS journals. His current research interests are in the evaluation of executive education and innovation. Previously he was a senior executive for over 20 years at IBM.

Dr. John Hindle is Head of Global Marketing for Accenture HR services, and a founding member of Knowledge Capital Partners. John has an extensive international business background, with over 30 years experience as a senior executive and adviser to companies in both the USA and Europe. Prior to his business career John was a university teacher, researcher and administrator. He holds an appointment as Adjunct Professor of Human and Organizational Development at Vanderbilt University and publishes widely in trade, popular and academic media. John may be emailed at John.hindle@vanderbilt.edu

Dr. Rudy Hirschheim is the Ourso Family Distinguished Professor of Information Systems at Louisiana State University. He has previously been on the faculties of University of Houston, Templeton College – Oxford, London School of Economics and McMaster University. His PhD is from the University of London. He was awarded an honorary doctorate by the University of Oulu (Finland) and is Fellow of the Association for Information Systems. He is Co-consulting Editor of the Wiley Series in Information Systems. He is Senior Editor of *Journal of the Association for Information Systems*; on the editorial boards of the journals: *Information and Organization; Information Systems Journal; Journal of Strategic Information Systems; Journal of MIS;* and *Journal of Information Technology.*

Dr. Thomas Kern is CIO & Executive Manager of KERN Global Language Services (www.e-kern.com). His areas of expertise are operational management of centralized and decentralized ICT services for more than 40 branches across the world. He has a strong background in ICT outsourcing, application service provision, ICT strategy and relationship management. He received his DPhil in Management Information Systems from Said Business School, University of Oxford. He has published more than 30 articles in Journals and European and International Conferences. He is co-author of two books *The Relationship Advantage: Sourcing, Technologies, and Management*, Oxford University Press 2001 and *Netsourcing: Renting Business Applications and Services over a*

Network, Financial Times, Prentice Hall, USA, 2002. E-mail: thomas.kern @e-kern.com

Dr. Julia Kotlarsky is Associate Professor of Information Systems at Warwick Business School. Her work revolves around managing knowledge, social and technical aspects of globally distributed software development teams, and IT outsourcing. Julia has published her work in a number of books and journals including *Communications of the ACM*, *MISQ Executive*, *Wall Street Journal* and many others. She is the co-founder of the annual Global Sourcing Workshop.

Dr. Ilan Oshri is Associate Professor of Strategy and Technology Management at Rotterdam School of Management erasmus. He is the co-editor of "Knowledge Processes in Globally Distributed Contexts" and "Outsourcing Global Services: Knowledge, Innovation and Social Capital" (Palgrave, 2008). His work has been published in numerous journals including *MISQ Executive*, *Communications of the ACM*, *IEEE Transactions on Engineering Management*, *European Journal of Information Systems*, *the Wall Street Journal* and many others. His main research interest lies in the area of learning, knowledge processes and innovation in global contexts. Ilan is the co-founder of the Global Sourcing Workshop (www.globalsourcing.org.uk).

Dr. Laura Poppo is an Associate Professor at the University of Kansas (lpoppo@ku.edu). She received her Ph.D. from The Wharton School of the University of Pennsylvania. Her research examines current theoretical perspectives in strategic management and sociology, such as transaction cost economics, knowledge-based view, and social institutional perspectives (such as trust, relational governance, managerial networks) with recent interests in emerging economies. Dr. Poppo serves on the editorial boards of *Organization Science, Strategic Management Journal, and International Journal of Strategic Change Management*.

Dr. Peter Reynolds is a Research Fellow in the Department of Information Systems at The University of Melbourne, Australia. He is completing his PhD in strategy and Entrepreneurship at the Australian Graduate School of management in 2008. Prior to this, Peter has spent over 10 years as a member of various CIO management teams for Australia's top-20 companies, including as Head of IT Strategy and then Chief Technology Officer for the Commonwealth Bank of Australia (CBA) from 1998 to 2003. His research is focused on IT-based strategic change and building internal capabilities and skills.

Dr. Joseph Rottman is an Associate Professor of Information Systems at the University of Missouri-St. Louis. He has conducted research and has spoken internationally on global sourcing, innovation diffusion and public sector IT. He has been engaged by Fortune 500 companies to assess their global sourcing strategies as well as public sector organizations seeking strategic leadership. He is author of *Offshore Outsourcing of IT Work* (Palgrave, 2008; co-author Mary Lacity). His journal publications have appeared in the *Sloan Management Review, IEEE Computer, MIS Quarterly Executive, Journal of Information Technology,* and *Information and Management.*

Dr. Peter Seddon is Associate Professor in the Department of Information Systems at the University of Melbourne. His teaching and research focuses on helping people and organizations gain greater benefits from their use of information technologies. His major publications have been in the areas of evaluating information systems success, packaged enterprise application software, IT outsourcing and accounting information systems. He is a Senior Editor of *MIS Quarterly* and is on the editorial board of *Journal of Information Technology.* He may be emailed at p.seddon@unimelb.edu.au

Professional Credits

Over the course of a 20 year publication record on IT outsourcing, the authors comment on which findings remain robust and which findings have significantly changed since initial publications. The authors have thus updated and revised material for this book. The editors and publishers are grateful for permission to reproduce in full or in part versions of our work that was initially published elsewhere.

Chapter 2, 'Transaction Cost Economics Applied to IT Outsourcing: Findings and Critique', by Mary C. Lacity and Leslie P. Willcocks. An initial version of this chapter was published by Elsevier Limited. in the *Accounting, Management and Information Technology*, Vol. 5, 3/4, 1996, 203–244.

Chapter 3, 'The Normative Value of Transaction Cost Economics in IT Outsourcing', by Laura Poppo and Mary C. Lacity. An initial version of this chapter was published by Springer (New York) in *Information Systems Outsourcing: Enduring Themes, New Perspectives, and Global Challenges*, Hirschheim, R., Heinzl, A. and Dibbern, J. (eds), Springer-Verlag, Berlin-Heidelberg-New York, 2006, pp. 259–282.

Chapter 4, 'Domberger's Theory of Contracting Applied to IT Outsourcing', by Peter Seddon, Sara Cullen, and Leslie P. Willcocks. An initial version of this chapter was published by Palgrave Macmillan Ltd. in *European Journal of Information Systems* Vol. 16, 3, 2007, pp. 237–254.

Chapter 5, 'Contracting and Relationship Theories Applied to IT Outsourcing', by Thomas Kern and Leslie P. Willcocks. An initial version of this chapter was published by Palgrave Macmillan Ltd. in *European Journal of Information Systems*, Vol. 11, 1, 2002, pp. 3–19.

Chapter 6, 'Outsourcing Myths and Contracting Realities' by Mary C. Lacity and Rudy Hirschheim. An initial version of this chapter was published by Massachusetts Institute of Technology, in *Sloan Management Review*, Vol. 35, 1, 1993, pp. 72–86.

Chapter 7, 'Making the Outsourcing Decision', by Mary C. Lacity, David Feeny and Leslie P. Willcocks. An initial version of this chapter was published by Massachusetts Institute of Technology in *Sloan Management Review*, Vol. 37, 3, 1996, pp. 13–25.

Chapter 8, 'Taking a Knowledge Perspective on IT and Business Process Outsourcing', by Leslie P. Willcocks, John Hindle, David Feeny, and Mary C. Lacity. An initial version of this chapter was published by Taylor and Francis in *Journal of Information Systems Management*, Vol. 21, 3, 2004, pp. 7–15.

Chapter 10, 'IT Offshore Outsourcing Practices', by Joseph W. Rottman and Mary C. Lacity. An initial version of this chapter was published in *MIS Quarterly Executive*, Vol. 3, 3, pp. 2004, 117–130.

Chapter 14, 'IT Offshore Outsourcing: Supplier Lessons on the Management of Expertise', by Ilan Oshri, Julia Kotlarsky and Leslie Willcocks. An initial version of this chapter was published in *MIS Quarterly Executive*, 2007, Vol. 6, 2, pp. 53–65.

Chapter 15, 'Playing Catch-Up' with Core IS Capabilities: The Secrets of Success', by Leslie Willcocks, Peter Reynolds and David Feeny. An initial version of this chapter was published in *MIS Quarterly Executive*, Vol. 6, 3, 2007, pp. 127–145.

Acknowledgements

First and foremost, we sincerely thank the now over 1,600 executives across the globe who participated in our research over the past 20 years. Without them our work just would not have been possible. Due to the sensitive nature of outsourcing, many participants requested anonymity and cannot be individually acknowledged. Participants who did not request anonymity are acknowledged in the appropriate places throughout this book. We also wish to acknowledge the supportive research environments from our respective institutions. During the 1990s we both found Templeton College, University of Oxford a special place to work and offer grateful thanks to all the staff and colleagues there who made research and study such a pleasure. Leslie is very grateful to all his colleagues at Warwick University and now London School of Economics for their tolerance and support over the years.

Obviously research work of this scope over such a long period is not just a two-person effort. Several colleagues who became friends made significant contributions and published with us in the earlier period, in particular Rudy Hirschheim, Wendy Currie, and Guy Fitzgerald. Latterly we have thoroughly enjoyed researching, digesting and writing with Thomas Kern, Joseph Rottman, Eric van Heck, Sara Cullen, Peter Seddon, Julia Kotlarsky, Ilan Oshri, and John Hindle. They provide intelligence, inspiration and hard work in equal measure and have been a joy to be with. Amongst all these David Feeny stands out as the person we owe most to. His insight and wisdom have been guiding lights.

Mary thanks Vice Chancellor Nasser Arshadi at the University of Missouri-St. Louis because his Office of Research provided or facilitated three research grants to support Mary's work. She also thanks her colleagues at UMSL, including Dean Keith Womer, Dr. Marius Janson, Dr. Kailash Joshi, Dr. Dinesh Mirchandani, Dr. Rajiv Sabherwal, Dr. Vicki Sauter, Dr. Ashok Subramanian, Dr. Joseph Rottman, and Karen Walsh.

Leslie would like to thank his circle of family and friends for their forbearance and humour, and especially Damaris, George, Catherine and Chrisanthi, not least for the getaway nights at the opera. Mary thanks her parents, Dr. and Mrs. Paul Lacity, and her three sisters: Karen Longo, Diane Iudica, and Julie Owings. She thanks her closest friends, Jerry Pancio, Michael McDevitt, Beth Nazemi, Val Graeser, and Katharine Hastings. Finally, her son, Michael Christopher, to whom all things in her life are dedicated.

As a further testimony to the value of global sourcing, we would like to acknowledge the great contribution of our global publishing team and especially Stephen Rutt and Emily Bown at Palgrave and Shirley Tan our copyeditor and coordinator.

Finally this book is dedicated to the memory of Mary's beloved sister Diane, and Leslie's beloved brother Rodger, both died this year. We miss you.

Part I
Introduction

1
Outsourcing Research: Towards More Informed Practice

Mary C. Lacity and Leslie P. Willcocks

Introduction: Developing the research base

This book, with its companion volume *The Practice of Outsourcing: From Information Systems To BPO and Offshoring* (Palgrave, 2009), draws upon rich case and survey research conducted between 1988 and 2008, a period that saw the rise of outsourcing to a global phenomenon. We, along with our co-authors, have examined every aspect of information technology outsourcing and most twists and turns in the market and practice, from both client and supplier perspectives. Academic research methods are extremely well equipped to explore and diagnose contemporary organizations. One fundamental aim we have shared has been to improve practice by disseminating the behaviors, arrangements and lessons that differentiated successful from failed sourcing outcomes. Our research base comprises literally hundreds of organizations from around the world across both private and public sectors. Our initial research projects focused on IT outsourcing. Since 1988, we have interviewed over 1,000 client and supplier stakeholders in over 500 organizations in North America, Europe and Asia Pacific and conducted five large-scale sample surveys. Our primary co-authors have been Sara Cullen, Wendy Currie, David Feeny, Guy Fitzgerald, Eric Van Heck, John Hindle, Rudy Hirschheim, Thomas Kern, Julia Kotlarsky, Ilan Oshri, Peter Reynolds, Joseph Rottman and Peter Seddon.

The first research base we draw upon for this book consists of 112 sourcing case histories (mainly in the area of IT) studied longitudinally from 1990 to 2001. These are described in Lacity, M. and Willcocks, L. (2001) *Global IT Outsourcing: In Search Of Business Advantage* (Wiley), but the cases are being continually updated through further research. The second is a study of relationships through seven case histories. This appears in Kern, T. and Willcocks, L. (2001) *The Relationship Advantage* (OUP, Oxford). The third is a 2000–5 longitudinal study of business process outsourcing practices, with a particular focus on four cases in aerospace and insurance. In 2000, Lacity, Feeny and Willcocks began to study business process outsourcing based on 70 interviews. We studied companies that outsourced business processes from human resources, policy administration, claims settlement and indirect procurement (see Lacity *et al.*, 2003; Feeny *et al.*, 2005; Willcocks, L. and Lacity, M., 2006). We also draw upon a fourth research stream consisting of ten cases of application service provision, published in Kern, T., Lacity, M. and Willcocks, L. (2002). *Netsourcing* (Prentice Hall, New York). A fifth research stream analyzed vendor capabilities and is represented in Feeny, D., Lacity, M. and Willcocks, L. (2005) "Taking the Measure of Outsourcing Providers", *Sloan Management Review 46, 3*. We also draw upon five outsourcing surveys carried out in USA, Europe and Australasia in 1993, 1997, 2000, 2001 and 2002 covering multiple sectors and over 900 organizations. A further research stream, by Sara Cullen, assessed 100 ITO/BPO initiatives of a variety of business functions during the decade from 1994 to 2003 to determine what worked and what did not work, what drove the various degrees of success and failure and the emerging lessons. The research is represented in Cullen, S. and Willcocks, L. (2004) *Intelligent IT Outsourcing* (Butterworth) and Cullen, S., Seddon, P. and Willcocks, L. (2005). "Managing Outsourcing: The Lifecycle Imperative", *MISQ Executive, 4, 1*.

In 2003, we began studying offshore outsourcing, primarily to Asian suppliers. Rottman and Lacity interviewed 238 people, including 53 supplier employees in India and 34 in China (Lacity and Rottman, 2008). Ilan Oshri, Julia Kotlarsky and Leslie Willcocks also began a large research project on offshore outsourcing. They interviewed some 110 executives in Mumbai, Gurgaon, Bangalore, Amsterdam, San Paulo, Zurich and Luxemburg. This work was extended to include knowledge, social capital and innovation issues related to global outsourcing (Oshri *et al.*, 2007a, b; 2008).

Combined, this work forms a 500 plus case research base held by the researchers at the London School of Economics Outsourcing Unit and the Universities of Melbourne and Missouri, St Louis Information Systems departments. (Including survey work the research base, by 2008 represented data from 1,400 plus organizations.) The research base covers all major economic and government sectors, including financial services, energy and utilities, defence/aerospace, retail, telecoms and IT, oil, transportation, central, state and local government, health care, industrial products and chemicals and is drawn from medium, large and multinational organizations based in Europe, USA and Asia Pacific. Most importantly, we have been able to track many of our cases over the life of their outsourcing contracts and indeed into their second and third generation, thus providing us with unique insights into clients' and suppliers' *a prior* expectations juxtaposed to actual outcomes.

We have utilized this combined, highly rich research output in many ways. One has to disseminate the results academically. As at 2008, we had between us co-authored over 14 books and 150 refereed journal and conference papers on the subject of outsourcing. There have also been numerous publications in practitioner journals, as newspaper articles and for trade magazines. These outputs express our desire not just to explore and understand outsourcing and its dynamics globally, but also to try to distill key issues and progress how sourcing practices can be improved. This has come together in the considerable number of client advisory engagements and keynote presentations we have carried out from the beginning of the 1990s through to the present day. Most recently these multiple objectives have come together in the founding of the Outsourcing Unit at the London School of Economics. The Outsourcing Unit represents a global network dedicated to research and its dissemination, education on sourcing and improvement of practice.

In this Introduction we bring together our thoughts on the theory and practice of outsourcing. Then, in the rest of the book, we provide detailed studies of applicable theory (Part II) followed by more practitioner-oriented chapters (Part III) that provide lessons gleaned from studying outsourcing in all its variants over the last 20 years. But first let us review the relevance of theory to the study and practice of outsourcing.

The relevance of theory

In 1945, Kurt Lewin – a father of modern social psychology – wrote, "nothing is so practical as a good theory." We further believe that the dual roles of theorist and practitioner are elemental to human nature. Any agent (whether she is manager or academic) is a *theorist* when creating abstractions and postulating relationships among the abstractions to make sense of reality. Searle (1997) calls this "world-to-mind" direction of fit. Any agent is a *practitioner* when applying abstractions to solve a problem, make a decision, or engage in any reasoned action. Searle calls this "mind-to-world" direction of fit. Thus, we all find ourselves theorists *and* practitioners.

Good theories shape practice and effective practices inform theory. In the context of IT outsourcing, there is no shortage of theory. Nearly 20 years of empirical work on IT outsourcing (ITO) has been guided by a number of theoretical perspectives from economics, strategy, sociology and systems science (see Table 1.1). Theories from economics include Transaction Cost Economics, Agency Theory and various theories on contracting. The main assumption across economic theories is that agents base outsourcing decisions and engage in contracts to minimize total costs and to mitigate risks, such as the risk that an agent or supplier will behave opportunistically. Theories from strategy include the Resource-Based View, Resource Dependency Theory, Game Theory, Auction Theory and various theories of firm strategy. The main assumption across strategic theories is that agents build or acquire resources to execute strategies that lead to "winning". Theories from sociology include Social/Relational Exchange Theory, Social Capital

Table 1.1 ITO Theories

Category	Theory	Foundational Reading	Brief Summary	IT Outsourcing Readings
Economic	Transaction Cost Theory	Coase (1937) Williamson (1975, 1979, 1981, 1985, 1991)	TCT generally addresses the question: why do firms exist? TCT specifically addresses the question: should companies make or buy resources? Make-or-buy decisions are presumed to be made on an economic basis, considering production and transaction costs. Agents match the attributes of the transaction (asset specificity, uncertainty, measurement, and frequency) to the most efficient governance form (market, hybrid, or hierarchy). The attributes indicate the extent to which opportunities exist for agents to behave opportunistically, which increases transaction costs due to increased needs for detailed contracts and monitoring.	Ang and Straub (1998) Aubert et al. (1996) Bahli and Rivard (2003) Barthélemy and Geyer (2005) Dibbern and Heinzl (2002) Grover et al. (1996) Heiskanen et al. (1996) Kishore et al. (2004) Knolmayer (2002) Lacity and Willcocks (1995) Lacity and Willcocks (1998) Loebbecke and Huyskens (2006) Loh and Venkatraman (1995) Miranda and Kim (2006) Nam et al. (1996) Ngwenyama and Bryson (1999) Oh et al. (2006) Poppo and Lacity (2002) Poppo and Zenger (1998) Qu and Brocklehurst (2003) Shelanski (1991) Tanriverdi et al. (2007) Tsang (2000) Walden (2005)

Table 1.1 ITO Theories – *continued*

Category	Theory	Foundational Reading	Brief Summary	IT Outsourcing Readings
	Agency Theory	Eisenhardt (1985, 1989) Sharma (1997)	AT purports that principal-agent relationships characterized by different goals and risk preferences – should be efficiently managed, particularly with appropriate contracts. Behavior-based contracts (such as time and materials) is appropriate when outcome uncertainty is high, the agent's risk aversion is high, outcomes are not easily measured. Outcome-based contracts (such as fixed price) are appropriate when the principal's risk aversion is high, outcomes are measurable, and tasks are programmable.	Bahli and Rivard (2003) Chalos and Sung (1998) Choudhury and Sabherwal (2003) Hall and Liedtka (2005) Hancox and Hackney (1999) Iyer et al. (2005)* Logan (2000)* Nelson et al. (1996) Oh et al. (2006)
	Contracting Theories	Domberger (1998) MacNeil (1980)	Several theories address contracting. Domberger basically argues that outsourcing is a sound decision if the net cost to the outsourcer drops as a result of outsourcing, provided there is no drop in service quality.	Gopal et al. (2003) Seddon et al. (2007)
Strategic	Resource-Based View	Barney (1991, 1999)	RBV purports that competitive advantage of a firm arises from developing and deploying unique, valuable, and costly-to-copy capabilities. RBV implies that companies should retain core capabilities, but that non-core capabilities do not have to be owned or controlled. Recent thinking focuses on complementary resources.	Alvarez-Suescun (2007) Barthélemy and Geyer (2004) Duncan (1998) Levina and Ross (2003) Roy and Aubert (2002) Straub et al. (2002) Tsang (2000) Wade and Hulland (2004)*

Table 1.1 ITO Theories – *continued*

Category	Theory	Foundational Reading	Brief Summary	IT Outsourcing Readings
	Resource Dependency Theory	Pfeffer and Salancik (1978) Pfeffer (1981, 1994)	RDT argues that an organization's dependence on external resources (outsourcing) is determined by the importance of the resource to the organization, the number of potential suppliers, and the cost of switching suppliers. Organizations try to minimize dependence when possible.	Grover *et al.* (1996) Grover *et al.* (1997) Oh *et al.* (2006) Teng *et al.* (1995)
	Firm Strategy	Chandler (1962) Miles and Snow (1978) Porter (1980, 1985) Prahalad and Hamel (1990)	Firms enact strategies to achieve a competitive advantage. Porter views that a firm's competitive advantage is either low cost producer (more efficient than rivals) or differentiator (firm differentiates itself from rivals). Miles and Snow proposed that organizations may be prospectors (seeking to innovate), defenders (seeking stability), analyzers (seeking stability in operations but innovation at the margins), or reactors (reacting to the environment). Prahalad and Hamel argue that the best strategy is to focus on core capabilities and outsource the rest.	Apte and Mason (1995) Bardhan *et al.* (2006) DiRomualdo and Gurbaxani (1998) Grover *et al.* (1994) Hall and Liedtka (2005) Loebbecke and Huyskens (2006) McLellan *et al.* (1995) Michell and Fitzgerald (1997) Slaughter and Ang (1996)

Table 1.1 ITO Theories – *continued*

Category	Theory	Foundational Reading	Brief Summary	IT Outsourcing Readings
	Game Theory/ Auction Theory	Nash (1951, 1953) Milgrom and Weber (1982)	Game Theory posits that an agent considers other agents' strategies before choosing a strategy to maximize his/her own return. Auction theory is a subset of game theory that examines how agents act in auction markets. These theories are applied to customer-supplier bidding and negotiations.	Bhargava and Sundaresan (2004) Chaudhury *et al.* (1995) Elitzur and Wensley (1997) Kern *et al.* (2002) Klotz and Chatterjee (1995) Wang *et al.* (1997) Whang (1992)
Social	Social/Relational Exchange Theory	Blau (1964) Ekeh (1974) Emerson (1972) Homans (1961, 1974) Rousseau (1995)	Relationships between customers and suppliers are based on trust developed over time (partnership advantage). Rousseau views a contract as mental beliefs and expectations parties have about their mutual obligations based on perceived promises of a reciprocal exchange.	Adler (2003/2004) Ang and Slaughter (2001) Goles (2001) Goles and Chin (2002) Grover *et al.* (1996) Klepper (1995) Koh *et al.* (2004) Lee and Kim (1999) Oza *et al.* (2006) Sabherwal (1999)
	Social Capital Theory	Nahapiet, J. and Ghosal (1998)	In general, the theory posits that social capital facilitates the exchange and recombination of existing intellectual capital to form new intellectual capital, and that an organization has an advantage over markets in this regard.	Chou *et al.* (2006) George (2006) Miranda and Kavan (2005)

Table 1.1 ITO Theories – *continued*

Category	Theory	Foundational Reading	Brief Summary	IT Outsourcing Readings
	Institutionalism	DiMaggio and Powell (1991)	The subset of this theory, institutional isomorphism studies how organizations eventually adopt similar practices through three mechanisms of influence: force, mimicking, and norms.	Ang and Cummings (1997) Barthélemy and Geyer (2004) Jayatilaka (2001) Jayatilaka (2002) Miranda and Kim (2006)
	Power Theories	Pfeffer (1981, 1994)	Organizational decision-making processes are characterized by the power and political tactics of stakeholders involved. Political tactics include the selective use of decision criteria, selective use of information, use of outside experts, building coalitions, and cooptation (swaying opposition by making them participants), framing, using interpersonal Influence, and timing. Sources of power include position of authority, ability to acquire or control resources that others value but few possess, location in the communication network, being in the right sub-unit, the ability to absorb uncertainty and personal characteristics.	Allen *et al.* (2002) Dibbern and Heinzl (2002) Lacity and Hirschheim (1993) Lee and Kim (1999) Peled (2001)

Table 1.1 ITO Theories – *continued*

Category	Theory	Foundational Reading	Brief Summary	IT Outsourcing Readings
	Innovation Diffusion	Rogers (1983)	ID posits that the rate at which *individuals* adopt innovations depends on attributes of the innovation, communication channels, and social norms. The rate at which *organizations* adopt innovations depends on leadership, characterization of the organization and system openness.	Hu *et al.* (1997) Loh and Venkatraman (1992b)
	Social Cognition	Fiske and Taylor (1991)	Social cognition theory studies how ordinary people think about other people (phenomenology) and how people think they think about people (naïve scientists)	Ho *et al.* (2003)
Systems Theories	General Systems Theory	von Bertalanffy (1968)	Many behavioral researchers believe social systems are like living organisms in the sense that both display wholeness, interact with their environment, exhibit strategies of self-maintenance, and experience cycles of birth, growth, maturity and death.	Marcolin and Ross (2005)

Table 1.1 ITO Theories – *continued*

Category	Theory	Foundational Reading	Brief Summary	IT Outsourcing Readings
	Systems Dynamics	Forrester (1996) Richardson (1996)	SD models are mathematical representations of the causal structure of systems. SD assumes that structure causes behavior	Dutta and Roy (2005)
	Modular Systems Theory	Sanchez and Mahoney (1996)	The extent to which a business process is loosely coupled, mature, and standardized enough to be separated from a firm's other business processes for outsourcing.	Tanriverdi *et al.* (2007)
Miscellaneous		Global Disaggregation		Apte and Mason (1995)
		Residual Rights Theory		Lee *et al.* (2004)

Theory, Institutionalism, Power Theories, Innovation Diffusion and Social Cognition. A common focus among these theories is the *relationships* among agents, including levels of trust and power, feelings of mutual obligation and social norms. Systems sciences view organizations as organisms that exchange resources across organizational boundaries and learn through feedback. When applied to IT outsourcing, systems approaches are used for modeling outsourcing and examining systems properties that facilitate outsourcing.

Why do ITO researchers use so many theories? One possible reason is that we examine so many different aspects of IT outsourcing. Researchers often use Transaction Cost Theory and Agency Theory to explore questions such as "What are the determinants of IT outsourcing?" "How do organizations govern transactions to minimize total costs?" and "How do organizations prevent agents from behaving opportunistically?" Researchers use game theory to answer, "How do buyers and suppliers behave during bidding and contract negotiations?" Researchers use Innovation Diffusion Theory to answer the question, "What determines the rate of adoption of IT outsourcing in a population of organizations?" Thus, theoretical eclecticism may be a consequence of the richness of the ITO research area. This reasoning celebrates the diversity in ITO research and considers it a healthy sign of progress (Benbasat and Weber, 1996).

Another possible reason for the adoption of so many theories is that ITO research is still in a pre-paradigm phase, characterized by competition between many distinct views. During this phase of scientific development, researchers do not take a common body of belief for granted. Each researcher builds his or her field anew from its foundations and the same phenomena are interpreted different ways (Kuhn, 1970). This reasoning views the diversity in ITO research as dangerous and unstable. Disciplines risk evaporation if a dominant paradigm does not create stability and identity (Benbasat and Weber, 1996).

According to Kuhn, a discipline becomes healthy and stable when a dominant paradigm emerges because it provides the best predictions. Several reviews of the literature have attempted to identify the emerging paradigm in ITO research (Dibbern *et al.*, 2004; Hui and Beath, 2001; Kakabadse and Kakabadse, 2000; Klein, 2002). A very broad review of the outsourcing literature that encompassed not only IT but other outsourcing domains concluded that the dominant paradigm emerging was not from economic theories but from relationship theories comparable with the Japanese keiretsu relationship model (Kakabadse and Kakabadse, 2000). In a review of only ITO research, however, Klein (2002) concluded that his most "*striking finding is the dominant influence of transaction cost theory*" (p. 26). Five years later, our Table 1.1 hints to a similar conclusion because Transaction Cost Economics (TCE) has the most empirical ITO applications. However, a review of the actual findings from these TCE applications produces mixed results across different studies (Miranda and Kim, 2006). Most interestingly, mixed results occurred *within* studies in that certain TCE propositions were supported and others were not. For example Ang and Cummings (1997) found support for asset specificity as a determinant of outsourcing in the context of large banks but not small banks. In another ITO review that examined TCE, the Resource-Based View and the relationship literature, the authors also found mixed results (Marcolin and Ross, 2005). Thus, rather than finding consistent predictions from this plethora of theories, we are finding apparent theoretical confusion. Or are we?

Marcolin and Ross (2005) argue that the mixed results from so many ITO empirical studies are due to equifinality. Equifinality is a property of systems in which the same final state may be reached from different initial conditions (von Bertalanffy, 1968). Thus, ITO researchers may observe several legitimate routes to IT outsourcing success (or failure). This conclusion is appealing because it resonates with what we witness in practice. Some organizations outsource the same transactions (data centers, applications development, systems maintenance) but experience very different results.

Besides equifinality, another way to reconcile the theoretical confusion is that one theory alone is not powerful enough to capture all the relevant constructs in IT outsourcing. To address the limitation of one theoretical perspective, many ITO researchers adopt multiple theoretical perspectives (Cheon *et al.*, 1995; Teng *et al.*, 1995; Ang and Cummings, 1997; Gallivan and Oh, 1999; Lacity and Hirschheim, 1993). A review of 84 publications studied by Dibbern *et al.* (2004), found that 18 articles adopted more than one theory, 13 of which included Transaction Cost Economics supplemented by one of the other theories from Table 1. When adopting multiple theories, some authors view the theories as *complementary*, offering different insights into the IT outsourcing phenomenon (Cheon *et al.*, 1995). Grover *et al.* (1995) developed a model of IT outsourcing based on constructs from Transaction Cost Economics, Agency Theory, Resource-Based View and Resource Dependence Theory. They conclude, "*While studies based on one theoretical perspective have been reported, opportunities exist to study the phenomenon in a more integrative manner, thereby facilitating a robust understanding*" (p. 98). Other researchers view the theories as *competing and* assess which theory best explained observed phenomena. Klein (2002) argues, "*researchers should adopt the habit of analyzing their data from at least two conflicting value perspectives*" (p. 31). The theory that generates the most intelligible insights and is most believable is the better theory.

More importantly than which theories to adopt or how many theories to adopt, IT researchers need to critically examine theories developed in other disciplines before importing them and applying them to IT contexts. Our own view of TCE in Chapter 2 is that a significant number of residuals (experiences not explained by TCE) and anomalies (experiences that contradict TCE) challenge the applicability of TCE to the IT outsourcing context. We found that residuals and anomalies existed because the nature of IT outsourcing decisions tend to violate many TCE assumptions. We noted, however, that TCE proponents could explain the residuals and anomalies by appealing to TCE exceptions, such as uncertainty and small number of suppliers, or to ambiguities in TCE language. We also noted what Hodgson (1994) described as the "regrettable malleability" of TCE constructs. TCE seemed cast as a high level general theory, its uncalibrated constructs permitting empirical data to be fitted to support the theory all too easily. This becomes especially problematic where, as in several IT outsourcing studies we have reviewed, TCE is assumed to be a fully explanatory theory and few tests of its predictiveness in terms of outsourcing success or failure are carried out. This finding also raised the question, not pursued in detail here, whether other non-IT focused empirical studies actually corroborate Transaction Cost Economics, as Williamson suggests, or also raise more questions than they answer. In fact reviews of the limited number of empirical studies are hardly decisive (Hodgson, 1994; Joskow, 1991; Shelanski and Klein, 1995) and suggest that at the very least alternative explanatory hypotheses should be considered.

In Chapter 3, Poppo and Lacity propose that the real value of Transaction Cost Theory may be *normative* rather than *description*. We note however, that other researchers have argued that TCE is bad for practice. Ghoshal and Morgan (1996), for example, theoretically argue that hierarchical controls create negative feelings for employees which increases the propensity to behave opportunistically – the exact behavior managers are hoping to avoid! Poppo and Lacity disagree. By examining two significant data sets, they found that managers who followed TCE tenants had better success with their sourcing decisions. The authors conclude that TCE logic is not intuitive to managers, but that managers may learn and apply TCE prescriptions over time. The evidence clearly suggests that managers learned from their mistakes in the 1980s and early 1990s and subsequently crafted more effective ITO contracts by the mid-1990s. Specifically, managers realized higher performance when they applied the TCE principles (1) to not outsource the most specialized activities and (2) to measure and benchmark outsourcing activities. However, the authors also found that managers realized higher performance when they complemented their use of customized contracts with supportive relational norms. This supports the view that multiple theoretical perspectives are complementary and are needed to capture the rich terrain of ITO.

In Chapter 4, Seddon, Cullen and Willcocks examine another economic theory of outsourcing determinants, Domberger's theory of the *Contracting Organization* (1998). Domberger explores the fundamental economic drivers and benefits of outsourcing. Domberger shows how specialization leads to outsourcing benefits (for both the outsourcing vendor and customer), how market discipline (competition) motivates vendors to share their benefits with their customers and how outsourcing can provide benefits to customers through flexibility and cost savings. Domberger's theories have been developed and tested in non-IT contexts (Domberger *et al.*, 1987, 1986, 1994, 2000). The main question Seddon, Cullen and Willcocks ask is whether Domberger's theory is applicable to the context of IT outsourcing. Based on a survey of 235 Australian senior IT leaders, the authors found strong support that Domberger's two constructs (*specialization* and *market discipline*) explained senior IT managers' satisfaction with IT outsourcing. Surprisingly, two constructs (*flexibility* and *cost savings*) did not. Most interesting, the authors found that cost savings were not the only benefits that a client firm derived from outsourcing. Non-monetary benefits such as opportunity costs avoided, growth opportunities, concentrating on its own core capabilities and flexibility options need to be factored into the overall cost-benefit equation.

In Chapter 5, Kern and Willcocks move beyond economic-only explanations of IT outsourcing by focusing on ITO relationships. The authors synthesize the major social and contracting theories used in outsourcing and created a new conceptual framework of ITO relationships. The framework is powerful because it includes both the client and supplier perspectives and identifies eight ways clients and suppliers interact. These eight ways include exchanges of products/services, finances, information, culture, resources, bonds, knowledge and vision. The framework is richly assessed based on in-depth case studies of client-supplier relationships. This work also shows the immense insights that multiple theoretical perspectives provide when combined in a coherent framework.

We therefore conclude that multiple theoretical perspectives are indeed good for practice, provided that theoretical assumptions are examined and empirically assessed in the ITO context.

Practice: Still on the learning curve

Information technology outsourcing (ITO) research has meaningfully and significantly addressed the call for academics to produce knowledge relevant to practitioners (Lee, 1999; Westfall, 1999). The ITO academic literature written for practitioners is widely cited and indicates that academics have clearly served to disseminate learning to practicing managers. In addition, thoughtful practitioners have published their IT outsourcing experiences in academic outlets (Cross, 1995; Huber, 1993), further fueling the ability of academics to abstract lessons from practice.

ITO research aimed at practitioners has examined all aspects of the phenomena from reasons why organizations outsourcing through to the long-term consequences of outsourcing from both client and supplier perspectives (see Table 1.2). Some authors enthusiastically portray outsourcing as a powerful practice for innovation and transformation (Linder, 2004;

Table 1.2   Academic Research for Practitioners

General Topic	Specific Topic	Noted Publications	
Outsourcing Intent	ITO expectations	DiRomualdo and Gurbaxani (1998) Lacity *et al.* (1994)	McLellan *et al.* (1995) Seddon *et al.* (2007)
	Innovation	Quinn (2000)*	
	Transformation	Lacity *et al.* (2003) Lacity *et al.* (2004)	Linder (2004) Willcocks and Lacity (2006)
Outsourcing Decisions	Case Studies	Applegate and Montealegre (1991): Eastman Kodak Cross (1995): BP Exploration Huber (1993): Continental Bank Lacity and Willcocks (2001): DuPont, Government of South Australia, Inland Revenue, British Aerospace	
	Outsourcing Decisions and Decision-making Frameworks	Arnett and Jones (1994) Clark *et al.* (1995) Cronk and Sharp (1995) Cullen *et al.* (2005) De Looff (1995) Fjermestad and Saitta (2005)	Insinga and Werle (2000)* Lacity *et al.* (1995) Lacity *et al.* (1996) Ross and Beath (2006) Sobol and Apte (1995)
	ITO Risks and Risk Mitigation	Aron *et al.* (2005) Aubert *et al.* (1998) Aubert *et al.* (1999) Currie (1998) Currie and Willcocks (1998)	Jurison (1995) King and Malhotra (2000) Sakthivel (2007) Vestring *et al.* (2005) Weinstein (2004)
	Strategic Outsourcing and Partnerships	DiRomualdo and Gurbaxani (1998) Gottfredson *et al.* (2005)* Gurbaxani (1996)	McFarlan and Nolan (1995) Quinn (1999)* Quinn and Hilmer (1994)* Rossetti and Choi (2005)

Table 1.2   **Academic Research for Practitioners** – *continued*

General Topic	Specific Topic	Noted Publications	
	Stock Market Reaction to ITO Decisions	Farag and Krishnan (2003) Hayes *et al.* (2000) Loh and Venkatraman (1992a)	Oh *et al.* (2006) Madison *et al.* (2006) Smith *et al.* (1998)
Engaging Suppliers	Costs	Barthélemy (2001)	
	Relationship Management	Kern *et al.* (2002) Kern and Willcocks (2001)	Kishore *et al.* (2003) Klepper (1995)
	Contracting	Lacity and Hirschheim (1993) Lichtenstein (2004)	Saunders *et al.* (1997)
Capabilities	Client Capabilities	Barney (1999)* Feeny and Willcocks (1998) Ranganathan and Balaji (2007)	Useem and Harder (2000)* Willcocks *et al.* (2007)
	Supplier Capabilities	Adler *et al.* (2005) Carmel (2006)	Feeny *et al.* (2005)
	Process Capabilities	Adler *et al.* (2005) Davenport (2005)	Harter *et al.* (2000) Jalote (2000)
Sourcing Models	Public Sector Outsourcing	Allen *et al.* (2002) Currie (1996)	Lacity and Willcocks (1997) Willcocks and Kern (1998)
	Application Service Provision	Bennett and Timbrell (2000) Dewire (2000)	Kern *et al.* (2002a, b) Susarla *et al.* (2003)
	Insourcing	Lacity and Hirschheim (1995) Hirschheim, R. (1998)	Hirschheim and Lacity (2000)

Table 1.2   Academic Research for Practitioners – *continued*

General Topic	Specific Topic	Noted Publications	
Offshore Outsourcing	Macroeconomic Effects	Harrison and McMillan (2006)* King (2004)	Matloff (2004) Pfannenstein and Tsai (2004)
	Client and Supplier Perspectives	Aron and Singh (2005), Carmel and Agarwal (2002) Carmel and Abbott (2007) Carmel and Tjia (2005) Farrell, D. (2006)* Kaiser and Hawk (2004) Krishna *et al.* (2004) Lacity and Rottman (2008) Levina and Vaast (2008)	Oshri *et al.* (2007a, 2007b) Ramingwong and Sajeev (2007) Rottman (2006) Rottman and Lacity (2004) Rottman and Lacity (2006) Shao and Smith David (2007) Venkatraman (2004) Wagner (2006) *
	County Comparisons and Capabilities	Apte (1997): US, Japan, Finland Barthélemy and Geyer (2001): France, Germany Barthélemy and Geyer (2004): France, Germany Bruno *et al.* (2004): North Africa Ein-Dor (2004): Eastern Europe Nair and Prasad (2004): India Qu and Brocklehurst (2003): China Zatolyuk and Allgood (2004): Ukraine	

* indicates that paper is not specific to IT outsourcing

Quinn, 2000). Some authors caution practitioners about the enormous risks and negative consequences of outsourcing. Notable titles include "The Outsourcing Compulsion" (Thomas and Wilkinson, 2006), "When Outsourcing Goes Awry" (Peisch, 1995), "Outsourced and Out of Control" (Weinstein, 2004), "The Outsourcing Bogeyman," (Drezner, 2004) and "On the Dark Side of Strategic Sourcing" (Rossetti and Choi, 2005).

Most authors, however, assume the perspective that clients and suppliers can both benefit from outsourcing, provided both sides properly manage the engagement. Prescriptions for ensuring success resolve around client and supplier capabilities, decision-making frameworks, sourcing models, risk mitigation, contract negotiations and post contract management. Academics have also studied how the stock market reacts to outsourcing announcements. Only one study found a significant 1% increase in stock price (Loh and Venkatraman, 1992a).

A brief history of academic research for practitioners

The first published outputs from academic research appeared in 1991, which documented companies pursuing large-scale *domestic* IT outsourcing (Applegate and Montealegre, 1991; Huber, 1993). More quantitative research and multiple-case studies followed, focusing on why firms outsource (Loh and Venkatraman, 1992b) and how firms benefit (or do not benefit) from IT outsourcing (Lacity and Hirschheim, 1993; Whang, 1992). Between 1994 and 2000, at least 79 other academic studies were published (Dibbern *et al.*, 2004), many geared towards practice.

The 17 years of research on domestic IT outsourcing has generated a good understanding of the practice. Overall, we learned *why* firms outsource (mostly to reduce costs, access resources, focus internal resources on more strategic work[1]), *what* firms outsource (mostly a portion of their overall IT portfolio), *how* firms outsource (mostly by formal processes) and IT outsourcing *outcomes* as measured by realization of expectations, satisfaction and performance (Dibbern *et al.*, 2004). Overall, we know that client readiness, good strategy, good processes, sound contracts and good relationship management are key success factors (Cullen *et al.*, 2005; Feeny and Willcocks, 1998; Teng *et al.*, 1995; Willcocks and Lacity, 2006).

Recently, much of the academic researcher has focused on *offshore* outsourcing. Offshore outsourcing research addresses macroeconomic issues, supplier capabilities in developing countries and specific client and supplier practices to ensure success. From the client perspective, researchers have found that offshore IT outsourcing poses additional challenges when compared to domestic IT outsourcing (Rottman and Lacity, 2006). For example, offshore outsourcing is more challenging because of time zone differences (Carmel, 2006), increased efforts in knowledge coordination (Kanawattanachai and Yoo, 2007) and boundary spanning (Levina and Vaast, 2008), the need for more controls (Choudhury and Sabherwal, 2003), cultural differences (Carmel and Agarwal, 2002; Carmel and Tjia, 2005; Krishna *et al.*, 2004), defining requirements more rigorously (Gopal *et al.*, 2003) and difficulties in managing dispersed teams (O'Leary and Cummings, 2007; Oshri *et al.*, 2007). Some of these issues are so difficult to manage that practitioners are turning to nearshore alternatives (Carmel and Abbott, 2007a).

Our articles for practitioners

For this volume, we include and update some of our best work written for practitioners. Chapter 6 addresses "Outsourcing Myths and Contracting Realities". This chapter is based on one of the first articles we published for practitioners (Lacity and Hirschheim, 1993). At that time, very little research had been conducted on what actually happens in client organizations when they outsourced IT. Based on 14 case studies in US organizations, the article examined three myths about outsourcing and proposed that clients need to sign much better contracts. Since its initial publication, clients and suppliers have indeed become much better at contracting. Defining services, setting prices and creating a flexible framework to adapt to business and technical changes are now norms in ITO contracts. Our research focus soon evolved from contractual issues to decision strategy and relationship management.

In Chapter 7, we present our ITO decision framework which guides practitioners to consider business, economic and technical factors. Originally published nearly 12 years ago, this framework is still remarkably relevant (Lacity, Willcocks and Feeny, 1996). When discussing business factors, we dismiss the traditional "core versus non-core" criterion because we found it was difficult for practitioners to differentiate IT activities on this basis. Instead, we guide practitioners to consider an IT activity's contribution to competitive advantage as well as to its critical support of daily business operations. In the discussion of economic factors, we challenge practitioners to examine the *practices* that lead to economic efficiency rather than just economies of scale. Surely, suppliers operate on a larger scale than internal IT departments, but economic efficiency depends more on practices such as standardization, centralization and tight controls than *size*. In the discussion of technical issues, we discuss a technology's maturity (stability, measurability and requirements certainty) and technology's integration with other business functions as the most important technical criteria to consider. This framework continues to be used by practitioners and is still widely cited by academics (225 citations as of 2007).

In Chapters 8 and 9, we present our research that addresses the specific issue of what happens to knowledge in the context of outsourcing. How is knowledge transferred to/from suppliers? How are knowledge investments protected and renewed? Chapter 8 is titled "Taking A Knowledge Perspective On IT and Business Process Outsourcing" and grew out of Willcocks, Hindle, Feeny and Lacity (2004). The chapter looks at the role social capital plays in knowledge exchange. Social capital is simply the idea that knowledge and resources are exchanged, work gets done and value is created through social relationships. The chapter compares how five approaches to back office transformation (do it yourself, hire consultants, outsource IT operations, outsource IT and the business process and create an enterprise partnership) help or hinder three aspects of social capital and knowledge exchange:

- Laying the foundation for trust (called the relational dimension of social capital)
- Creating shared language, codes and systems of meaning among parties (called the cognitive dimension of social capital)
- Designing social linkages among people (called the structural dimension of social capital)

In Chapter 9, Rottman and Lacity discuss five practices to transfer and protect knowledge investments in the context of offshore outsourcing of IT work. The practices were used by a US Manufacturing Company. This company had the best outcomes from offshore outsourcing in terms of innovation, cost and speed among 25 US client firms studied. One of their most interesting practices was to divide their intellectual property across three Indian suppliers. This company views their IP as a large puzzle in which no one supplier can re-assemble the entire IT puzzle from their individual pieces.

In Chapter 10, Rottman and Lacity discuss 20 practices that were learned across all the US clients studied. Based on Rottman and Lacity (2004), the chapter compares domestic and offshore outsourcing practices. Five practices apply equally to both domestic and offshore, ten practices are more important to offshore and five practices are unique to offshore sourcing. The practices unique to offshore include giving customers a choice of sourcing locations, elevating the customer's Capability Maturity Model certification to work better with offshore suppliers, managing bottlenecks to relieve the substantial time zone differences and waiting to establish the ideal in-house/onsite/offshore ratio until the relationship has stabilized. Together, the 20 practices can help CIOs swiftly move through the learning curve, mitigate risks, work with offshore suppliers and achieve satisfactory costs and service levels.

While much of our research has targeted the capabilities and practices CIOs need to ensure outsourcing success, Chapter 11 is aimed at the client CEO. CEOs must enable their CIOs to meet outsourcing objectives in part by setting the supplier selection criteria. In this chapter, we show CIOs how to assess supplier capabilities, configure supplier options (such as sole sourcing versus multi-sourcing) and bid effectively. The chapter is based on the considerable work we have carried out since 2000 studying supplier strategies and capabilities. This is combined with insights from research and advisory work we have carried out on actually setting up and running outsourcing arrangements.

In Chapter 12, we examine eight stakeholders within client and supplier organizations and discuss how they must be managed during six phases of an outsourcing engagement. This chapter is developed out of one of our most widely cited book chapters that originally appeared in Zmud's *Framing the Domains of IT Management* (Lacity and Willcocks, 2000). We argue that most outsourcing research only distinguishes between two supplier stakeholders – the client and supplier. While this high-level organizational unit of analysis is an important part of understanding outsourcing, it does not fully capture the rich stakeholder landscape *within* client and supplier organizations. We discuss the need to manage four client stakeholders (senior management, IT management, business unit managers/users and IT staff) and four supplier stakeholders (senior management, alliance/engagement managers, supplier's delivery team and subcontractors). Each stakeholder has different expectations, perceptions and roles to play in the life of an outsourcing engagement.

Chapter 13 distills the 20 most important client and supplier lessons extracted from our entire body of research. Originally based on Lacity and Willcocks (2003), the client lessons focus on four ITO processes:

- assessing the in-house IT portfolio
- evaluating market options for the best sourcing models and best suppliers
- crafting contracts to align customer and supplier expectations and incentives and
- managing supplier relationships.

Major supplier lessons are also identified, which call for superior supplier capability and integrity in selling, negotiating and delivering IT services.

In Chapter 14, Oshri, Kotlarsky and Willcocks identify eight practices for managing globally dispersed teams. This chapter focuses primarily on the supplier-side capabilities. Based on 120 plus interviews in Tata Consultancy Services, practices address organizational structures, knowledge management processes and system development methods. Developed further from Oshri *et al.* (2007a, b), the chapter looks ahead five years as to the capabilities both clients and suppliers need to manage globally dispersed expertise and provides advice to clients on how to leverage a potential knowledge dividend inherent in outsourcing.

Chapter 15, entitled "Playing 'Catch-Up' with Core IS Capabilities", is one of our most valued contributions to practice. In 1998, Feeny and Willcocks initially identified nine core IS capabilities clients need in-house to effectively manage IT. These nine capabilities are leadership, informed buying, business systems thinking, relationship building, contract facilitation, architecture planning and design, vendor development, contract monitoring and making technology work (Feeny and Willcocks, 1998). Since its initial publication, many large companies have adopted the core capabilities model, including DuPont and Commonwealth Bank in Australia. In this chapter, Willcocks, Reynolds and Feeny show how client organizations actually build these capabilities over time through process, cultural and structural mechanisms (Willcocks *et al.*, 2007).

The authors demonstrate that retained core capabilities provide the single most powerful client key to control and risk mitigation in outsourcing, but also comment that building such capabilities is the area most neglected in practice. Given this is the case, the chapter provides a suitable conclusion to a book dedicated to showing how academic research and theory can be utilized to vitally inform and improve practice.

Note

1 Besides these rational reasons, some studies find personal agendas dominating large-scale outsourcing decisions (Hall and Liedtka, 2005; Lacity and Hirschheim, 1993).

References

Adler, T. (2003/2004) "Member Trust in Teams: A synthesized Analysis of Contract Negotiation in Outsourcing of IT Work," *The Journal of Computer Information Systems,* Vol. 44, 2, pp. 6–16.

Adler, P., McGarry, F., Talbot, W. and Binney, D. (2005) "Enabling Process Discipline: Lessons from the Journey to CMM Level 5," *MIS Quarterly Executive,* Vol. 4, 1, pp. 215–227.

Ajzen, I. and Fishbein, M. (1980) *Understanding Attitudes and Predicting Social Behavior,* Englewood Cliffs, New Jersey: Prentice-Hall.

Alchain, A. and Demsetz, H. (1972) "Production, Information Costs and Economic Organization," *American Economic Review,* Vol. 62, pp. 777–795.

Aldrich, H. (2006) *Organizations and Environments,* Englewood Cliffs, New Jersey: Prentice Hall.

Allen, D., Kern, T. and Mattison, D. (2002) "Culture, Power and Politics in ICT outsourcing in higher education," *European Journal of Information Systems,* Vol. 11, pp. 159–173.

Alvarez-Suescun, A. (2007) "Testing resource-based propositions about IS sourcing decisions," *Industrial Management & Data Systems,* Vol. 107, 6, pp. 762–779.

Ang, S. and Slaughter, S. (2001) "Work Outcomes and Job Design for Contract Versus Permanent Information Systems Professionals on Software Development Teams," *MIS Quarterly,* Vol. 25, 3, pp. 321–350.

Ang, S. and Cummings, L. (1997) "Strategic Response to Institutional Influences on Information Systems Outsourcing," *Organization Science,* Vol. 8, No. 3, pp. 235–256.

Ang, S. and Straub, D. (1998) "Production and Transaction Economies and IS Outsourcing: A Study of the U.S. Banking Industry," *MIS Quarterly,* Vol. 22, 4, pp. 535–552.

Applegate, L. and Montealegre, R. (1991) "Eastman Kodak Organization: Managing Information Systems Through Strategic Alliances," *Harvard Business School* Case 9–192–030, Boston, Massachusetts.

Apte, U. and Mason, R. (1995) "Global Disaggregation of Information-Intensive Services," *Management Science,* Vol. 41, 7, pp. 1250–1262.

Apte, U., Sobel, M., Hanaoka, S., Shimada, T., Saarinen, T., Salmela, T. and Vepsalainen, A. P. J. (1997) "IS Outsourcing Practices in the USA, Japan and Finland: A Comparative Study," *Journal of Information Technology,* Vol. 12, pp. 289–304.

Arnett, K. and Jones, M. (1994) "Firms that Choose Outsourcing: A Profile," *Information & Management,* Vol. 26, pp. 179–188.

Aron, R. and Singh, J. (2005) "Getting Offshoring Right," *Harvard Business Review,* Vol. 83, 12, pp. 135–143.

Aron, R., Clemons, E. and Reddi, S. (2005) "Just Right Outsourcing: Understanding and Managing Risk," *Journal of Management Information Systems,* Vol. 22, 2, pp. 37–55.

Aubert, B. A., Dussault, S., Patry, M. and Rivard, S. (1999) "Managing the Risk of IT Outsourcing," *Proceedings of the 32nd Annual Hawaii International Conference on System Sciences.*

Aubert, B., Patry, M. and Rivard, S. (1998) "Assessing the Risk of IT Outsourcing," *Proceedings of the 31st Annual Hawaii International Conference on System Sciences,* pp. 685–691.

Aubert, B., Rivard, S. and Patry, M. (1996) "A Transaction Cost Approach to Outsourcing Behavior: Some Empirical Evidence," *Information & Management,* Vol. 30, 2, pp. 51–64.

Bahli, B. and Rivard, S. (2003) "The information technology outsourcing risk: a transaction cost and agency theory-based perspective," *Journal of Information Technology*, Vol. 18, 3, pp. 211–221.

Bardhan, I., Whitaker, J. and Mithas, S. (2006) "Information Technology, Production Process Outsourcing and Manufacturing Plant Performance," *Journal of Management Information*, Vol. 23, 2, pp. 13–40.

Barney, J. (1991) "Firm Resources and Sustained Competitive Advantage," *Journal of Management*, Vol. 17, 1, pp. 99–120.

Barney, J. (1999) "How a Firm's Capabilities Affect Boundary Decisions," *Sloan Management Review*, Vol. 40, 3, pp. 137–145.

Barthélemy, J. (2001) "The Hidden Costs of IT Outsourcing," *Sloan Management Review*, Vol. 42, 3, pp. 60–69.

Barthélemy, J. and Geyer, D. (2001) "IT Outsourcing: Evidence from France and Germany," *European Management Journal*, Vol. 19, No. 2, pp. 195–202.

Barthélemy, J. and Geyer, D. (2004) "The Determinants of Total IT Outsourcing: An Empirical Investigation of French and German Firms," *The Journal of Computer Information Systems*, Vol. 44, 3, pp. 91–98.

Barthélemy, J. and Geyer, D. (2005) "An empirical investigation of IT outsourcing versus quasi-outsourcing in France and Germany," *Information & Management*, Vol. 42, 4, pp. 533–652.

Benbasat, I. and Weber, R. (1996) "Research commentary: Rethinking 'diversity' in information systems research," *Information Systems Research*, Vol. 7, 4, pp. 389–399.

Bennett, C. and Timbrell, G. (2000) "Application Service Providers: Will They Succeed?" *Information Systems Frontiers*, Vol. 2, 2, pp. 195–211.

Bhargava, H. and Sundaresan, S. (2004) "Computing as Utility: Managing Availability, Commitment and Pricing Through Contingent Bid Auctions," *Journal of Management Information Systems*, Vol. 21, 2, pp. 201–227.

Blau, P. (1964) *Exchange and Power in Social Life*, New York: Wiley.

Bruno, G., Esposito, G., Iandoli, L. and Raffa, M. (2004) "The ICT Service Industry in North Africa and Role of Partnerships in Morocco," *Journal of Global Information Technology Management*, Vol. 7, 3, pp. 5–26.

Carmel, E. (2006) "Building Your Information Systems from the Other Side of the World: How Infosys Manages Time Zone Differences," *MIS Quarterly Executive*, Vol. 5, 1, pp. 43–53.

Carmel, E. and Agarwal, R. (2002) "The Maturation of Offshore Sourcing of Information Technology Work," *MIS Quarterly Executive*, Vol. 1, 2, pp. 65–78.

Carmel, E. and Abbott, P. (2007) "Why Nearshore Means That Distance Matters," *Communications of the ACM*, Vol. 50, 10, pp. 40–46.

Carmel, E. and Tjia, P. (2005) *Offshoring Information Technology: Sourcing and Outsourcing to a Global Workforce*, Cambridge: Cambridge University Press.

Chalos, P. and Sung, J. (1998) "Outsourcing Decisions and Managerial Incentives," Decision Sciences, Vol. 29, No. 4, pp. 901–919.

Chandler, A. (1962) *Strategy and Structure*, Cambridge, MA: MIT Press.

Chaudhury, A., Nam, K. and Rao, H. R. (1995) "Management of Information Systems Outsourcing: A Bidding Perspective," *Journal of Management Information Systems*, Vol. 12, 2, pp. 131–159.

Cheon, M., Grover, V. and Teng, J. (1995) "Theoretical Perspectives on the Outsourcing of Information Systems," *Journal of Information Technology*, Vol. 10, pp. 209–210.

Chou, T., Chen, J. and Pan, S. (2006) "The Impacts of Social Capital on Information Technology Outsourcing Decisions: A Case Study of Taiwanese High-Tech Firms," *International Journal of Information Management,* Vol. 26, pp. 249–256.

Choudhury, V. and Sabherwal, R. (2003) "Portfolios of Control in Outsourced Software Development Projects," *Information Systems Research,* Vol. 14, 3, pp. 291–314.

Clark, T., Jr., Zmud, R. and McCray, G. (1995) "The Outsourcing of Information Services: Transforming the Nature of Business in the Information Industry," *Journal of Information Technology,* Vol. 10, pp. 221–237.

Coase, R. H. (1937) "The Nature of the Firm," *Economica,* Vol. 4, pp. 386–405.

Cronk, J. and Sharp, J. (1995) "A Framework for Deciding What to Outsource in Information Technology," *Journal of Information Technology,* Vol. 10, pp. 259–267.

Cross, J. (1995) "IT outsourcing: British Petroleum's competitive approach," *Harvard Business Review,* Vol. 73, 3, pp. 94–103.

Cullen, S., Seddon, P. and Willcocks, L. (2005) "Managing Outsourcing: The Life Cycle Imperative," *MIS Quarterly Executive,* Vol. 4, 1, pp. 229–246.

Cullen, S. and Willcocks, L. (2004) "IT Outsourcing: Carving the Right Strategy," *General Management Review,* Jan–March, pp. 1–6.

Currie, W. (1996) "Outsourcing in the Private and Public sectors: An Unpredictable IT Strategy," *European Journal of Information Systems,* Vol. 4, 4, pp. 226–236.

Currie, W. (1998) "Using Multiple Suppliers to Mitigate the Risk of IT Outsourcing at ICI and Wessex Water," *Journal of Information Technology,* Vol. 13, pp. 169–180.

Currie, W. and Willcocks, L. (1998) "Analyzing Four Types of IT Sourcing Decisions in the Context of Scale, Client/Supplier Interdependency and Risk Mitigation," *Information Systems Journal,* Vol. 8, 2, pp. 119–143.

Davenport, T. (2005) "The Coming Commoditization of Processes," *Harvard Business Review,* Vol. 83, 6, pp. 101–108.

De Looff, L. (1995) "Information Systems Outsourcing Decision Making: A Framework, Organizational Theories and case Studies," *Journal of Information Technology,* Vol. 10, pp. 281–297.

Dewire, D. (2000) "Application Service Providers," *Information Systems Management,* Vol. 17, No. 4, pp. 14–19.

Dibbern, J. and Heinzl, A. (2002) "Outsourcing of Information Systems in Small and Medium Sized Enterprises: A Test of Multi-Theoretical Model," in *Information Systems Outsourcing: Enduring Themes, Emergent Patterns and Future Directions,* R.A. Hirschheim, A. Heinzl and J. Dibbern (eds), Berlin, Heidelberg, New York: Springer-Verlag, pp. 77–99.

Dibbern, J., Goles, T., Hirschheim, R. and Bandula, J. (2004) "Information Systems Outsourcing: A Survey and Analysis of the Literature," *Database for Advances in Information Systems,* Vol. 34, 4, Fall 2004, pp. 6–102.

DiMaggio, P. and Powell, W. (1991) "The Iron Cage Revisited: Institutional Isomorphism and Collective Rationality in Organizational Fields," in *The New Institutionalism in Organizational Analysis* (Powell and DiMaggio eds), Chicago: The University of Chicago Press, pp. 63–82.

DiRomualdo, A. and Gurbaxani, V. (1998) "Strategic Intent for IT Outsourcing," *Sloan Management Review,* Vol. 39, 4, pp. 67–80.

Domberger, S. (1998) *The Contracting Organization: A Strategic Guide to Outsourcing.* Oxford: Oxford University Press.

Drezner, D. (2004) "The Outsourcing Bogeyman," *Foreign Affairs,* Vol. 83, 3, p. 22.

Duncan, N. (1998) "Beyond Opportunism: A Resource-based View of Outsourcing Risk," *Proceedings of the 31st Annual Hawaii International Conference on System Sciences,* pp. 675–684.

Dutta, A. and Roy, R. (2005) "Offshore Outsourcing: A Dynamic Causal Model of Counteracting Forces," *Journal of Management Information Systems*, Vol. 22, 2, pp. 15–36.

Earl, M. (1996) "The Risks of Outsourcing IT," *Sloan Management Review*, Vol. 37, 3, pp. 26–32.

Ein-Dor, P. (2004) "IT Industry Development and the Knowledge Economy: A Four Country Study," *Journal of Global Information Management*, Vol. 12, 4, pp. 23–49.

Eisenhardt, K. (1985) "Control: Organizational and Economic Approaches," *Management Science*, Vol. 31, 2, pp. 134–150.

Eisenhardt, K. (1989) "Agency Theory: An Assessment and Review," *The Academy of Management Review*, Vol. 14, 1, pp. 57–76.

Ekeh, P. (1974) *Social Exchange Theory: The Two Traditions*, Boston: Harvard University Press.

Elitzur, R. and Wensley, A. (1997) "Game Theory as a Tool for Understanding Information Services Outsourcing," *Journal of Information Technology*, Vol. 12, pp. 45–60.

Emerson, R. (1972) "Exchange Theory, Part I: A Psychological Basis for Social Exchange" and "Exchange Theory, Part II: Exchange Relations and Network Structures," in *Sociological Theories in Progress*, J. Berger, J., Zelditch, M. and Anderson, B. (eds), New York: Houghton Mifflin.

Farag, N. and Krishnan, M. (2003) "The Market Value of IT Outsourcing Investment Announcements: An Event-study Analysis," *Proceedings of the 9th Americas Conference on Information Systems*, pp. 1623–1629.

Farrell, D. (2006) "Smarter Offshoring," *Harvard Business Review*, Vol. 84, 6, p. 84.

Feeny, D. and Willcocks, L. (1998) "Core IS Capabilities for exploiting Information Technology," *Sloan Management Review*, Vol. 39, 3, pp. 9–21.

Feeny, D., Lacity, M. and Willcocks, L. (2005) "Taking the Measure of Outsourcing Providers," *Sloan Management Review*, Vol. 46, 3, pp. 41–48.

Fiske, S. and Taylor, S. (1991) *Social Cognition*, New York: McGraw Hill.

Fjermestad, J. and Saitta, J. (2005) "A Strategic Management Framework for IT Outsourcing," *Journal of Information Technology Case and Application Research*, Vol. 7, 3, pp. 42–60.

Forrester, J. (1996) *Industrial Dynamics*, Waltham, Massachusetts: Pegasus Communications.

Gallivan, M. and Oh, W. (1999) "Analyzing IT Outsourcing Relationships as Alliances among Multiple Clients and Vendors," *Proceedings of the 32nd Annual International Conference on System Sciences*, Hawaii, pp. 1–15.

George, B. (2006) *Exploring Information Systems Outsourcing: The Role of Social Capital*, unpublished Ph.D. thesis, University of Houston.

Ghoshal, S. and Morgan, P. (1996) "Bad for Practice: A Critique of Transaction Cost Theory," *Academy of Management Review*, Vol. 21, pp. 13–47.

Goles, T. (2001) *The Impact of the Client/Vendor Relationship on Outsourcing Success*, unpublished Dissertation, University of Houston.

Goles, T. and Chin, W. (2002) "Relational Exchange Theory and IS Outsourcing: Developing a Scale to Measure Relationship Factors," in *Information Systems Outsourcing in the New Economy*, R. Hirschheim, A. Heinzl and J. Dibbern (eds), Berlin, Heidelberg, New York: Springer-Verlag, 2002, pp. 221–250.

Gopal, A., Sivaramakrishnan, K., Krishnan, M. and Mukhopadhyay, T. (2003) "Contracts in Offshore Software Development: An Empirical Analysis," *Management Science*, Vol. 49, 12, pp. 1671–1683.

Gottfredson, M., Puryear, R. and Phillips, S. (2005) "Strategic Sourcing: From Periphery to the Core," *Harvard Business Review,* Vol. 83, 2, pp. 132–139.

Grover, V., Cheon, M. and Teng, J. (1996) "The Effect of Service Quality and Partnership on the Outsourcing of Information Systems Functions," *Journal of Management Information Systems,* Vol. 12, 4, pp. 89–116.

Grover, V., Teng, J. and Cheon, M. (1997) "Towards a Theoretically-based Contingency Model of IS Outsourcing", in *Strategic Sourcing of Information Systems: Perspectives and Practices,* Willcocks, L. and Lacity, M. (eds), Wiley, Chichester, pp. 78–101.

Grover, V., Cheon, M. and Teng, J. (1994) "An evaluation of the impact of corporate strategy and the role of information technology on IS functional outsourcing," *European Journal of Information Systems,* Vol. 3, 3, pp. 179–191.

Gurbaxani, V. (1996) "The New World of Information Technology Outsourcing," *Communications of the ACM,* Vol. 39, 7, pp. 45–46.

Hall, J. and Liedtka, S. (2005) "Financial Performance, CEO Compensation and Large-Scale Information Technology Outsourcing Decisions," *Journal of Management Information Systems,* Vol. 22, 1, pp. 193–222.

Hancox, M. and Hackney, R. (1999) "Information Technology Outsourcing: Conceptualizing Practice in the Public and Private sector," *Proceedings of the 32nd Annual Hawaii International Conference on System Sciences.*

Harrison, A. and McMillan, M. (2006) "Dispelling Some Myths About Offshoring," *The Academy of Management Perspectives,* Vol. 20, 4, pp. 6–22.

Harter, D., Krishnan, M. and Slaughter, S. (2000) "Effects of process maturity on quality, cycle time and effort in software product development," *Management Science,* Vol. 46, 4, pp. 451–467.

Hayes, D., Hunton, J. and Reck, J. (2000) "Information Systems Outsourcing Announcement: Investigating the Impact on the Market Value of Contract Granting and Receiving Firms," *Journal of Information Systems,* Vol. 14, 2, pp. 109–125.

Heiskanen, A., Newman, M. and Similä, J. (1996) "Software Contracting: A Process Model Approach," *Proceedings of the International Conference on Information Systems,* pp. 51–62.

Hill, C. and Jones, G. (2001) *Strategic Management,* Houghton: Mifflin.

Hirschheim, R. (1998) "Backsourcing: An Emerging Trend?," *Infoserver,* http://www.infoserver.eom/sep1998/html/academic.html, September.

Hirschheim, R., Heinzl, A. and Dibbern, J. (eds) (2002) *Information Systems Outsourcing: Enduring Themes, Emergent Patterns and Future Directions,* Berlin: Springer-Verlag.

Hirschheim, R. and Lacity, M. (2000) "The Myths and Realities of Information Technology Insourcing," *Communications of the ACM,* Vol. 43, No. 2, pp. 99–107.

Ho, V. Ang, S. and Straub, D. (2003) "When subordinates become IT contractors: Persistent managerial expectations in IT outsourcing," *Information Systems Research,* Vol. 14, 1, pp. 66–86.

Hodgson, G. (1994) "Corporate Culture and Evolving Competences: An Old Institutionalist Perspective on the Nature of the Firm," Paper presented at *The Conference of Transaction Cost Economics and Beyond,* Erasmus University, Rotterdam, Netherlands, June.

Homans, G. (1961) *Social Behavior: Its Elementary Forms,* New York: Harcourt Brace Jovanovich (revised 1974).

Hoopes, D., Madsen, T. and Walker, G. (2003) "Guest editors' introduction to the special issue: Why is there a resource-based view? Toward a theory of competitive heterogeneity," *Strategic Management Journal,* Chichester: Vol. 24, 10, pp. 889–902.

Hu, Q., Saunders, C. and Gebelt, M. (1997) "Research Report: Diffusion of Information Systems Outsourcing: A Reevaluation of Influence Sources," *Information Systems Research,* Vol. 8, 3, pp. 288–301.

Huber, R. (1993) "How Continental Bank Outsourced its 'Crown Jewels'," *Harvard Business Review,* Vol. 71, 1, pp. 121–129.

Hui, P. and Beath, C. (2001) "The IT Sourcing Process: A Framework for Research," University of Austin, Texas: http://disc-nt.cba.uh.edu/chin/speakerseries/The %20IT %20Sourcing %20Process.pdf.

Insinga, R. and Werle, M. (2000) "Linking outsourcing to business strategy," *The Academy of Management Executive,* Vol. 14, 4, pp. 58–71.

Iyer, A., Schwarz, L. and Zenios, S. (2005) "A Principal-Agent Model for Product Specification and Production," *Management Science,* Vol. 51, 1, pp. 106–120.

Jalote, P. (2000) *CMM in Practice,* Boston: Addison Wesley.

Jayatilaka, B. (2001) "Information Systems Outsourcing: Transitions and Antecedents," unpublished Dissertation, University of Houston.

Jayatilaka, B. (2002) "IT Sourcing: A Dynamic Phenomenon: Forming an Institutional Theory Perspective, in *Information Systems Outsourcing in the New Economy,* R. Hirschheim, A. Heinzl and J. Dibbern (eds), Berlin, Heidelberg, New York: Springer-Verlag, 2002, pp. 100–130.

Jeyaraj, A., Rottman, J. and Lacity, M. (2006) "A Review of the Predictors, Linkages and Biases in IT Innovation Adoption Research," *Journal of Information Technology,* Vol. 21, 1, pp. 1–23.

Joskow, P. (1991) "The Role of Transaction Cost Economics in Antitrust and Public Utility Regulatory Policies", *Journal of Law Economics and Organization,* Vol. 7, special issue, pp. 53–83.

Jurison, J. (1995) "The Role of Risk and Return in Information Technology Outsourcing Decisions," *Journal of Information Technology,* Vol. 10, pp. 239–247.

Kaiser, K. and Hawk, S. (2004) "Evolution of Offshore Software Development: From Outsourcing to Co-Sourcing," *MIS Quarterly Executive,* Vol. 3, 2, pp. 69–81.

Kakabadse, N. and Kakabadse, A. (2000) "Critical review – outsourcing: A paradigm shift," *The Journal of Management Development,* Vol. 19, 8, pp. 670–729.

Kanawattanachai, P. and Yoo, Y. (2007) "The impact of knowledge coordination on virtual team performance over time," *MIS Quarterly,* Vol. 31, 4, pp. 783–808.

Kern, T. and Willcocks, L. (2001) *The Relationship Advantage: Information Technologies, Sourcing and Management,* Oxford: Oxford University Press.

Kern, T., Lacity, M. and Willcocks, L. (2002a) *Net Sourcing: Renting Business Applications and Services Over a Network,* Upper Saddle River, NJ: Prentice-Hall.

Kern, T., Willcocks, L. and Lacity, M. (2002b) "Application Service Provision: Risk Assessment and Risk Mitigation," *MIS Quarterly Executive,* Vol. 1, 2, pp. 113–126.

Kern, T., Willcocks, L. and Van Heck, E. (2002) "The Winners Curse in IT Outsourcing: Strategies for Avoiding Relational Trauma," *California Management Review,* Vol. 44, 2, pp. 47–69.

King, W. (2004) "Outsourcing and the Future of IT," *Information Systems Management,* Vol. 21, 4, pp. 83–84.

King, W. and Malhotra, Y. (2000) "Developing a Framework for Analyzing IS Outsourcing," *Information and Management,* Vol. 37, pp. 323–334.

Kishore, R., Agarwal, M. and Rao, H.R. (2004) "Determinants of Sourcing During Technology Growth and Maturity: An Empirical Study of e-Commerce Sourcing," *Journal of Management Information Systems,* Vol. 21, 3, pp. 47–82.

Kishore, R., Rao, H., Nam, K., Rajagopalan, S., Chaudhury, A. (2003) "A Relationship Perspective on IT Outsourcing," *Communications of the ACM*, Vol. 46, 12, pp. 86–92.

Klein, H.K. (2002) "On the Theoretical Foundations of Current Outsourcing Research," in *Information Systems Outsourcing: Enduring Themes, Emergent Patterns*, R. A. Hirschheim, A. Heinzl and J. Dibbern (ed.), Berlin, Heidelberg, New York: Springer, pp. 24–44.

Klepper, R. (1995) "The Management of Partnering Development in I/S Outsourcing," *Journal of Information Technology*, Vol. 10, pp. 249–258.

Klotz, D.E. and Chatterjee, K. (1995) "Dual Sourcing in Repeated Procurement Competitions," *Management Science*, Vol. 41, No. 8, pp. 1317–1327.

Knolmayer, G. (2002) "Cybermediaries Supporting the Management of Independent Workers: A Case Study of Extended Outsourcing Relationships," in *Information Systems Outsourcing: Enduring Themes, Emergent Patterns and Future Directions*, R. A. Hirschheim, A. Heinzl and J. Dibbern (eds), Berlin, Heidelberg, New York: Springer-Verlag, pp. 432–448.

Koh, C., Ang, S. and Straub, D. (2004) "IT Outsourcing Success: A Psychological Contract Perspective," *Information Systems Research*, Vol. 15, 4, pp. 356–373.

Krishna, S., Sahay, S. and Walsham, G. (2004) "Managing Cross-Cultural Issues in Global Software Outsourcing," *Communications of the ACM*, Vol. 47, 4, pp. 62–66.

Kuhn, T. (1970) *The Structure of Scientific Revolutions*, Chicago: University of Chicago Press.

Lacity, M., Feeny, D. and Willcocks, L. (2003) "Transforming a back-office function: Lessons from BAE Systems' Experience With an Enterprise Partnership," *MIS Quarterly Executive*, Vol. 2, 2, pp. 86–103.

Lacity, M., Feeny, D. and Willcocks, L. (2004) "Commercializing the Back Office at Lloyds of London: Outsourcing and Strategic Partnerships Revisited," *European Management Journal*, Vol. 22, 2, pp. 127–140.

Lacity, M. and Hirschheim, R. (1993) "The Information Systems Outsourcing Bandwagon," *Sloan Management Review*, Vol. 35, 1, pp. 73–86.

Lacity, M. and Hirschheim, R. (1995) *Beyond the information systems outsourcing bandwagon: the insourcing response*, Chichester; New York: Wiley.

Lacity, M., Hirschheim, R. and Willcocks, L. (1994) "Realizing Outsourcing Expectations: Incredible Promise, Credible Outcomes", *Journal of Information Systems Management*, Vol. 11, 4, pp. 7–18.

Lacity, M. and Rottman, J. (2008) *Offshore Outsourcing of IT Work*, London: Palgrave.

Lacity, M. and Willcocks, L. (1995) "Interpreting Information Technology Sourcing Decisions from a Transaction Cost Perspective: Findings and Critique," *Accounting, Management and Information Technologies*, Vol. 5, No. 3/4, pp. 203–244.

Lacity, M. and Willcocks, L. (1997) "Information Systems Sourcing: Examining the Privatization Option in USA Public Administration," *Information Systems Journal*, Vol. 7, pp. 83–108.

Lacity, M. and Willcocks, L. (1998) "An empirical investigation of information technology sourcing practices: Lessons from experience," *MIS Quarterly*, Vol. 22, No. 3, pp. 363–408.

Lacity, M. and Willcocks, L. (2000) "Relationships in IT Outsourcing: A Stakeholder Perspective," in *Framing the Domain of IT Management*, Robert Zmud (ed.), Pinnaflex, pp. 355–384.

Lacity, M. and Willcocks, L. (2001) *Global Information Technology Outsourcing: In Search of Business Advantage*, Chichester: Wiley.

Lacity, M. and Willcocks, L. (2003) "Information Technology Sourcing Reflections," *Wirtschaftsinformatik*, Special Issue on Outsourcing, Vol. 45, 2, pp. 115–125.

Lacity, M., Willcocks, L. and Feeny, D. (1995) "IT Outsourcing: Maximize Flexibility and Control," *Harvard Business Review*, Vol. 73, 3, pp. 84–93.

Lacity, M., Willcocks, L. and Feeny, D. (1996) "The Value of Selective IT Sourcing," *Sloan Management Review*, Vol. 37, No. 3, pp. 13–25.

Lee, A. (1999) "Rigor and Relevance in Information Systems Research: Beyond the Approach of Positivism Alone," *MIS Quarterly*, Vol. 23, 1, pp. 29–34.

Lee, J., Miranda, S. and Kim, Y. (2004) "IT Outsourcing Strategies: Universalistic, Contingency and Configurational Explanations of Success," *Information Systems Research*, Vol. 15, 2, pp. 110–131.

Lee, J. and Kim, Y. (1999) "Effect of Partnership Quality on IS Outsourcing Success: Conceptual Framework and Empirical Validation," *Journal of Management Information Systems*, Vol. 15, No. 4, pp. 29–61.

Levina, N. and Ross, J. (2003) "From the Vendor's Perspective: Exploring the Value Proposition in IT Outsourcing," *MIS Quarterly*, Vol. 27, 3, pp. 331–364.

Levina, N. and Vaast, E. (2008) "Innovating or Doing as Told? Status Differences and Overlapping Boundaries in Offshore Collaboration," *MIS Quarterly*, Special Issue on Offshoring, forthcoming.

Lewin, K., "The Research Center For Group Dynamics at Massachusetts Institute of Technology," *Sociometry*, Vol. 8, pp. 126–135.

Lichtenstein, Y. (2004) "Puzzles in Software Development Contracting," *Communications of the ACM*, Vol. 47, 2, pp. 61–65.

Linder, J. (2004) "Transformational Outsourcing," *Sloan Management Review*, Vol. 45, 2, pp. 52–58.

Loebbecke, C. and Huyskens, C. (2006) "What drives netsourcing decisions? An empirical analysis," *European Journal of Information Systems*, Vol. 15, 4, pp. 415–423.

Logan, M. (2000) "Using Agency Theory to Design Successful Outsourcing Relationships," *International Journal of Logistics Management*, Vol. 11, 2, pp. 21–32.

Loh, L. and Venkatraman, N. (1992a) Stock Market Reaction to IT Outsourcing: An Event Study. Sloan School of Management, MIT, Cambridge, 1992.

Loh, L. and Venkatraman, N. (1992b) "Diffusion of Information Technology Outsourcing: Influence Sources and the Kodak Effect," *Information Systems Research*, Vol. 3, 4, pp. 334–358.

Loh, L. and Venkatraman, N. (1995) "An Empirical Study of Information Technology Outsourcing: Benefits, Risks and Performance Implications," *Proceedings of the 16th International Conference on Information Systems*, Amsterdam, The Netherlands, pp. 277–288.

Madison, T., San Miguel, P. and Padmanabhan, P. (2006) "Stock Market Reaction to Domestic Outsourcing Announcements by U.S. Based Client and Vendor Firms," *Journal of Information Technology Case and Application Research*, Vol. 8, 4, pp. 6–26.

Matloff, N. (2004) "Globalization and the American IT Worker," *Communications of the ACM*, Vol. 47, 11, pp. 27–30.

Macneil, I. (1980) *The New Social Contract: An Inquiry into Modern Contractual Relations*, New London: Yale University Press.

Marcolin, B. and Ross, A. (2005) "Complexities in IS Sourcing: Equifinality and Relationship Management," *Database for Advances in Information Systems*, Vol. 36, 4, pp. 29–46.

Mayer, R., Davis, J. and Schoonnan, F. (1995) "An integrative model of organizational trust," *Academy of Management Review*, Vol. 20, 3, pp. 709–734.

McFarlan, F. W. and Nolan, R. (1995) "How to Manage an IT Outsourcing Alliance," *Sloan Management Review*, Vol. 36, 2, pp. 9–24.

McLellan, K., Marcolin, B. and Beamish, P. (1995) "Financial and Strategic Motivations Behind IS Outsourcing," *Journal of Information Technology*, Vol. 10, pp. 299–321.

Michalisin, M., Smith, R. and Kline, D. (1997) "In search of strategic assets", *International Journal of Organizational Analysis*, Vol. 5, 4, pp. 360–388.

Michell, V. and Fitzgerald, G. (1997) "The IT Outsourcing Market-Place: Vendors and their Selection," *Journal of Information Technology*, Vol. 12, pp. 223–237.

Milgrom, P. and Weber, R. (1982) "A Theory of Auctions and Competitive Bidding," *Econometrica*, Vol. 50 No. 5, pp. 1089–1122.

Miles, R. and Snow, C. (1978) *Organizational Strategy, Structure and Process*, New York: McGraw-Hill revised 2003 by Stanford University Press, Stanford.

Miranda, S. and Kim, Y. (2006) "Professionalism Versus Political Contexts: Institutional Mitigation and the Transaction Cost Heuristic in Information Systems Outsourcing," *MIS Quarterly*. Vol. 30, 3, pp. 725–753.

Miranda, S. and Kavan, B. (2005) "Moments of governance in IS outsourcing: conceptualizing effects of contracts on value capture and creation," *Journal of Information Technology* Vol. 20, 3, pp. 152–169.

Nair, K. and Prasad, P. (2004) "Offshore Outsourcing: A SWOT Analysis of a State in India," *Information Systems Management*, Vol. 21, 3, pp. 34–40.

Nahapiet, J. and Ghoshal, S. (1998) "Social Capital, Intellectual Capital and the Organizational Advantage," *Academy of Management Review*, Vol. 23, 2, pp. 242–265.

Nam, K., Rajagopalan, S., Rao, H.R. and Chaudhury, A. (1996) "A Two-Level Investigation of Information Systems Outsourcing," *Communications of the ACM*, Vol. 39, No. 7, pp. 36–44.

Nash, J.F. (1953) "Two-Person Cooperative Games," Econometrica, Vol. 21, pp. 128–140.

Nash, J. (1951) "Non-Cooperative Games," *The Annals of Mathematics* (54:2), pp. 286–295.

Nelson, P., Richmond, W. and Seidmann, A. (1996) "Two dimensions of software acquisition," *Communications of the ACM*, Vol. 39, No. 7, pp. 29–35.

Ngwenyama, O. and, Bryson, N. (1999) "Making the Information Systems Outsourcing Decision: A Transaction Cost Approach to Analyzing Outsourcing Decision Problems," *European Journal of Operational Research*, pp. 351–367.

O'Leary, M.B. and Cummings, J.N. (2007) "The Spatial, Temporal, and Configurational Characteristics of Geographic Dispersion in Teams," *MIS Quarterly*, 31(3), pp. 433–452.

Oh, W., Gallivan, M. and Kim, J. (2006) "The Market's Perception of the Transactional Risks of Information Technology Outsourcing Announcements," *Journal of Management Information Systems*, Vol. 22, 4, pp. 271–303.

Oshri, I., Kotlarsky, J. and L.P. Willcocks (2007a) "Managing Dispersed Expertise in IT Offshore Outsourcing: Lessons from Tata Consultancy Services," *MISQ Executive*, 6(2), pp. 53–65.

Oshri, I., Kotlarsky, J. and L.P. Willcocks (2007b) "Global Software Development: Exploring Socialization in Distributed Strategic Projects, *Journal of Strategic Information Systems*, 16(1), pp. 25–49.

Oshri, I., Kotlarsky, J. and Willcocks, L. (eds) (2008). *Outsourcing Global Services: Knowledge, Social Capital and Innovation*. London: Palgrave.

Oza, N., Hall, T., Rainer, A. and Grey, S. (2006) "Trust in Software Outsourcing Relationships: An Empirical Investigation of Indian Software Companies," *Information and Software Technology*, Vol. 48, pp. 345–354.

Peisch, R. (1995) "When outsourcing goes awry," *Harvard Business Review*, Vol. 73, 3, pp. 24–33.

Peled, A. (2001) "Outsourcing and Political Power: Bureaucrats, Consultants, Vendors and Public Information Technology," *Public Personnel Management*, Vol. 30, 4, pp. 495–514.

Pfannenstein, L. and Tsai, R. (2004) "Offshore Outsourcing: Current and Future Effects on American I.T. Industry," *Information Systems Management*, Vol. 21, 4, Fall 2004, pp. 72–80.

Pfeffer, J. (1981) *Power in Organizations*, Marshfield, Mass: Pitman Pub.

Pfeffer, J. (1994) *Managing With Power: Politics and Influence in Organizations*, Boston: Harvard Business School Press.

Pfeffer, J. and Salancik, G. (1978) *The External Control of Organizations: A Resource Dependence Perspective*, New York: Harper and Row; reprinted by Stanford University Press, Stanford, 2003.

Poppo, L. and Zenger, T. (1998) "Testing Alternative Theories of the Firm: Transaction Cost, Knowledge-Based and Measurement Explanations for Make-or-Buy Decisions in Information Services," *Strategic Management Journal*, Vol. 19, pp. 853–877.

Poppo, L. and Lacity, M. (2002) "The Normative Value of Transaction Cost Economics: What Managers Have Learned About TCE Principles in the IT Context," in *Information Systems Outsourcing in the New Economy*, Hirschheim, R., Heinzl, A. and Dibbern, J. (eds), Springer-Verlag, Berlin-Heidelberg-New York, pp. 235–276.

Porter, M. (1980) *Competitive Strategy: Techniques for Analyzing Industries and Competitors*, New York: Free Press.

Porter, M. (1985) *Competitive Advantage: Creating and Sustaining Superior Performance*, New York, London: Free Press; Collier Macmillan.

Prahalad, C.K. and Hamel, G. (1990) The core competence of the corporation. *Harvard Business Review*, Vol. 68, pp. 79–91.

Qu, Z. and Brocklehurst, M. (2003) "What Will it Take for China to become a Competitive Force in Offshore Outsourcing? An Analysis of the Role of Transaction Costs in Supplier Selection," *Journal of Information Technology*, Vol. 18, pp. 53–67.

Quinn, J. (1999) "Strategic Outsourcing: Leveraging Knowledge Capabilities," *Sloan Management Review*, Vol. 40, 4, pp. 9–21.

Quinn, J. (2000) "Outsourcing Innovation: The New Engine of Growth," *Sloan Management Review*, Vol. 41, 4, pp. 13–28.

Quinn, B.J. and Hilmer, G.H. (1994) "Strategic outsourcing", *McKinsey Quarterly*, No. 1, pp. 47–69.

Ranganathan, C. and Balaji, S. (2007) "Critical Capabilities for Offshore Outsourcing of IS," *MIS Quarterly Executive*, Vol. 6, 3, pp. 147–164.

Ramingwong, S. and Sajeev, A. (2007) "Offshore Outsourcing: The Risk of Keeping Mum," *Communications of the ACM*, Vol. 50, 8, pp. 101–103.

Richardson, G. (1996) *Modeling for Management*, Aldershot, UK, Datmouth.

Rogers, E. (1983) *Diffusion of Innovations*, New York: The Free Press.

Ross, J. and Beath, C. (2006) "Sustainable IT Outsourcing: Let Enterprise Architecture by Your Guide," *MIS Quarterly Executive*, Vol. 5, 4, pp. 181–192.

Rossetti, C. and Choi, T. (2005) "On the Dark Side of Strategic Sourcing: Experiences from the Aerospace Industry," *The Academy of Management Executive*, Vol. 19, 1, p. 46.

Rottman, J. (2006) "Successfully Outsourcing Embedded Software Development," *IEEE Computer*, Vol. 39, 1, pp. 55–61.

Rottman, J. and Lacity, M. (2004) "Twenty Practices for Offshore Sourcing," *MIS Quarterly Executive*, Vol. 3, 3, pp. 117–130.

Rottman, J. and Lacity, M. (2006) "Proven Practices for Effectively Offshoring IT Work," *Sloan Management Review*, Vol. 47, 3, pp. 56–63.

Rottman, J. and Lacity, M. (2006) "Knowledge Transfer Is The Key To Successful Strategic Outsourcing," Achieving Competitive Advantage Through Collaborative Partnerships: The Outsourcing Project, published by CxO Research, Ltd, pp. 16–19.

Rousseau, D. M. (1995) *Psychological Contract in Organizations: Understanding Written and Unwritten Agreements*, Newbury Park, CA: Sage Publications.

Roy, V. and Aubert, B. (2002) "A Resource-Based Analysis of IT Sourcing," *Database for Advances in IS,* Vol. 33, 2, pp. 29–40.

Sabherwal, R. (1999) "The Role of Trust in Outsourced IS Development Projects," *Communications of the ACM*, Vol. 42, 2, pp. 80–86.

Sakthivel, S. (2007) "Managing Risk in Offshore Development," *Communications of the ACM*, Vol. 50, 4, pp. 69–75.

Sanchez, R. and Mahoney, J. (1996) "Modularity, flexibility and knowledge management in product and organizational Design", *Strategic Management Journal*, Vol. 17, pp. 63–76.

Saunders, C., Gebelt, M. and Hu, Q. (1997) "Achieving success in information systems outsourcing," *California Management Review,* Vol. 39, 2, pp. 63–80.

Searle, John (1997) *The Construction of Social Reality,* New York: The Free Press.

Seddon, P., Cullen, S. and Willcocks, L. (2007) "Does Domberger's Theory of Contracting Explain Why Organizations Outsource IT and the Levels of Satisfaction Achieved?" *European Journal of Information Systems* Vol. 16, 3, pp. 237–254.

Shao, B. and Smith David, J. (2007) "The impact of offshore outsourcing on IT workers in developed countries," *Communications of the ACM*, Vol. 50, 2, pp. 89–95.

Sharma, A. (1997) "Professional as agent: Knowledge asymmetry in agency exchange," *Academy of Management Review*, Vol. 22, 3, pp. 758–798.

Shelanski, H. (1991) *Empirical research in transaction cost economics: a survey and assessment.* University of California, Berkeley, Department of Economics.

Shelanski, H. and Klein, P. (1995) "Empirical Research in Transaction Cost Economics: A Review and Assessment," *Journal of Law, Economics, and Organization,* Vol. 11, 2, pp. 335–361.

Simon, H. (1947) *Administrative behavior: a study of decision-making processes in administrative organization*, New York: Macmillan.

Simon, H. (1957) *Models of Man: Social and Rational,* New York: Wiley.

Simon, H. (1976) *Administrative Behavior*, New York: Free Press.

Slaughter, S.A. and Ang, S. (1996) "Employment Outsourcing in Information Systems," *Communications of the ACM*, Vol. 39, 7, pp. 47–54.

Smith, M., Mitra, S. and Narasimhan, S. (1998) "Information Systems Outsourcing: A Study of Pre-Event Firm Characteristics," *Journal of Management Information Systems*, Vol. 15, 2, pp. 61–93.

Sobel, M. and Apte, U. (1995) "Domestic and Global Outsourcing Practices of America's most Effective IS Users," *Journal of Information Technology*, Vol. 10, pp. 269–280.

Straub, D., Weill, P. and Stewart, K. (2002) "Strategic Control of IT Resources: A Test of Resource-Based Theory in the Context of Selective IT Outsourcing," Working paper, Georgia State University and MIT Sloan School of Management.

Susarla, A., Barua, A. and Whinston, A.B. (2003) "Understanding the Service Component of Application Service Provision: An Empirical Analysis of Satisfaction with ASP Services," *Management Information Systems Quarterly*, Vol. 27, 1, pp. 91–123.

Tanriverdi, H., Konana, P. and Ge, L. (2007) "The Choice of Sourcing Mechanisms for Business Processes" *Information Systems Research*, Vol. 18, 3, pp. 280–302.

Teng, J., Cheon, M. and Grover, V. (1995) "Decisions to Outsource Information Systems Functions: Testing a Strategy-Theoretic Discrepancy Model," *Decision Sciences*, Vol. 26, No. 1, pp. 75–103.

Thomas, A. and Wilkinson, T. (2006) "The Outsourcing Compulsion," *Sloan Management Review*, Vol. 48, 1, pp. 10–14.

Tsang, E. (2000) "Transaction cost and resource-bases explanations of joint ventures: A comparison and synthesis," *Organization Studies*, Vol. 21, 1, pp. 215–242.

Useem, M. and Harder, J. (2000) "Leading Laterally in Company Outsourcing," *Sloan Management Review*, Vol. 41, 2, pp. 25–36.

Venkatraman, N.V. (2004) "Offshoring Without Guilt," *Sloan Management Review*, Vol. 45, 3, pp. 14–16.

Vestring, T., Rouse, T. and Reinert, U. (2005) "Hedge Your Offshoring Bets," *Sloan Management Review*, Vol. 46, pp. 27–29.

Van De Ven, A. (1989) "Nothing Is Quite So Practical as a Good Theory," *Academy of Management Review*, Vol. 14, 4, pp. 486–489.

Von Bertalanffy, L. (1968) *General Systems Theory: Foundations, Development and Applications*, New York, George Braziller.

Wade, M. and Hulland, J. (2004) "The Resource Based View and IS Systems Research: Review, Extension and Suggestions", *MIS Quarterly*, Vol. 28, 1, pp. 107–142.

Wagner, D. (2006) "Success Factors in Outsourcing Service Jobs," *Sloan Management Review*, Vol. 48, 1, p. 7.

Walden, E. (2005) "Intellectual Property Rights and Cannibalization in Information Technology Outsourcing Contracts," *MIS Quarterly*, Vol. 29, 4, pp. 699–721.

Wang, E., Barron, T. and Seidmann, A. (1997) "Contracting Structures for Custom Software Development: The Impacts of Informational Rents and Uncertainty on Internal Development and Outsourcing," *Management Science*, Vol. 43, 12, pp. 1726–1744.

Whang, S. (1992) "Contracting for Software Development," *Management Science*, Vol. 38, 3, pp. 307–324.

Weinstein, L. (2004) "Outsourced and Out of Control," *Communications of the ACM*, Vol. 47, 2, p. 120.

Westfall, R. (1999) "An IS Research Relevance Manifesto," *Communications of the AIS*, Vol. 2, 14, http://cais.asinet.org/articles/2–14/article.htm.

Willcocks, L., Cullen, S. and Lacity, M. (2006) "The CEO Guide to Selecting Effective Suppliers," LogicaCMG, London, 29 pages.

Willcocks, L. and Kern, T. (1998) "IT Outsourcing as Strategic Partnering: The case of the UK Inland Revenue," *European Journal of Information Systems*, Vol. 7, 1, pp. 29–45.

Willcocks, L., Hindle, J., Feeny, D. and Lacity, M. (2004) "Information Technology and Business Process Outsourcing: The Knowledge Potential," *Journal of Information Systems Management*, Vol. 21, 3, pp. 7–15.

Willcocks, L. and Lacity, M. (2006) *Global Sourcing of Business and IT Services*, United Kingdom: Palgrave.

Willcocks, L., Reynolds, P. and Feeny, D. (2007) "Evolving IS Capabilities to Leverage the External IT Services Market, *MIS Quarterly Executive*, Vol. 6, 3, pp. 127–145.

Williamson, O. (1981) "The Economics of Organization: The Transaction Cost Approach," *American Journal of Sociology*, Vol. 87, 3, pp. 548–577.

Williamson, O. (1985) *The Economic Institutions of Capitalism: Firms, Markets, Relational Contracting*, New York, London: Free Press, Collier Macmillan.

Williamson, O. (1991) "Comparative Economic Organization: The Analysis of Discrete Structural Alternatives," *Administrative Science Quarterly*, Vol. 36, 2, pp. 269–296.

Williamson, O. (1979) "Transaction Cost Economics: The Governance of Contractual Relations," *Journal of Law and Economics*, Vol. 22, 2, October 1979, pp. 233–261.

Williamson, O. (1975) *Markets and Hierarchies: Analysis and Antitrust Implications: A Study in the Economics of Internal Organization*, New York: The Free Press.

Zatolyuk, S. and Allgood, B. (2004) "Evaluating a Country for Offshore Outsourcing: Software Development Providers in the Ukraine," *Information Systems Management*, Vol. 21, 3, pp. 28–33.

Part II
Theories

2
Transaction Cost Economics Applied to IT Outsourcing: Findings and Critique

Mary C. Lacity and Leslie P. Willcocks

Introduction

As noted in the introduction, Transaction Cost Economics (TCE) is one of the most widely adopted theories used to study IT outsourcing (ITO) decisions. Early ITO articles argued that TCE is a useful framework for studying ITO decisions for various reasons (Clark *et al.*, 1995; Cronk and Sharp, 1995; De Looff, 1995; Jurison, 1995; Klepper, 1993, 1995; Lacity and Hirschheim, 1993a; Beath, 1987). First, TCE specifically addresses sourcing decisions, that is, the decision to produce a good or service internally or purchase it externally. Second, TCE captures the widely-held perception that organizational members make sourcing decisions based upon an economic rationale and that outsourcing should reduce costs (Anthes, 1990, 1991; Hamilton, 1989; Hammersmith, 1989; Kass, 1990; Kelleher, 1990; Krass, 1990; Morse, 1990; O'Leary, 1990; Oltman, 1990; Rochester and Douglas, 1990). Third, many practitioners use "TCE-speak" to explain why outsourcing is predicted to reduce IT costs: IT is most efficiently provided by external vendors because it is a commodity service (translated into "TCE-speak" as a "non-specific asset") (Ward, 1991; Ambrosio, 1991). Fourth, TCE has enjoyed an abundance of empirical and theoretical academic attention in other organizational contexts (Anderson, 1994; Bowen and Jones, 1986; Griesinger, 1990; Hill, 1990; Hennart, 1991a, 1991b; Hesterly *et al.*, 1990; Joskow, 1985; Lieberman, 1991; Malone, 1987; Malone *et al.*, 1987; Pisano, 1990; Robins, 1987; Walker and Poppo, 1991). More recent ITO studies have rigorously tested TCE propositions and frequently found mixed results (Miranda and Kim, 2006). Most interestingly, mixed results occurred *within* studies in that certain TCE propositions were supported and others were not. For example Ang and Cummings (1997) found support for asset specificity as a determinant of outsourcing in the context of large banks but not small banks. How can these mixed results be explained?

In this chapter, we interpret 61 sourcing decisions made by 145 participants in 40 US and UK organizations from a transaction cost perspective.

We analyzed the success and failure of participants' sourcing decisions to determine whether they outsourced or insourced the "right" transaction types using the "right" contracts as predicted by TCE. A significant percentage of anomalies – 87.5% – resulted from this analysis. We present two interpretations of these anomalies – one interpretation maintains the integrity of a TCE perspective, and an alternative interpretation challenges the applicability of TCE to the IT outsourcing context. These two interpretations serve as the *thesis* and *antithesis* of a Hegelian approach to inquiry. After presenting both positions, we propose two alternatives which may lead to a *synthesis* of the debate.

Transaction Cost Theory: Williamson's governance framework

TCE's major constructs as defined by Oliver Williamson (1975, 1979, 1981, 1985, 1991 and 1994) – costs, transaction type, threat of opportunism, uncertainty and information impactedness – are briefly explained below. Although TCE theorists have preceded (Coase, 1937) and succeeded Williamson (Pitelis, 1991), he is widely recognized as the major author and spokesperson of TCE, as evidenced by over 40,000 citations of his work as of December 2007. Williamson's constructs were the foundation for our research.

Williamson developed Transaction Cost Economics when he became troubled by a discrepancy between economic theory and organizational reality. Economic theory predicts that goods and services are most efficiently produced in specialized organizations that are able to achieve economies of scale. Williamson questioned, however, why the twentieth century witnessed the growth of large bureaucracies that produce many goods and services internally (Perrow, 1986). Williamson proposes that costs are comprised of not only production costs – the costs of capital, labor and materials – but transaction costs. Transaction costs, which are synonymous with coordination costs, consist of the costs of monitoring, controlling and managing transactions. Thus, managers consider total costs (production costs plus transaction costs) when selecting among sourcing alternatives.

In general, Williamson argues that production costs are lower with outsourcing due to vendor economies of scale achieved through mass production efficiencies and labor specialization. In general, however, Williamson argues that transaction costs are lower with insourcing because internal organizations presumably administer an efficient system of rewards and punishments to discourage employee opportunism. In contrast, organizations must incur transaction costs during contract negotiations/monitoring to prevent vendor opportunism.

In practice, production and transaction costs are often difficult to assess. Williamson, however, provides a heuristic for estimating costs based on the inherent nature of the transaction type which favors insourcing or outsourcing. Transaction type is classified based on two dimensions: the frequency of occurrence and the degree of asset specificity. The *frequency of occurrence* refers to the number of times the buyer seeks to initiate the transaction. Transaction frequency may either be occasional or recurrent. *Asset specificity* refers to the degree to which assets are redeployable for alternative uses or users. A transaction type is highly asset specific if it cannot readily be used by other organizations because of its site specificity (location), physical asset specificity (degree of customization of the product or service), or human asset specificity (the degree of specialized knowledge required to produce the transaction). Asset specificity may be non-specific (highly standardized), idiosyncratic (highly customized to a specific organization), or mixed (some aspects of the transaction are standard while others are customized). Using the two dimensions – frequency and asset specificity – Williamson creates a framework for categorizing the most efficient governance mechanism. In order for the inherent efficiencies of outsourcing or insourcing to be realized, Williamson admonishes that appropriate contracts must be negotiated to prevent excessive coordination costs (see Table 2.1).

The framework in Table 2.1 assumes a degree of certainty exists. If a *high degree of uncertainty* surrounds the transaction, the relative appeal of outsourcing diminishes due to the increasing coordination costs incurred to develop an appropriate contract. For example, an organization may be able to define its telecommunications needs today, but their future needs may be highly uncertain given the unpredictable effect of new technologies, changes in business needs, mergers, acquisitions, etc. Williamson proposes that organizations have three alternatives when faced with a high degree of uncertainty: sacrifice design features to make the transaction more standardized, surround the transaction with an elaborate contract, or insource. Under extreme circumstances (which Williamson describes as "externalities"), a high degree of uncertainty paired with the threat of opportunism results in *information impactedness*. Williamson defines information impactedness as follows:

> It exists in circumstances in which one of the parties to an exchange is much better informed than is the other regarding underlying conditions germane to the trade and the second party cannot achieve information parity except at great cost – because he cannot rely on the first party to disclose the information in a fully candid manner (Williamson, 1975, p. 14).

Williamson argues that information impactedness will not impair outsourcing negotiations if any of the following conditions hold: parties do not behave opportunistically, the condition of unbounded rationality is achieved, or large number of suppliers exist. When all three of these

Table 2.1   Efficient Sourcing Strategies

Frequency	Asset Specificity		
	Non-specific	Mixed	Idiosyncratic
Occasional Frequency	*Outsource with Classical Contract Rationale*: For non-specific assets, the market achieves economies of scale on production costs. Transaction costs are minimal because the buyer does not need to monitor the vendor. Thus, classical contracts (i.e. standard contracts) , such as a computer store's return policy or the software manufacturer's warranty, serve to temper the threat of vendor opportunism.	*Outsource with Neo-classical Contract Rationale*: Hierarchies cannot obtain economies of scale for transactions only needed occasionally, thus the market has superior economies of scale on production costs. Transaction costs are minimized with neo-classical contracts in which all foreseeable contingencies are specified and the effects of enforceable contingencies are minimized by providing for third-party arbitration to resolve principal-agent disputes. The contract always serves as the original reference to coordinate the transaction.	
Recurrent Frequency		*Outsource with Relational Contract Rationale:* Market has superior economies of scale on production costs for the standard part of the transaction. Relational contracts, where mutual obligations of both parties are spelled out, minimize transaction costs because both parties have incentive to sustain the relationship–the company gets a steady supply, the vendor gets a steady stream of revenue.	*Insource* *Rationale*: Hierarchies can realize economies of scale as readily as vendors because assets are specialized to a single user. Because production costs are approximately equal, the decision criterion focuses on transaction costs. Transaction costs for outsourcing are more costly than insourcing because the contractual agreement needs to be more complex.

Source: Adapted from Williamson (1979)

assumptions are violated, Williamson suggests that insourcing is the most efficient governing mechanism.

Williamson's framework also assumes that there are a large number of providers in the market place. He maintains that markets with a large number of suppliers minimize opportunism because "rivalry among large numbers of bidders will render opportunistic inclinations ineffectual" (Williamson,

1975, p. 27). If this assumption is violated, *a small number of suppliers* increases the threat of opportunism. In order to minimize the threat of opportunism in the case of a small number of suppliers, organizations must negotiate appropriate contracts.

Williamson's theory can be summarized with the following proposition:

P1: When production and transaction costs are considered, outsourcing is more efficient than insourcing for all transactions except:
(a) recurrent-idiosyncratic transactions
or
(b) asset-specific transactions with a high degree of uncertainty
or
(c) transactions with a small number of suppliers

Research methodology

We sought to study organizations that had made substantial outsourcing decisions. Although outsourcing, in its most basic form, includes the external purchase of any good or service, we were not interested in studying traditional forms of outsourcing, such as the purchase of off-the-shelf software or the use of contract programmers and management consultants. These practices are well understood and pose little risk to practitioners. Instead, we were interested in decisions that span multiple systems, deal with the provision and management of IT products and services and represent at least 20% of the IT budget. Using these criteria, we studied 19 organizations in the United States and 21 organizations in the United Kingdom. As can be seen in Table 2.2, the cases represent a wide range of sourcing decisions including data center operations, system development, systems support, telecommunications and/or personal computers.

In total, participants in the 40 organizations made 61 sourcing decisions. Fourteen decisions resulted in *total outsourcing* when participants transferred IT assets, leases and staff to third-party vendors representing at least 80% of their IT budgets. Fifteen decisions resulted in *total insourcing* when participants decided to retain the management and provision of at least 80% of the IT budget internally. Thirty-two decisions resulted in *selective sourcing* when participants decided to source selected IT functions from external providers while still providing between 20–80% of the IT budget internally.

We interviewed 145 participants (see Table 2.2). At each case site, we conducted face-to-face interviews with individuals directly involved in the outsourcing decision on behalf of the organization or outsourcing vendor. The interviews each lasted for one to three hours. Interviewees included senior business executives and chief information officers (or equivalent

Table 2.2 Case Study Profiles

#	Industry & Size In Terms of Sales* and Mips	Case Study Participants	Sourcing Decision(S)[1]	Year of Decisions	# of Bids	Type of Contract	Expected Cost Savings	Cost Savings Achieved?	Initiator of the Decisions
1	U.S. Commercial Bank * 180 MIPS	1. VP of IS 2. Financial Manager 3. Manager of IS Group 4. Outsourcing Consultant	Total Outsourcing – 10 years	1990	1	Neo-classical	15–18%	Yes, as of 1994	Senior Manager
2	U.S. Diversified Services * 135 MIPS	5. Manager of IS 6. VP of Operationing Division 7. Vendor Account Manager 8. VP of Computer Utility 9. Outsourcing Consultant	(a) Total Insourcing (b) Total Outsourcing – 10 years	(a) 1988 (b) 1988	(a) 0 (b) 1	(a) N/A (b) Relational	(a) 0% (b) 20%	(a) none (b) No, customer threatened to sue vendor	(a) IT Manager (b) Senior Manager
3	U.S. Metals * <150 MIPS	10. Manager of IS 11. Manager of Systems 12. Manager of Purchasing 13. Vendor Account Manager 14. Outsourcing Consultant	Total Outsourcing – 10 years Development	1990	2	Neo-classical, with major loopholes	16%	Unable to determine	IT Manager
4	U.S. Transportation * <300 MIPS	15. Chief Financial Officer	Total Outsourcing – 10 years	1991	1	Neo-classical	20%	Unable to determine	Senior Manager

Table 2.2 Case Study Profiles – *continued*

#	Industry & Size In Terms of Sales* and Mips	Case Study Participants	Sourcing Decision(S)[1]	Year of Decisions	# of Bids	Type of Contract	Expected Cost Savings	Cost Savings Achieved?	Initiator of the Decisions
5	U.S. Mining * 150 MIPS	16. Controller 17. Vendor Account Manager	Total Outsourcing – 10 years	1991	1	Neo-classical, with loopholes quantified	Savings anticipated but not	Some anticipated savings achieved	Senior Manager
6	U.S. Aerospace * < 300 MIPS	18. Director of Processes and Tools	Total Outsourcing – 10 years	1993	1	Neo-classical	No savings estimated	Unable to determine	Senior Manager
7	U.S. Chemicals * <150 MIPS	19. Manager of Data Processing	(a) Total Outsourcing – 7 years (b) Total Insourcing – Return In-house	(a) 1984 (b) 1988	(a) 1 (b) 0	(a) Relational (b) N/A	(a&b) Savings anticipated but not quantified	(a) No, terminated contract early due to excessive costs	(a) Senior Manager (b) IT Manager
8	U.S. Rubber & Plastics * < 150 MIPS	20. VP of IS	(a) Total Outsourcing – 7 years (b) Total Insourcing – Return In-house	(a) 1987 (b) 1991	(a) 1 (b) N/A	(a) Relational (b) N/A	(a&b) Savings anticipated but not quantified	(a) No, IT costs rose to 4% of sales; contract terminated early	(a) Senior Manager (b) IT Manager
9	UK Clothing & Housewares Retailer * < 150 MIPS	21. Director of Logistics 22. Contract Manager 23. Vendor Account Manager 24. Branch Manager	Total Outsourcing – 10.5 years	1993	4	Neo-classical for present performance, Relational for contingencies	25%	Too early to determine	IT Managers

Table 2.2 Case Study Profiles – *continued*

#	Industry & Size In Terms of Sales* and Mips	Case Study Participants	Sourcing Decision(S)[1]	Year of Decisions	# of Bids	Type of Contract	Expected Cost Savings	Cost Savings Achieved?	Initiator of the Decisions
10	UK Oil * < 150 MIPS	25. Manager of IT 26. In-house Consultant 27. In-house Consultant 28. Vendor Account Manager 29. Contract Manager	(a) Selective: Diverse Services, 3 years (b) Selective: Accounting Services, 4 years (c) Total Outsourcing (3 contracts) Client Servers, WANs, Data Centers – 5 years	(a) 1988– 1990 (b) 1991 c) 1993	(a) 4 (b) 3 (c) 6	(a) Neo-classical (b) Neo-classical (c) Neo-classical with Relational aspects	(a) 15–20% (b) 20% (c) 20–25%	(a) Yes (b) Most (c) Some savings, less than 20%	(a) IT Managers (b) Senior Managers (c) Senior Managers
11	European Electronics * <150 MIPS	30. IS Director 31. Vendor IS Manager 32. Senior Manager 33. Marketing Manager	(a) Selective: Software Development & Support – 5 years (b) Total Outsourcing : Telecommunications and Data Centers – annually renewable	(a) 1989 (b) 1991	(a) 1 (b) 1	(a & b) Neo-classical with relational aspects	(a & b) No cost savings estimated, desire to create variable IT costs	(a& b) Some cost savings	(a&b) Senior & IT Managers
12	UK insurance <50 MIPS	34. IS Director 35. Vendor Account Manager 36. Senior Manager 37. Consultant	(a) Total Outsourcing – 1 year (b) Selective Outsourcing – Systems Maintenance – 1 year (c) Total Insourcing – 1 year	(a) 1990 (b) 1991 (c) 1993	(a) 1 (b) 1 (c) 2	(a) Neo-classical (b) Neo-classical (c) Neo-classical	(a) No (b) 25–30% (c) 30%	(a) No (b) Yes (c) Yes	(a&b&c) Senior & IT Managers

Table 2.2 Case Study Profiles – *continued*

#	Industry & Size In Terms of Sales* and Mips	Case Study Participants	Sourcing Decision(S)[1]	Year of Decisions	# of Bids	Type of Contract	Expected Cost Savings	Cost Savings Achieved?	Initiator of the Decisions
23	UK Water Company 20 MIPS	72. Business Manager 73. IS Director 74. Manager of Operations 75. Vendor Account Manager	Selective – Customer Billing System – 5 years	1991	2	Neo-classical	20%	Yes	IT Manager
24	U.S. Petroleum Refining < 150 MIPS	76. Director of IS 77. Controller 78. Manager of Network Services 79. Data Center Manager 80. Supervisor of Technical Support 81. Manager of Applications	Selective-Data Center – 5 years	1991	2	Neo-classical	16%	Unable to determine	IT Manager
25	UK Retail and Distribution * < 300 MIPS	82. Principal, IT Consultant 83. Group IS Director 84. Vendor Account Manager 85. Business Manager	(a) Selective – Corporate Telecommunications – 3 years (b) Selective – Telecommunications – 2.5 years	(a) 1990 (b) 1992	(a) 3 (b) 3	(a) Classical (b) Neo-classical	(a) 20% (b) 30%	(a) Yes (b) Yes	(a&b) IT Managers

Table 2.2 Case Study Profiles – *continued*

#	Industry & Size In Terms of Sales* and Mips	Case Study Participants	Sourcing Decision(S)[1]	Year of Decisions	# of Bids	Type of Contract	Expected Cost Savings	Cost Savings Achieved?	Initiator of the Decisions
26	UK Chemicals Manufacturer * <150 MIPS	86. Group IT Manager 87. Manager of Applications Development 88. Manager of European & UK Operations 89. Manager of IT Development	(a) Selective: System Support – 2 years (b) Selective: Development & Support – 2 years (c) Selective: Development & Support – 3 years	(a) 1985 (b) 1991 (c) 1992	(a) 3 (b) 1 (c) 4	(a&b&c) Neo-classical	(a) 40% (b) 30% (c) 20%	(a) 50% over 8 years (b) Some (c) Most	Senior and IT Managers
27	UK Food Manufacturer * 76 MIPS	90. Manager of IT Services 91. Managing Director of Group Services 92. Consultant 93. Senior Manager	(a) Total Insourcing (b) Selective – Factory Software Development – 2.5 years	(a) 1990 (b) 1991	(a) 2 (b) 3	(a) N/A (b) Neo-classical	(a) 20–30% (b) 25%	(a) Yes (b) No	(a) IT Manager (b) Business & IT Managers
28	UK Consumer Product Manufacturer * <150 MIPS	94. Director of IS 95. Manager of Operations 96. Manager of Operations 97. Vendor Account Manager	(a) Total Outsourcing – 5 years (b) Selective – Data Center – 3 years	(a) 1985 (b) 1988	(a) 5 (b) 4	(a) Neo-classical (b) Neo-classical	(a) 15% (b) 20%	(a) No (b) Yes	(a) Senior & IT Managers (b) Business and IT Managers
29	U.S. Commercial Bank * < 150 MIPS	98. Contract Manager 99. Vendor Consultant 100. Senior Business Manager 101. Data Center Manager	Selective – Data Centers – 5 years	1992	5	Neo-classical	25%	Yes	Senior Business Manager

Table 2.2 Case Study Profiles – *continued*

#	Industry & Size In Terms of Sales* and Mips	Case Study Participants	Sourcing Decision(S)[1]	Year of Decisions	# of Bids	Type of Contract	Expected Cost Savings	Cost Savings Achieved?	Initiator of the Decisions
30	UK Commercial Bank * < 150 MIPS	102. Managing Director of IT 103. Manager of IT Operations 104. Vendor Account Manager 105. Senior Manager	(a) Selective – Systems Support – 3 years (b) Selective – Systems Support & Enhancement – 2 years	(a) 1991 (b) 1992	(a) 4 (b) 4	(a) Neo-classical (b) Neo-classical	(a) 15–20% (b) 20%	(a) Yes (b) Yes	Business and IT Managers
31	UK Glass and Plastics Manufacturer * 40 MIPS	106. Group IS Director 107. Vendor Account Manager 108. Manager of IS	Selective – Data Center and Systems Development – 2 years + renewed for 3 years	1992	5	Neo-classical for data center, Relational for other aspects	24%	Yes	Senior and IT Managers
32	UK Brewing & Distribution* < 300 MIPS	109. Director of Systems Services 110. Vendor Director 111. Contract Manager 112. Production Manager	Selective – Central Systems Development & Support – 5 years	1993	4 informal	Neo-classical with Relational elements over 5 years	Cost increase over 2 years, Break even	1st year cost increase	IT Managers
33	UK Clothing & Food Retailer * 150 MIPS	113. Operating Services Manager 114. Senior Business Manager 115. Senior Business Manager 116. Vendor Account Manager 117. Manager of IT	(a) Selective-Data Center – 3 years (b) Selective – PC Maintenance – 3 years (c) Selective – Mainframe Maintenance – 3 years	(a) 1988 (b) 1988 (c) 1990	(a) 3 (b) 4 (c) 2	(a) Neo-classical (b) Neo-classical (c) Neo-classical	(a) None (b) 15% (c) 20%	(a) N/A (b) Yes (c) Yes	IT Managers

Table 2.2 Case Study Profiles – *continued*

#	Industry & Size In Terms of Sales* and Mips	Case Study Participants	Sourcing Decision(S)[1]	Year of Decisions	# of Bids	Type of Contract	Expected Cost Savings	Cost Savings Achieved?	Initiator of the Decisions
34	UK Food Manufacturer* <50 MIPS	118. Manager of IS 119. Manager of Software Development 120. Manager of Systems Management 121. Vendor Account Manager	(a) Selective – Factory Software Development – 2 years (b) Selective – Data Center – 3 years	(a) 1988 (b) 1992	(a) 4 (b) 5	(a) Neo-classical with Relational aspects (b) Neo-classical	(a) None (b) 30-33%	(a) No, Costs doubled (b) Yes, so far	(a) Senior Manager (b) IT Manager
35	UK Electricity Supply* <100 MIPS	122. Manager of IT Operations 123. Contract Manager 124. Services Manager	Selective – Distributed PC Networks & UNIX Servers – 2 years	1992	6	Neo-classical	30%	Yes, as of 1994	Divisional Manager
36	UK Public Health Authority (PSB) <100 MIPS	125. Director of IS 126. IS Staff Member 127. IS Staff Member 128. Contract Manager 129. Regional Manager	Selective – Data Center and Software Packages – 5 years	1991	4	Neo-classical	20-25%	Yes	IT Manager
37	UK County Council (PSB) <50 MIPS	130. Manager of IS 131. Department Manager 132. Vendor Consultant 133. Outsourcing Consultant 134. Contract Manager	(a) Selective – Data Center & Tele-communications – 5 years (b) Selective – Office Systems Support – 4 years	(a) 1991 (b) 1992	(a) 6 (b) 1	(a) Neo-classical (b) Neo-classical	(a) 20% (b) 17%	(a) Yes, 20-22% (b) Yes	(a&b) IT, Finance & Business Service Managers

Table 2.2 Case Study Profiles – *continued*

#	Industry & Size In Terms of Sales* and Mips	Case Study Participants	Sourcing Decision(S)[1]	Year of Decisions	# of Bids	Type of Contract	Expected Cost Savings	Cost Savings Achieved?	Initiator of the Decisions
38	UK Broadcasting Corporation * (PSB) <100 MIPS	135. Director of IS 136. Contract Manager 137. Production Manager	(a) Insourcing (b) Selective – Data Center – 7 years	(a) 1988 (b) 1992	(a) 1 (b) 5	(a) N/A (b) Neo-classical	(a) 25% (b) 35%	(a) Yes (b) Yes	(a) Senior & IT Managers (b) IT Manager
39	UK Aviation Authority * <100 MIPS	138. Manager – Internal IT 139. Contract Manager 140. Vendor Consultant 141. Vendor Manager	(a) Selective – Payroll & Financial Systems – 5 years (b) Selective – PCs and Networks – 4 years (c) Selective – Financial Packages – 5 years	(a) 1988 (b) 1989 (c) 1990	(a) 2 (b) 3 (c) 1	(a) Classical (b) Neo-classical (c) Neo-classical	(a) 15% (b) Some (c) Some	(a) none (b) minimal (c) minimal	(a) Senior Manager (b) IT Manager (c) IT Manager
40	UK Water Company <100 MIPS	142. Director of IS 143. Vendor Manager 144. Contract Manager 145. Senior Manager	Selective – Data Center – 3 years	1994	3	Neo-classical	15–20%	too early	Senior Managers

1 Some companies evaluated outsourcing on multiple occasions
2 PSB = Public Sector Body
* = U.S. *Fortune 500 or Financial Times European 1000*

title) who initiated the sourcing evaluations, consultants hired to assist contract negotiations and vendor account managers responsible for the execution of the resulting contract. We also interviewed IT personnel responsible for gathering technical and financial information. During the interviews, we sought to understand the participants' perceptions of the motivations, evaluation processes and consequences of their sourcing decisions. In this sense, we assumed an interpretive perspective with the goal of understanding the information systems outsourcing phenomenon from the participants' viewpoint (Orlikowski and Baroudi, 1991).

In addition to the interviews, we gathered relevant documentation such as the outsourcing request for proposals, outsourcing bids, internal bids, bid analysis criteria, outsourcing contracts, benchmarks, annual reports and organizational charts. We used the documentation to corroborate participants' statements and to analyze contract specifics.

All interviews were tape-recorded and transcribed into 1,120 single-spaced pages. After reflecting upon participants' similar experiences across both sides of the Atlantic Ocean, we sought to formalize the body of evidence with a sourcing theory. Although we had collected ample anecdotes of successes and failures, we believe that a contribution to knowledge requires a higher level of abstraction and interpretation:

> Discovering truth is really a matter of creatively incorporating events into theories to make sense of them. Administrative science is essentially an interpretive exercise, a sense-making activity in which truth is defined by the rules of intelligibility embodied in theoretical schemata....the interpretive framework, not the observations, contribute to our knowledge (Astley, 1985, p. 498).

For reasons already cited, we selected TCE as a potential theoretical framework. From an interpretive perspective, we do not assume that TCE (or any theory) describes an objective reality, but rather we view theories as products of people used to help ascribe meaning to existence. From an interpretive perspective, theories are assumed to encapsulate "explanations of human intentions" (Chua, 1986), "linguistic products of research" (Astley, 1985), or "perceptual filters" (Allison, 1972). The common element in all these descriptions is that theories are assumed to be social constructions of reality, not objective formulations of truth. Therefore, our decision to analyze our evidence from a transaction cost perspective was based upon our need for a coherent, formal interpretation of sourcing decisions rather than an attempt to support or refute TCE in a Popperian sense (Popper, 1988). If TCE provides a useful interpretation, we would expect to see that decision-makers make sourcing decisions as described by Williamson in Table 2.1. To analyze this proposition, we mapped the participants' transactions types (frequency and asset specificity) and contract types into Williamson's framework of efficient sourcing strategies.

Mapping transaction types We mapped systems development as an occasional transaction because participants systematically perceived system development as a one-time transaction. Although systems continue to evolve through enhancements, these on-going activities were described by participants as systems maintenance or systems support rather than systems development. Participants perceived systems maintenance, systems support, data center operations, PC support, end user support, ana-lyst training, user training and telecommunications as on-going activities. We mapped these to Williamson's framework as recurrent transactions.

To assess the asset specificity of the transaction, we relied on participants' views of the transaction. To illustrate our categorizations, we provide the following examples. Participants from FIRMS 18, 29 and 32 view data center operations as a support commodity rather than a strategic asset requiring specialized knowledge. We therefore classified these transactions as "non-specific":

> FIRM18 does not have a desire to be a leader from a technological standpoint. Competitive advantage and things like that did not enter into the reason for data processing, people don't see it as a tool for that...I needed to determine what was the most cost-effective way to deliver computer resources to the organization. Our outsourcing evaluation was limited to evaluation of the processor. And receiving the service much like when you flip on a light switch and get electricity – Director of IS, FIRM18

> We looked upon datacenters as just being a tool, a big PC on your desk, to provide a hardware service, but we did not see it as being an intelligent service and therefore it could be outsourced. – Contract Manager, FIRM29

> IT is not seen as the stuff of competitive edge by and large. It's viewed as a facilitator...we don't see our business as being particularly demanding on IT compared to a bank or airline...it's more support, really. – System Services Director, FIRM32

When participants perceived that transactions required specialized knowledge, we classified the transactions as "idiosyncratic". For example, participants from FIRMS 1, 25 and 29 perceive that applications development requires specific business expertise. At FIRM1, 20% of the IT budget is generated by developing applications for the Treasury Department, for which the internal IT department possessed a significant business expertise. The

IT manager therefore limited the scope of the decision to data processing, which represented 80% of her budget:

> We did look at applications because we felt we needed to do that; the conclusion to the study, not unlike our gut feeling, is that we are best to manage that ourselves. – VP of IS, FIRM1

Participants from FIRM25 and FIRM29 also perceive a significant business expertise is required to develop applications:

> We would not outsource instrumental color matching which is done within our research community. They use a lot of IT skills and we really do not want any knowledge about formulations or physical equipment used to become generally available. – Contract Manager, FIRM25

> Our most successful franchise is the foreign exchange dealing and customer environment. The systems we built up to support this in terms of trading and back office operational support are considered marketplace leaders and we would not want to relinquish control of that. – Contract Manager, FIRM29

Because participants in half of the sourcing decisions used an entire IT department as a unit of analysis rather than treating individual IT activities separately, we characterized the 14 total outsourcing and 15 total insourcing decisions as "mixed-recurrent". Participants perceived that some IT functions involved in the transaction, such as some new system development projects, required highly specialized skills while they perceived that other IT functions, such as data processing, were standard. In total, the entire transaction possesses both standard (non-specific) and customized (idiosyncratic) attributes and will be performed over the next five to ten years (as evidenced by the RFP), thus suggesting a mixed-recurrent transaction.

Mapping contract types To categorize contract types into classical, neo-classical and relational, we analyzed participants' perceptions of the contract and the level of detail evident in the contracts (see "Type of Contract" Column in Table 2.2).

As Williamson notes, classical contracts do not require the buyer to engage in specialized contracting. We thus categorized two contracts as "classical" because participants signed the vendor's standard contract:

> All we had was a contract written by the vendor. – Contract Manager, FIRM25

Basically the vendor drew up the contract and it was put to us. – IT Manager, FIRM39

Williamson argues that neo-classical contracts include special contractual clauses that serve as the original reference to coordinate the transaction (Williamson, 1979). We classified 34 contracts as "neo-classical" because participants included special requirements such as detailing contingencies, measures of performance, service levels and penalties for non-performance. For example, FIRM24's contract is classified as "neo-classical" because of the level of detail specified in the contract as well as the IT Manager's perception that the document will serve as the original reference:

A lot of people at (the outsourcing vendor) were uncomfortable with this (contract). In fact, their VP said, "Can't we put this thing in the drawer?" I said, "Yeah, but this is still the operating agreement." – Director of IS, FIRM24

We initially categorized only three contracts as "relational" because the contracts failed to detail contingencies, implying that the contracts would not be used as original references, but that the parties would commit to solving disputes under the trust and spirit of partnership (Henderson, 1990). For example, we categorized FIRM2's contract as "relational" because participants failed to articulate service levels, measures of performance, or penalties for non-performance. FIRM2's CEO declared after a few high level meetings with the vendor, "let's make a marriage," thus corroborating the categorization of the contract as relational.

We had trouble categorizing eight contracts as either "neo-classical" or "relational" because they included aspects of both. For the first year or two of the contract, data processing requirements were fully specified, connoting a neo-classical contract. However, participants realized that technology and business requirements would change in the long run and agreed that the vendors would adapt in the spirit of a partnership. For example, we classified FIRM31's contract as "neo-classical with relational aspects":

The organization was looking for a minimum fixed price contract with provision to add other things as they materialized. The organization was in the throws of reorganization and could only define quite high-level deliverables. To put a boundary around the contract, we did it by resourcing level – the vendor will deliver these things or substitutions thereof by mutual agreement...The organization wanted a very flexible arrangement which is where the trust things come in.

The service level was based around existing services. We spent the first 3 months of the contract securing the service, settling it down and defining and agreeing the service levels. – Vendor Account Manager, FIRM31

For the purposes of mapping the cases to Williamson's framework, however, we categorized these mixed contracts as "relational" because participants perceived that their outsourcing vendors would operate as partners for the duration of the contract.

Data anomalies

In Table 2.3, we highlighted Williamson's predictions of efficient sourcing decisions by shading the boxes, then mapped our cases into the framework. Only 13 of the 61 sourcing decisions map as predicted by Williamson.

In order to interpret the anomalies (i.e. contradictions), however, we limit our analysis to the 40 sourcing decisions for which financial success or failure were clearly demonstrated (see "Cost Savings Achieved" column in

Table 2.3 All Sourcing Decisions Mapped to TCE Framework (n=61 sourcing decisions)

| Transaction Type | Insource | Outsource | | |
		Classical Contract	Neo-classical Contract	Relational
Non-specific/ Occasional Non-specific/ Recurrent	38a	25a, 39a	1,10a,23,24, 25b,26a,28b,29, 30a,33abc,34b, 36,37ab,38b, 39bc,40	
Mixed/ Occasional Idiosyncratic/ Occasional			27b	34a
Mixed/ Recurrent	2a,7b,8b,12c, 14,15,16,17,18, 19,20,21,22,27a		3,4,5,6,10b, 12ab,26bc,28a, 30b,35	2b,7a,8a,9,10c, 11ab,13,31,32
Idiosyncratic/ Recurrent				

☐ Predicted by TCE

Table 2.2). In this way, we can determine if the anomalies are attributed to the fact that participants made wrong sourcing decisions. Thus, Williamson's framework would adequately explain the data. When successes and failures are mapped into Williamson's framework, only three of the 33 sourcing successes and two of the seven sourcing failures are readily explained (see Table 2.4), resulting in anomalies for 87.5% of the cases.

In 30 sourcing decisions made in 27 companies, participants experienced successful sourcing decisions, although they did fall into Williamson's framework. We categorized these 30 sourcing decisions into four anomalies:

Anomaly 1. FIRM38 (decision "a") successfully insourced a non-specific recurrent asset rather than outsourced this as predicted by Williamson.

Table 2.4 Successful and Unsuccessful Outcomes Mapped to TCE Framework (n=40 sourcing decisions)

| Transaction Type | Insource | | Outsource | | | | | |
| | | | Classical Contract | | Neo-classical Contract | | Relational | |
	Failure	Success	Failure	Success	Failure	Success	Failure	Success
Non-specific/ Occasional & Non-specific/ Recurrent		38a	39a	25a		1,10a, 23,25b, 26a,28b, 29,30a, 33bc,34b, 36,37ab, 38b		
Mixed/ Occasional & Idiosyncratic/ Occasional					27b		34a	
Mixed/Recurrent		12c, 17, 19, 20, 21, 22, 27a			28a	5,10b, 12b, 26bc, 30b,35	2b,7a, 8a	10c,31
Idiosyncratic/ Recurrent								

☐ Success predicted by TCE
■ Failure predicted by TCE

Anomaly 2. FIRMS 1, 10a, 23, 25b, 26a, 28b, 29, 30a, 33bc, 34b, 36, 37ab and 38b all successfully outsourced non-specific transactions using a neo-classical contract rather than a classical contract as predicted by Williamson.

Anomaly 3. FIRMS 12c, 17, 19, 20, 21, 22 and 27a successfully insourced mixed-recurrent transactions rather than outsourced using a relational contract as predicted by Williamson.

Anomaly 4. FIRMS 5, 10b, 12b, 26bc, 30b and 35 successfully out-sourced mixed-recurrent transactions using neo-classical contracts rather than outsourced using a relational contract as predicted by Williamson.

In five sourcing decisions, participants experienced failures even though they made sourcing decisions as described by Williamson. We organized these five sourcing decisions into the following three anomalies:

Anomaly 5. FIRM39a outsourced a non-specific asset using a classical contract as predicted by Williamson, but the transaction resulted in failure.

Anomaly 6. FIRM27b outsourced an idiosyncratic/occasional transaction using a neo-classical contract as predicted by Williamson, but the trans-action resulted in failure.

Anomaly 7. FIRMS 2b, 7a and 8a outsourced mixed-recurrent transac-tions using relational contracts as predicted by Williamson, but these transactions resulted in failure.

A Hegelian approach to anomaly interpretation

After the mappings generated anomalies for 87.5% of the cases, we began to speculate how to interpret them. We chose a Hegelian approach – a dialectic process by which a *thesis* and *antithesis* serve to uncover contradic-tions which lead to a new, higher-stage of development called a *synthesis* (Churchman, 1971; Burrell and Morgan, 1979). Although Hegelians ini-tially used this approach to explain historical developments – such as the development of Feudalism, Capitalism and Communism – the Hegelian approach to inquiry has been adopted in many social contexts (Stevenson, 1987). For example, our justice system is based on a thesis (prosecution), antithesis (defence) and synthesis (verdict).

We adopted a Hegelian approach by asking: How would staunch TCE proponents and staunch TCE opponents interpret the anomalies? Presumably, TCE proponents would defend the following thesis: *transaction cost economics explains the IT outsourcing data*. That is, TCE proponents would defend TCE by dismissing, explaining, or re-interpreting the "apparent" anomalies. Alternatively, TCE opponents could defend the antithesis: *transaction cost economics does not explain the IT outsourcing data*. Although we have tried to present the thesis and antithesis as neutrally as possible, Churchman warns that subscribers to either position will assume a "mood of opposition":

> Now the very effort to maintain one's convictions in the thesis generates opportunity for the deadliest enemy…the antithesis is not the contradictory of the thesis, but rather its deadliest enemy. It is an anti-conviction of forcefulness at least as great as the conviction. (Churchman, 1971, pp. 172–173)

The aim of arguing for both a thesis and an antithesis is to uncover contradictions or false assumptions in either view. By examining both positions, we aim to generate a debate within the academic community on the applicability of using TCE to explain the IT outsourcing phenomenon. We believe this debate is important because adoption of theories from other disciplines needs to be critically examined within our own discipline. We argue that a synthesis of the debate may lead to supplementing TCE with additional theories to increase its explanatory powers in the context of IT outsourcing. Or alternatively, we as a discipline may develop a more narrow, but IT-specific theory to explain and predict IT sourcing behaviors.

Thesis: A TCT explanation of anomalies

TCE proponents could explain all the data anomalies within the TCE framework by appealing to exceptions or by re-interpreting TCE language. Possible explanations for each anomaly follow:

Anomaly 1. FIRM38 successfully insourced a non-specific-recurrent asset (data center operations) rather than outsourced this as predicted by Williamson. In reality, TCE proponents could argue that this anomaly is explained by an analysis of production costs. FIRM38 operated five large mainframes, which placed them well within the theoretical level of economies of scale, which Real Decisions and Compass estimate to begin at 150 MIPs. In the exception case when internal production costs are equivalent to a vendor, transaction costs become the main criterion for evaluating outsourcing. As Williamson predicts, insourcing becomes the preferred option because transaction costs will be minimized.

Anomaly 2. FIRMS 1, 10a, 23, 25b, 26a, 28b, 29, 30a, 33bc, 34b, 36, 37ab and 38b all successfully outsourced non-specific transactions using a neo-classical contract, rather than a classical contract as predicted by Williamson. Upon further reflection, TCE proponents could argue that these transactions may actually be mixed assets rather than non-specific assets. We originally categorized these transactions as non-specific because participants used terms to connote a non-specific asset, such as "commodity", "utility", "electricity", "cafeteria", "laundry service", "mail room". Thus, participants uttered language that suggests a non-specific asset. However, upon analysis of their behavior as documented in the contract, participants detailed many contingencies, thus suggesting that the transaction is not "non-specific" as defined by Williamson. IT "commodities" are therefore not equivalent to the TCE concept of "commodities". Thus, the ambiguities in the language of TCE provides one explanation for the discrepancy in Table 2.4.

Anomaly 3. FIRMS 12c, 17, 19, 20, 21, 22 and 27a successfully insourced mixed-recurrent transactions rather than outsourced using a relational contract as predicted by Williamson. TCE proponents could provide explanations consistent with a TCE perspective for all seven of these anomalies.

At FIRM12, participants decided to outsource when they started the insurance organization. Rather than invest capital to erect an internal IT department, they outsourced to a vendor. However, the exception of a small number of suppliers existed, as only one vendor in the marketplace was able to provide total outsourcing services for this large organization (see "Number of Bids" column in Table 2.2). As a result, the vendor behaved opportunistically and over-charged FIRM12. Thus, this anomaly can be explained by TCE – the exception of a small number of suppliers promoted vendor opportunism which increased transaction costs to the point where it became more efficient to insource.

In FIRMS 17, 20, 21, the internal IT departments decided to consolidate their own data centers to achieve economies of scale in data processing. Through consolidation, these organizations achieved theoretical economies of scale. Under the exception case when internal production costs are equivalent to a vendor, transaction costs become the main criterion for evaluating outsourcing. As Williamson predicts, insourcing becomes the preferred option because the transaction costs will be minimized.

At FIRM19, participants also consolidated two data centers into one data center that operates at 56 MIPs. Although this data center size is less than the theoretically efficient size, FIRM19 is classified as a success because they reduced costs by 54%. A TCE proponent could provide several explanations. A TCE proponent could claim that data center operations at this site are idiosyncratic and thus specialized knowledge of the business enables FIRM19's IT staff to operate more efficiently than a vendor. Alternatively, TCE proponents could also claim that FIRM19 is considered a success merely because they eliminated a very inefficient practice of operating two small data centers. Because FIRM19 failed to create a formal request for proposal (RFP), we have no comparison against external vendor bids; thus it is difficult to determine whether outsourcing vendors could still improve cost efficiency.

At FIRM22, data center costs were high because a unionized labor force enacted inefficient work practices such as requiring supervisors on every shift, preventing supervisors from touching the hardware and requiring both a manager and technician to be brought in for emergencies. Although FIRM22's IT managers had tried to negotiate better terms, the labor union resisted. Only after the request for proposal attracted two external bids did the labor union agree to allow the internal IT department to include revised union rules in their internal bid. The internal bid won and FIRM22 subsequently reduced costs by 46%. TCE proponents could explain this experience by claiming that the labor union was really the exception of a monopoly supplier that behaved opportunistically. The threat of competition rendered opportunism ineffectual, as Williamson predicts.

At FIRM27, participants operate a 76 MIP data center that has similar average costs to 200 MIP data centers, as determined by a benchmarking service and an outsourcing evaluation. Thus, a TCE proponent could argue that because production costs are comparable to a vendor, transaction costs become the sole criterion. As Williamson predicts, insourcing becomes the preferred option because transaction costs will be minimized.

Anomaly 4. FIRMS 5, 10b, 12b, 26bc, 30b and 35 successfully outsourced mixed-recurrent transactions using neo-classical contracts rather than outsourced using a relational contract as predicted by Williamson. This anomaly can be explained from a TCE perspective by appealing to the exception of a high degree of uncertainty. One could argue these transactions were highly uncertain due to the length of the contact (ten years for FIRM5), unspecified requirements for new applications development (FIRM26), or unspecified enhancements and corrections for systems support (FIRM10, FIRM12, FIRM30). Williamson notes that under a high degree of uncertainty, organizations must surround the transaction with an elaborate contract to reduce the threat of opportunism.

Anomaly 5. FIRM39a outsourced a non-specific asset (payroll & financial systems) using a classical contract as predicted by Williamson, but the transaction resulted in failure. This anomaly can be explained from a TCE perspective by appealing to language ambiguities. TCE proponents could argue that the transaction was more asset-specific than the participants originally perceived. As FIRM39 subsequently experienced, many "commodity" type applications, such as payroll, require specific customization. FIRM39's failure to detail the specifics of the contract led to unexpected excess charges. Thus, a TCE proponent could conclude that FIRM39's failure is explained by the fact that the asset was more specific than participants perceived and thus participants should have signed a neo-classical contract rather than a classical contract.

Anomaly 6. FIRM27b outsourced an idiosyncratic/occasional (factory software development) transaction using a neo-classical contract as predicted by Williamson, but the transaction resulted in failure. TCE proponents could explain the failure by arguing that the exception of a high degree of uncertainty increased transaction costs. The Systems Director explains that the users kept changing the system requirements, resulting in the vendor charging extra fees:

> [The vendor] would almost certainly say that it failed because FIRM27 kept changing their minds and new developments kept coming in. – Systems Director, FIRM27.

Williamson notes that transaction costs increase with a high level of uncertainty and recommends that buyers sacrifice design features to make the asset more standard, surround the transaction with an elaborate contract, or insource – tactics FIRM27 failed to pursue.

Anomaly 7. FIRMS 2b, 7a and 8a outsourced mixed-recurrent transactions using relational contracts as predicted by Williamson, but these transactions resulted in failure. A TCE proponent could provide a transaction cost perspective by appealing to the exceptions of a high degree of uncertainty and a small number of suppliers. Williamson argues that under these exceptions, the threat of opportunism will significantly increase transaction costs. In all three of these cases, TCE proponents could appeal to these exceptions. A high degree of uncertainty existed because these organizations signed contracts for 7–10 years, naively assuming that their information needs would remain stable over the contract period. The participants failed to account for the degree of uncertainty in changing business needs and advances in information technology. As a result, participants were charged stiff fees to accommodate change. The Manager of IS from FIRM2 explains:

> The vendor makes sense in a stable environment where resource requirements and growth can be realistically predicted and the organization can provide [the vendor] with a complete and detailed forecast of the services. Deviations are costly and if they do not fit [the vendor's]

operating standards, extremely costly to obtain. – Manager of IS, FIRM2

During the mid-1980s when these contracts were signed, only one vendor (the same vendor in all three cases) submitted a bid. This vendor was virtually the only vendor in the marketplace large enough to provide total outsourcing services for large *Fortune* 500 organizations. As Williamson predicts, the small number of suppliers enabled the vendor to behave opportunistically. All three participating organizations were charged stiff excess fees for services they assumed were covered in the contract. At FIRM2, for example, the participants received one monthly bill for $500,000 worth of excess charges. The participants had no recourse because they signed a relational contract that provided few details for the services and service levels they expected to receive from the vendor. TCE proponents could thus explain the anomaly by appealing to the exceptions of high degree of uncertainty and small number of suppliers.

IT and TCE exceptions

Throughout our analysis, we noted that TCE proponents could explain the anomalies from P1 by appealing to TCE exceptions of high uncertainty, recurrent-idiosyncratic transactions, a small number of suppliers, or by appealing to language ambiguities. In this section, we discuss why the unique nature of information technology triggers TCE exceptions.

1. Information technology evolves rapidly – exception of high degree of uncertainty.
2. The underlying economics of information technology changes rapidly – exception of high degree of uncertainty.
3. The penetration of information technology to all business functions is ubiquitous – exception of recurrent idiosyncratic transactions.
4. The switching costs to alternative information technologies and IT suppliers is high – exception of small number of suppliers.
5. Customers are often inexperienced with information technology outsourcing – exceptional condition of information impactedness.

1. Information technology evolves rapidly. Because information technology evolves so rapidly, IT outsourcing decisions – particularly decisions which may result in long-term contracts – are always surrounded by a high degree of uncertainty. Although participants from 11 organizations initially perceived that outsourcing vendors would reduce the uncertainty associated with new IT, many discovered that outsourcing actually locks them into older technologies. Senior managers, in particular, found keeping up with the rapid evolution of IT an overwhelming task. They reasoned that by outsourcing IT, the vendors would help them keep abreast of new IT advancements. In reality, participants found that vendors are motivated to maintain the same level of technology rather than implement advancements. For example, FIRM2 signed a ten-year total outsourcing contract in 1988. At that time, the majority of systems were running on mainframe technology. With the advent of client-server technology, FIRM2 participants wanted to migrate to the smaller platform but found their outsourcing contract erected significant obstacles. In the end, business unit leaders used discretionary funds to build client-server technologies while still paying on the ten-year contract for the increasingly obsolescent mainframe.

Other organizations experienced the same fate as FIRM2. The manager of data processing from FIRM7 complains that his vendor was motivated to simply run the technology "into the ground":

> I think you find with outsourcing that any innovation in technology comes from your own people. Requirements from users on your staff. But basically the [outsourcing vendor] just cranks it. And so we were operating old software. Some of it was written in the 1960s. All batch. – Manager of Data Processing, FIRM7

The purchasing manager from FIRM3 argues that access to new technologies can be very costly:

> None of it is cheap. I guess there is a perception that once you have an outsourcer hooked in that you have a conduit to all this expertise, but you pay. – Purchasing Manager, FIRM3

Because of the uncertainty associated with rapid IT evolution, participants felt (in hindsight) that contracts over three years in duration lock customers into older technologies.

2. The underlying economics of information technology changes rapidly. Although price/performance improvements occur in every industry, in few industries do the underlying economics shift as fast as IT. A mainframe MIP that cost $1 million in 1965 costs less than $30,000 in 1995. Today's computing resources will cost 20 to 30% less next year (Benjamin and Blunt, 1992). The rapid change in the underlying economics causes extreme uncertainty and thus makes it difficult for decision-makers to evaluate costs of outsourcing bids. While a 10% discount on IT for the next ten years may be appealing to a senior executive today, by next year he or she may be paying the vendor above-market prices for computer resources.

3. The penetration of information technology to all business functions is ubiquitous. Many senior executives we interviewed treated the IT outsourcing decision in much the same way they treated other outsourcing decisions. For example, one senior executive questioned why he should treat outsourcing IT any differently than outsourcing advertising. The answer is that unlike advertisements – and unlike many other products and services – IT cannot be easily isolated from other organizational functions. IT penetrates every business function in the value chain as well as all support activities (Porter and Millar, 1985).

The ubiquitous nature of IT penetration makes outsourcing difficult because idiosyncratic knowledge of an organization is required for most IT activities. When participants tried to isolate IT activities for outsourcing, they often discovered that changes to the outsourced function affect other areas of the business. The vendors typically lacked the specialized knowledge to cope with organizational interfaces outside the boundaries of the IT outsourcing contract. For example, FIRM34 outsourced the development of factory automation. Soon into the contract, participants realized that the new system had profound implications for the existing systems in almost every department in the business. Although the vendor had specialized technical knowledge on factory software, they lacked the specialized business knowledge to cope with interfaces. The system took four years to develop instead of two.

Even IT activities described by participants as "commodities", such as data center operations, payroll and PC support, requires specific adaptation – and thus specialized knowledge – of a particular organization. For example, participants often used "commodity" language to refer to their data centers. In actuality, data centers are hardly homogeneous. Different organizations use different hardware configurations, operating software, software utilities, facilities for cooling/lighting/fire prevention, levels of software automation and disaster recovery strategies and provide different service levels. Specialized knowledge of a given organization's production schedule is also a critical skill – knowing what users run what systems at what times with what particular problems can make the difference between a successful and unsuccessful data center.

Thus, the exception of TCE's recurrent-idiosyncratic transactions is more the general rule in the IT outsourcing context – a high degree of physical asset specificity requires customization of IT products and services. In addition, a high degree of human asset specificity requires specialized business knowledge to create the product or service.

4. The switching costs to alternative information technologies and IT suppliers is high. Because much of TCE relies on ample competition to dissuade vendor opportunism, the situation of a small number of suppliers is treated as an exception. In the area of IT, high switching costs make the circumstances of a small number of suppliers the norm rather than the exception. Once participants sign with an outsourcing vendor, the threat of opportunism is extremely likely because the switching costs to another vendor or to an in-house IT function are extremely expensive. As the CFO from FIRM4 notes:

> Once you sign with a vendor, you have no options other than onerous contract terms, so when you get into a situation it's a lose/lose for both parties. What are you going to do? Sue them? Fire them? Stop buying services? There is nobody else, in a short period of time, who you can buy services from. – CFO, FIRM4

Although some participants terminated relationships with outsourcing vendors, this was done at great expense. For example, participants from FIRM7 and FIRM8 paid a stiff penalty to terminate the contract early. They made investments in hardware and software, built new data centers and hired a new IT staff. These extreme cases demonstrate that IT outsourcing almost always involves the exception of a small number of suppliers.

5. Customers are often inexperienced in information technology outsourcing. Participants were at a significant disadvantage when negotiating contracts with outsourcing vendors. While vendors sign large contracts as often as every month, participants typically had no experience with negotiating large outsourcing contracts. Because of customers' inexperience with outsourcing and the likelihood that the vendor will take advantage of their ignorance, the exception of information impactedness results. Due to information asymmetry, the vendors were able to negotiate deals which strongly favored their position. Several examples illustrate the point. Participants from FIRM2 did not question the vendor's "change of character clause." This clause stipulates that any changes in functionality are subject to excess fees. When FIRM2 changed from one word processing package to another, the vendor charged them a stiff excess fee, appealing to the change of character clause. At FIRM1, the vendor had a clause that stated that FIRM1 would pay any fees associated with transferring software licensing agreements. Participants were more than shocked when their major software provider charged then $500,000 to transfer their software licenses to the outsourcing vendor.

In summary, TCE proponents could provide a strong argument to explain the data anomalies from a TCE perspective by appealing to the exceptions of high uncertainty, highly idiosyncratic transactions, a small number of suppliers, or by appealing to language ambiguities.

Antithesis: TCE assumptions are violated in the context of IT outsourcing

Thus far, we have discussed how TCE proponents could explain the anomalies resulting from a transaction cost interpretation of IT outsourcing decisions.

Although strong arguments can be made to explain the anomalies from a TCE perspective, an alternative interpretation is that anomalies exist because the context of IT outsourcing decisions violates the following TCE assumptions:

1. Decision-makers select among alternatives based on economic efficiency
2. Organizational goals are aligned with individual goals
3. Information is used to make rationally bounded decisions
4. The market will always provide cheaper production costs through economies of scale
5. The transaction is the appropriate unit of analysis

1. Decision-makers select among alternatives based on economic efficiency. Williamson argues that decision-makers use cost efficiency as the sole criterion:

> The criterion for organizing transactions is assumed to be the strictly instrumental one of cost-economizing. Essentially this takes two parts: economizing on production expense and economizing on transaction costs (Williamson, 1979, p. 245).

Although Williamson recognizes that politics play a role in organizational processes, he assumes an organization must be economically viable in the long run. He argues that economizing is a more super-ordinate construct than political strategizing:

> I furthermore aver that, as between economizing and strategizing, economizing is much the more fundamental...More importantly, I maintain that a strategizing effort will rarely prevail if a program is burdened by significant cost excesses in production, distribution, or organization. All the clever ploys and positioning, aye, all the king's horses and all the king's men, will rarely save a project that is seriously flawed in first-order economizing respects. (Williamson, 1991, p. 75).

We analyzed the transcribed interviews to determine the reasons participants made sourcing decisions. We found that of the 257 reasons cited by participants for initiating outsourcing decisions, 190 (64%) could be readily explained by TCE, but 67 (26%) could not. For the sake of parsimony, we have categorized these 257 reasons into 18 categories (See Table 2.5).[1] In aggregate, the first 12 categories of reasons can be readily interpreted from a transaction cost perspective. But TCE opponents could argue that the remaining six categories of reasons – which represent at least one participant's view in 32 (80%) of the 40 cases – are not readily explained by

Table 2.5 **Participants' Reasons for Sourcing Decisions**

Reason Cited	Case Numbers
Transaction Cost Theory Reasons:	
TCT R1: Reduce Costs	1,2,3,4,5,7,8,9,10abc,11ab,12bc,13,17,19, 20, 21,22,23,24,25ab,26abc,27ab,28ab,29, 30ab,31,33bc,34b,35,36,37ab,38ab,39abc, 40
TCT R2: Improve Cost Controls	1,10bc,20,32
TCT R3: Restructure IT budgets	4,6,9,10bc,11ab,16,23,25ab,28ab,29,32, 36,38b,40
TCT R4: Return to Core Business Competencies	6,9,10bc,11ab,12c,13,22,28ab,29,31,32, 37ab,38b,39bc
TCT R5: Government Pressure for Market Testing	13,36,37ab,38
TCT R6: Devolution of Organization/ Management Structures	9,10c,11ab,31,36,38b
TCT R7: Facilitate Mergers & Acquisitions	3, 18, 24
TCT R8: Start-up New Companies/ Privatization	7,11b,12a,14,23,35,40
TCT R9: Improve Technical Service	1,3,5,7,8,9,13,25ab,26abc,27b,28ab,30ab, 35,39abc,40
TCT R10: Access to Technical Talent	1,3,5,8,9,11a,12a,13,23,25ab,26abc,27b, 28a,30ab,31,32,33bc,34a,35,37ab,39abc,40
TCT R11: Access to Vendor Technologies	1,3,8,12a,13,23,27b,31,34ab,35,39a
TCT R12: Focus the Internal IT Staff on Core Technical Activities	1,26b,28b,29,30ab,32,33abc,34b,36,40
Residuals:	
RESIDUAL 1: Prove Efficiency of In-house IT	2a,12bc,14,15,18,19,27a,38a
RESIDUAL 2: Justify New Resources for In-house IT	2,14,18
RESIDUAL 3: Expose Exaggerated Outsourcing Claims	15,17,19,27b,36,38a
RESIDUAL 4: Break the Glass Ceiling by Being Perceived as a "Good Corporate Citizen"	11ab,13,14,18,23,24,25ab,26c,27b,28a,31, 32,35,36,38b,40
RESIDUAL 5: Eliminate Troublesome IT activities	5,17,21,28a,30ab,34a,39a
RESIDUAL 6: Duplicate Success of Published Outsourcing Cases	1,5,9,11ab,13,20,21,22,23,26c,27b,28ab,29, 30ab,31,37ab,38a,39a,40

TCE.[2] We have labelled these "residuals" because these experiences are "left unexplained" by TCE. TCE opponents could interpret these "residuals" as political motives pursued by a particular person within a stakeholder group. Rather than making decisions based on economic efficiency, these participants in part based decisions on personal agendas.

Residual 1: Prove Efficiency of in-house IT. IT managers from eight of the organizations (20%) initiated cursory outsourcing evaluations to prove efficiency, fearing that senior executives would conduct sourcing evaluations if they did not assume the initiative. These IT managers did not create formal requests for proposals, solicit external vendor bids, nor provide any economic rationale for maintaining a policy of insourcing. A participant from FIRM15, for example, initiated an outsourcing evaluation when he heard rumors that senior managers had contacted EDS:

> If you don't look at outsourcing, somebody will do it for you – Director of Advanced Technology, FIRM15

Residual 2: Justify new resources for in-house IT. IT managers from three of the organizations (7.5%) initiated outsourcing evaluations to justify resource requests. By bundling resource requests with an "objective" evaluation which demonstrates that the resource could not be more efficiently acquired through outsourcing, participants predicted that senior managers were more likely to grant approval. One participant explained how he partly used an outsourcing evaluation to justify an upgrade:

> ...I was building a base I guess to upgrade to a CPU with a five-year lease on it...While it was an outsourcing study, it was also designed to enhance my personal credibility when it came time to ask for bucks. – Manager of DP, FIRM14

Residual 3: Expose exaggerated outsourcing claims. IT managers from six of the organizations (15%) initiated outsourcing evaluations in hopes of exposing the exaggerated outsourcing claims propagated in the trade press. For example, one participant wrote a white paper to expose exaggerated claims as part of his outsourcing evaluation. The following is an extract from the participant's report to senior management:

> Outsourcing has gained considerable notoriety recently not so much because it is a new idea, but because of who is doing it. Prominent examples of organizations that have chosen to outsource some or

all of their functions include Eastman Kodak, American Standard, First City Bancorp, Purina, Heinz, and Trane. Effective and cost efficient performance are most frequently cited as the motivation behind outsourcing. To date, many of these newsworthy examples of outsourcing have been done by organizations that were either in or headed for financial trouble.

Residual 4: Break the glass ceiling. IT managers from 16 of the organizations (40%) initiated outsourcing evaluations to break the glass ceiling. By showing that they are willing to outsource some of their IT kingdom, IT managers demonstrate to senior managers that they are business people, not technocrats, and therefore deserve executive status. For example, the IT Manager at FIRM18 considered outsourcing partly to demonstrate his corporate citizenship:

> I mean as good corporate citizens, we were trying to do what was right – so did that help? Since then, I've been to two officer meetings, so I guess it did. – Former Director of IS, currently Treasurer, FIRM18

Residual 5: Eliminate a troublesome IT activity. Senior managers from seven of the organizations (17.5%) initiated outsourcing evaluations because they were most anxious to unload the burdensome IT function to an outsourcing vendor. Peter Keen once noted to one of the authors that some CEOs question: "You mean if I outsource, I can get rid of that IT guy?" At FIRM5, for example, the Controller was most anxious to rid himself of the entire IT department which reported through him. When asked whether he regretted outsourcing his strategic coal and mineral systems, he responded:

> People say that you should keep applications. I ask, why would you do that? That's the biggest headache. – Controller, FIRM5

Residual 6: Imitate success of published outsourcing cases. Senior managers from 19 organizations (47.5%) jumped on the outsourcing bandwagon in an effort to imitate the widely-publicized outsourcing success stories propagated in the trade press. When asked why they considered outsourcing, participants responded by pointing to outsourcing exemplars, such as Kodak, or to competitors that outsourced. For example, one participant from FIRM1 explains that her boss outsourced because other major banks had done so:

> So he really felt, and I think quite correctly, that outsourcing was something people were talking about. Other organizations had

done it, especially in banks that were the same size as us. – VP of IS, FIRM1

2. Organizational goals are aligned with individual goals. Williamson assumes that all members of an organization are motivated to make cost efficient decisions because internal rewards and punishments align individual goals with corporate goals. Therefore, Williamson recognizes that decision-makers pursue personal agendas, but only those agendas aligned with corporate goals will be rewarded with perks, bonuses, salary increases, or promotions. In the long run, decision-makers who pursue personal agendas not in accordance with corporate goals will be punished through demotions or even termination. This assumption precludes a stakeholder view of organizations, arguing instead that all organizational members share common goals.

In the context of IT sourcing decisions, TCE opponents could argue that a stakeholder perspective sheds significant understanding on sourcing decisions. In our cases, for example, at least three stakeholder groups possessed different views and agendas for IT. Senior management often viewed IT as a support function and pursued IT cost-minimization as an agenda. Users often viewed IT as critical to their business and often pursued service excellence as an agenda. IT Managers, placed in the precarious position of trying to provide excellent service at a minimum cost, often pursued a compromise strategy. As a result, senior management did not receive the desired level of cost cuts, nor did users receive the desired level of service. Thus, IT was often perceived as providing an expensive, sub-standard service. Amidst the different perspectives and agendas for IT, participants initiated outsourcing decisions to promote the interests of their different stakeholder groups. To demonstrate the value of a stakeholder approach, TCE opponents could point to FIRM17.

At FIRM17, senior managers wanted IT to cut costs, users wanted IT to increase service, and IT Managers were unable to please either group. IT Managers tried to appease senior management's desire to reduce costs by consolidating data centers, but the users resisted because they perceived consolidation would result in service degradation. A senior manager explains his stakeholder's perceptions of IT:

All we see is this amount of money that they have to write a check for every year. Year after year after year. Where is the benefit? MIS says, "Well, we process data faster than we did last year." They say, "so what?" MIS says, "Well we can close the ledger faster." And they say, "So what? Where have you increased revenue? All you do is increase costs, year after year after year and I am sick of it. All I get are these esoteric benefits and a bunch of baloney on how much technology has advanced. Show me where you put one more dollar on the income statement. – Corporate Manager of Planning, FIRM17

A Strategic Business Unit Leader explains why he was unwilling to allow IT to consolidate data centers to save costs. Service excellence was worth more to him than cost efficiency:

> If it cost me five million more dollars to have this in my business unit and be able to control it and make it responsive to my needs, it's worth five million dollars to me. – Division Manager, Chemicals Business Unit, FIRM17

Senior management finally empowered the IT department to consolidate data centers by threatening business unit leaders with outsourcing. Once an RFP was created, the IT Manager explained to his users that his internal bid must include data center consolidation to compete with vendor bids. The users agreed. The internal IT won the bid and the IT Manager subsequently reduced IT costs by 43%. The IT Manager explains:

> This is critical: this is the first time someone handed an MIS guy a stick. In the past, if a company came and said, "I want this new piece of software, I need it." bingo, we went out and bought it. That doesn't happen anymore. – Corporate Manager of Technology, FIRM17

FIRM17 demonstrates the value of a stakeholder perspective in understanding outsourcing decisions. Although an economic benefit resulted from the sourcing decision, an analysis of stakeholder groups' perceptions and levels of power yields much understanding of the outsourcing decision.

3. Information is used to make rationally bounded decisions. Williamson's work is largely influenced by Herb Simon's theories on organizations and decision-making. In particular, Williamson adopts Simon's concept of bounded rationality (Simon, 1976). Like Simon, Williamson assumes that decision-makers identify some alternatives (but not *all* possible alternatives due to bounded rationality), evaluate the cost efficiency of these alternatives by gathering information, then select the low-cost alternative. This decision model assumes that decision-makers select an outcome only *after* analyzing alternatives.

In some of our cases, TCE opponents could argue that participants selected an outcome *before* the decision process and merely selectively gathered information to justify their preferences. But in some of our cases, particularly where no economic justification was given for the decision

(FIRM14, FIRM15, FIRM16, FIRM18), TCE opponents could argue that participants selectively used information to promote their a priori preferences rather than to reduce uncertainty. Consider the use of information at FIRM24.

According to the IT Manager at FIRM24 who made the outsourcing decision, he wanted to outsource the data center to avoid relocating it when the entire corporation relocated to another state. According to five participants from FIRM24, the IT Manager decided to outsource the data center to break the glass ceiling by being perceived as a business person and selectively used information to support his outsourcing preference. His subordinate, the Data Center Manager, explains:

> I can only speak from my own observations. I got the feeling that he [the IT Manager] just wanted to make his mark. To give the illusion that he proactively made a decision. It was a project that was highly visible. He got some press, that sort of thing. That's really what I felt the agenda was – Data Center Manager, FIRM24

The IT Manager's first outsourcing evaluation resulted in maintaining the data center in-house because no vendor bids were lower than current IT costs. The participants explained that FIRM24 adopts best practices for cost reduction, such as purchasing only used equipment, which enables them to achieve average costs similar to a vendor. During the second evaluation, however, several participants suggested that the IT Manager "stacked the deck" in favor of outsourcing by including a relocation cost in the internal bid but not on the external bids:

> We made some sort of biased analysis so it would show that we were going to save money, but that's not the case...That kind of ties in with when you know the answer your boss wants, the smart thing is to give him that answer...We had a trump card...this whole locating to the new city wild card. This is the item that swung the deal from costing you money [to outsource] to saving you money. – Supervisor of Technical Support

> We put in the one-time cost of relocating the data center [on the internal bid], but we didn't put some one-time costs on the other side [the external bid]. – Manager of Computer and Network Services

> They were basically thinking, and this is twisted logic, that the data center belonged...they couldn't imagine the data center being here and the corporate offices being elsewhere, but it's okay to have the data center in an alternative site in the instance of outsourcing? They are still

going to make a phone call to have something done. – Supervisor of Technical Support

4. The market will always provide cheaper production costs through economies of scale. Williamson assumes that vendors possess inherent economies of scale that allow them to incur lower average costs through mass production efficiencies and labor specialization. Mass production is presumed to reduce average costs by allocating fixed costs over more units of output and by receiving volume discounts on inputs. Labor specialization is presumed to reduce costs by allocating workers to focus on tasks at which they are most adept. It is only transaction costs that are cheaper with a hierarchy. In the context of IT, TCE opponents could argue that internal IT departments have equivalent/superior cost advantages over vendors for many IT cost drivers, other than just transaction costs.

Based on our research, the major cost drivers are data center operating costs, hardware purchasing costs, software licensing costs, labor costs to acquire both business and technical expertise, shareholder costs (the need to generate a profit), research and development costs, marketing costs, opportunity costs, and transaction costs (see Table 2.6). Through this analysis, TCE opponents could argue:

- Vendors only possess an inherent cost advantage for IS functions whose cost drivers are dominated by new technologies, R&D costs, and opportunity costs
- Large internal IS departments possess equivalent or superior cost advantage as vendors for data center operating costs, hardware purchasing costs, and software licensing costs.

Table 2.6   Economies of Scale: Cost Advantages of Insourcing and Outsourcing

Costs:	Small is Department	Large is Department	Outsourcing Vendor
Technical expertise			Advantage
Opportunity cost			Advantage
Business expertise	Advantage	Advantage	
Transaction costs	Advantage	Advantage	
Shareholder costs	Advantage	Advantage	
Marketing costs	Advantage	Advantage	
Data Center costs		Advantage	Advantage
Hardware costs		Advantage	Advantage
Software costs		Advantage	Advantage
R&D costs			Advantage

- Any internal IT department – whether large or small – possess superior cost advantage for business expertise costs, marketing costs, and shareholder costs.

Thus, the relative advantage of outsourcing or insourcing a given IT activity depends on the major cost drivers of that particular activity.

Data Center Operating Costs. In the area of data processing, benchmarking organizations have assessed that theoretical economies of scale are achieved at 150 MIPS, approximately equal to the size of one large IBM mainframe. In 20 of the 40 organizations, the data centers we studied were at least equivalent to theoretical economies of scale of 150 MIPs (see Table 2.2). Thus, organizations which operate a large mainframe have the critical mass associated with cost efficiency. In cases where organizations operate multiple smaller data centers, cost efficiency could be achieved through data center consolidation. We also note that smaller organizations can achieve similar average costs to a vendor, such as FIRM27, even though they operate data centers below the 150–200 MIP range. As documented in Lacity and Hirschheim (1993b), small organizations are often willing to lag one or two generations behind, allowing them to capitalize on the large savings of the used computer market.

Hardware Purchasing Costs. Suppliers are willing to offer large customers volume discounts, which lead to lower purchasing costs. In IS, most hardware suppliers do indeed offer their larger clients significant discounts off published price lists. Thus, large organizations typically purchase heavy iron for approximately the same costs as outsourcing vendors. For example, one consultant claims that mainframes that retail for $15 million dollars may be sold to large organizations such as Exxon or EDS for as little as $11 million. Thus, large internal IS departments and outsourcing vendors accrue comparable hardware purchasing costs. Smaller organizations may indeed be at a disadvantage. FIRM22, for example, diligently tried to negotiate lower costs with their hardware suppliers. Due to their size, the suppliers were unwilling to offer the same volume discounts enjoyed by their larger customers.

Software Licensing Costs. As discussed in Lacity and Hirschheim (1993a), at one time vendors possessed an inherent cost advantage over internal IS departments because of site licenses. With site licenses, outsourcing vendors spread licensing fees over multiple customers, yielding lower average software costs than internal IS departments. As a backlash to lost revenues due to outsourcing, software houses have restructured their licensing practices. Instead of offering site licenses, software houses now offer group licenses for which the customer is charged according to the size of machine. Thus, large-sized internal IS departments possess a comparable cost advantage to vendors for software licenses.

Business Expertise Costs. The cost of acquiring business expertise is a major cost driver, particularly in the areas of IT strategy formulation, applications development, and applications support. The critical skill required to deliver these functions is understanding how business requirements can be met through available technology. TCE opponents could point to the following quotes to illustrate participants' perceptions that internal IT staff possess an inherent advantage in providing business expertise. The first two quotes are from participants whose organizations outsourced at least 80% of their IT budget and maintained an internal IT staff for business-critical IT functions:

> I guess the most significant problem we face – and we are trying to compensate for it – is the loss of FIRM3's perspective relative to running the business. For that risk, we determined that we would never turn over the strategic planning and decision-making direction part of the business to [the outsourcing vendor] – Manager of IS, FIRM3

> We kept a certain amount of what I call value-added people…People like systems analysts, applications programmers, things like business people develop, capacity planning people. Those are the people that really know your business. They add value. – CFO, FIRM4

The following two quotes are from participants whose organizations outsourced all IT functions, including business-critical applications. They perceive that the outsourcing vendor focuses too much on technical issues rather than business issues:

> They [the vendor] are more technical, less user-oriented. They are more technically-oriented and less functionally-oriented, less industry-oriented. So if you were to grade them overall, I lost. – VP of an Operating Division, FIRM2

> Change seems to take an awfully long time with an outsourcing vendor basically because it takes a long time to explain your business to the folks. – VP of IS, FIRM8

Most internal IS departments possess superior knowledge of their users' business requirements. As organizational employees, internal IS managers and systems analysts understand the idiosyncratic business requirements for delivering a cost effective service. For example, every organization possesses significant quirks even in their allegedly "commodity" type applications such as payroll, inventory control, purchasing, order processing, etc. As any business person will attest, it is the exceptions that potentially cripple an application. Internal IS staff typically have acquired significant understanding of these quirks and thus have an inherent advantage over vendors.

Technical Expertise Costs. The cost of acquiring technical expertise is also a major IS cost driver, particularly for emerging technologies. Almost all participants perceived that vendors have a cost advantage as far as technical expertise because vendors invest more capital and labor to develop new technologies than internal IT departments. The following quotes capture participants' perceptions:

A lot of areas needed some new software capabilities to stay competitive. There wasn't a chance in the world that the current (internal) staff was going to be able to provide support necessary to get those things on-line. – Manager of Purchasing, FIRM3

Their staff [the vendor's] that they support us with now is smaller than what we had. And because of the depth of their organization, they are able to support us with a smaller staff. – Controller, FIRM5

The only exceptions were in the total outsourcing cases where the internal staff transferred to the vendor, thus equivocating the level of technical expertise.

[The vendor] took over all the people as they usually do. So what happens in that environment is that your unqualified IS people that you had become your unqualified [vendor] people. So you are no better off. – VP of IS, FIRM8

Shareholder Costs. Outsourcing vendors must generate a profit for their shareholders, whereas internal IS departments merely need to recover costs. Some participants claimed that this cost driver alone provides internal IS departments with a significant cost advantage. As one IS manager notes:

[Outsourcing vendors] are not a small organization by any stretch of the imagination...But those guys look for a gross margin of 50 to 60%. So can they do it cheaper? – VP of IS, FIRM8

Although increased competition in the market suggests that 50–60% margins are no longer reasonable, vendors still look for 15% margins.

Research and Development Costs. IS research and development costs are incurred to fuel the development of new technologies. Few internal IS departments have the critical mass to justify large expenditures in research and development. Rather, vendors possess an inherent advantage because they can recover R&D costs by selling the new technology, tools, and methods to many customers. Also included in R&D costs are the costs of environmental scanning and retraining staff. Here too, a vendor possesses an inherent cost advantage. An outsourcing vendor can recover the costs of environmental scanning by selling selected technologies to multiple customers. In addition, an outsourcing vendor can efficiently train their staff, which may include as many as 50,000 people. Most internal IS departments simply are too small to achieve cost advantages in these areas.

Marketing Costs. Marketing costs are incurred to attract IS customers. For internal IS departments, marketing costs are minimal because internal users are a captive audience. Outsourcing vendors, however, incur considerable costs to attract customers and submit bids. Thus, internal IS departments possess an inherent advantage over vendors in the area of marketing.

Opportunity Costs. Opportunity costs are an important cost driver, but are often ignored because they are not captured in accounting calculations. When management chooses to focus resources in one area, they lose the opportunity to apply those resources elsewhere. In IS, some senior managers consider opportunity costs in their sourcing decisions. Willcocks and Fitzgerald (1994) describe several organizations that decided to outsource their legacy systems so that the internal IS department could focus on the development of more strategic applications. Even though these legacy systems could have been efficiently run and maintained in-house, the opportunity cost of not developing strategic applications was sufficiently high to warrant outsourcing.

To use Table 2.6 as a guideline for sourcing decisions, consider an example of the proposed development of a medical supply organization's first client server application to support product development. The two primary cost drivers are likely technical expertise associated with the new technology and business expertise associated with medical supply development. The costs of technical expertise suggest outsourcing, while the costs of business expertise suggest insourcing. To minimize development costs, this organization can access vendor technical expertise while still maintaining control over applications development. For example, rather than outsource the entire development to an outsourcing vendor, this organization can maintain managerial control, use the internal IS staff to determine business requirements, and merely hire vendor resources to transfer learning about the new client-server technology. In this scenario, the organization can exploit the inherent efficiencies of both internal IS departments and vendors.

In summary, TCE opponents could argue that the nature of information technology economies of scale violates Williamson's assumption that the market will always provide cheaper production costs. This violation explains several of the anomalies: in many cases, participants successfully insourced IT rather than outsourced to a vendor.

5. The transaction is the appropriate unit of analysis. Williamson's unit of analysis is the individual transaction. As such, the model assumes decisions have initial entry and exit points defined by the transaction. In the sourcing context, the decision begins when an organizational member initiates an outsourcing evaluation for a particular IT transaction. The decision terminates with a decision to insource or outsource. In the IT outsourcing context, TCE opponents could argue that using the transaction as the unit of analysis overlooks the broader historical context which sheds significant understanding on outsourcing decisions. By understanding senior management's view of IT developed over years of service, outsourcing decisions can be better understood. Consider FIRM16. If the unit of analysis is simply the transaction, a very limited understanding arises. The initial entry point was a letter sent by the vendor to the CEO:

> There was a letter, the chairman of the board of [the outsourcing vendor] wrote a letter to our CEO saying that they would be most interested in paying substantial cash for our whole IS organization. That includes all the people and they would be very happy to meet with him, and discuss that with him. – VP of IS, FIRM16

According to the VP of IS, the CEO sent him the letter and asked him to guess how much money the vendor would pay for FIRM16's IT assets. The VP of IS guessed $250 to $400 million. The CEO promptly told the VP of IS to decline the offer:

> He says, "I'm not interested in letting other people," that's the CEO talking, "have access to our data. So prepare a letter back to the chairman of the [outsourcing vendor] and say we appreciate your offer but at this time we consider our IT as part of the strategic work that we have..." He washed his hands of it and he was through with it. – VP of IS, FIRM16

From a TCE perspective, the whole decision took less than two weeks from entry to exit points. Given that FIRM16 was about to go bankrupt, the CEO's decision seems irrational until one learns of the VP of IS's 35-year history of marketing systems to senior management. The VP of IS marketed systems by changing the accounting structure to a profit center, by soliciting customers outside of FIRM16 to raise revenue and create a marketing mentality among his IT staff, by demonstrating efficiency through benchmarking, and by training senior executives through "Valuing IT" courses. Through these efforts, the CEO perceived that IT was a core competency that adds value to his organization. This explains why he promptly dismissed the outsourcing solicitation even though his organization was facing bankruptcy. Without a historical perspective, it is very difficult to make sense of FIRM16's outsourcing decision.

In summary, TCE opponents could argue that anomalies are largely attributed to the violations of TCE's assumptions in the IT outsourcing decision context. TCE opponents have previously criticized TCE's failure to consider the power of stakeholders within organizations (Bradach and Eccles, 1989; Collin and Larsson, 1993; Francis, 1983; and Perrow, 1986). Others have criticized TCE's unrealistic assumptions, such as the assumption that market-based resources are available (Bauer and Cohen, 1983; Dugger, 1983; Dietrich, 1994a,b; and Etzioni, 1988). Finally, several researchers claim that the transaction cost is a poor unit of analysis because it ignores the broader contextual issues – such as organizational learning, that influence sourcing decisions (Collin, 1993; Dietrich, 1994a, b; Elg and Johansson, 1993).

Conclusions: towards a synthesis?

As we did not aim to corroborate or refute TCE in the Popperian sense, we have ignored this issue but tended to assume an interpretive perspective. In particular, we asked ourselves: "Does TCE explain the empirical findings?" To answer this question, we mapped 40 sourcing decisions to Williamson's framework of efficient governance structures. We found that the original mapping to the framework only explained five sourcing decisions and generated 35 anomalies. We noted that TCE proponents could explain these anomalies by appealing to the exceptions of small number of suppliers, high uncertainty, recurrent-idiosyncratic transactions, or language ambiguities. Thus, TCE proponents could explain all of the data, but their arguments generate the following question: *Do IT academics and IT practitioners benefit from a theoretical framework that treats the general case of IT sourcing decisions as TCE exceptions?*

We also noted that TCE opponents could attack the theory by showing that the unique nature of IT violates the major TCE assumptions. But even TCE opponents do not deal a fatal blow because all theories make simplifying assumptions. The question merely becomes: *What simplifying assumptions are useful in understanding the complex reality of IT sourcing?*

Although a Hegelian approach to inquiry promises a synthesis of the contradictions and questions that arise from an analysis of a thesis and antithesis, our aims are more modest. First, we hope that this paper serves to stimulate debate among the IT academic community on the applicability of using TCE as an explanator of IT sourcing decisions. Second, we propose two possible alternatives which may lead to a synthesis. The first alternative is to supplement a TCE explanation with other theories. The second alternative is to develop an IT sourcing theory based on assumptions that address the general case of IT sourcing. The pursuit of these alternatives is the subject of future research.

We believe TCE could be supplemented with two other organizational theories to address the apparent violation of three TCE assumptions and to explain all the IT sourcing *motives* uttered by participants. Although IS academics have called for multiple theoretical perspectives, we note that the elegance of grand theories lies in parsimony. The suggestion to adopt multiple theoretical perspectives must be balanced with the value of the additional explanatory power.

As previously noted, TCE opponents could argue that in 80% of our cases (26% of the reasons uttered), at least some political motivations were cited by participants. These "residuals" seemed to violate three TCE assumptions: economic efficiency as sole decision criterion, alignment of individual and organizational goals, and the use of information to reduce uncertainty. Violations of these assumptions have been widely addressed by Principal-Agency Theory (PAT). PAT assumes that agents (such as internal managers) often behave in a manner that is inconsistent with maximizing the benefit of the principals (such as shareholders and bond holders) (Jensen and Meckling, 1976). Principals need to develop incentives or increase monitoring to prevent agent opportunism. Failure to do so results in some of the political behaviors witnessed in Table 2.5, such as using cursory IT outsourcing evaluations to "prove" efficiency, to justify new IT resources, to expose exaggerated claims, to be perceived as the "good corporate citizen", or to eliminate troublesome IT activities. By extending TCE to include aspects of PAT, 92% of the reasons participants cited for initiating outsourcing can be explained.

We also feel that the remaining 8% (which represents utterances made by at least one participant in 19 of the 40 organizations) can be explained by institutional isomorphism (DiMaggio and Powell, 1983). Institutional isomorphism assumes that organizations are more similar than dissimilar due to coercion, norms, and mimicry. With coercion, one organization pressures another organization to conform – such as a powerful customer demanding that all suppliers adopt electronic data interchange (Green and Hirschheim, 1993). With norms, professional organizations encourage conformity through membership, publications, seminars, and conferences. With mimicry, only the early adopters are assumed to make rational decisions – other organizations merely attempt to mimic their success. The mimicry concept captures the essence of Residual 6 articulated by participants: they initiated outsourcing decisions because another company has done it.

The benefit of this proposed synthesis is that a wide variety of behaviors can be understood from a limited number of perspectives. The drawback of this proposed synthesis is the seemingly inconsistent assumptions, particularly with the type of interpretation suggested by institutional isomorphism as contrasted with TCE and PAT. This trade-off – completeness versus consistency – is a property of any formal system of logic (Godel, 1931). Thus, we can either adopt a simplified theory which is internally consistent but cannot explain the entire phenomenon, or we can adopt multiple theoretical perspectives that completely explain the data but yield logical inconsistencies.

We believe that a second possible synthesis may result from a theoretical framework that addresses IT sourcing decisions and outcomes as a general case rather than as exceptions to an extant general administrative, economic, or organizational theory. Such a theoretical framework should predict IT sourcing successes and failures. Two major "critical success factors" which arise from our research would be a good starting point for the development of such a theory:

Successful sourcing depends on treating IT as a portfolio. Our data suggest that sourcing decisions should not treat an entire IT department as a single strategic asset to be totally insourced, or conversely, a single commodity to be totally outsourced. Instead, successful IT sourcing treats IT as a portfolio of activities, which calls for a selective sourcing approach. Our data indicate that selective sourcing was more successful than total outsourcing and total insourcing. Of the selective sourcing cases where success or failure was clearing demonstrated, 22 of the 25 (88%) selective outsourcing decisions were successful. Contrast this with total outsourcing where only three of the seven (42%) decisions were successful. Although all eight of the insourcing decisions were successful, participants believed that the threat of competition motivated the IT staff to strive for improvements. Without the outsourcing threat, participants do not believe the internal IT staff could have reduced costs by up to 54%.

Successful outsourcing is associated with short-term, detailed contracts. Our data suggest that short-term and detailed contracts – which last only as long as requirements are stable – are associated with successful outcomes. The average duration of our selective sourcing cases – which were largely successful – was only 3.32 years compared with the average duration of our total outsourcing cases – which were less successful – of 8.6 years. Participants believed that short-term, detailed contracts are more successful than long-term relational contracts for three reasons:

First, technology and business conditions typically cannot be predicted past a three-year time horizon, thus original contracts become increasingly outdated as time progresses. Although participants attempted to address future technologies by appealing to "strategic partnerships" defined in relational contracts, such arrangements often failed because vendors and participants did not share risks and rewards. In actuality, every dollar out of the customer's pocket in terms of excess fees or hidden contractual costs went into the vendor's pocket. For example, when new technologies arose – such as client server technology – vendors often saw this as an opportunity to supplement payments from the original contract by charging excess fees. In hindsight, many participants noted that contracts lasting more than three years increase the threat of vendor opportunism. After three years, participants could not define with certainty their information technology requirements.

Second, short-term detailed contracts also ensure that a customer's fixed prices will not be out of step with market prices. Vendors prefer long-term contracts because they can capitalize on the dramatic 20%–30% price/performance improvements. In the short term, vendors can offer a low bid to secure the contract, knowing that as time progresses, their internal costs will decline, thus increasing their profits.

Third, short-term contracts motivate vendor performance because they realize customers may opt to switch vendors when the contract has expired – thus stripping them of the power of sole provider. Short-term contracts afford selective sourcers an opportunity to adapt requirements to changes in business or technology, to once again access market prices, and to minimize the monopolistic power of their vendors.

In summary, we believe the debate we presented is important because theories adopted from other disciplines need to be critically examined within our own discipline. We argue that a synthesis of the debate may lead to supplementing TCE with additional theories to increase its explanatory powers in the context of IT sourcing decisions. Or alternatively, we as a discipline may develop a more narrow, but IT specific, theory to explain and predict IT sourcing behaviors.

Notes

1 See Lacity *et al.*, 1994 for a full description of these reasons.
2 Participants may have been more likely to articulate economic motives because these are deemed as legitimate (Pfeffer, 1981; 1992). In many of our interviews, participants uttered "political" motives only after establishing a rapport with us. As a consequence, we suspect that political motives may have played a larger role in IT sourcing decisions than suggested by the percentage of political utterances.

References

Allison, G. (1971) *Essence of Decision*, Massachusetts: Little, Brown & Organization, Boston.
Ambrosio, J. (1991) "Outsourcing at Southland: Best of Times, Worst of Times", *Computerworld*, Vol. 25, 12, p. 61.
Anderson, E. (1994) "Transaction Cost Analysis and Marketing," Paper presented at *The Conference of Transaction Cost Economics and Beyond*, Rotterdam, Netherlands: Erasmus University.
Ang, S. and Cummings, L. (1997) "Strategic Response to Institutional Influences on Information Systems Outsourcing," *Organization Science*, Vol. 8, No. 3, pp. 235–256.

Anthes, G. (1991) "Perot Wins 10-year Outsourcing Deal," *Computerworld*, Vol. 25, 14, p. 96.

Anthes, G. (1990) "HUD set to Outsource IS," *Computerworld*, Vol. 24, 49, p. 1, 119.

Astley, W. (1985) "Administrative Science as Socially Constructed Truth," *Administrative Science Quarterly*, Vol. 30, 4, pp. 497–513.

Bauer, M. and Cohen, E. (1983) "The Invisibility of Power in Economics: Beyond Markets and Hierarchies, in *Power, Efficiency, and Institutions*, Francis, A., Turk, J. and Willman, P. (eds) London, Hienemann, pp. 81–104.

Beath, C. (1987) "Strategies For Managing MIS Projects: A Transaction Costs Approach," *Proceedings of the Fourth International Conference on Information Systems*, pp. 72–80.

Benjamin, R. and Blunt, J. (1992) "Critical IT Issues: The Next Ten Years," *Sloan Management Review*, Vol. 33, 4, pp. 7–19.

Bowen, D. and Jones, G. (1986) "Transaction Cost Analysis of Service Organization-Customer Exchange," *Academy of Management Review*, Vol. 11, 2, pp. 428–441.

Bradach, J. and Eccles, R. (1989) "Price, Authority and Trust: From Ideal Types to Plural Forms," *Annual Review of Sociology*, Vol. 15, pp. 97–118.

Burrell, G. and Morgan, G. (1979) *Sociological Paradigms and Organizational Analysis*, Portsmouth, New Hampshire: Heinemann.

Chua, W. (1986) "Radical Developments in Accounting Thought," *The Accounting Review*, Vol. LXI, 4, pp. 601–632.

Churchman, C.W. (1971) *The Design of Inquiry Systems*, New York: Basic Books.

Clark, T., Jr., Zmud, R. and McCray, G. (1995) "The Outsourcing of Information Services: Transforming the Nature of Business in the Information Industry," *Journal of Information Technology*, Vol. 10, 4, pp. 221–237.

Coase, R. (1937) "The Nature of the Firm," *Economica*, Vol. 4, 16, pp. 386–405.

Collin, S.V. (1993) "The Brotherhood of the Swedish Sphere: A Third Institutional Form for Economic Exchange," *International Studies of Management and Organization*, Vol. 23, 1, pp. 69–86.

Collin, S.V. and Larsson, R. (1993) "Beyond Markets and Hierarchies: A Swedish Quest for a Tripolar Institutional Framework," *International Studies of Management and Organization*, Vol. 23, 1, pp. 3–12.

Cronk, J. and Sharp, J. (1995) "A Framework for Deciding What to Outsource in Information Technology," *Journal of Information Technology*, Vol. 10, 4, pp. 259–267.

De Looff, L. (1995) "Information Systems Outsourcing Decision Making: A Framework, Organizational Theories and case Studies," *Journal of Information Technology*, Vol. 10, 4, pp. 281–297.

Dietrich, M. (1994a) *Transaction Cost Economies and Beyond*, London: Routledge.

Dietrich, M. (1994b) "Opportunism, Learning and Organisational Evolution: Transaction Costs and Beyond," Paper presented at *The Conference of Transaction Cost Economics and Beyond*, Netherlands: Erasmus University, Rotterdam.

DiMaggio, P. and Powell, W. (1983) "The Iron Cage Revisited: Institutional Isomorphism and Collective Rationality in Organizational Fields," *American Sociological Review*, Vol. 48, 2, pp. 147–160.

Dugger, W. (1983) "The Transaction Cost Analysis of Oliver E. Williamson: A New Synthesis?" *Journal of Economic Issues*, Vol. 17, pp. 95–114.

Elg, U. and Johansson, U. (1993) "The Institutions of Industrial Governance," *International Studies of Management and Organization*, Vol. 23, 1, pp. 29–46.

Etzioni, A. (1988) *The Moral Dimension: Toward a New Economies*, New York: Free Press.

Francis, A. (1983) "Markets and Hierarchies: Efficiency or Domination?" in *Power, Efficiency, and Institutions*, Francis, A., Turk, J. and Willman, P. (eds), London: Hienemann.

Green, C. and Hirschheim, R. (1993) *EDI: Adoption Rationale and Its Relationship to Implementation Activity*, white paper for the University of Houston's Information Systems Research Center.

Griesinger, D. (1990) "The Human Side of Economic Organization," *Academy of Management Review*, Vol. 15, 3, pp. 478–499.

Godel, K. (1931) "On Formally Undecidable Propositions in Principia Mathematica," *Monatcheft fur Mathematik und Physik*, Vol. 38, pp. 173–198.

Hamilton, R. (1989) "Kendall Outsources IS Chief," *Computerworld*, Vol. 23, 46, pp. 1,4.

Hammersmith, A. (1989) "Slaying the IS Dragon with Outsourcery," *Computerworld*, Vol. 23, 38, pp. 89–93.

Henderson, J. (1990) "Plugging into Strategic Partnerships: The Critical IS Connection," *Sloan Management Review*, Vol. 30, 3, pp. 7–18.

Hennart, J.F. (1991a) "The Transaction Costs Theory of Joint Ventures: An Empirical Study of Japanese Subsidiaries in the United States," *Management Science*, Vol. 34, 4, pp. 483–497.

Hennart, J.F. (1991b) "Control in Multi-National Firms: The Role of Prices and Hierarchy," *Management International Review*, Vol. 31, pp. 71–96.

Hesterly, W., Liebeskind, J. and Zenger, T. (1990) "Organizational Economics: An Impending Revolution in Organizational Theory?" *Academy of Management Review*, Vol. 15, 3, pp. 402–420.

Hill, C. (1990) "Cooperation, Opportunism, and the Invisible Hand: Implications for Transaction Cost Theory," *Academy of Management Review*, Vol. 15, 3, pp. 500–513.

Jensen, M. and Meckling, W. (1976) "Theory of the Firm: Managerial Behavior, Agency Costs, and Ownership Structure," *Journal of Financial Economics*, pp. 305–360.

Joskow, P. (1985) "Vertical Integration and Long Term Contracts: The Case of Coal Burning Electric Generating Plants, *Journal of Law, Economics, and Organization*, Vol. 1, 1, pp. 33–79.

Jurison, J. (1995) "The Role of Risk and Return in Information Technology Outsourcing Decisions," *Journal of Information Technology*, Vol. 10, 4, pp. 239–247.

Kass, E. (1990) "EDS Shifts to the Fast Lane," *Information Week*, Issue 268, pp. 30–34.

Kelleher, J. (1990) "The Dollars and Sense of Outsourcing: Sometimes a Great Notion," *Computerworld*, Vol. 24, 2, pp. 76–77.

Klepper, R. (1993) "Efficient Outsourcing Relationships," Paper at the Outsourcing of Information Systems Services Conference, University of Twente, the Netherlands, May 20–22.

Klepper, R. (1995) "Outsourcing Relationships," in *Managing Information Technology Investments with Outsourcing* (Khosrowpour, ed.), Harrisburg: Idea Group Publishing, pp. 218–243.

Krass, P. (1990) "The Dollars and Sense of Outsourcing," *Information Week*, Issue 259, February 26, pp. 26–31.

Lacity, M. and Hirschheim, R. (1993a) *Information Systems Outsourcing: Myths, Metaphors, and Realities*, Chichester: Wiley.

Lacity, M. and Hirschheim, R. (1993b) "The Information Systems Outsourcing Bandwagon," *Sloan Management Review*, Vol. 35, 1, pp. 73–86.

Lacity, M., Hirschheim, R. and Willcocks, L. (1994) "Realizing Outsourcing Expectations: Incredible Promise, Credible Outcomes", *Journal of Information Systems Management*, Vol. 11, 4, pp. 7–18.

Lieberman, M. (1991) "Determinants of Vertical Integration: An Empirical Test," *The Journal of Industrial Economics*, Vol. XXXIX, 5, pp. 451–466.

Malone, T. (1987) "Modelling Coordination in Organizations and Markets," *Management Science*, Vol. 33, 10, pp. 1317–1332.

Malone, T., Yates, J. and Benjamin, R. (1987) "Electronic Markets and Electronic Hierarchies," *Communications of the ACM*, Vol. 30, 6, pp. 484–497.

Miranda, S. and Kim, Y. (2006) "Professionalism Versus Political Contexts: Institutional Mitigation and the Transaction Cost Heuristic in Information Systems Outsourcing," *MIS Quarterly*, Vol. 30, 3, p. 725–753.

Morse, P. (1990) "Big Business in Outsourcing," *ComputerData*, Vol. 15, 1, p. 23.

O'Leary, M. (1990) "The Mainframe Doesn't Work Here Anymore," *CIO*, Vol. 6, 6, pp. 27–35.

Oltman, J. (1990) "21st Century Outsourcing," *Computerworld*, Vol. 24, 16, pp. 77–79.

Orlikowski, W. and Baroudi, J. (1991) "Studying Information Technology in Organizations: Research Approaches and Assumptions," *Information Systems Research*, Vol. 2, 1, pp. 1–28.

Perrow, C. (1986) *Complex Organizations*, New York: Random House.

Pfeffer, J. (1981) *Power in Organizations*, Massachusetts: Pitman Publishing, Marshfield.

Pfeffer, J. (1992) *Managing with Power*, Massachusetts: Harvard Business School Press, Boston.

Pisano, G. (1990) "The R&D Boundaries of the Firm: An Empirical Analysis," *Administrative Science Quarterly*, Vol. 35, 1, pp. 153–176.

Pitelis, C. (1991) *Market and Non-Market Hierarchies: Theory of Institutional Failure*, Oxford: Blackwell.

Popper, K. (1988) "Science: Conjectures and Refutations," in *Philosophy of Science* Klemke, E., Hollinger, R. and Kline, A. (eds), Prometheus Books, New York, pp. 19–27 (Based on lectures given at Cambridge, 1953).

Porter, M. and Millar, V. (1985) "How Information Gives You Competitive Advantage," Harvard Business Review, Vol. 63, 4, pp. 149–160.

Robins, J. (1987) "Organizational Economics: Notes on the Use of Transaction Cost Theory in the Study of Organizations," *Administrative Science Quarterly*, Vol. 32, 1, pp. 68–86.

Rochester, J. and Douglas, D. (eds) (1990). "Taking An Objective Look at Outsourcing," *I/S Analyzer*, Vol. 28, 8, pp. 1–16.

Simon, H. (1976) *Administrative Behavior*, New York: The Free Press.

Stevenson, L. (1987) *Theories of Human Nature*, Oxford: Oxford University Press.

Walker, G. and Poppo, L. (1991) "Profit Centers, Single-Source Suppliers, and Transaction Costs," *Administrative Science Quarterly*, Vol. 36, 1, pp. 66–87.

Ward, B. (1991) "Hiring Out: Outsourcing Is the New Buzzword in the Management of Information Systems," *Sky Magazine*, Vol. 20, 8, pp. 37–45.

Willcocks, L. and Fitzgerald, G. (1994) *A Business Guide to IT Outsourcing*, London: Business Intelligence.

Williamson, O. (1975) *Markets and Hierarchies: Analysis and Antitrust Implications. A Study in the Economics of Internal Organization*, New York: The Free Press.

Williamson, O. (1979) "Transaction Cost Economics: The Governance of Contractual Relations," *Journal of Law and Economics*, Vol. 22, 2, pp. 233–261.

Williamson, O. and Ouchi, W. (1981) "Markets and Hierarchies: Origins, Implications, Perspectives," in Van de Ven, A. and Joyce, W., *Perspectives in Organizational Design and Behavior*, New York: John Wiley & Sons.

Williamson, O. (1985) *The Economic Institutions of Capitalism*, New York: Free Press.

Williamson, O. (1991) "Strategizing, Economizing, and Economic Organization," *Strategic Management Journal,* Vol. 12, pp. 75–94.

Williamson, O. (1991) "Comparative Economic Organization: The Analysis of Discrete Structural Alternatives," *Administrative Science Quarterly,* Vol. 36, 2, pp. 269–296.

Williamson, O. (1994) "Efficiency, Power, Authority, and Economic Organization," Paper presented at *The Conference of Transaction Cost Economics and Beyond,* Rotterdam, Netherlands: Erasmus University.

3
The Normative Value of Transaction Cost Economics in IT Outsourcing

Laura Poppo and Mary C. Lacity

Introduction

In the previous chapter, Lacity and Willcocks found that 61 actual IT out-sourcing (ITO) decisions did not map well to Transaction Cost Economics (TCE). Our findings were initially written in 1995 when large scale ITO decisions were still novel. As time progressed, other researchers found better results with ITO tests of TCE propositions. For example, Poppo and Zenger (1998) found that asset specificity and measurement accuracy did have the effects on ITO as predicted by TCE (although uncertainty did not). In 2002, Lacity and Poppo began discussing their TCE results in the context of ITO. This chapter is the result of that collaboration.

After re-analyzing our two data sets, we concluded that the real value of TCE may be *normative* rather than *descriptive*. We found that managers who followed TCE tenants had better success with their sourcing decisions. We conclude that TCE logic is not intuitive to managers, but that managers may learn and apply TCE prescriptions over time. The evidence clearly suggests that managers learned from their mistakes in the 1980s and early 1990s and subsequently crafted more effective ITO contracts by the mid-1990s. Specifically, managers realized higher performance when they applied the TCE principles (1) to not outsource the most specialized activities, and (2) to measure and benchmark outsourcing activities. However, we also found that managers realized higher performance when they complemented their use of customized contracts with supportive relational norms. This supports the view that multiple theoretical perspectives are complementary and are needed to capture the rich terrain of ITO.

Sourcing decisions in practice

Consider the following stories regarding the performance of outsourced of IT services (Lacity and Willcocks, 2001):

> A US Food company paid twice the original contract price due to excess fees triggered by undocumented requirements. In hindsight, participants

believe the wrong activity was outsourced. They perhaps should have bought-in supplier expertise to work on an in-house project development team, rather than contract management and delivery of the system to a third party.

A United Kingdom public sector body (PBS) signed a fixed-fee for service, ten-year, £1 billion contract for most of PSB1's product and services. In 1994, the IT Director referred to the supplier as a "strategic partner". By 1995, excess fees included £100,000 for unexpected software license transfer fees, an additional £5 million a year to cover inaccuracies in the original tender documents, and an additional £15 million a year for hardware maintenance. Furthermore, PSB could not meet some of the contractual terms, such as specifying requirements for 48 skill types 13 months in advance.

The stories suggests the outsourcing firm incurred huge levels of hidden or unanticipated costs in the outsourcing IT activities, had a poor understanding of the work-to-be-done, and chose an inadequate form of governance. If asked about the success of outsourcing, the customers acknowledge disappointment.

These stories are inconsistent with the optimal governance, and thus performance, of exchanges, as outlined by TCE. Interestingly, in most empirical contexts, the basic propositions of TCE are widely supported leading Williamson (1999: 1092) to claim it "is an empirical success story" and Joskow (1988: 81) to acknowledge "this empirical work is in much better shape than much of the empirical work in industrial organization generally." TCE affirms that as assets become increasingly specialized, firms vertically integrate to avoid the transaction costs associated with market governance (see Shelanski and Klein, 1995 for a review of the literature). For exchanges characterized by low or mixed levels of asset specificity, market exchanges, supported by classical and/or neo-classical contracts, efficiently coordinate exchange.

The IT context presents several challenges when crafting optimal market arrangements that are not found in many technologies (Lacity and Willcocks, 1996). First, information technology evolves rapidly, and depreciates faster, making lock-in arrangements potentially disastrous. Second IT economics changes rapidly and unpredictably. For example, while a 10% discount today may appeal to outsourcer companies, that same price may be 50% above market value next year. Third, high switching costs from one supplier to another – or even bringing the IT activity back in-house – creates power asymmetries in favor of suppliers. Finally, because of their relative inexperience in negotiating deals, managers who were outsourcing IT were at a significant disadvantage when negotiating contracts with suppliers. In this paper, we show how managers have learned to mediate hazards idiosyncratic to IT by better outsourcing choices, better contracts, and better relationship management.

Specifically, we examine whether TCE principles apply to the outsourcing of IT. We first review the TCE framework, and advance several theoretical challenges to this framework from strategists, namely that social relationship and supporting cooperative norms, can constitute an effective governance device. Next, we review two sets of studies that have examined the governance of IT (Poppo and Zenger, 1998; Poppo and Zenger, 2001; Poppo *et al.*, 2001; Lacity and Willcocks, 1996, 2001). These two studies employ very different methodologies: Lacity and Willcocks focus on interviews and induction; where as Poppo and Zenger use surveys and econometric models. Yet, their findings are consistent and complementary. Major lessons based on the findings of the two research studies include:

1. TCE logic is not intuitive, and managers learned through their mistakes in the 1980s how to craft more effective contracts in the mid-1990s;
2. Managers realize higher performance when they apply the TCE principle to not outsource the most specialized activities;
3. Managers realized higher satisfaction when they apply the TCE principle to measure and benchmark outsourcing activities; and
4. Managers realize higher performance when they complement their use of customized contracts with supportive relational norms, or when they merely invest in such relational norms.

The outsourcing phenomenon from the lenses of economics and strategy

Transaction Cost Economics

For organizational economics, the central question underlying the outsourcing of information technology and services, is how to choose, in a manner that maximizes performance, which service or activity to outsource. The outsourcing choice is predicated on the proposition that managers must match the IT activity, which differs in attributes, to governance forms, which differ in performance (Williamson, 1991b). The governance choice depends, therefore, on the comparative performance of the alternative forms, given the exchange attributes. Governance forms include: 1) coordinating the exchange of the service or product on a spot market in which price, quantity, and quality is readily observed, 2) using a more complex (hybrid) market arrangement in which contracts and social norms are used to govern the exchange, 3) employing ownership (vertical integration) to control the assets. Thus, according to *TCE not all IT* activities should be outsourced; some are better governed and yield higher performance when kept in-house.

TCE focuses on three exchange attributes that are likely to challenge market forms of governance: asset specificity, uncertainty, and measurement (Williamson, 1985, 1991a; Alchian and Demsetz, 1972). The attributes indicate situations in which opportunities exist for either one or both parties in a market exchange to be opportunistic: that is, to lie, cheat, or misrepresent information in such a way that one party benefits and the other party suffers losses. When opportunism arises, performance of the exchange suffers and the costs of managing the exchange (transaction costs) increase. The attributes, their challenges, and their optimal governance are detailed below.

Asset specificity, by definition, requires significant relationship-specific investments in physical and/or human assets that are non-redeployable to alternative uses or users. For example, an information service provider may customize an application to the clients' work setting. Similarly, the client may need to develop a unique understanding of the provider's procedures, approach, and language to effectively utilize their services. In outsourcing such exchanges, the continuity of an exchange becomes vital to its effectiveness. Severing the relationship results in the forfeiture of the value of these specialized investments. Unexpected changes or unmet expectations may lead to threats to terminate the relationship, or alternatively, both contractual parties may seek to appropriate returns from these specialized investments. To safeguard against such hold-up behavior, managers adopt neo-classical contracts (i.e. relational contracts), which promote the longevity of relationship by specifying not only required actions and conditions of contractual breach, but also a framework for resolving unforeseen disputes and norms of trust, mutuality, and solidarity, which foster adaptations and project exchange into the future, despite the disputes that arise from unexpected events (Macneil, 1978; Williamson, 1991b).

Despite the positive governance features of relational contracts, TCE predicts that for the most extreme levels of specialized assets, vertical integration is the optimal governance choice. Ownership has demonstrative advantages over relational contracts in the ease and cost of highly consequential adaptations, which invariably arise during the course of exchange (Williamson, 1991b, p. 280). Firms have access to fiat, which can quickly resolve disputes. Moreover, information disclosure can be more easily accessed and more accurately assessed, and proposals for change are likely to require less documentation. Finally, incentives and informal organization are likely to support a more team-based approach to dispute resolution.

Difficulty in measuring the performance of exchange partners also challenges market exchanges. Markets succeed when they can effectively link rewards to productivity – that is they can measure productivity and pay for it accordingly (Alchian and Demsetz, 1972). When performance is difficult to measure, parties have incentives to limit their efforts toward fulfilling the agreement. Managers have two choices. They can realize lower performance because of their inability to measure performance, or expend resources to improve performance measurement by creating more complex contracts that specify delivered service levels or facilitate the monitoring of a supplier's behaviors as well as by developing social norms of trust, mutuality, and bilaterialism. For example, clauses may specify third party monitoring, disclosure of necessary documents to justify work done, and if possible, the use of benchmarks to gauge the performance of the work done. Social norms, if properly maintained, mitigate the negative effects of performance measurement, by effectively replacing self-interest with more cooperative behavior, which enhance information disclosure. Thus, as measurement becomes more difficult, we expect managers to develop more relational contracts, which enable them to accurately measure and reward productivity.

The agency literature is ambiguous as to whether vertical integration is superior to relational contracts for difficult performance measurement. When managers find it difficult to meter the activity and thus performance of their employees, they cannot implement high-powered incentives in which pay is a function of performance (Eisenhardt, 1988; Brown, 1990; Poppo and Zenger, 1998). Similar to more complex market arrangements, managers can develop rules and policies to facilitate monitoring and information disclosure, and have access in informal structures or norms to support cooperation and unity of employees.

Uncertainty, the third hazard, challenges market exchange by requiring the parties to adapt to problems raised from unforeseeable changes. In general, markets marvel at autonomous adaptation, in which price serves as a sufficient statistic (Williamson, 1991b: 287), such as changes in demand and supply. For more complex forms of adaptation that require coordination among parties, simple market governance, however, is no longer adequate. In order to facilitate coordination, contracts become necessarily more customized by adding information disclosure and dispute-resolution procedures to facilitate the bargaining and negotiations that will invariably arise from technological or business changes. While contract customization is a necessary response to conditions of uncertainty arising from technological change, it is an inferior governance solution to vertical integration, which has access to fiat, better information disclosure and incentives.

In situations in which transactions involve mixed attributes, such as uncertainty and asset specificity or difficult performance measurement, devising effective contracts becomes even more critical. Contracts must specify clauses not only to protect investments in specialized assets or to measure the performance of the party, but also to facilitate adjustments as adaptations become necessary. Absence such customization, market-based arrangements struggle with costly haggling and adaptation issues. Williamson (1985, p. 80) further proposes that "unless an appropriate market-assisted governance structure can be devised, such transactions may 'flee' to one of the polar extremes as the degree of uncertainty increases." That is, firms may choose to procure a standard product or to vertically integrate if contracts cannot be sufficiently customized to safeguard the parties from opportunistic behavior. Thus, uncertainty may also act in conjunction with specialized assets and difficult performance measurement to increase the customization of contingent contracts, and in extreme cases, result in vertical integration.

Theoretical counter-attacks and alternatives to TCE

Transaction Cost Economics assumes that formal controls and ownership are the most efficient mechanisms to offset costly adaptations that occur when specialized assets and uncertainty arise. Some strategists argue, however, that Transaction Cost Economics overstates the desirability of either integration or explicit contractual safeguards in such exchange settings (Granovetter, 1985; Bradach and Eccles, 1989; Dyer and Singh, 1998; Gulati, 1995; Uzzi, 1997). They counter that when parties share an expectation of future exchange, and thus, value continuance of exchange, relational norms, most notably trust, but also mutuality and bilaterialism, offset self-interest and opportunism in market exchanges by promoting cooperation. Moreover, such social relationships reduce transaction costs by facilitating negotiations and reducing the need to craft contracts. These theorists view relational norms as substitutes for complex, explicit contracts or vertical integration.

A more extreme position, taken by some, is that formal controls may even undermine a firm's capacity to develop relational norms. That is, the use of formal contracts or formal controls within the firm signal an initial distrust of the other party, and therefore undermines the creation of trust and the display of cooperation (Ghoshal and Moran, 1996). Macaulay explains, for example, "Not only are contract and contract law not needed in many situations, their use may have, or may be thought to have, undesirable consequences. ... Detailed negotiated contracts can get in the way of creating good exchange relationships between business units (1963, 64)." He argues that some firms discourage the use of an elaborate contract because it "indicates a lack of trust and blunts the demands of friendship, turning a cooperative venture into an antagonistic horsetrade" (p. 64). Thus, if trust is present, formal contracts are at best an unnecessary expense and at worst counter-productive.

A second attack on the transaction cost view stems from a variant of the resource-base view of the firm, the knowledge-base view of the firm. Both the resource-base view and the knowledge view advance that competitive advantage stems from an ability of firms to exploit resources. Resources constitute assets that are rare, difficult to imitate, and non-substitutable, which managers acquire at a price less than the return that they produce (Barney, 1986, 1991). The knowledge position applies this logic to the vertical integration decision. Conner (1991, 140) explains: firms realize value from integrating assets that are highly specific to existing operations because "the in-house team is likely to produce technological knowledge, skill, or routines that fit better with the firm's current activities", when compared to the outsourced alternative. Thus, relatedness (that is, co-specialization) is the source of value creation. Efficiency gains are also realized from specific, related investments because of shared language, routines, and culture, resulting in more efficient communication and transfer of know-how (Demsetz, 1988; Kogut and Zander, 1992; Monteverde, 1995). The knowledge position, thus, offers an alternative motivation for vertical integration: rather than to avoid opportunism in market exchanges, firms invest in co-specialized assets to increase the productive value of such assets.

Research approaches

This paper relies on two separate sources of empirical data. The first source of data is based on a survey of key informants from the *Directory of Top Computer Executives* (Poppo and Zenger, 1998; Poppo and Zenger, 2001; Poppo *et al.*, 2001). Key informants were top computer executives of US-based operations who held one of two positions: 1) the senior corporate information technology manager who provided overall guidance and planning for information services, or 2) the manager who had control over major data processing facilities in operating departments, divisions, or subsidiaries. The use of a single key informant in evaluating exchange performance is consistent with prior studies (Goodman *et al.*, 1995; Mohr and Spekman, 1994) and should not threaten measurement validity (Anderson and Narus, 1990; Heide and John, 1990).

The directory, which has been in existence since 1972, included top computer executives of companies with an annual data processing budget of $250,000 or more. Also included in this directory were all *Fortune 500* companies. By using this broad population of key informants, we sought to enhance the external validity of the study. Most previous studies of governance choice constrain their analysis to single firms or single industries.

We obtained 181 responses and of these 152 were usable. Each respondent provided data on 9 IS functions. Therefore, although the sample size varied by analysis, partly due to missing data, the core sample was 9 IT functions across 152 companies for a total sample of 1,368 information service exchanges. We tested for a response bias, and analyses indicated that no significant mean differences existed between early and late respondents on a sample of questionnaire items. Thus, there was no evidence of obvious response bias in the sample, other than the a slight under-representation of manufacturing companies.

The survey, requested information on nine commonly used information services: data entry; data center operations; network design; network operations (data); network operations (voice); end user support; training and education; applications development; and applications maintenance. For each information service we collected data on a number of theoretical constructs as well as control variables (see Table 3.1 for measurement of the theoretical constructs). Over 50% of the sample provided information services totally in-house and 70% of the sample outsourced 10% or less. Our

Table 3.1 Measurement of Primary Theoretical Constructs

Theoretical Construct	Measurement
Performance	Managerial satisfaction with: 1) the overall cost of the service; 2) the quality of the output or service; and 3) the vendor's responsiveness to problems or inquiries (cronbach alpha = .84).
Negotiation cost	Level of agreement with: 1) negotiations of financial adjustments to the contract were typically difficult and lengthy, and 2) when unexpected changes arise, at least one party was dissatisfied with negotiated outcomes (cronbach alpha = .81).
Relational norms	Level of agreement with: 1) the buyer has an extremely collaborative relationship with the vendor; 2) both parties share long and short-term goals and plans; and 3) the buyer can rely on the vendor to keep promises (cronbach alpha = .78).
Contractual complexity	Level of agreement with: the formal contract is highly customized and required considerable legal work.
Asset specificity	1) To what degree must individuals acquire company-specific or division-specific information to adequately perform the IS function?; 2) To what degree is your approach to this function (or set of applications) custom-tailored to the company?; and 3) How costly would it be to switch outsourcing vendor? (Consider the time required to locate, qualify, train, make investments, conduct testing, and develop a working relationship) (cronbach alpha = .83).
Measurement difficulty	To what degree is it easy to measure the collective performance of those individuals who perform this function? (1 = very difficult, 7 = very easy). (reverse scored)
Technological change	1) To what degree are the underlying skills associated with this IS function (or set of applications) rapidly changing?; and 2) To what degree is the optimal configuration of hardware and software required to perform this function (or set of applications) rapidly changing? (cronbach alpha = .84).

pilot testing indicated that applications maintenance and applications development were categorically different from the other information services. Outsourcing, particularly partial outsourcing, was far more prevalent. IT managers were very likely to outsource some application-based projects while internally sourcing others. Hence, for these two information services, key informants provided separate information on the attributes for those applications they outsourced and those that they internally sourced.

Note: Questionnaire items, unless stated otherwise, were measured using a 7-point scale in which '1' represented 'low degree' and '7' represented 'high degree'.

The second source of data was based on 116 sourcing decisions, published in Lacity and Willcocks (2001). Lacity and Willcocks interviewed 271 people about 116 sourcing decisions made in 76 organizations. They wanted to get as many perspectives on IT sourcing decisions as possible, and therefore sought interviews with multiple stakeholders in each organization. The 271 participants included 64 IT managers, 56 supplier managers, 52 chief information officers, 45 senior business executives, and 24 consultants and IT experts. All interviews were tape recorded and transcribed in over 2,000 pages.

A variety of industries in a number of countries participated in the study. The cases represent public and private sectors, service and manufacturing sectors, and consumer and industrial products from over three continents (see www.umsl.edu/~lacity/cases.htm).

Unlike many IT outsourcing studies, Lacity and Willcocks collected data on outcomes and levels of success and failure. They first assessed expectations, then assessed whether expectations have been met, then compared the two to determine the extent of success.

When asking participants to describe sourcing expectations, they also asked participants to provide evidence of their expectations, such as archived documents. For example, if a participant cited cost savings as an expectation, they provided evidence such as a press clipping after the contract was signed indicating expected savings during the life of the contract. Not surprisingly, participants cited a variety of expectations (anticipated and hoped-for outcomes) and reasons (justifications or explanations) for their sourcing decisions. Four categories were used to capture 12 "expectations/ reasons" cited by participants for sourcing: financial, business, focus strategy, and technical (see Lacity and Willcocks, 2001, p. 150). The four most commonly cited expectations/reasons were IT cost reduction, better service, ability to focus IT staff on core IT activities, and financial restructuring the IT cost structure.

Participants were also asked to what extent their expectations had been realized. Rather than solely base this on opinion, participants were asked to support their opinions with substantial evidence, including documents, budgets, press announcements, memos, reports, etc. The resulting indicator of success had four possible outcomes:

- YES, participants achieved most of their expectations
- NO, participants did not achieve most of their expectations
- MIXED results-participants achieved some major expectations but other major expectations were not achieved
- TOO EARLY TO TELL whether expectations were achieved

In this paper, we dropped the 14 decisions that do not have outcomes from the analyses as well as the 17 insourcing cases. Thus, findings are based on 85 outsourcing decisions with discernible outcomes.

Lessons Learned and principles applied by IT managers

We had many discussions and interpretations of our perspective research studies. Initially, it appeared that our studies were contradictory: Lacity and Willcocks (1996, 2001) suggested that TCE propositions were not largely supported in IT; while Poppo and Zenger (1998; 2001) suggested they were. We then realized that Lacity and Willcocks study spanned the 1980s as well as the 1990s, a time period that includes the initial emergence as well as some maturing use of IT outsourcing; where as Poppo and Zenger's data was in the early 1990s. This prompted a new analysis of the Lacity and Willcocks (2001) data. By dividing the data across two time periods, new and interesting findings concerning the applicability of TCE principles to IT outsourcing were found. These lessons, and our respective supporting data, are described in detail in this section.

Lesson 1: TCE logic is not intuitive, and managers learned through their mistakes in the 1980s how to craft more effective contracts in the mid-1990s;

Finding: Specifically, contracts created since 1991 have higher relative frequency of success than contracts created in the 1980s.

Corollary: Contracts created since 1991 have lower relative frequency of failure than pre-1991 contracts.

The following conclusions are based on data collected by Lacity and Willcocks (2001) (See Table 3.2). The contract date was analyzed to determine whether customers were getting better at negotiating contracts. We classified decisions into two categories: "1984–1991" and "1992–1998". We chose 1991/1992 as the cut-off point because contracts studied span 15 years, thus the cut-off represents the midpoint. Using these two categories, we

Table 3.2   Contract Date (n=85 outsourcing decisions with discernible outcomes)

Year Decision Was Made	YES, most expectations met	NO, most expectations not met	Mixed Results	Total
1984–1991	14 (48.3%)	12 (41.4%)	3 (10.3%	29
1992 to 1998	41 (73.2%)	8 (14,3%)	7 (12.5%)	56
Total number of decisions	55 (64.7%)	20 (23.5%)	10 (11.8%)	85

classified the 85 outsourcing contracts with discernible outcomes as follows:

- 29 contracts were signed between 1984 and 1991 (34%)
- 56 contracts were signed after 1994 and 1998 (66%).

It is evident that 73% of newer contracts were successful compared to 48% of older contracts as successful. Conversely, only 14% of new contracts failed compared to 41% of older contracts failing.

We offer two explanations for the poor success rates of older contracts. First, customers had little experience with IT outsourcing in the 1980s. Prior to 1992, most organizations insourced the majority of their information technology, and thus lacked the skills to evaluate outsourcing, craft optimal contracts, or manage suppliers. Second, the outsourcing market was not mature – the number of suppliers were much fewer than today, and services were less differentiated. The major deals studied prior to 1992 were nearly all awarded to EDS or IBM. Clearly the absence of competition combined with little customer experience with IT outsourcing transactions, contributed to the failure rates.

In contrast, deals made after 1991 had a success rate of 73%. Next, we elaborate on the two major factors for improvement: customer learning and more supplier competition.

Customer Learning. First and foremost, significant customer learning about make-or-buy decisions, crafting contracts, and managing suppliers have served to significantly improve outsourcing transactions since 1991. The sources of customer learning include: the customer's own mounting experience with outsourcing (via incremental outsourcing) as well as the infusion of best practices from external consultants and legal firms.

Concerning incremental outsourcing, some of the Lacity and Willcocks (2001) participants adopted this outsourcing strategy precisely to develop an in-house knowledge base learnt from the initial outsourcing experience. With incremental outsourcing, organizations outsourced a small and discrete part of its IT activities, such as third-party maintenance or shared processing services. The experience gained from this first incremental approach was then fed back into further outsourcing. In two cases, a petrochemical company and an electric utility, organizations found themselves ultimately engaging in total outsourcing.

Another very important factor in customer learning is the wide spread-use of key IT outsourcing consultants and IT outsourcing legal firms. We are witnessing an institutional isomorphic effect where outside experts, such as Technology Partners International (TPI) and Gartner Group, seed client organizations with similar standards and methods. In addition, all customers with outsourcing contracts over $1 billion belong to the ITTUG group, which provides many opportunities for information exchange. In this way, organizational learning is transferred across organizations, and proven practices are more quickly disseminated.

Taking a deeper look into TPI will serve to illustrate the effect these consulting firms on customer learning. Since 1989, Technology Partners International's mission has been to assist clients with the evaluation, negotiation and management of sourcing transactions. Denny McGuire, CEO and founder of the company, used to negotiate contracts for one of the major IT outsourcing suppliers. Thus, he knew the supplier's strategies, cost structures, practices, and contracts – and thus transferred this knowledge to customers who hired him. TPI now has over 100 professional consultants who average more than 20 years of experience in information technology and business processes across industries. TPI has the processes and experience to assist clients with total transactions value ranging from $50 million to over $4 billion. TPI consultants have assisted in over 300 client sourcing transactions valued at more than $175 billion. Considering that the entire US outsourcing market is $250 billion a year, we certainly understand the impact TPI has had on customer learning.

On the legal side, nearly every mega-deal involves the legal services of Shaw Pittman or Millbank Tweed. On the technology consulting and benchmarking side, Gartner Group and Compass are involved in nearly every mega-deal. The overall effect of these external constituents is the dissemination of best practices. In particular, mega-deal contracts are now templated, with all the customer costs, service levels, performance measures, mechanisms of change, and other clauses nearly identical. Although each organization participating in the research regards these practices as "competitive secrets", practices are nearly identical across mega-contracts. A typical mega-deal contract now contains 30,000 lines, over 600 service level agreements, and over 50 different pricing mechanisms.

Post-contract management practices are also becoming increasingly standardized, such as external benchmarking of data centers, networks, desktops, and applications; color-coded problem resolution systems, joint supplier/customer teams to resolve disputes; and responsibility matrices to clearly define customer responsibilities and supplier responsibilities (for example at BAe, DuPont, Inland Revenue, Government of South Australia use these practices).

Increased Competition. The second major factor is the increased number of suppliers in the marketplace since 1991. Once dominated by a few big players (EDS and IBM), the IT outsourcing market had fragmented into many niche services. As competition in the outsourcing market increases, companies have more power to bargain for shorter contracts, more select services, and better financial packages. For example, in the 1980s, a US chemicals company and a US Rubber Manufacturer, received only one supplier bid from EDS. In 1992, a UK public sector body received many responses, *"We put an advert in the press looking for interested parties, and had about 22 responses."* (Manager of IS) In 1993, a US Petroleum company reviewed a list of 115 potential suppliers. By 2000 we were noting in our advisory work many more players and ways organizations were contemplating using them, as we predicted in our 1995 *Harvard Business Review* article (Lacity, Willcocks and Feeny, 1995). However, suppliers capable of delivering a consistent service globally on even a specific aspect of IT were, even in 2000, still few and far between.

Lesson 2: Managers realize higher performance when they apply the TCE principle to not outsource the most specialized activities.

As stated earlier, TCE argues that for the most extreme levels of specialized assets, vertical integration is the optimal choice. We view the entire information technology function as a *portfolio*-some of the IT portfolio is highly asset specific while some of the IT portfolio is non-specific (see for example, Feeny and Willcocks, 1998). This suggests that the optimal governance structure for IT is selective sourcing, where the most specialized aspects of IT is retained in house and the mixed and least specialized IT is outsourced. That is, total outsourcing (defined here as outsourcing more than 80% of the annual IT budget) would likely not be optimal for most firms.

Both Lacity and Willcocks (2001) and Poppo and Zenger (1998) find evidence that supports Conclusion #2.

Finding: Mangers that use selective outsource experience higher levels of met expectations that those that use total outsourcing.

First, the Lacity and Willcocks (2001) data shows that selective outsourcing in both time periods had a higher frequency of success than total outsourcing (see Table 3.3). Looking at the earlier contracts (1984 to 1991), selective outsourcing had a higher relative frequency of success (63%) compared to total outsourcing (20% successful.) In the later contracts (1992–1998), selective outsourcing had a higher relative frequency of success (87%) compared to total outsourcing (44% successful.)

Table 3.3   The Performance Effects of Selective vs. Total Outsourcing Over Time (n=85 outsourcing decisions with discernible outcomes)

Year Decision Was Made	YES, most expectations met	NO, most expectations not met	Mixed Results	Total
Selective outsourcing	12 (63%)	7 (37%)	0	19
Total outsourcing	2 (20%)	5 (50%)	3 (30%)	10
1984 to 1991 Totals	14	12	3	29
Selective outsourcing	3 (87%)	3 (8%)	2 (5%)	38
Total outsourcing	8 (44%)	5 (28%)	5 (28%)	18
1992 to 1998 Totals	41	8	7	56
Total number of decisions	55	20	10	85

With selective outsourcing, organizations can select the most capable and efficient source – a practice some participants referred to as "best-of-breed" sourcing. The most commonly outsourced functions were mainframe data centers, software development and support services, telecommunications/networks, and support of existing systems. In most cases, suppliers were judged to have an ability to deliver these IT products and services less expensively than internal IT managers. Sometimes, the ability to focus in-house resources to higher-value work also justified selective outsourcing.

For total outsourcing, performance is much lower. In 10 of the 28 total outsourcing cases (36%) with discernible outcomes, however, expectations were not realized. Participants encountered one or more of the following problems:

- excess fees for services beyond the contract or excess fees for services participants assumed were in the contract (poor contracts or poor management of uncertainty)
- "hidden costs" such as software license transfer fees (poor contracts)
- fixed-prices that exceeded market prices two to three years into the contract (no mechanisms for change in the contract)
- inability to adapt the contract to even minor changes in business or technology without triggering additional costs (poor contracts)
- lack of innovation from the supplier (poor vendor selection or improper contractual motivation)

- deteriorating service in the face of patchy supplier staffing of the contract

As expected, total outsourcing remains problematic, most likely because too many knowledge specific activities are transferred to the supplier. Poor contracts are to be expected: that is, there is no optimal contract for governing specialized IT activities.

Finding: When outsourcing IT, managers experience increasingly lower performance as assets become increasingly specialized.

As noted above, many of the reasons cited by participants for the failure of total outsourcing are contractual in nature. While managers told Lacity and Willcocks that better contract design and incentives may improve performance, Poppo's and Zenger's (1998) results suggest that managers may be too optimistic about the effective use of effective contracts. Regardless of the type of contract, specific assets damage the performance of market governance by creating hold-up hazards. Because specific assets are of lesser value in alternative uses, partners in an exchange have incentives to appropriate returns from these specialized investments through post-contractual bargaining or threats of termination. Thus, increasing asset specificity leads to the diminishing effectiveness of market governance. Our results suggest that significant performance losses accrue as firms choose to coordinate firm-specific IT activities in the market. Markets simply lack effective mechanisms for resolving coordination problems and opportunism that arise as exchanges become increasingly specialized.

Finding: Surprisingly, managers do not experience increasingly better performance in-house as IT assets become increasingly specialized.

As stated earlier, customizing physical assets and developing firm-specific human assets enable firms to reduce production costs, innovate, and meet product specifications. Ideally, these investments should help provide strategic advantage. However, Poppo and Zenger (1998) find no evidence that such specialized assets generate the type of performance return envisioned by their managers. This finding does not suggest that markets are preferred – by integrating managers avoid the transaction costs associated with outsourcing specialized IT activities. Yet, this result does suggest that merely increasing specialization of the IT activity does not generate an incremental improvement in performance. Generating advantage from specialized investments is a very difficult task – sometimes it's a function of luck; sometimes it's a good idea; most of the time, it's a risky investment that turns out to be the wrong path because you paid too much to generate a return, or your competition can copy it or trump it with superior alternative. Poppo and Zenger's (1998) result is particularly disappointing for the knowledge-base view, and they suggest that at the time of their study, firms may have been disappointed with their IS/IT because of their inability to keep abreast of the latest developments, given the rapidly changing and evolving applications in the early 1990s.

Finding: Consistent with TCE, increased specialization of assets is met with increased contract customization.

We also explored when IT managers are more likely to invest in more customized contract design. Recall that TCE advances that managers craft increasingly complex contracts in response to exchange hazards. Poppo and Zenger (2001) find that managers do not increasingly customize their contracts to respond to the hazards of difficult performance measurement and technological change. Rather, they customize contracts to protect their investment in specialized assets. Because specialized assets have no value in alternative uses, if an exchange relationship is prematurely terminated, managers are not likely to have recouped their investment. Through contractual complexity, managers specify penalties for early termination, and this formal record facilitates, if need be, the court "picking up the pieces" and resolving termination issues. This result confirms the non-triviality of specialized assets and its importance in the governance decision.

Taken together, these results suggest that neo-classical contracts have adaptive limits when it comes to technological change and the more hazardous situation of both technological change and difficult performance measurement. This result is broadly consistent with Williamson's (1985, 80) argument that managers will flee from hybrid forms of governance which are ill-suited to deal with the problems of adaptation and haggling, and suggests that optimal contracts may not exist.

Lesson 3: Managers realize higher satisfaction when they apply the TCE principle to measure and benchmark the performance of IT activities.

Finding: When IT managers could not easily measure the performance of an outsourced activity, they were less satisfied with its cost performance.

Finding: IT managers were less satisfied with the cost, quality, and responsiveness of internal activities when they could not easily measure its performance.

Consistent with the agency theory and property rights literature, our results (Poppo and Zenger, 2001) confirm the role of measurement difficulty as a determinant of governance performance in both markets and within firms. Difficulty in measuring the internal performance of an activity leads to assessments of lower internal performance along all dimensions – cost, quality, and responsiveness. This finding is entirely consistent with the predictions of principal-agent models. Imprecise measurement constrains the incentive intensity of rewards and low powered rewards limit performance. While managers may employ centralized decision-making and behavioral monitoring to mitigate measurement problems, these governance devices appear to fail as output measures become increasingly imprecise. In order to improve performance, managers need to apply benchmarking and more effective monitoring devices just like they do to evaluate outsourced IT.

Our results are less consistent in demonstrating that measurement difficulty damages the performance of markets. Consistent with predictions in the property rights literature, measurement difficulty appears to strongly damage cost performance. However, contrary to prediction, measurement difficulty has only insignificant negative effects on quality and responsiveness as performance measures. Reputations for quality and responsiveness are important for vendors to maintain even when measurement difficulty creates opportunities for short-term gains.

Alternatively, the IT managers satisfaction with quality and responsiveness may occur because of contractual specification. We have already noted that a typical mega-contract now can include over 600 service level agreements. Service level agreements essentially define the service, how the service will be measured, how the service will be reported, escalation procedures for a missed service level, and even penalties for non-performance. Ironically, none of the mega-deals studied in Lacity and Willcocks (2001) were able to manage 600 plus service levels, particularly on a global basis, but no participant regretted the detailed SLAs-they are there if they need them. Instead, customers tended to focus on a few key measures. But the point is that the service levels in the contract now are treated as a baseline measure. In long-term contracts, customers expect the suppliers to *improve* service level performance. The challenge became: how can the customer contractually obligate the supplier to improve performance? Enter external benchmarking.

Many mega-contracts now require that service levels and unit prices be periodically benchmarked, typically every three years. Benchmarking is the practice of comparing a customer's IT performance against a reference group of similar organizations. The idea is that customers contractually obligate suppliers to be in the top X% of service performance and the bottom X% of unit price. Thus, benchmarks become contractual obligations to reduce costs and improve service levels. But how do they work in practice?

Based on TPI and Garter's influence on contracts, benchmarks are organized into "towers", including telecommunications, desktops, midrange, and applications. A balanced scorecard approach is typically adopted, using a number of measures to determine an overall bill of health for each tower. In general, external benchmarking firms such as Gartner and Compass, competently measure the cost and service of technical platforms such as IBM mainframe data centers, UNIX midrange computing, or LAN performance. But Lacity and Willcocks (2001) found that both customers and suppliers agree that benchmarking is still immature in a number of areas, particularly desktop computing and applications. In addition, suppliers may contest results of the benchmark. For example, a few customers found that the suppliers' application productivity was low and costs were high, as assessed by a benchmarking firm using function point metrics. The customers wanted the suppliers to lower their prices and improve service. But the suppliers argued that the application productivity depends not only on the supplier's performance, but on the quality of the applications inherited from the customer. Over-customization and jury-rigged legacy systems required a significant amount of supplier support. Is it fair to compare the supplier's performance of these old systems against the best-of-breed productivity in a bench marker's database?

> Our experience, being honest, is that I haven't been terribly happy with the benchmarking process. This is not happy for CSC nor BAe. It's just the process seems to be a little bit naive. – Contract Manager for British Aerospace

Despite the immaturity of benchmarking, it does provide evidence that managers are trying to better measure supplier performance and to motivate suppliers to improve performance while reducing unit costs over time.

Lesson 4: Managers realize higher performance when they complement their use of customized contracts with supportive relational norms. They also realize higher performance when investing in just relational norms.

> **Finding: The larger the investment in social relationships, the higher the managers' satisfaction of the IT vendors' cost, quality, and service goals and the lower the negotiation costs.**

> **Corollary: Managers experience lower performance and greater negotiation costs from IT vendors that they have known for years and years**

Both sociologists and strategists criticize TCE for its relative neglect of the role of social relations in economic exchange. Both Poppo and Zenger (2001) and Poppo *et al.* (2001) find strong support that social norms enhance exchange performance, and help managers realize more equitable outcomes and less difficult negotiations to unexpected changes. Thus, contrary to TCE relational norms appear to operate as a viable governance choice, and offers a wider range of performance improvements that would be specified by the TCE framework. Yet, it is important to note that our data also shows a dark side of social relations. Merely contracting with a known party is not sufficient to produce performance improvements. In fact, our data (Poppo *et al.*, 2001) suggest, to the contrary, that managers experience lower performance from such vendors. Given the high degree of technological change, it is not surprising that a reliance on a vendor because of past use is not sufficient to produce expected performance levels. Managers must continually assess supplier capabilities and their internal IT demands, in order to select the best IT supplier, and therefore, achieve performance expectations.

> **Finding: Managers appear to complement their investment in contract customization with the development of social relations, and in doing so improve the performance of the outsourced activity.**

TCE and legal scholars argue that social relationships are a necessary complement to contracts, while some strategists argue that it's a substitute for contracts. Both are at best an unnecessary expense, and at worse counterproductive. Consistent with the notion of complements, our results (Poppo and Zenger, 2001) show that managers tend to employ greater levels of relational norms as their contracts become increasingly customized, and to employ greater contractual complexity as they develop greater levels of relational governance. We suggest that customized contracts narrow the domain around which parties can be opportunistic. Customized contracts specify contingencies, adaptive processes, and controls likely to mitigate opportunistic behavior and thereby support relational governance. However, customized contracts do not guarantee the intent of mutuality, bilateralism, and continuance when conflict arises. Relational governance complements such adaptive limits of contracts by fostering continuance of the exchange and entrusting both parties with mutually agreeable outcomes.

Contractual complexity and relational governance not only function as complements, but also, as complements, improve managerial satisfaction with exchange performance, which is clearly inconsistent with a substitution perspective. Taking into account the positive relationship between relational governance and contract customization, the results of our models show that managerial satisfaction with the cost, quality, and service of the outsourced service improves as the exchange is increasingly governed through relational norms and through more complex contracts. Note, however, that our performance measure generally ignores the costs associated with increasing the complexity of contracts and developing relational norms, which is necessary to thoroughly test the substitution argument.

> A good contract does not ensure a good relationship, but a bad contract does ensure a bad relationship. – Bob Ridout, Chief Information Officer, DuPont

The quotation underscores the finding that customers and suppliers must create social norms to complement their use of contracts. The Lacity and Willcocks (2001) nomenclature use the term "post contract management" to capture the social norms instituted on successful deals. Several practices that are becoming common on large deals include an intensive off-site, team building exercise between customer and supplier representatives just after the contract is signed. The purpose is to reorient both sides away from the adversarial positioning that occurs during contract negotiations towards a more cooperative positioning after the contract is signed. Another common practice is joint customer/supplier task forces to resolve conflicts. Here, lower level employees are evaluated on how well the team resolves conflicts, rather than how well they defended their perspective organizations. The operating principle of each team is to be fair, not to exploit any contract inefficiencies. If joint teams cannot resolve a problem, it is typically escalated up the chain of command, ultimately to the general contract managers.

More formally, Lacity and Willcocks (2001) expanded three post contract management capabilities (first identified by Feeny & Willcocks, 1998) to help ensure outsourcing success.

Contract facilitation. Both users and suppliers place high value on effective contract facilitators. Although contract facilitation is sometimes set up to manage excessive user demand and cost overruns with suppliers, in general it is a coordinating role. But a fundamental task would seem to be that of managing expectations on all sides. The role of contract facilitation in such situations is demonstrated by this manager commenting on the UK Inland Revenue Service deal with EDS:

> There is always some hot spot somewhere that's not working entirely the way either side is expecting. And usually it's a misunderstanding of what people can expect from the contract and relationship. So once you get in there, it's not always difficult to find some way to improve the relationship. It's just that you don't always know until there is a bit of a stand-off.

Contractual adjustments. As organizations exploit the burgeoning external market for IT services, contract monitoring and adjustment becomes a core IT capability. While the contract facilitator is working to "make things happen" on a day-to-day basis, the contract monitor is ensuring that the business position is protected at all times. Effective contract monitoring involves holding suppliers to account against both existing service contracts and the developing performance standards of the services market. It enables the production of a "report card" for each supplier that highlights their achievement against external benchmarks and the standards in the contract. Nor would it seem that the role is about merely monitoring a static contract. According to one contract manager:

> We've come to the conclusion that actually it has to be a much more dynamic, moving, changing thing rather than a set-in-stone thing. We've been jointly working (client and vendor) to realign the mechanisms so that they produce the results more in keeping with what we went after. But the important factor is that we anticipate to do the same thing in two to three years time, and then two to three years after that. Not because we got it wrong, but because of the changes in technologies and user requirements.

Supplier development. The single most threatening aspect of IT outsourcing is the substantial switching costs. To outsource successfully requires considerable organizational effort over an extended period of time. In one case, it took more than 50 person-years to arrive at a contract for a ten-year deal worth around $700 million. Sizable implementation requirements followed. To subsequently change suppliers may require equivalent effort. Hence it is in the company's interest to maximize the contribution of existing suppliers, and also, when outsourcing, to guard against what we call "mid-contract sag." A supplier may be meeting the contract after two or more years, but none of the much talked-about added value of outsourcing materializes. As one IT Services Director commented in an aerospace company:

> Yes [the supplier] can achieve all the things that were proposed – but where is this famous "added-value service"? We are not getting anything over and above what any old outsourcer could provide.

In supplier development, organizations look beyond existing contractual arrangements to explore the long-term potential for suppliers to create the "win-win" situations in which the supplier increases its revenues by providing services that increase business benefits. A major retail multinational has many ways to achieve this, including an annual formal meeting:

> It's in both our interests to keep these things going and we formally, with our biggest suppliers, have a meeting once a year and these are done at very senior levels in both organizations. There are certain things

we force on our suppliers, like understanding our business and growing the business together...and that works very well.

While joint understanding of each other's business is important, and relational norms assure such cooperation, it is unwise to think that such partnership will create value-added service. Such specialization is generally beyond the scope of market arrangements, and requires vertical integration.

Finding: Managers' decision to invest in relational norms appears to be largely a response to IT vendors they have done business with, and not a "calculative" response of how to most effectively mitigate market hazards.

The mechanisms through which relational governance attenuates exchange hazards are both economic and sociological in nature. Economists emphasize the rational, calculative origins of relational governance, emphasizing particularly expectations of future exchanges that prompt cooperation in the present. Sociologists emphasize socially derived norms and social ties that have emerged from prior exchange (Uzzi, 1997, 45). Trust is therefore considered a trait that becomes embedded in a parti-cular exchange relation. In essence, once an exchange partner is granted "trustworthy" status, they are expected to behave in a trustworthy fashion in the future. We (Poppo *et al.*, 2001) find no evidence the managers are using a calculative approach of when an investment in social relations is worthwhile. Market hazards, such as technological change, difficult performance measurement, and technological change, do not prompt greater levels of relational norms. Instead, managers appear to link their development of relational norms to IT vendors that have survived (in effect, those that they have done business with for years and years).

Conclusion

Our review, based on the results of two very different research approaches, shows that IT managers enjoy higher performance when they use the prescriptions offered by TCE to determine what to outsource and how to structure the governance of the outsourced activity. We find, in particular: 1) Managers should not outsource their most specialized, knowledge intensive IT, but will experience greater satisfaction if left in-house, 2) Managers realize higher satisfaction when they apply the TCE principle to measure and benchmark outsourcing activities, and 3) Managers realize higher performance when they complement their use of customized contracts with supportive relational norms.

Yet, our review also suggests two important caveats: 1) Managers do not easily intuit the results of efficient governance, but learn through their mistakes, and 2) Managers should develop supporting social norms and practices to govern their outsourced activity, a governance device that is largely ignored, and thus undervalued in TCE.

The fact that managers need to learn the framework as well as how to apply the framework suggests that any dramatic change in how business is done represents a potential short-term source of competitive advantage. That is, managers who learn quickly and without huge financial mistakes how to best govern may realize higher economic performance than those who learn slowly. This issue is especially germane to IT at this time because the rules of how to outsource are changing. One recent development is the "commodization" of IT outsourcing transaction process, including RFPs, bids, and contract negotiations through IT outsourcing exchanges. Currently, the Everest Group and the Outsourcing Institute have such exchanges. The Everest Group, for example, already has 400 suppliers in the exchange. ScotiaBank, for example, used the Everest Group exchange to find a supplier and negotiate a $23 million customer relationship management project. (It is interesting to note that the bank hired TPI to help with the RFP). The entire process took two months as opposed to the normal six month process for this size deal. EDS won a $150 million contract through the same exchange. The exchange is challenging some of EDS's established regional compensation mechanisms. For example, the EDS person credited with the $150 million sale made their entire year's quota by February! Thus, although IT has not become a commodity, the coordination processes are becoming increasingly commoditized. Managers who realize how to make this process more efficient are likely to generate economic returns, a source of advantage, until it is replicated by others.

While empirical work validates the TCE framework for the make-or-buy decision, it remains an empirical question as to whether "ownership" dominates the governance device of social norms. Thus, some of the most interesting questions, such as the relative efficiency of relational norms compared to ownership or the substitution of "partnerships" for vertical integration remain an avenue for empirical inquiry. The issue is particular germane to IT as technology continues to change, evolve, and reinvent itself. It's unlikely that firms who do not have a capability in IT can keep abreast of such changes as efficiently as an IT specialist. If a firm believes IT is germane to competitive advantage, then it may well be better off partnering with an IT firm than pursuing integration. Yet, practitioners need to keep in mind that optimal governance of a partnership, including the social norms, may need to be learned, just as IT managers have learned the criticality of well-specified contracts.

References

Alchian, A. and Demsetz, H. (1972) "Production, information costs, and economic organization," *American Economic Review*, Vol. 62, pp. 777–795.

Anderson, J.C. and J.A. Narus (1990) "A model of the distributor's firm and manufacturer firm working partnerships", *Journal of Marketing*, 54, pp. 42–58.

Barney, J. (1986) "Strategic factor markets: Expectations, luck, and business strategy," *Management Science*, Vol. 32, pp. 1231–1241.

Barney, J. (1991) "Firm resources and sustained competitive advantage," *Journal of Management*, Vol. 17, pp. 99–120.

Bradach, J. and R. Eccles (1989) "Price, authority, and trust: From ideal types to plural forms," *Annual Review of Sociology*, Vol. 15, pp. 97–118.

Brown, C. (1990) "Firms' choice of method of pay," in Ronald G. Ehrenberg (ed.), *Do Compensation Policies Matter*, Cornell University: ILR Press, pp. 165–182.

Conner, K. (1991) "A historical comparison of resource-based theory and five schools of thought within industrial organization economics: Do we have a new theory of the firm?" *Journal of Management*, Vol. 17, pp. 121–154.

Demsetz, H. (1988) "The theory of the firm revisited," *Journal of Law, Economics, and Organization*, Vol. 4, 1, pp. 141–162.

Dyer, J. and H. Singh. (1998) "The relational view: Cooperative strategy and sources of interorganizational competitive advantage," *Academy of Management Review*, Vol. 23, pp. 660–679.

Eisenhardt, K. (1988) "Agency and Institutional Explanations of Compensation in Retail Sales," *Academy of Management Journal*, Vol. 31, pp. 488–511.

Feeny, D. and Willcocks, L. (1998) "Core IS Capabilities For Exploiting Information Technology," *Sloan Management Review*, Vol. 39, 3, pp. 9–21.

Ghoshal, S. and Moran P. (1996) "Bad for practice: A critique of the transaction cost theory," *Academy of Management Review*, Vol. 21, pp. 13–47.

Goodman, P.S., M. Fichman, F.J. Lerch and P.R. Snyder (1995) "Customer-firm relationships, involvement and customer satisfaction", *Academy of Management Journal*, 38(5), pp. 1310–324.

Granovetter, M. (1985) "Economic Action and Social Structure: The Problem of Embeddedness," *American Journal of Sociology*, Vol. 91, 3, pp. 481–510.

Gulati, R. (1995) "Social structure and alliance formation patterns: A longitudinal analysis," *Administrative Science Quarterly*, Vol. 40, pp. 619–652.

Heide, J. and G. John (1990) "Alliances in industrial purchasing: The determinants of joint action in buyer–supplier relationships", *Journal of Marketing Research*, 27, pp. 24–36.

Joskow, P. (1988) "Asset Specificity and the Structure of Vertical Relationships: Empirical Evidence," *Journal of Law, Economics, and Organization*, Vol. 4, pp. 95–118.

Kogut, B. and Zander, U. (1992) "Knowledge of the firm, combinative capabilities, and the replication of technology," *Organization Science*, Vol. 3, pp. 383–397.

Lacity, M., and Willcocks, L. (2001) *Global Information Technology Outsourcing: Search for Business Advantage*, Wiley: Chichester.

Lacity, M. and Willcocks, L. (1996) "Interpreting Information Technology Sourcing Decisions From A Transaction Cost Perspective: Findings and Critique," *Accounting, Management and Information Technology*, Vol. 5, 3/4, pp. 203–244.

Lacity, M., Willcocks, L. and Feeny, D. (1995) "IT Outsourcing: Maximize Flexibility and Control," *Harvard Business Review*, Vol. 73, 3, pp. 84–93.

Macaulay, S. (1963) "Non-contractual relations in business: A preliminary study," *American Sociological Review*, Vol. 28, pp. 55–69.

Macneil, I.R. (1978) "Contracts: Adjustment of Long-term Economic Relations Under Classical, Neoclassical and Relational Contract Law," *Northwestern University Law Review*, Vol. 72, pp. 854–905.

Mohr, J. and R. Spekman (1994) "Characteristics of partnership success: Partnership attributes, communication behavior, and conflict resolution techniques", *Strategic Management Journal*, 15(2), pp. 135–142.

Monteverde, K. (1995) "Technical dialog as an incentive for vertical integration in the semiconductor industry", *Management Science*, 41(10), pp. 1624–1638.

Poppo, L. and Zenger, T. (1998) "Testing alternative theories of the firm: Transaction cost, knowledge-based, and measurement explanations for make-or-buy decisions in information services," *Strategic Management Journal*, Vol. 19, pp. 853–877.

Poppo, L. and Zenger, T. (2001). Do Formal Contracts and Relational Governance Function as Substitutes or Complements?, working paper.

Poppo, L., Zhou, Z., and Zenger, T. (2001). On the Road to Social Relations? Examining the Limits of Relational Norms, working paper.

Shelanski, H. and Klein, P. (1995) "Empirical Research in Transaction Cost Economics: A Review and Assessment," *Journal of Law, Economics, and Organization*, Vol. 11, 2, pp. 335–361.

Teece, D. (1988) "Technological change and the nature of the firm," in G. Dosi, *et al.* (eds) *Technical Change and Economic Theory*, London: Pinter Publishers, pp. 256–281.

Uzzi, B. (1997) "Social structure and competition in interfirm networks: The paradox of embeddedness," *Administrative Science Quarterly*, Vol. 42, pp. 35–67.

Williamson, O. (1985) *The Economic Institutions of Capitalism*. New York: The Free Press.

Williamson, O. (1991a) "Strategizing, economizing, and economic organization," *Strategic Management Journal*, Vol. 12, pp. 75–94.

Williamson, O. (1991b) "Comparative economic organization: The analysis of discrete structural alternatives," *Administrative Science Quarterly*, Vol. 36, pp. 269–296.

Williamson, O. (1999) Strategy research: Governance and competence perspectives, *Strategic Management Journal*, Vol. 20, pp. 1087–1108.

4
Domberger's Theory of Contracting Applied to IT Outsourcing

Peter Seddon, Sara Cullen and Leslie P. Willcocks

Introduction

This chapter contributes an interpretation of Domberger's theory of *The Contracting Organization* for use in an IT outsourcing context, then presents a preliminary test of the validity of that theory using data from a survey of 235 senior IT managers. Our conclusion is that Domberger's theory appears to be a useful lens for understanding IT outsourcing, and that a further study using purpose-collected data is therefore warranted. Phrased differently, his four types of benefit of contracting – namely Specialization, Market Discipline, Flexibility, and Cost Savings – appear to be a good way of summarizing senior IT managers' explanations of why their organizations chose to outsource IT. We also conduct a preliminary test of the extent to which these four factors can explain a purchasing organization's satisfaction with IT outsourcing.

FOR RELEASE: Thursday, March 1, 2001

Telstra Selects EDS For Major Outsourcing Contract For Billing and Shared Services

Australia's Largest Telco Set To Reduce Costs, Increase Speed-to-Market and Improve Delivery Quality

MELBOURNE, Australia – Telstra, Australia's largest telecommunications company, has awarded EDS a major five-year contract worth approximately US $300 million (AUD $500 million) to provide software maintenance and development for its billing functions and shared services.

"This alignment with EDS will allow Telstra to significantly reduce IT costs through process efficiency, increase our speed-to-market for infrastructure and solutions that support customer initiatives and improve quality of information and delivery," Dwight King, Telstra's managing director of business and wholesale, said. "We are confident this relationship will contribute to the long-term success of both companies."

(TPI 2001)

Typical of many announcements of IT outsourcing deals, the above press release announces that Telstra, a technologically sophisticated, US$10 billion per annum vendor of telecommunications services across Australia, had chosen to outsource management of its billing functions to one of the world's largest IT outsourcing specialists, EDS. The contract itself is not remarkable. What is surprising, though, was that Telstra decided to award the contract to EDS although it was a 23% shareholder in a major competitor of EDS, namely IBM Global Services Australia (GSA) (IBM, 1997). Evidently managers in Telstra recognized that, in line with our remarks in the Introduction to this book, competition in the IT outsourcing market is a prime source of outsourcing benefits, so they were even prepared to outsource to their competitor. This study explores the impact of competition and three other factors – specialization, flexibility, and cost savings – on the benefits to the purchaser of IT outsourcing services.

Since Kodak's initial foray into outsourcing (Applegate and Montealegre, 1991), IT outsourcing has emerged as an important tool for enabling organizations around the world to gain access to specific IT skills and services, focus on their core competencies, and in some cases, reduce the cost of IT service provision. Its economic impact is now huge. For 2004–5, revenues of US-based vendors EDS and CSC were US$21B and US$14B respectively (EDS, 2005; CSC, 2005). In India, the National Association of Software and Services Companies reported that 2004–5 export revenue for the country's IT service providers was US$12B (NASSCOM, 2005). These figures, which do not include major vendors IBM Global Services or Accenture, and recent studies reported in Willcocks and Lacity (2006), suggest that IT outsourcing revenues worldwide were in excess of US$200 billion by the end of 2005. Further, with continued growth of outsourcing in countries such as India (NASSCOM, 2005), increase in outsourcing revenues seems assured, with Willcocks and Lacity (2006) and Willcocks and Craig (2007) estimating that there would be a 7% per annum growth in revenues between 2006–12.

During this period of IT outsourcing growth, much has been learned about what works and what does not. Numerous conceptual models for understanding when firms should and should not outsource, and how they should outsource, have been proposed. Ten studies that illustrate the range of insights are as follows. First, Loh and Venkatraman (1992) propose and test a model of when firms outsource based on Compustat-style accounting ratios. Second, Lacity and Hirschheim (1995) argue that most cost reductions achievable through outsourcing can equally well be achieved by the in-house IT function if it is given freedom to reorganize. They present 11 generic cost-reduction strategies that internal IS departments can implement to reduce costs. Third, Grover *et al.* (1998) propose a contingency model of IT outsourcing based on four theories – resource-based theory, resource-dependency theory, transaction-cost theory, and agency-cost theory – that they hope will "provide guidance in examining the various aspects of the outsourcing phenomenon in a consistent and cumulative manner." Fourth, Ang and Straub (1998) propose a model in which four factors – production cost advantage, transaction cost, financial slack, and firm size – determine the degree of outsourcing. Their tests showed the two strongest factors were production cost advantage and firm size, the former driven by economies of scale. Fifth, Greaver (1999) provides a practitioner viewpoint, with 21 different reasons for outsourcing, grouped under six headings – Organizationally-driven, Improvement-driven, Financially-driven, Revenue-driven, Cost-driven, and Employee-driven.

Sixth, Hui and Beath (2001) provide a comprehensive review of 143 papers and books in this much-studied area, including some useful tables summarizing the theoretical bases of the different studies. The four main theoretical bases are as follows: (1) transaction-cost economics (2) other economic theories such as agency theory and production-cost economics (3) resource-based view/core competencies, and (4) social exchange/trust/relationship theories. Seventh, Lacity and Willcocks (2001) present a list of six "proven practices" for IT outsourcing (p. xiii) and three frameworks for guiding outsourcing decisions (Ch. 5) induced from their large database of in-depth case studies of IT outsourcing. Eighth, Levina and Ross (2003) provide a detailed theoretical analysis of the ways that specialization and complementarities between core competencies enable vendor firms to create value for their customers. Ninth, Cullen and Willcocks (2003) and Cullen *et al.* (2005a) present a lifecycle process model of 54 steps that potential IT outsourcing customers should follow to reduce the risk of problems arising from IT outsourcing. Tenth, in a 97-page review of the literature, Dibbern *et al.* (2004) review 74 studies from 1992– 2000 (see their Table 29, pp. 99–102) and present "a roadmap of the IS outsourcing literature, highlighting what has been done so far, how the work fits together under a common umbrella, and what the future directions might be" (p. 6).

With 143 studies reviewed by Hui and Beath (2001) and 74 by Dibbern *et al.* (2004) there is clearly no shortage of studies of when, what, how, and why a firm should outsource IT. However, the literature has produced little clear-cut advice on the keys to success with outsourcing. Cullen *et al.* (2005b) argue that this is because outsourcing can be configured in so many different ways that sound advice for managing one IT outsourcing portfolio may be quite inappropriate for another portfolio. However, some things are common to all outsourcing arrangements. Outsourcing is a principal-agent relationship (Jensen and Meckling, 1976) where a client organization (the principal) purchases services from a vendor firm (the agent). Further, such inter-organizational relationships have been studied for years (Williamson, 1975, 1985, 2000). Surely, therefore, despite the diversity of possible configurations (Cullen *et al.*, 2005b), there must be some fundamental principles that provide insight into all outsourcing arrangements?

The purpose of this study is to provide a preliminary test of one set of fundamental economic principles that seeks to explain why firms outsource. This explanation, which comes from Domberger's (1998) book *The Contracting Organization*, stands out as an empirically backed attempt to provide an explanation of the main economic incentives for what Domberger calls "contracting out". In the 15 years prior to writing his book, Domberger had conducted a series of empirical studies, surveys, and meta-analyses of "contracting out" of simple services such as refuse collection by 60 municipalities in the UK (Domberger *et al.*, 1986), domestic service costs for 1,500 UK hospitals (Domberger *et al.*, 1987), cleaning contracts for 68 bus companies in Sydney, Australia (Domberger *et al.*, 1994), and 48 hardware and software maintenance contracts in Sydney, Australia (Domberger *et al.*, 2000). In repeated studies, his findings were that after controlling for other factors that affected costs, organizations that contracted out service provision were able to save about 20% of the cost without a drop of service quality. Hodge's (2000) meta-analysis of 28 empirical studies – including three from Domberger *et al.*'s several studies – confirms this finding. Hodge's (2000, 113) histogram of cost savings from various studies shows that although contracting out sometimes resulted in cost increases, and although cost savings differed with different types of services, contracting out resulted in statistically significant cost savings for most services studied.

In his book, *The Contracting Organization*, Domberger goes well beyond services such as refuse collection, managing prisons, and water treatment to a much broader range of contracted services. Based on his in-depth knowledge of the literature on contracting and outsourcing, including the work of Coase (1937) on why firms exist, Williamson (1975, 1985) on transaction-cost economics, a wide range of empirical studies of contracting for different services in various settings (including IT outsourcing, e.g., Domberger *et al.* (2000)), and examples of well-known cases of contracting organizations (e.g., the keiretsu that supply 80% of Toyota car parts, Nike with its two tiers of contract suppliers doing all the manufacturing, and so-called "virtual" organizations such as Benetton), Domberger presents an economic analysis of benefits and costs of contracting. His basic position is that outsourcing is a sound decision if the net cost to the outsourcer drops as a result of outsourcing, provided there is no drop in service quality. Domberger's contribution is his identification and explanation of four fundamental economic drivers of the benefits of contracting out.

Many IT researchers will argue that Domberger's analysis is too simple, for example, that IT outsourcing is much more complex than the outsourcing of refuse collection. Lacity and Willcocks (2001, 183–185), for instance, have argued that IT is not just another resource like advertising, or even human resources. They identify five reasons why IT contracting should be treated differently. In their words:

1. "IT is not a homogeneous function, but comprises a wide variety of IT activities."

2. "IT capabilities continue to evolve at a dizzying pace; thus, predicting IT needs past a three-year horizon is wrought with uncertainty."
3. "There is no simple basis for gauging the economics of IT activity."
4. "Economic efficiency has more to do with IT practices than inherent economies of scale."
5. "Most distinctively of all, large switching costs are associated with IT sourcing decisions." (pp. 183–185)

If authors such as Lacity and Willcocks are correct, Domberger's arguments may well break down when applied to IT outsourcing (because IT outsourcing is different from generic outsourcing). Alternatively, if Domberger is correct, his theory will explain benefits, even for IT outsourcing. Hence the research question addressed in this chapter:

Does Domberger's theory of "The Contracting Organization" explain reasons for IT outsourcing and levels of satisfaction with benefits from IT outsourcing?

To answer this question we use a two-step process. First, we use a principal-components analysis of data from 235 respondents to a survey of senior IT managers in 1,000 large organizations to see if Domberger's four classes of benefit are consistent with managers' reasons for outsourcing. Our conclusion is that Domberger's theory *does* appear to be a useful lens for understanding IT outsourcing. Second, we test a model (discussed shortly) that seeks to explain organizational satisfaction with benefits from outsourcing, using Domberger's four factors. Two of four factors were found to be important. Surprisingly, given the importance attributed to cost savings in the main IT outsourcing literature, e.g. see Lacity and Willcocks (1998), cost savings were not important in explaining satisfaction with benefits from outsourcing in this study.

The remainder of this chapter is structured in five main sections. Section 2 summarizes theoretical arguments from Domberger's (1998) book: *The Contacting Organization*. Section 3 formulates a tentative model of Organizational Satisfaction with IT outsourcing. Section 4 provides details of survey data available for this study. Section 5 uses principal-components analysis of reasons those managers gave for outsourcing, to test the validity of Domberger's benefits categories. Finally, Section 6 tests the explanatory power of Domberger's four factors in explaining variance in organizational satisfaction with benefits from IT outsourcing.

One thing we do not do here is to discuss a very important factor that is often reported as driving success in IT outsourcing, namely partnering (or relationships). Grover *et al.* (1996), for instance, report that what they called "partnership" was a major factor in explaining perceptions of outsourcing success. More recently, Lacity and Willcocks (2000b), Goles (2001), Kern and Willcocks (2002), Alborz *et al.* (2005), and Willcocks and Cullen (2005) have argued that relationship management is a key determinant of success with IT outsourcing. The importance of sound relationship management is accepted but not studied in this paper. Our focus here is on the fundamental economic drivers of benefits from IT outsourcing discussed by Domberger (1998) and summarized in his Table 3.1, p. 51 (reproduced below as Table 4.1).

Domberger's theory of the "contracting organization"

According to Domberger (1998) the benefits of "contracting out", as he calls it, come from the four sources defined in Table 4.1. Table 4.1 is a verbatim copy of Domberger's (1998) Table 3.1 (p. 51). As discussed below, the table is initially a little hard to understand because the first two benefits are benefit *drivers* rather than benefits *per se*, whereas the last two benefits are much more directly benefits to the purchasing organization. Moreover, the first benefit driver, specialization, can lead to benefits to both client

Table 4.1   "A Summary of Benefits from Contracting"*

Title	Definition	Assessment
Specialization	Concentrating on those activities in which the organization has established a distinctive capability, letting others produce supporting goods and services.	Specialization leads demonstrable economic benefits. By concentrating on activities in which an organization is relatively more efficient, total value added is maximized. It also facilitates the exploitation of scale economies.
Market discipline	Identifies conditions in which the purchaser is separated from the provider and a formal transaction takes place under contract.	Market discipline provides a range of benefits, namely, focus by the purchaser on outputs not inputs, competition (contestability) between suppliers, choices by purchasers, and innovative work practices.
Flexibility	The ability to adjust the scale and scope of production upwards or downwards at low cost and rapid rate.	Networks of small organizations linked to their clients via contract can adjust more quickly and at lower cost to changing demand conditions compared to integrated organizations.
Cost savings	Lower resource costs of service delivery compared to in-house production.	International studies show that significant cost savings are achieved by contracting, on average of the order of 20%. As a rule, efficiency gains need not lead to lower quality.

*This table, including the heading, is a verbatim copy from Domberger's (1998) Table 3.1, p.51.

and vendor, if both parties specialize. To summarize benefits from the perspective of the purchasing organization, the authors have constructed a second table, Table 4.2, presented at the end of this section. Table 4.2 is the authors' attempt to apply Domberger's theory to predict benefits *to the purchaser* of outsourcing IT services.

Specialization

The first benefit driver in Table 4.1 is specialization. Benefits from specialization have been recognized and discussed since the time of Adam Smith (1776). Specialization is a fundamental driver of economic organization in Western societies today. Consistent with the literature on economies of scale, production-cost advantages (Ang and Straub, 1998), core competency (Hamel and Prahalad, 1996), and complementary sets of core competencies (Levina and Ross, 2003), Domberger (1998, Ch. 5, pp. 75–92) argues that if a firm contracts out something it is not so good at, it can devote its energies to doing more of what it is good at, and both parties will benefit:

- When contracting out leads to specialization and economies of scale in the *service provider*, the service provider benefits.
- Where contracting leads to specialization in the *purchasing* firm, the benefits are likely to be found not in lower costs, but in greater revenue and profit. All other things being equal, revenue and profit will increase because the purchaser will benefit from its own economies of scale, offer a better quality or lower cost product or service in its own marketplace, and so attract more customers or induce existing customers to buy more. It will often be very hard to link these benefits to the decision to outsource.

Recall that Domberger's arguments apply to outsourcing generally, not just IT outsourcing. In IT outsourcing terms, an excellent example of both service-provider and purchaser specialization is provided by the 1998 outsourcing deal between IBM and AT&T (AT&T, 1998). In this example, *both* parties to the contract, i.e., both *purchaser* and *provider*, seem likely to gain specialization benefits. There were three parts to the deal:

(1) IBM sold its Global Network business to AT&T for $5 billion in cash;
(2) IBM outsourced a significant portion of its global networking needs to AT&T in a contract worth US$5 billion over five years that involved transferring 5,000 employees to AT&T;
(3) AT&T outsourced certain applications processing and data center management operations to IBM in a deal worth US$4 billion over ten years that involved transferring 2,000 employees to IBM.

In this case, specialization means that *each* party becomes stronger in what it does well. In the usual glowing terms associated with such announcements,

IBM's then CEO, Lou Gerstner, explained that he expected AT&T to do a better job managing its network than IBM could do itself:

"We are delighted that AT&T will be the new home for our Global Network operation." "With this agreement, the network will receive the management focus and resources necessary to maintain its standing as a world-class provider of connectivity to IBM and millions of customers."

In return, IBM gets to expand its own data center business and benefit from potential economies of scale from focusing on that area of its business.

The first row in Table 4.2 shows how the authors expect Domberger's specialization benefits to flow through to the purchaser of outsourcing IT services. There are three points. First, the purchaser may see benefits in terms of increased revenue and profitability from concentration on its own core business. As noted above, this benefit is unlikely to be recognized in conventional measures of cost savings. Second, the purchaser will have access to more expert knowledge and skills, a particular benefit for smaller organizations. In one organization we interviewed, the CIO said that as a result of outsourcing, his firm now wasted less money on false starts and failed projects. The outsourcing vendor had more knowledge of which technologies worked and which did not, and this resulted in fewer pilot projects and fewer mistakes in his own organization. As for increased revenue and profitability, these opportunity-costs-avoided benefits are unlikely to be recognized in conventional measures of cost savings. Third, the service provider's benefits from specialization do not automatically flow through to the purchasing firm. Rather, as discussed in the next section, Market Discipline plays a major role in determining the extent to which the purchasing firm might see additional benefits, e.g. in the form of higher quality services and/or lower costs.

Market discipline

The second benefit driver in Table 4.1 is "Market Discipline". Domberger (1998, Ch. 3, pp. 38–48) regards market discipline as a source of benefit from contracting for two reasons. First, competition creates incentives for service providers to deliver services at lower cost (for example, through adopting innovative work practices) and higher standards than they would feel motivated to deliver in a non-competitive environment. Lacity and Hirschheim's (1995) arguments – that in-house service provision can be just as cheap as outsourcing – seem to revolve around this issue: competition leads to changes in patterns of service delivery that in turn lead to lower costs. Domberger argues that it is the threat of competition that drives the benefits, not whether the service provider is in-house or an external vendor.

Review the press release in the Introduction to this chapter. In awarding the US\$300 million contract to EDS, not to its normal partly-owned vendor (IBM Global Services Australia), Telstra showed that it was keenly aware of the benefits of competition. A second source of benefit from market discipline is that it requires the client organization to consider carefully the nature of the service required prior to contracting, and to develop measures to judge service quality. Such measures, Domberger says, are often not articulated clearly prior to contracting out. In addition to clarification of goals, definition of performance measures means that once a contract is in force, the performance measures provide the basis for a constructive dialog concerning strengths and weaknesses of service delivery and the nature of the relationship.

The second row in Table 4.2 shows how the authors expect Domberger's Market-Discipline benefit drivers to flow through to the purchaser of outsourcing IT services. There are two points. First, competitive pressures, or "contestability" as Domberger calls it in Table 4.1, can result in lower costs and a smoother flow of higher quality services. It is through this market-discipline mechanism that any benefits the vendor has gained through specialization and the adoption of innovative work practices may flow through to the purchaser. Second, clearer definition of services required can result in purchasing only those services actually needed. From a cost-saving and control point of view, this is good. In-house IT staff are often asked to undertake projects that have not been officially approved. Irrespective of whether they are likely to create value for the organization, unofficial projects are less likely under an outsourcing service provision arrangement.

Flexibility

The third benefit in Table 4.1, flexibility, can be achieved by offering many smaller contracts to different providers for shortish time periods, e.g. three to seven years (Domberger, 1998, 131), or moving from a fixed- to more variable-cost regime for provision of IT services. Domberger does not discuss who benefits from flexibility, but we argue that flexibility benefits are likely to accrue mainly to the purchaser, although the vendor may benefit if it is able to attract more business. IBM's current "On Demand" initiative (IBM, 2005) promises customers flexibility benefits.

A good example of an outsourcing deal motivated by the desire to increase flexibility is American Express's decision to outsource its "worldwide computer systems and web sites", which process "approximately one billion transactions daily" to IBM Global Services for US\$4B over seven years (IBM, 2002). After the September 11, 2001, terrorist attack in New York, American Express' profits dipped to half their 1999–2003 average level in 2001, a dip of about US\$1.3B (American Express, 2004). Its decision to outsource to IBM early the next year was motivated by its discovery during 2001 that it could not easily reduce IT costs to increase profitability.

Because of high switching costs (Lacity and Willcocks, 2001: 185) and need for integration of services, there may be fewer flexibility benefits to be had from contracting for IT than for other services. For example, at the end of an outsourcing contract, the vendor's staff have detailed knowledge of their customer's needs that are often not easily transferable to another party. Therefore, it may not be easy to switch from one IT service provider to another.

Cost savings

The fourth benefit in Table 4.1 is cost savings. Some, but by no means all, of the benefits mentioned above will flow through to the purchaser as cost savings. If the vendor can simplify, innovate, gain specialization benefits, or otherwise produce at lower cost, and if competition motivates the vendor to pass on some of those benefits to the purchaser, the overall cost to the purchaser can fall without degradation of service quality. Outsourcing to low-wage economies such as India and China, is a simple and rapidly growing way of procuring IT services at a lower cost.

The final row in Table 4.2 shows how the authors expect Domberger's cost savings benefits to flow through to the purchaser of outsourcing IT services. There are four points. First, Domberger's studies of benefits of contracting generic services indicated to him that contracting out can often lead to cost savings of the order of 20%. It is possible that cost savings of a similar order might be realized for at least some IT services purchased from some vendors. Second, the current growth of "offshore" outsourcing to India shows that cost savings are clearly possible if resource costs, e.g. programming labor costs, are much lower in one labor market than in another. Third, although outsourcing involves additional costs for vendor contract management, it also saves money through not having to manage resources internally. These savings at least partly compensate for such contract management costs. Finally, cost savings are hard to measure (Seddon, 2001). Because of the rapid rate of technological innovation in IT, costs of services prior to contracting out rapidly lose relevance for making judgments about cost savings. Often the only meaningful approach for assessing cost savings is to using benchmarking to compare cost of similar services to other organizations.

Summary

Table 4.2 is the authors' attempt to apply Domberger's theory from Table 4.1 to IT outsourcing for the purchasing organization. Some benefits may appear as cost savings; others will be less tangible. An example of a "less tangible" benefit might be that because of better advice, a firm makes fewer mistaken investments in inappropriate technologies as a result of outsourcing. Though real, such benefits are unlikely to appear in a conventional financial analysis of benefits from outsourcing.

Table 4.2   Interpreting Domberger's Benefits for the *Purchaser* in an IT Outsourcing Context

Benefit Driver	How the *Purchasing* Organization will Benefit
Specialization	• The purchaser may see benefits in terms of increased revenue and profitability from concentration on its own core business. This benefit will not be recognized in conventional measures of cost savings. • The purchaser will have access to expert knowledge and skills, a particular benefit for smaller organizations. Such expertise may lead to improved IT services and fewer failed projects. These benefits are unlikely to be recognized in conventional measures of cost savings.
Market discipline	• Competitive pressure is crucial to the purchaser achieving cost savings whilst maintaining quality: "as a rule, efficiency gains need not lead to lower quality" (Domberger, 1998:21). • Clearer definition of services required can result in purchasing only those services actually needed. This can lead to cost savings.
Flexibility	• The purchaser may find it easier to add and change vendors for different services, or purchase more or fewer services from existing vendors, than to build and maintain services in-house. For example, if demand for IT services drops, it is often easier to revise or not to renew a contract than to manage redundancies of internal staff. • For the IT industry, switching costs are high, however (see Lacity and Willcocks, 2001), which may reduce flexibility benefits from IT outsourcing. • Contracting out can provide scale and scope, numerical, functional and financial flexibilities.
Cost savings	• Contracting out can achieve cost savings of the order of 20% (Domberger, 1998:31). • Cost savings is a major driver for the current trend towards so-called 'offshore' outsourcing where firms in high-wage countries purchase IT services from firms in low-wage countries (a form of virtual immigration). • The purchaser will see cost savings if the vendor gains from specialization AND competition motivates the vendor to share those benefits. • Cost savings should be measured relative to the cost of providing comparable services in-house. Because of changing needs and technologies over the life of the contract, cost savings are very hard to measure. Benchmarking is often the only viable option.

A model of organizational satisfaction with it outsourcing

Recall that the research question driving this study is *"Does Domberger's Theory of 'The Contracting Organization' explain reasons for IT outsourcing and levels of satisfaction achieved?"* Here we use the simple model in Figure 4.1 to answer the second half of this question. The model assumes that Domberger's four factors (see Table 4.1) are valid for IT outsourcing and hypothesizes that each independently causes variance in *Satisfaction of the Organization with IT Outsourcing*. (This assumption is tested and confirmed valid in Analysis step 1.) The model in Figure 4.1 is the authors' interpretation of Domberger's Table 4.1. Testing the model enables us to explore the relative importance of each factor in determining satisfaction. Note that although Grover *et al.* (1996) found that *Partnership* (communication, trust, cooperation, and satisfaction) was a prime determinant of both *Satisfaction* and overall success, *Partnership* is not tested as an independent variable in this study because it is not in Domberger's list of benefits (see Table 4.1).

The choice of the benefits construct "Satisfaction of Purchasing Organization with IT Outsourcing" for the dependent variable in the model in Figure 1 was considered carefully. Domberger's Table 3.1 (our Table 4.1) has the simple heading: "A summary of benefits from contracting". It does not say how benefits should be measured. In addition, as mentioned earlier, Domberger's first two factors are drivers of benefits, whereas the latter two are more directly benefits per se, so the choice of benefits measure is not clear. Moreover, although Domberger's basic position is that outsourcing is a sound decision if the net cost to the outsourcer drops as a result of outsourcing, provided there is no drop in service quality – which suggests that the benefits construct in Figure 4.1 should be framed in terms of a tradeoff between costs and service quality – Table 4.2 shows that purchasing organizations may also benefit through a range of non-monetary benefits from

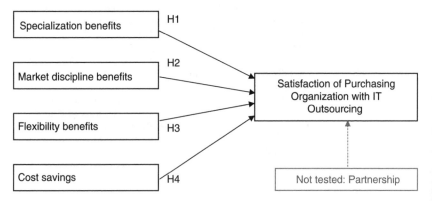

Figure 4.1   Explaining Organizational Satisfaction with IT Outsourcing

outsourcing. Ideally, the benefits construct in our model should reflect all these benefits.

Consistent with comments from Levina and Ross (2003: 351) who say: "Since the value of outsourcing to the client is very hard to measure, most researchers have focused on client satisfaction (Goles, 2001; Lacity and Willcocks, 1998; Saunders *et al.*, 1997)", we elected to use *Satisfaction of the purchasing organization with IT outsourcing* as the dependent variable in our model. Satisfaction is an appropriate measure of benefits for two reasons:

- Judgments about Satisfaction involve a weighing up of costs and benefits. Naylor *et al.* (1980), for instance, define satisfaction as "the result of the individual taking outcomes that have been received and evaluating them on a pleasant-unpleasant continuum".
- A key conclusion from Cullen *et al.*'s (2005c) study on outcomes from outsourcing is that satisfaction is always a valid outcomes measure whereas more specific measures are not always valid. As an example of a potentially flawed more-specific measure, the frequently used Grover *et al.* (1996) success instrument asks eight questions about things like economies of scale, cost control, access to technology, core focus, and access to staff. The instrument assumes these outcomes are relevant to all organizations. However, if not all organizations have these outcomes as goals for their outsourcing arrangements, the measure would be flawed for those organizations. By contrast, a manager assessing satisfaction will use his/her own organization's goals, which means that satisfaction is always a valid measure

Thus we chose *Satisfaction* as our dependent variable in Figure 4.1.

The survey

To test the applicability of Domberger's theory to IT outsourcing, we use data from an Australian survey of senior IT managers concerning their perceptions of the benefits or otherwise of IT outsourcing (Cullen *et al.*, 2001). The survey was the third in a series of three-yearly studies in Australia (the first two being Cullen (1994) and Cullen (1997)) designed to understand what organizations outsource, why they outsource, and their success with outsourcing. Although not specifically designed to answer the questions posed in this study, answers to the questions it asked (on reasons for outsourcing, outcomes from outsourcing, and satisfaction) contained almost all the data needed to provide a *preliminary* test of Domberger's theory. (As shown later, the only area not well covered was the measure for Domberger's Market-Discipline factor.) Our goal in this study was not to reach a definitive conclusion about the validity or otherwise of Domberger's theory. It was simply to use existing data to make a preliminary assessment of the potential validity of Domberger's theory. If the preliminary assessment proved positive, it would be worthwhile to conduct a full-blown study with purpose-collected data at some later date. In this study we report the results of that preliminary assessment.

For the survey, IT outsourcing was defined as:

> "A significant contribution by external suppliers in the management and provision of physical and/or human resources associated with the organization's IT function and services. This does not include the use of contract programmers and analysts or consultants working under the organization's direct control, nor the cost of purchasing packaged software."

Questions in our survey were based on a combination of questions from: (a) a survey that had been conducted by Lacity and Willcocks (2000a) on IT outsourcing practices in the US and the UK (highlights from the UK & US study are reproduced in Appendix A to Lacity and Willcocks (2001: 332–339)), and (b) two prior surveys conducted in Australia by Sara Cullen (one in 1994, the other in 1997). This multi-source approach to the questionnaire design was adopted so that results from this study could be compared with prior studies.

In late 1999, near the height of the dot-com boom, our survey of IT sourcing practices was mailed to senior IT managers in 1,000 large Australian organizations. The list of organizations included what we judged to be the 500 largest organizations, by employment, and a 50% random sample from the next 1,000 largest organizations. It included both private- and government-sector organizations. Particular care (including many phone calls to check contact information) was taken in developing a list of names of CIOs and senior IT managers in each organization. Despite the efforts made to ensure accurate mailing addresses, a number of surveys were returned, chiefly because the named person in charge of IT was no longer with the organization. Details were updated and re-mailed to the organizations concerned or, if the organization was no longer operational, a random replacement was selected from the remaining 500 next-largest organizations. The survey asked about what was being outsourced, reasons for and against outsourcing, and outcomes from outsourcing. After one follow-up letter in January 2000, we had received 235 responses. The response rate of 23.5% is higher than usual for surveys of this nature.

Australian Bureau of Statistics (ABS) figures indicate that around the time of the survey there were 2,400,000 people employed by 3,220 "private-sector organizations with more than 200 employees" (ABS, 2001) in Australia, and 1,500,000 people employed by an unspecified number of government organizations (ABS, 2002) in Australia. Comparable figures from our respondents are 436,000 and 137,000 employees, respectively. In other words, our respondents represent organizations employing 18% of all employees in "private-sector organizations with 200 or more employees", and 12% of all employees in government organizations in Australia. This is a significant slice of the workforce in large Australian organizations.

Contextual information from respondents

In order to have confidence in the analysis that follows it is important to understand as much as possible about the respondents and their firms. For that reason, contextual information about the respondents' industries, organization sizes, IT budgets, and degree of involvement with IT outsourcing (which is substantial) is now presented.

Details of the number of respondents, by industry, are provided in Table 4.3. A number of respondents came from what we have termed "smaller" organ-

Table 4.3   **Respondents by Industry**

Industry	Number of Smaller Organizations	Number of Larger Organizations	Number of Respondents	Percentage of Respondents
State Government	15	26	41	18%
Manufacturing	14	16	30	13%
Health and community services	6	16	22	10%
Local government	19	1	20	9%
Federal Government	10	9	19	8%
Finance and insurance	10	8	18	8%
Tertiary education		12	12	5%
Electricity, gas, and water	6	4	10	4%
Transport and storage	3	7	10	4%
Mining	3	6	9	4%
Communication services	3	4	7	3%
Wholesale trade	5	1	6	3%
Other (six different industries)	7	17	24	11%
Total	101	127	228	100%

izations. In this study such organizations have less than 1,000 employees, while "larger" organizations have 1,000 or more employees. Figure 4.2 shows the number of employees in the organizations that responded to the survey. Annual IT budgets for those organizations are shown in Figure 4.3. In short, it appears that a broad range of industries and organizations of different sizes is represented.

Percentage of IT budget outsourced

The percentage of IT budget outsourced by responding organizations is shown in Figure 4.4. 97% of surveyed organizations indicated that they spend a portion of their IT budgets on outsourcing, the average being 28%. The combined annual IT outsourcing budget for the 231 respondents to this question was approximately A$1.7 billion. Extrapolating this figure based on the ratio of employees in the respondent firms to employees in similar organizations Australia-wide, we estimate total Australian IT outsourcing expenditure was of the order of A$5–8 billion in 2000. Expenditure on IT

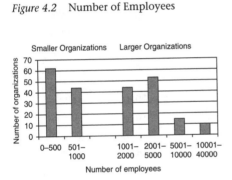

Figure 4.2   Number of Employees

Employees	Number of Respondents
0–500	62
501–1000	44
1001–2000	44
2001–5000	53
5001–10000	15

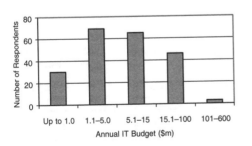

Figure 4.3   Annual IT Budgets

IT Budget (A$m)	Number of Respondents
Up to 1.0	30
1.1–5.0	69
5.1–15	65
15.1–100	46
101–600	3

Percentage of IT Budget Outsourced, by Respondent Size

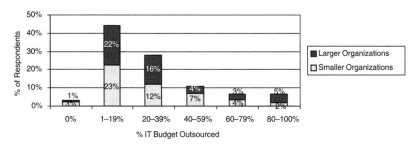

Figure 4.4 Percentage of IT Expenditure Outsourced

Source: Survey data from 231 respondents. 'Larger organization' have more than 1,000 employees.

outsourcing was not industry-specific; it spanned all 19 industry sectors surveyed. As shown in Figure 4.4, larger organizations outsourced slightly more of their IT, but the difference was not great.

What do these organizations outsource?

Respondents were given a list of 22 IT services and asked to indicate for each service, whether it: (a) had not been formally considered for outsourcing; (b) had been considered and rejected; (c) was under current consideration for outsourcing; (d) had already been partially outsourced; or (e) had already been fully outsourced. Results are summarized in Exhibit 1 in the Appendix. The most frequently outsourced services related to infrastructure, and stable, mature operations. Over half the respondents outsourced hardware support and maintenance, systems implementation, applications development and applications support and maintenance, WAN (wide area network) services, and cabling/infrastructure in premises, and education/training. Generally, both smaller and larger organizations shared similar outsourcing patterns. However, *ad-hoc* or project-based activities such as systems implementation, applications development and communications were fully or partially out-sourced 10–15% more frequently by smaller firms. Smaller organizations were less likely to retain the skills, tools and/or infrastructure required to deliver intermittent services or one-off projects.

Analysis step 1: Do Domberger's benefit categories apply to IT outsourcing?

The first goal here is to test whether Domberger's four benefits categories adequately describe benefits from IT outsourcing. Respondents were given a list of 21 possible reasons for outsourcing and asked to "tick all that applied" as primary or secondary reasons. Most questions came from Lacity and

Willcocks (2000a) and Cullen (1994, 1997), based on their extensive first-hand experience of issues that were important to managers involved in IT outsourcing. The questions were intended to provide a comprehensive list of reasons for outsourcing. They are very similar to Cullen *et al.*'s (2005c) slightly more comprehensive list of 25 reasons. Table 4.4 shows the survey results, sorted by primary reason.

Table 4.4   Reasons for Outsourcing IT Services

Rationale	Percentages of respondents			
	Not a reason	Secondary reason	Primary reason	Primary & secondary combined)
1 Access to better or more skills/ expertise	9%	31%	60%	91%
2 Unable to provide services internally	28%	23%	49%	72%
3 Concentration on core business	23%	33%	43%	76%
4 Better match of resource supply to demand	28%	33%	38%	71%
5 Access to better or more technology	22%	41%	37%	78%
6 Better use of in-house personnel	27%	38%	35%	73%
7 Obtain better service	30%	35%	34%	69%
8 Improve flexibility for the business	35%	34%	31%	65%
9 Reduce cost	42%	30%	28%	58%
10 Compliance with outsourcing mandate	56%	16%	28%	44%
11 Allow more flexible work practices	49%	29%	22%	51%
12 Enhance management control	49%	34%	17%	51%
13 Rationalize assets	62%	22%	16%	38%
14 Change users' accountability	49%	37%	14%	51%
15 Reduce staff numbers	55%	32%	14%	46%
16 Shift from capital to operating expense	62%	25%	13%	38%
17 Industry or economic development	73%	17%	11%	28%
18 Dissatisfaction with internal providers	74%	20%	7%	27%
19 Temporary solution	84%	10%	5%	15%
20 Get penalties for non performance	85%	11%	3%	14%
21 Improve cash flow	89%	9%	2%	11%

The number of respondents ranges from 186 to 200.

The most popular reasons – those that were cited by more 50% of organizations as either primary or secondary – are highlighted in bold.

Principal-components analysis of all 21 reasons that IT managers identified as reasons why their organizations outsourced was used to identify underlying factors. Principal components analysis is used in situations where, as Tabachnick and Fidell (1989, p. 597) explain, "the researcher is interested in discovering which variables in the set form coherent sub-sets that are relatively independent of one another." In our case, the goal was to see if statistical analysis would identify (a) any common themes underlying the 21 reasons in Table 4.4, and (b) if any of those themes were related to Domberger's four factors. This is a quite strong test because the list of 21 reasons had been prepared by experts in the outsourcing field, based on lessons from at least four prior surveys, quite independently of Domberger's theory. Except for the knowledge that both Domberger and various associates, on the one hand, and Willcocks, Lacity, and Cullen, on the other, had a good understanding of reasons why organizations outsourced, we had no a priori grounds for expecting that the factors from analysis of our data would correspond to those from Domberger.

For the analysis, responses to questions summarized in Table 4.4 were scored 0 (zero) if respondents indicated the item was not a reason for their organization outsourcing, 1 if the item was a "secondary or supporting reason", and 2 if it was a "primary or driving reason" for their organization outsourcing. Due to missing responses to some questions, only 168 responses were used in the analysis. The rotated factor matrix is shown in Table 4.5.

The first three factors are readily interpretable as three of Dombeger's four sources of benefits from contracting, namely specialization, cost savings, and flexibility, respectively. The best label for the fourth factor in Table 4.5 might be *Better Service*, rather than *Market Discipline*, although items 18 and 7 could be interpreted as indicators of market discipline. It is a pity there were not more questions in our questionnaire about *Market Discipline* to provide a clearer indicator of the fourth factor.

In short, despite arguments presented earlier to the effect that IT outsourcing is different from outsourcing of generic services like refuse collection, Domberger's four types of benefits from contracting – specialization, cost saving, flexibility, and something closely related to market discipline – appear to be a good way of summarizing senior IT managers' explanations of why their organizations chose to outsource IT. This is a very important conclusion. The implication is that Domberger's "theory" of contracting (which was developed to explain contracting for many different types of services, not just IT) *does* seem to explain IT outsourcing decisions. This, in turn, means that organizations considering outsourcing, and researchers who study outsourcing, should look for these types of benefit drivers or benefit drivers for IT outsourcing deals.

Table 4.5 Principal-Components Analysis of Reasons for Outsourcing
Coding: Not a reason = 0, Secondary reason = 1, Primary reason = 2
Factors: 1=Specialization; 2=Cost savings; 3=Flexibility; 4=Market discipline (Better service?)

Factors	Specialization	Cost Savings	Flexibility	Market Discipline	?	?
	1	2	3	4	5	6
1 Access to better or more skills/expertise	.794					
6 Better use of in-house personnel	.780					
4 Better match of resource supply to demand	.698					
5 Access to better/more technology	.667					
3 Concentration on core business	.504					−.426
13 Rationalize assets		.757				
9 Reduce cost		.705				
16 Shift from capital to operating expense		.645				
15 Reduce staff numbers		.637				
21 Improve cash flow		.619				
12 Enhance management control		.440				
11 Allow more flexible work practices			.701			
14 Change users' accountability			.677			
8 Improve flexibility for the business	.507		.558			
18 Dissatisfaction with internal providers				.739		
7 Obtain better service				.561		
17 Industry or economic development					.751	
10 Compliance with outsourcing mandate					.692	
20 Get penalties for non performance				.433	.623	
19 Temporary solution						.774
2 Unable to provide services internally						.622

Principal Components Analysis, Extraction Method: Maximum Likelihood. Rotation Method: Varimax with Kaiser Normalization. Listwise deletion of missing values; 21 questions, n=168; eigenvalues<1 (4.41, 2.38, 1.69, 1.39, 1.22, and 1.12). Cumulative % of total variance explained: 21%, 32%, 40%, 47%, 53%, 58%.

Analysis step 2: Testing the model of purchasing organization satisfaction

The dependent variable

The dependent variable in the model in Figure 4.1 is "Satisfaction of the Purchasing Organization with IT outsourcing". Reasons why this dependent variable is a good one for studying outsourcing were discussed earlier. To measure satisfaction, respondent IT managers were given two prompts:

"Overall, our organization is satisfied with the benefits from outsourcing"

"Our organization is satisfied with the performance of our service provider"

and asked to rate their own overall success with IT outsourcing (which may involve a number of contracts) on a seven-point scale. The first question is similar to the overall satisfaction question from Grover *et al.* (1996, p. 115), with anchors strongly disagree to strongly agree. The second question is based on a question from Lacity and Willcocks (2000a) that asked respondents to rate supplier performance from poor, through satisfactory, to excellent. Results for the first question above are shown in Figure 4.5. They show that (a) 50% of the 192 respondents rated their overall satisfaction as 5 or above (the most frequent score was 5, from 63 respondents, shown by the 32.8% bar in Figure 4.5); (b) 21% of respondents were neutral about their organization's satisfaction (score of 4); and (c) 29% indicated their organizations were dissatisfied with their outsourcing arrangements (scores of

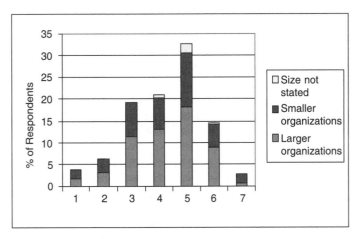

Figure 4.5   Overall Satisfaction with IT Outsourcing (192 respondents)

3 or below). Responses to the second prompt were similar (Pearson correlation, $r=0.814$, $p<0.000$). Our *Satisfaction* measure for the regression analysis that follows is an average of responses to these two prompts (Cronbach-alpha reliability statistic 0.897). The distribution of satisfaction scores was independent of industry, organizational size, or percentage of IT

Table 4.6   Outcomes from IT Outsourcing

Outcome	Percentages of Respondents				Number of Respondents
	Worse	None	Moderate Result	Substantial Result	
2 Access to services could not provide internally	2%	8%	47%	43%	191
1 Access to better or more skills/expertise	2%	12%	45%	41%	188
6 Better use of in-house personnel	2%	13%	59%	26%	170
4 Better match resource supply to demand	3%	17%	56%	23%	172
3 Concentration on core business	1%	20%	57%	22%	166
5 Access to better or more technology	1%	29%	49%	21%	175
7 Obtained better service	8%	18%	58%	17%	173
8 Improved flexibility for business	6%	26%	53%	14%	172
12 Enhanced management control	5%	28%	52%	15%	165
15 Reduced staff numbers	3%	40%	40%	17%	162
16 Shift from capital to operating expense	1%	35%	46%	18%	130
14 Changed users' accountabilities	1%	43%	48%	8%	167
11 Allowed more flexible work practices	4%	38%	46%	12%	161
10 Compliance with outsourcing mandate	1%	40%	35%	25%	126
13 Rationalized assets	2%	43%	44%	12%	147
20 Have penalties for non-performance		59%	36%	4%	135
17 Industry or economic development		65%	28%	6%	124
9 Reduced cost	22%	36%	35%	7%	173
18 Dissatisfaction with internal providers	2%	67%	26%	4%	123
19 Temporary solution	1%	66%	28%	5%	104
21 Improved cash flow	4%	69%	21%	6%	121

outsourced. Service quality apparently did not suffer. In fact, the data from the survey (questions 7 and 9 in Table 4.6) actually showed a positive correlation (r=0.46, p<0.01) between cost savings and service quality improvement!

Independent variables: Domberger's four constructs

In addition to the 21 questions on *reasons for* outsourcing, summarized in Table 4.4, respondents were given a matching list of 21 possible *outcomes from* outsourcing and asked to classify outcomes into "substantial result", "moderate result", "none", "worse", and "not applicable" and asked to "please tick all that apply" for all outcomes that applied to their organization. Table 4.6 shows the percentages of organizations that ticked each box. The table is sorted in descending order by the sum of "moderate result" and "substantial result", i.e., most frequent outcomes. The most satisfactory outcomes – those where high numbers of organizations reported moderate or substantial results – are highlighted in bold. Also highlighted in bold is the least satisfactory outcome – reduced costs – where significant numbers of respondents reported the situation was worse as a result of IT outsourcing. Since few organizations would willingly pay more for service provision than it would cost to provide the service in-house, one might expect failure to achieve cost savings to cause considerable dissatisfaction. This issue is explored in the regression analysis below.

Principal-components analysis (PCA) was again used, this time to test whether responses to these *outcomes* questions grouped consistently with the way the 15 similar questions about Reasons for Outsourcing were grouped earlier in the survey (see Table 4.5). Responses were scored –1 if respondents indicated the outcome was worse than before outsourcing, 0 (zero) if there was no change, 1 for a moderate result, and 2 for a substantial result. Because of listwise deletion of missing values (many respondents indicated that some outcomes were not applicable to their organizations) only 85 observations were used in the analysis. The rotated-factor matrix and expected item loadings are shown and discussed in Exhibit 2 in the Appendix. Since the sample size is small and the ratio of observations to items is only 6:1 the analysis cannot be relied upon for defining factors (Tabachnick and Fidell, 1989: 603). Nonetheless, two factors are readily interpretable as Dombeger's *Specialization* and *Cost savings* factors. The third and fourth factors, *Market discipline* and *Flexibility*, are not clearly interpretable.

Since this second PCA was based on such a small sample, we decided to use the 5+6+3+2=16 questions highlighted in the first PCA, in Table 4.5, to define variables for testing the model in Figure 4.1. After examining Cronbach-alpha reliability coefficients (reported in Exhibit 3 in the Appendix) using data on outcomes summarized in Table 4.6, we decided to drop two questions and use responses to the following outcomes questions for computing scores for the four independent variables: *Specialization:* Q.1, 3, 4, 5, and 6 (Cronbach alpha = 0.81); *Market discipline:* Q.7 only (Obtain better service); *Flexibility:* Q.8, 14 (Cronbach alpha = 0.61); and *Cost savings:* Q.9, 12, 13, 15, 16, and 21 (Cronbach alpha = 0.75). The frequency of "not applicable" responses in the dataset created a problem for analysis. As discussed in more detail in Exhibit 3 in the Appendix, we decided to use the SPSS *mean* function, which ignores missing values, to compute scores for the five variables in Figure 4.1, and ordinary least squares (OLS) regression as our analysis tool.

Testing the model of satisfaction with IT outsourcing

Results from OLS regression analysis to test the model in Figure 4.1 using the outcomes data summarized in Table 4.6 are shown in Figure 4.6. Probability-values (p-values) from SPSS's OLS regression analysis procedure are meaningful indicators of possible non-null coefficients in the population if the sample data are representative of the population (Seddon and Scheepers, 2005). Since our data do appear to come from a quite representative sample of the population, we argue that the p-values are likely to be meaningful here. P-values for standardized path coefficients for *Specialization* benefits and *Market discipline* benefits were both less than 0.05, i.e., they were significant at conventional levels for significance tests. P-values for *Flexibility* and *Cost savings* were not significant at conventional levels. (Details of the analysis are shown in Exhibit 4 in the Appendix.) In other words, only two of Domberger's four factors were significantly associated with Satisfaction of the Purchasing Organization with IT Outsourcing. The test in Figure 4.6 thus provides limited support for the view that Domberger's four factors explain variance in benefits from IT outsourcing.

It is most surprising that *Cost savings* was not significant. Cost saving heads the list of reasons for IT outsourcing in McLellan *et al.* (1995), DeLooff

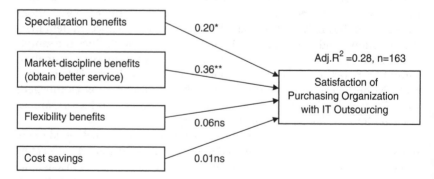

Significance: **=p<0.01, *=p<0.05, ns=not significant

Figure 4.6   Do Domberger's Four Factors Explain Variance in Overall Satisfaction with IT Outsourcing?

(1995), Sobel and Apte (1995), Lacity and Willcocks (1998: 369), Ang and Straub (1998: 543), and Lacity and Willcocks (2000a: 27–28). No organization, public or private, will willingly spend more than it needs to on service provision of any kind. Our conclusion is that cost saving is important, but at the time the survey data were collected (at the height of the dot-com boom), cost savings achieved was not a driver of satisfaction with IT outsourcing.

Discussion

The purpose of the analyses in the preceding two sections was to provide a preliminary test of Domberger's theory using data that had been collected for another purpose. The preliminary indications are encouraging. However, lack of purpose-collected data, and missing values in the dataset caused problems. First, the 21 questions used to collect the data summarized in Tables 4.4 and 4.6 were not designed from the outset to measure Domberger's factors. As a result, the *Market discipline* construct was measured for the regression analysis with a single scale "Obtained better service". Second, the questionnaire asked respondents to "tick all that apply". This meant that many respondents did not answer all questions, or indicated that questions were not applicable, so what SPSS treats as "missing data" caused problems in the Step-2 analysis. As discussed in Exhibit 3 in the Appendix, we solved this in part by using the SPSS *mean* function to deal with non applicable/missing responses. Third, we used coarse 3 and 4-point scales for reasons for, and outcomes from, outsourcing, respectively. Seven-point Likert scales would have been better for factor analysis. Despite these limitations, the first four factors shown in Table 4.5 correspond to Domberger's, and two of those factors are clearly evident in Exhibit 2 in the Appendix. In short, further testing of Domberger's theory with purpose-collected data seems warranted.

With respect to the generalizability of our findings, the data formed a large sample, that appears to be representative of large organizations in Australia, collected just before the end of the dot-com bubble. Although this timing is unlikely to affect the factor analysis in Table 4.5 (which assesses the extent to which scores on certain questions tend to covary), the relative importance of items shown in Tables 4.4 and 4.6, and of the relative importance of Domberger's four variables explaining variance in Satisfaction with outsourcing (see Figure 4.6) may not apply today in Australia or other western countries.

Conclusion

This study makes three contributions to the literature on IT outsourcing. First and most importantly, we show that Domberger's theory of The Contracting Organization *does* seem valid in an IT context. Despite some arguments from authors such as Lacity and Willcocks (2001:183–185), this study has found that Domberger's four factors do appear to provide a simple way of summarizing senior IT managers' explanations of the reasons why their organizations decided to outsource IT service provision. Evidence of the probably validity of Domberger's factors was presented in the form of the principal components analysis of the reasons IT managers from 235 largest Australian organizations gave for their organization's decision to outsource some IT service provision. Those reasons are summarized in Table 4.4, with the factor analysis reported in Table 4.5. Further testing of Domberger's theory, with purpose-collected data, therefore appears warranted.

The attraction of Domberger's theory, compared to the many other theories reviewed in Chapters 2, 3, and 5, and by Hui and Beath (2001) and Dibbern *et al.* (2004) (e.g., transaction-cost economics, agency theory, production-cost economics, resource-based view, social-exchange theory) is that it explores the fundamental economic drivers of benefits from outsourcing. Domberger shows how specialization leads to outsourcing benefits (for both the outsourcing vendor and customer), how market discipline (competition) motivates vendors to share their benefits with their customers, and how outsourcing can provide benefits to customers through flexibility and cost savings. It is important to note that cost savings are not the only benefits that a client firm can derive from outsourcing; non-monetary benefits such as opportunity costs avoided through access to better advice, growth opportunities through concentrating on its own core capabilities, and flexibility options need to be factored into the overall cost-benefit equation.

Our second contribution is the exploration of the extent to which Domberger's four benefit categories explain benefits to the purchasing organization of IT outsourcing, and the finding that (at least in late 1999 when data were collected for this study) *Cost savings* was not significantly associated with *Satisfaction with IT outsourcing*. Two factors, *Specialization* and *Market Discipline* (better service), were significant at $p<0.05$, however, *Flexibility* and *Cost savings* were not significantly associated with Satisfaction. Again, further testing of Domberger's theory with purpose-collected data therefore appears warranted. The relatively low coefficients of determination in this regression (Adjusted $R^2 = 0.28$) may be due, at least in part, to the non-inclusion in the analyses of relationship management/partnership. As explained earlier, in prior studies, relationship management has been shown to be an important driver of success, e.g., Grover *et al.* (1996), Alborz *et al.* (2005), but was not included in this study because it is not one of Domberger's four factors.

The third and final contribution of this chapter is the descriptive data in Tables 4.4 and 4.6, Figure 4.5, and Exhibit 1 in the Appendix. These Tables and the Figure provide a useful large-sample snapshot of what was outsourced, reasons for outsourcing, outcomes from outsourcing, and organizational satisfaction with IT outsourcing in Australia at the height of the dot-com bubble.

References

Alborz, S., Seddon, P.B. and Scheepers, R. (2005) The Quality-of-Relationship Construct in IT Outsourcing, *Proceedings of Pacific-Asia Conference on Information Systems (PACIS)*, Bangkok: 1118–1131

American Express (2004) 2003 Annual Report, http://www.onlineproxy.com/amex/ 2004/ nonvote/ar/AXP_annual03.pdf (viewed October, 2005)

Ang, S. and Straub, D.W. (1998) "Production and Transaction Economies and IS Outsourcing – A Study of the US Banking Industry," *MIS Quarterly*, 22, 4: 535–552.

Applegate, L.M. and Montelegre, R (1991) *Eastman Kodak Company: Managing Information Systems through Strategic Alliances*, Harvard Business School, MA, Case 9–192–030.

AT&T (1998) *AT&T to Acquire IBM's Global Network Business for $5 Billion*, Press Release http://www.att.com/news/1298/981208.cha.html (viewed October 2005)

Australian Bureau of Statistics (ABS) (2001) Business Operations and Industry Performance, Australia: 1999–2000 *(Cat.no. 8140.0)* Released 25 October 2001

Australian Bureau of Statistics (ABS) (2002) Wage and salary earners, Australia. *(ABS Cat. 6248.0)* September Quarter 2001, Released 24 January 2002.

Coase, R.H. (1937) The nature of the firm. *Econometrica* 4: 386–405.

CSC (2005) *2005 Annual Report*, http://www.csc.com/investorrelations/uploads/ CSC_AR05.pdf (viewed October 2005)

Cullen, S. (1994) *IT Outsourcing: The Myths Exploded*, Melbourne: Touche and Tohmatsu.

Cullen, S. (1997) *Information Technology Outsourcing Survey*. Deloitte and Touche Consulting Group, Melbourne.

Cullen, S., Seddon, P.B., and Willcocks, L.P. (2005a) "Managing Outsourcing: The Process Imperative", *MIS Quarterly Executive* (4,1), 2005: 229–246.

Cullen, S., Seddon, P.B., and Willcocks, L.P. (2005b) "IT Outsourcing Configuration: Research into Defining and Designing Outsourcing Arrangements", *Journal of Strategic Information Systems*, 14, 4 357–387.

Cullen, S., Seddon, P.B., and Willcocks, L.P. (2005c) "IT Outsourcing Success: A multidimensional, contextual perspective of outsourcing outcomes", Working Paper, Department of Information Systems, The University of Melbourne.

Cullen, S., Willcocks, L.P., and Seddon, P.B. (2001) *Information Technology Outsourcing Practices in Australia*, Melbourne, Australia: Deloitte Touche Tohmatsu, http:// www.cullengroup.com.au/publications/2001%20ITO%20report.pdf

Cullen S and Willcocks L.P. (2003) *Intelligent IT Outsourcing: Eight Building Blocks to Success*. Oxford: Butterworth-Heinemann.

DeLooff, L.A. (1995) Information systems outsourcing decision making, A framework, organizational theories and case studies, *Journal of Information Technology*, Vol. 10, 4: 281–297.

Dibbern, J., Goles, T., Hirschheim, R. and Jayatlilaka, B. (2004) "Information Systems Outsourcing: A Survey and Analysis of the Literature," *ACM DataBase*, 35:4, 6–102.

Domberger, S. (1998) *The Contracting Organization: A Strategic Guide to Outsourcing*. Oxford: Oxford University Press.

Domberger, S., Fernandez, P., and Fliebig, D.G. (2000) Modelling the price, performance and contract characteristics of IT outsourcing, *Journal of Information Technology*, Vol. 15, No. 2, June: 107–118.

Domberger, S., Hall, C., and Li, E. (1994) *The determinants of quality in competitively tendered contracts*. Working Paper, Graduate School of Business, University of Sydney, Australia.

Domberger, S., Meadowcroft, S.A. and Thompson, D.J. (1986) Competitive Tendering and Efficiency: The case of refuse collection. *Fiscal Studies* 7(4) November: 69–87.

Domberger, S., Meadowcroft, S.A. and Thompson, D.J. (1987) The impact of competitive tendering on the costs of hospital domestic services. *Fiscal Studies* 8(4): 39–54.

EDS (2005) *2004 Annual Report*, http://www.eds.com/investor/annual/2004/downloads/2004_annual_report_excerpt.pdf (viewed October 2005)

Goles, T. (2001) *The Impact of The Client-Vendor Relationship on Information Systems Outsourcing Success.* Unpublished Ph.D., University of Houston, Houston.

Greaver, M.F. II. (1999) *Strategic Outsourcing: A Structured Approach To Outsourcing Decisions and Initiatives.* AMACOM, American Management Association, New York

Grover, V., Cheon, M.J. and Teng, J.T.C. (1996) The effect of service quality and partnership on the outsourcing of information systems functions, *Journal of Management Information Systems*, Vol. 12, No. 4: 89–112.

Grover, V., Teng, J.T.C., and Cheon, M.J. (1998) Towards a theoretically-based contingency model of information systems outsourcing, in Willcocks and Lacity (eds) *Strategic Sourcing of Information Systems*, Wiley, Chichester, 79–102.

Hamel, G. and Prahalad, C.K. (1996) *Competing for the Future*, Boston: Harvard Business School Press.

Hodge, G.A. (2000) *Privatization: An International Review of Performance* Westview Press, Boulder

Hui, P.P., and Beath, C.M. (2001) The IT Sourcing Process: A Framework for Research, University of Austin, Texas: http://disc-nt.cba.uh.edu/chin/speakerseries/The%20IT%20Sourcing%20Process.pdf (viewed October 2005)

IBM (1997) "IBM, Lend Lease and Telstra Announce Strategic Alliance Agreement Creates Services Joint Ventures and Largest Data Center in Southern Hemisphere", http://www-7.ibm.com/nz/services/success/telstra2.html (viewed April 2004)

IBM (2002) American Express Teams with IBM in Industry-Leading Technology Services Initiative, Media Release, 25 Feb 2002, http://www-1.ibm.com/press/PressServletForm.wss?MenuChoice=pressreleases&TemplateName=ShowPressReleaseTemplate&SelectString=t1.docunid=886&TableName=DataheadApplicationClass&SESSIONKEY=any&WindowTitle=Press+Release&STATUS=publish (viewed October 2005)

IBM (2005) On demand business. http://www-306.ibm.com/e-business/ondemand/us/overview/overview.shtml (viewed October 2005)

Jensen, M.C. and Meckling, W. (1976) "Theory of the Firm: Managerial behavior, agency costs and ownership structure", *Journal of Financial Economics*, 305–360.

Kern, T. and Willcocks, L. (2002) *The Relationship Advantage: Information Technologies, Sourcing, and Management*, Wiley, Chichester.

Lacity, M. and Hirschheim, R. (1995) *Beyond the Information Systems Outsourcing Bandwagon: The Insourcing Response*, Wiley, Chichester.

Lacity, M. and Willcocks, L.P. (1998) "An Empirical Investigation of Information Technology Sourcing Practices: Lessons From Experience," *MIS Quarterly* (22:3), September: 363–408.

Lacity, M. and Willcocks, L.P. (2000a) *Inside Information Technology Outsourcing: A State-of-the-Art Report.* Templeton Research, Templeton College, Oxford.

Lacity, M. and Willcocks, L.P. (2000b) "Relationships in IT Outsourcing: A Stakeholder Perspective," In *Framing The Domains of IT Management Research: Glimpsing The Future through The Past.*, R. W. Zmud (ed.), Pinnaflex Educational Resources, Inc., Cincinnati, OH.

Lacity, M. and Willcocks, L.P. (2001) *Global Information Technology Outsourcing: In Search of Business Advantage*, Wiley, Chichester.

Levina, N. and Ross, J.W. (2003) From The Vendor's Perspective: Exploring the Value Proposition in Information Technology Outsourcing, *MIS Quarterly* (27, 3): 331–364.

Loh, L. and Venkatraman, N. (1992) "Determinants of Information Technology Outsourcing: A Cross-sectional analysis," *Journal of Management Information Systems* (9,1) Summer: 7–24.

McLellan, K., Marcolin, B.L. and Beamish, P.W. (1995) Financial and strategic motivations behind IS outsourcing. *Journal of Information Technology*, Vol. 10, No. 4: 299–321.

NASSCOM (2005) NASSCOM announces Top 20 IT Software and Service Exporters in India, Press Release, June 16, http://www.nasscom.org/artdisplay.asp?Art_id=4413

Naylor, J.C. Prichard, R.D. and Ilgen, D.R. (1980) *A Theory of Behavior in Organizations*. Academic Press, New York

Saunders, C., Gebelt, M. and Hu, Q. (1997) "Achieving Success in Information Systems Outsourcing," *California Management Review* (39:2), Winter: 63–79.

Seddon P.B. (2001) The Australian Federal Government's Clustered-Agency IT Outsourcing Experiment, *Communications of the AIS*, Vol. 5, Article 13. http://cais.isworld.org/articles/default.asp?vol=5&art=13 (viewed October 2005)

Seddon, P.B. and Scheepers, R. (2005) The Case for Greater Discussion of Other-Settings Generalizability in IS Research Papers, Working Paper, Department of Information Systems, The University of Melbourne, Melbourne.

Sobel, M. and Apte, U. (1995) Domestic and Global Outsourcing practices of America's Most Effective IS Users, *Journal of Information Technology*, 10, 4: 269–280.

Smith, A. (1776) The Wealth of Nations: An enquiry into the nature and causes. Republished in numerous places. e.g. http://www.econlib.org/library/Smith/smWN.html (viewed October 2005)

Tabachnick, B.G. and Fidell, L.S. (1989) *Using Multivariate Statistics*, 2nd ed. Harper-Collins, New York.

TPI (2001) Telstra Selects EDS For Major Outsourcing Contract For Billing and Shared Services. Press Release, TPI, New York http://www.tpi.net/about/displayNews.aspx?NewsTypeID=5&spid=71&id=392 (viewed October 2005).

Willcocks, L. and Craig, A. (2007) *The Outsourcing Enterprise 4: Retaining Core Capabilities*. LogicaCMG, London.

Willcocks, L. and Cullen, S. (2005) *The Outsourcing Enterprise 2: The Power of Relationships*, LogicaCMG, London.

Willcocks, L. and Lacity, M. (2006) *Global Sourcing of Business and IT Services*, Palgrave, London.

Williamson, O.E (1975) *Markets and Hierarchies*, New York: The Free Press.

Williamson, O.E. (1985) *The Economic Institutions of Capitalism*, New York: The Free Press.

Williamson, O.E. (2000) "The New Institutional Economics: Taking Stock, Looking Ahead", *Journal of Economic Literature*, 38, 595–613.

Appendix

Exhibit 1:   Percentage of Respondents Outsourcing, by Activity

IT Service/Activity	Not formally considered or N/A	Considered & Rejected Outsourcing	Considering Outsourcing	Partially Outsourced	Fully Outsourced	Number of Respondents
Mainframe & Data Centre Operations						
Hardware Support & Maintenance	12%	4%	6%	34%	45%	228
Systems Implementation	24%	3%	4%	60%	9%	227
Applications Development	26%	10%	4%	42%	19%	228
Applications Support & Maintenance	27%	10%	5%	44%	14%	228
Systems Integration	43%	9%	5%	32%	10%	227
Operations & Facilities Management	33%	18%	9%	21%	19%	228
Disaster Recovery	40%	9%	12%	20%	18%	228
Client/Server and Desktop						
Hardware Support & Maintenance	11%	6%	7%	43%	34%	229
Systems Implementation	20%	9%	6%	58%	8%	232
Applications Support & Maintenance	19%	11%	7%	50%	13%	233
Applications Development	27%	9%	5%	45%	13%	233
Systems Integration	39%	11%	7%	36%	7%	231
Operations & Facilities Management	38%	15%	11%	22%	14%	230
Disaster Recovery	44%	11%	10%	24%	11%	232
IT Management and Support						
Education & training	15%	3%	5%	58%	19%	232
Help desk	36%	22%	13%	9%	19%	233
Asset Management	63%	11%	7%	13%	6%	230
IT Strategic Planning	65%	21%	1%	13%	0%	231
Communications						
Network services between & beyond premises (WAN Services)	9%	3%	7%	37%	44%	233
Cabling & infrastructure in premises	17%	5%	5%	35%	38%	231
Operations & Facilities Management	31%	14%	10%	20%	24%	231
LAN services	36%	16%	10%	18%	20%	233

Exhibit 2: Principal-Components Analysis of Outcomes from Outsourcing

Principal Components Analysis, listwise deletion of missing values; 15 questions,
n=85; eigenvalues>1
Coding: Worse = –1, No change = 0, Moderate result = 1, Substantial result = 2
**Expected Factors: 1=Specialization; 2=Cost savings; 3=Market discipline;
4=Flexibility**

	Factor			Expected factor loadings (from Table 5)			
	1	2	3	1	2	3	4
1 Access to better or more skills/expertise	.741			X			
4 Better match resource supply to demand	.727			X			
8 Improved flexibility for business	.726						X
6 Better use of in-house personnel	.722			X			
3 Concentration on core business	.712			X			
5 Access to better or more technology	.662			X			
7 Obtained better service	.648					X	
11 Allowed more flexible work practices	.602						X
21 Improved cash flow		.779			X		
16 Shift from capital to operating expense		.739			X		
13 Rationalized assets		.697			X		
9 Reduced cost		.662			X		
15 Reduced staff numbers		.592			X		
14 Changed users' accountabilities		.429					X
18 Dissatisfaction with internal providers			.864			X	

Extraction Method: Maximum Likelihood. Rotation Method: Varimax with Kaiser Normalization

Comment on the Principal-Components Analysis Factor Structure: Four factors were
expected, but only three factors had eigenvalues greater than one. Eleven of fifteen
items have loaded on the expected factors. Because of listwise deletion of responses
with missing values (some "missing" values due to instructions to "tick all that

apply" and some due to respondents indicating that a possible outcome was "not applicable") only 85 observations were used in the analysis. Since the sample size is small and the ratio of observations to items is only 6:1 the analysis cannot be relied upon for defining factors (Tabachnick and Fidell 1989: 603). Despite this, two of the three factors above are readily interpretable as Domberger's *Specialization* and *Cost savings* factors. The third and fourth factors, *Market discipline* and *Flexibility*, are not clearly interpretable.

Exhibit 3:   Reliability of Scales for Outcomes from Outsourcing

	Special-ization	Market discipline	Flexi-bility	Cost Savings
1. Scale questions (based on expected PCA of questions on *expected* benefits in Table 5)	Q.1,3,4,5,6	Q.7,18	Q.8,11,14	Q.9,12,13,15,16,21
2. Cronbach alpha for the questions in row 1	0.81	0.42	0.51	0.72
3. Questions used for calculating variable scores for regression analysis	Q.1,3,4,5,6	Q.7 only	Q.8, 14	Q.9,12,13,15,16,21
4. Cronbach alpha for the questions in row 3	0.81	n/a	0.61	0.72

Comment on the scale reliability

Because of the low reliability of intended scales for Market Discipline and Flexibility (see alphas in row 2 of the above table), two questions were dropped, and only the questions in row 3 of Exhibit 3 were used for computing variable scores in the regression analysis.

Use of the SPSS mean function to avoid miscoding "not applicable" responses

One commonly used technique for dealing with missing values is to impute a value from data that are not missing. However, it is not valid to impute values for missing cells when respondents have identified a question as *not applicable*. We used the SPSS *mean* function to solve this problem. First, we coded both (a) non responses and (b) outcomes respondents identified as "not applicable" as "missing" in our SPSS data file. Second, since the SPSS *mean* function ignores missing values, not applicable responses were ignored when SPSS calculated the mean score for the corresponding variable.

For example, if a respondent checked Question 21 (improved cash flow) as an outcome that was not applicable, we stored that response as a blank cell in SPSS. The mean score for Cost savings for that respondent would be based on the remaining questions answered. If none of Q.9,12,13,15,16,21 were answered, SPSS would treat the score for Cost savings as missing, and through listwise deletion of missing values, the response would dropped from the regression analysis. Only 163 of the 235 responses had non-missing responses to all five variables included in the regression analysis in Exhibit 4.

Exhibit 4: OLS Regression Testing of the Model in Figure 1

Descriptive Statistics

	Mean	Std. Devi-ation	N	Pearson Correl-ations	SAT	SPEC	MKT	FLEX	COST
Satisfaction	4.195	1.342	163	SAT	1.000	0.458	0.514	0.367	0.195
Specialization	1.017	0.539	163	SPEC	0.458	1.000	0.629	0.609	0.274
Market Discipline	0.816	0.795	163	MKT	0.514	0.629	1.000	0.521	0.312
Flexibility	0.702	0.664	163	FLEX	0.367	0.609	0.521	1.000	0.369
Cost Savings	0.532	0.568	163	COST	0.195	0.274	0.312	0.369	1.000

Model Summary

R	R Square	Adjusted R Square	Std. Error of the Estimate
0.544	0.296	0.279	1.140

ANOVA

	Sum of Squares	df	Mean Square	F	Sig.
Regression	86.51	4	21.627	16.639	0.000
Residual	205.37	158	1.300		
Total	291.88	162			

Coefficients

	Unstandardized Coefficients		Standardized Coefficients		
	B	Std. Error	Beta	T	Sig.
(Constant)	3.114	0.198		15.749	0.000
Specialization	0.487	0.236	0.196	2.063	0.041
Market Discipline	0.604	0.150	0.358	4.021	0.000
Flexibility	0.119	0.180	0.059	0.661	0.510
Cost Savings	0.018	0.172	0.008	0.108	0.914

5
Contracting and Relationship Theories Applied to IT Outsourcing

Thomas Kern and Leslie P. Willcocks

Introduction

Information technology (IT) outsourcing ventures have been termed successful or less successful in achieving their expected outsourcing objectives according to the operational effectiveness of the ensuing client-supplier relationship. Yet, even now, researchers and practitioners know little about the actual operational characteristics of these outsourcing relationships. This lack of insight on outsourcing relationships forms the rationale for the research on which this chapter is based. An attempt at bridging the gap is made by adopting the IMP group's dyadic "Interaction Approach" to shed some light on the crucial dimensions of IT outsourcing relationships. Exploratory research into twelve organizations identified the potential of the "interaction approach", but also highlighted its various limitations. Despite these, we find that the "Interaction approach" represents a very useful foundation for delimiting such relationships. The "Interaction" approach also helps to identify a number of management issues that warrant careful consideration if IT outsourcing relationship management is to be improved. Our more recent work (Kern and Willcocks, 2001; Willcocks and Cullen, 2005) confirms that relationships remain a problematic area in outsourcing, and that the Interaction approach retains considerable potency for analyzing outsourcing arrangements.

IT outsourcing describes a process whereby an organization decides to contract-out or sell the firm's IT assets, people and/or activities to a third party supplier, who in exchange provides and manages these assets and services for a agreed fee over an agreed time period (Loh and Venkatraman, 1992; Lacity and Hirschheim, 1993; Lacity and Willcocks, 2001). Although not exactly a new approach (Earl, 1991), IT outsourcing achieved a global service market size of US$86 billion in 1996, rising to US$200 billion. by 2006 (Lacity and Willcocks, 2001; Lacity and Willcocks, 2006). For those organisations where the decision to outsource was eventually made and contract negotiations led to an agreement, the ensuing concern for management was:

how to handle the venture and manage the relationship to achieve the outsourcing objectives.

By relationship we mean:

> "the state of being connected or related; the mutual dealings, connections, or feelings that exist between two parties, countries, people, etc. (Collins Dictionary of English Language, 1986, p. 1289)."

IT outsourcing tends to be more complex than most other forms of outsourcing, such as cleaning, catering or accounting, due to the fact that IT pervades, affects and shapes most organizational processes in some way. To this extent, the evolving outsourcing relationship will take on a mission critical status in maintaining key support services and functions for an organisation's processes. Willcocks *et al.* (1996), and Chapter 4 of the present volume, point to other characteristics that make IT outsourcing distinctive: IT is not a homogeneous function, but comprises a variety of IT activities; IT capabilities evolve at a dizzying pace, making IT outsourcing wrought with uncertainty; there is no simple basis for gauging the economics of IT activity, and of IT outsourcing; and most distinctively of all, large switching costs are associated with IT sourcing decisions.

It thus comes as a surprise, that little is known to date about the outsourcing relationship's operational dimensions, and its management. There have been a few notable exceptions, for example Kern, 1999; Klepper, 1994; 1995; Lacity and Willcocks, 2001; McFarlan and Nolan, 1995; Willcocks and Kern, 1998; Willcocks and Choi, 1995 – all of whom studied IT outsourcing relationships, but they were mostly inconclusive (but see Oshri *et al.*, 2008). In turn, for many organizations, the post-contract management phase in which the outsourcing relationship takes its true shape, still proves extremely problematic to predict and manage, and is often beyond what was initially anticipated and planned for. British Petroleum Exploration (Cross, 1995; Kern and Blois, 2000), the UK Inland Revenue (Willcocks and Kern, 1998; Lacity and Willcocks, 2001), Sainsburys (Bravard and Morgan, 2006) and Xerox Corporation (Kern and Willcocks, 2000) are just a few examples that highlight the relationship management problems clients and suppliers were experiencing in their outsourcing ventures throughout the 1993–2007 period.

To date, most IT outsourcing research has focused on its determinants, costs, benefits, the decision process, vendor selection and contracting, whereas the relationship has all too often been neglected (see Kern, 1999, Klepper and Jones, 1998; Willcocks and Cullen, 2005; Willcocks and Lacity, 1998). This disregard seems paradoxical as the relationship's impact on the overall outsourcing initiative, be it developmental, selective or total outsourcing, has been shown to make the difference between success, less success and even failure of such ventures (see Davis, 1996; Kern, 1999; Lacity and Willcocks, 2001; Klepper and Jones, 1998; McFarlan and Nolan, 1995; Willcocks and

Kern, 1998). This raises the underlying research question of this chapter: what key dimensions define an outsourcing relationship and how do organizations manage their relationships in relation to addressing these dimensions?

Following a literature review of representative research on the outsourcing relationship, we identify Håkansson's "Interaction approach" as a guiding conceptual framework for describing dyadic client-supplier relationships. As other Information Systems (IS) researchers have already shown, the Interaction approach has proven particularly valuable for investigating dyadic relationships in an IT/IS environment (see for example Cunningham and Tynan, 1993; Leek, *et al.*, 2000). Building on these positive findings, it seems rational to build on the Interaction approach as a basis for launching an exploratory investigation into client-supplier relationships in IT outsourcing.

This chapter presents three streams of research into IT outsourcing relationships. The first reviews the existing research, which leads us to present Håkansson's (also referred to as the "Nordic schools") Interaction framework as a conceptual framework for exploring outsourcing relationships. The second part presents a set of exploratory findings into relationship practice in 12 (client and supplier) organizations undertaken in parallel to our theoretical research into outsourcing relationships. The findings are then analyzed using the main dimensions of the Interaction approach. The findings point to the limitations and potential usefulness of the framework, and also enable us to identify suggestions for improving relationship practice in outsourcing.

Reviewing IT outsourcing relationship approaches

The paucity of research on outsourcing relationships was highlighted by the small number of conceptual and empirical studies identified for the period 1990–2000. Only five studies were found in our search[1] (i.e. Davis, 1996; Klepper, 1994 and 1995; McFarlan and Nolan, 1995; Willcocks and Choi, 1995). Clearly our literature search was very focused, and we realize that many researchers have alluded to the importance of partnering or relationship management, but few actually address the issue conceptually or empirically (cf. Fitzgerald and Willcocks, 1994; Halvey and Murphy, 1995; Lacity and Hirschheim, 1993; Johnson, 1997; Mylott, 1995). One should add that the period 2001–8 also throws up very few detailed studies of the relationship in outsourcing arrangements (see Willcocks and Cullen, 2005; Oshri *et al.*, 2008)

Looking just at the 1990–2000 period, McFarlan and Nolan (1995), Klepper (1994, 1995), and Davis (1996) are the only three conceptual studies on the outsourcing relationship, although strictly speaking Davis (1996) and Klepper (1995) did also apply their frameworks to two case studies. McFarlan and Nolan's (1995) approach is more of an aggregation of helpful conceptual pointers, that has strong similarities to a checklist of the evolution, and hence handling, of an outsourcing alliance. The issues they raise seem good management practice, but are very general, with little empirical support to show how companies have handled the proposed management sugges- tions. Moreover, their subsequent generalization that outsourcing arrange- ments are in essence strategic alliances has been shown by Willcocks and Choi (1995) to be a dangerous assumption, as not even total outsourcing ventures entail some of the underlying characteristics that are integral to the alliance concept, such as detailed risk-reward sharing arrangements (Child and Faulkner, 1998).

Klepper's (1994) first conceptual approach, on the other hand, is based on a rigorous framework developed by Anderson and Narus (1990) in the mar- keting field, which he subsequently amends by integrating the concept of organizational adaptation to explain the dynamic and changing dimensions of the outsourcing relationship. The behaviorally focused model has at its core the dimensions "outcomes" and "relative dependence", from which unidirec- tional trust, influence, functionality of conflict, co-operation, and conflict are suggested to lead to satisfaction – all of which are particularly relevant to the IT outsourcing relationship (Kern, 1997). The model is clearly restricted, though, in its focus on behavioral dimensions, thus providing little insights into exogenous and endogenous influences, such as the contract (Willcocks and Kern, 1998). Klepper's model also disregards the bi-directional influence that behaviors such as cooperation-conflict (cf. Axelrod, 1984) and influence- dependence (cf. Emerson, 1962) will have, which empirical findings have revealed (Kern and Silva, 1998; Willcocks and Kern, 1998).

Klepper's (1995) second relationship approach is again based on a concep- tual model from the marketing field (by Dwyer, Schurr and Oh, 1987) which this time addresses the developmental stages of partnering relationships. He presents a life-cycle model of awareness, exploration, expansion and com- mitment, which are pervaded by processes of attraction, communication, bargaining, development and exercise of power, norm development, and expectation development that supposedly lead to deeper relations. This consti- tutes an interesting approach with yet again a behavioral focus. Again, Klepper (1995) neglects the contract and its effect on the resulting relationship; nor does he explain how structures and management processes evolve, even though they must surely underpin relationship development. It also seems that relations evolve in a vacuum unaffected by external factors or the other party. The inconclusiveness of the model, as shown by its use in retrospectively analysing two case studies, led Klepper (1995, p. 257) to concede that:

"in the future an effort should be made to combine elements of several theories to obtain a better understanding of the mechanisms by which partnerships evolve and how this process can be managed."

Davis (1996) seems to follow Klepper's advice, elaborating an intricate web of economic and sociological theories to arrive at a "strawman" model that supposedly aids decision-makers in their analysis of the best control mechanism (price, trust, authority) to enforce in an outsourcing relationship. The resulting framework describes the outsourcing context (both endogenous and exogenous factors), the elements of organizational design (operating processes, structures, management systems and human resource management policies) in a matrix prescribed by control mechanisms (price, authority, trust), which, when combined, are suggested to lead to sources of IT value creation. The three parts provide some of the essential ingredients of outsourcing relationships, alluding to the context, intention, structure, management processes, and likely outcome, but he too ignores the contract dimension. Moreover, the reasons behind how the different dimensions were derived, and hence why only these three control mechanisms seem appropriate, were not apparent. Davis's theoretical eclecticism is confusing, as he not only relies on theory but also on consultancy frameworks, and provides few justifications for his choices.

A different approach was taken by Willcocks and Choi (1995) who provided the only empirically-driven study that attempted to explain their findings by use of a relationship framework from another discipline. To analyse their three case studies, they essentially use Henderson's (1990) strategic partnership framework in an effort to determine the validity of their argument regarding partnering. Henderson's prescriptive model identifies predisposition, commitment, and mutual benefits as factors in the "context"; shared knowledge, mutual dependence on distinctive competency and resources, and organizational linkage are "action" factors, that combined with the former determine partnerships. Willcocks and Choi (1995) identify a number of shortcomings of Henderson's framework when used to discuss IT outsourcing relationships (for which it was not originally developed). These include its neglect of contract, difficulty of building mutual dependence in outsourcing, disregard of costs, the downplay of risk-reward arrangements, the influence of exogenous factors, and the lack of discussion on maintaining a strategic partnership. However, they conclude that the approach provides a good starting point, yet no conclusive insights became apparent and the emphasis, as in Klepper's study, is on the need for further research and on the necessity to combine elements from several theories.

Table 5.1 summarizes the 1990–2000 studies, which demonstrates clearly that our understanding of outsourcing relationships was, as at 2000, truly at an early stage – no common framework had been identified or formulated upon which knowledge and relationship management could be developed. (One can report that this largely remained the case as at 2008). Secondly, little overlap was found between the different studies, thus making the elicitation of common elements impossible. Thirdly, the majority of approaches were found to be conceptually or empirically inconclusive. Conceptually frameworks focused either on the behaviors, management aspects, and/or evolution, yet none truly focused on the interactions, the structure and the

Table 5.1   Main Findings from Outsourcing Relationship Research 1990–2000

Researchers	Key Findings
McFarlan & Nolan (1995)	• Structuring the alliance – areas to outsourcing, vendor selection, contacting and transition problems • Alliance management – involve senior management, performance measurement, develop a management infrastructure
Klepper (1994)	• Integrates concept of organizational adaptation with Anderson & Narus's (1990) model • Suggests following dimensions: outcomes and relative dependence, trust, influence, functionality of conflict, cooperation, conflict and satisfaction
Klepper (1995)	• Uses Dwyer, Schurr & Oh's (1987) evolutionary partnering framework • Stages of development include awareness, exploration, expansion and commitment • Additional dimensions: attraction, communication, bargaining, development and exercise of power, norm development, and expectation development
Davis (1996)	• Focuses on control mechanisms (price, trust, authority) • Framework describes: outsourcing context (endogenous and exogenous factors) and organizational design (operating processes, structures, management systems & HRM policies)
Willcocks & Choi (1995)	• Uses Henderson's (1990) strategic partnership framework • Dimensions: 'context' – predisposition, commitment, mutual benefits; 'action factors' – shared knowledge, mutual dependence on distinctive competency and resources and organizational linkages.

context. In turn, when it came to using the proposed frameworks and approaches, research studies proved inconclusive in their attempts to explain the relationship situation. Finally, we identified two prevailing perspectives underlying outsourcing relationships, these being an "economic view"[2] and a "partnering view".[3] This means that the "contracting perspective" has been largely ignored (Willcocks and Kern, 1998). Indeed the little relationship research carried out in the IT outsourcing field has focused primarily on the partnering, i.e. behavioral dimension.

   To alleviate some of these weaknesses, our search through the literature on relationship frameworks and practice focused on dyadic frameworks that encapsulated the relationship context, the relationship structure, the interactions and processes and the behavioral dimensions that define the relational atmosphere. This led to the identification of the dyadic Interaction approach. As Cunningham and Tynan (1993), and Leek, Turnbull and Naude (2000) had already argued before us, the Interaction approach in particular lends itself to exploring business relationships in the IT environment due to its rather precise focus on the interactions that pervade and define business relationships. Building on this notion, we further note that the Interaction approach since the 1980s had received substantial empirical validation in the marketing (Håkansson, 1982), but also in the IS literature (Cunningham and Tynan, 1993; Leek, *et al.*, 2000), alleviating possible concerns over theoretical and empirical rigour and validity. Moreover, the framework's integration of context, structure, interactions and behaviours offers a potential comprehensiveness lacking in alternative conceptualizations. The final reason for selecting the Interaction approach was that it is clearly based in both economic and sociological theories, thus coinciding with what our review had shown as essential grounding for a framework that could assist in the exploration of IT outsourcing relationships.

The IMP group's interaction approach

The industrial market and purchasing group (IMP group), also referred to as the "Nordic school", has been particularly influential in providing insights into buyer-supplier exchange relationships. This international group was formed when discrepancies were identified between the basic models of economic and marketing theory and industrial buyer-supplier relationships. In essence, existing models were found to be inconsistent. In particular, the IMP group found that the existing models all assumed competitive, "free market", and "adversarial relationships" as being the norm, yet buyer-supplier relations often showed signs of closeness and even social "embeddedness" (Cunningham and Tynan, 1993; Granovetter, 1985, Uzzi, 1997). This then determined the IMP's research agenda into the "interaction between companies when both parties recognise their mutual interdependence and are interested in each other's resources" (Håkansson, 1982: 14).

Theoretical origins

The Interaction approach draws upon the inter-organizational theory, marketing and purchasing literatures, and also transaction cost theory (see Chapters 2 and 3) in order to substantiate its distinctive constructs and dimensions (for more details see Håkansson, 1982). The inter-organizational research is classifiable into three categories according to its interplay between the organization and its environment. First, there are those studies that focus on the organization as being dependent upon its environment. Secondly, there are studies where an organization acts as part of a "group of interacting units" (Håkansson, 1982: 11). Thirdly, there are studies of groups of organizations in a societal context. In parallel in the marketing and purchasing literatures, we found studies similarly distinguishable as organizational, distribution and social system focused. Finally, transaction cost theory focused the IMP on transactions and points of deficiencies in markets and organ-

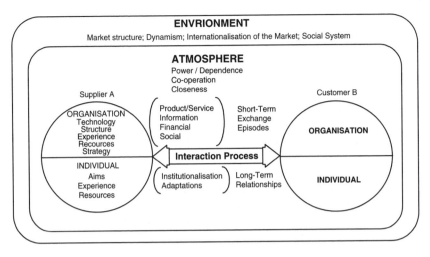

Figure 5.1 'Interaction Approach' adopted from Håkansson (1982)

izations, resulting in negotiated contracts between buyers and suppliers (Cunningham, 1980). The IMP group argues that buyers favor the market arrangement over hierarchies, because of lower overall costs, once transaction and production costs had been considered (see Chapter 2).

The interaction model

Figure 5.1 reproduces the basic interaction model. Its focus is on both the short-term episodes and general long-term relationships of dyadic buyer-supplier ventures, which essentially conform to the present study's concern with IT outsourcing relationships. The model recognizes that participants are commonly confronted with a complex pattern of interactions between and within organizations, and that the interactions essentially become institutionalized into a set of roles that each organization expects the other to perform. Cunningham (1980: 325) notes that "the interaction between companies is a dynamic process, varying in intensity and may require significant adaptations by either or both parties." Thus, it may involve both conflict and co-operation.

Four main groups of variables describe and influence the interaction:

- the elements of the interaction process;
- the parties involved, i.e. both the organizations and individuals;
- the environment within which the interaction takes place; and
- the "atmosphere" affecting and affected by the interaction.

Together, these variables comprise what many now consider to be the key element of business-to-business and services marketing, i.e. the interaction exchange relationship (Cunningham and Tynan, 1993). The model has proved robust enough to be applied to a wide range of different inter-organizational exchange relationships and has enriched the marketing and business literature with useful insights over the past decade (Ford, 1990). The core part of the model are the four exchange episodes:

- products and/or service exchanges;
- information exchanges;
- financial exchanges; and
- social exchanges.

The products and service bought and sold are the core interactions and exchanges, but may entail a number of risks depending on their complexity. Information exchange is essential, and has several aspects of interests including content (technical or financial), its media of communication, and the degree of formality with which it occurs. Financial exchange reveals the importance of the relationship. Social exchange helps to reduce uncertainty, especially in situations of cultural or spatial disparity. Formalization, trust, understanding, flexibility and integrity are important aspects of social exchange, as Cunningham (1980) suggests.

Clearly, a number of characteristics of the *parties to the interaction* will have important effects on the interaction process. Firstly, *technology* determines not only how parties might interact, but also defines the product and manufacturing process of both parties which in effect ties the two parties together. Secondly, *organization size, structure and strategy* determines the relative size and power of the participants. The *experience* issue determines whether companies have had experience with similar arrangements. This identifies the relative position of the individuals in the relationship. Finally, at least two *individuals*, one from each organization will be the key interface point in the relationship. However, usually many individuals at different levels in the hierarchy and across the organization will be involved (Lacity and Willcocks, 2001).

Interactions generally cannot be analysed in isolation from organizational environments. The following aspects of the environment are particularly relevant. *Market structure* determines the rate of change, the concentration of suppliers and buyers, and the number of alternative relationships available for the participants. The degree of *dynamism* influences either party's ability to predict and forecast changes in the market that in turn may affect the relationship. Håkansson (1982, p. 20) also notes that it affects the "...opportunity costs of dependence on a single or small number of relationships." *Internationalization of the market* may influence either organization's motivation to develop international relationships. The reason being it may affect the organization's structure, sales arrangements, know-how required technology, language, and trade legislation. Finally, the *social system* surrounding the relationship defines the real barriers to interacting between the organizations. Such aspects as protocols, procedures, experiences and ways of behaving when dealing with particular industries and organization will influence relations.

Finally, the working *atmosphere* that characterizes the relationship in many ways will also influence its operations. IMP found that "atmosphere" could be best described in terms of power/dependence, the degree of conflict or co-operation, and the overall social distance between the contributing organisations. Generally the atmosphere evolves through specific exchange episodes and long-terms exchange experiences with the partner. Cunningham (1980, p. 328) elaborates "it is a product of the relationship and it also mediates the influences of the three groups of variables" [see above].

Together these elements define the Interaction approach.

Research approach

Using this Interaction approach as a guiding framework, our subsequent research strategy was one of seeking qualitative data that would give further insight into the nuances of relationship practice in IT outsourcing. Adopting an interpretivist standpoint, and endeavoring to ascertain a dual perspective of both client and supplier practices, we undertook an exploratory study in late 1996. For this we contacted organizations who had outsourced for at least one year and also contacted their respective supplier(s). From the start we found that a qualitative research method of multiple respondents covering the perspective of both parties would be appropriate for exploring relationship practice in outsourcing, since the understanding of the relationship in this research project depended on the "knowledge of reality as socially constructed by the individual human actors" (Walsham, 1995). In turn, the authors interviewed 14 participants, including IT managers, contract managers, account executives, general managers, and support managers in client and supplier organizations in the early months of 1997. The differing and multiple perspectives provided a rich picture in this otherwise often "messy and iterative process" (Parkhe, 1993, p. 228).

Data collection

Questions addressing the contract, post-contract management, relationship management, the nature of a working relationship and the evolution of a relationship were posed, with a strong emphasis on what characteristics influenced relationship operationalization. The interviews were scheduled for one hour but in many cases lasted anywhere up to three hours. All interviewees were assured anonymity, to promote openness. Interviews were tape-recorded, transcribed, and posted to interviewees for validation. Findings were further corroborated by the collection and the ensuing analysis of secondary documentation, such as magazine and newspaper articles, internal

Table 5.2 Clients Organizations and Interviewees

Client Company & Interviewee	Industry	Origin	Outsourced	Start of Deal	Length of Deal	Size of Deal	No. of People Transferred	Customer of Vendor Company
Client A Business Support Manager	Retailing & Stores	British	Total	1993	10 years	£1bn	120	**Supplier B**
Client B Group IS Manager	Chemicals manufacturer	British	Selective (Europe) 1. telecomms network 2. data center, software support & legacy systems 3. desktop systems & phones	1. 1994 2. 1995 3. Late 1996	1. 3 years 2. 5 years 3. 4 years	1.<10mn 2. £75mn 3. £40mn	1. <10 2. 400 3. <10	1. **Confidential** 2. **Supplier B** 3. **Confidential**
Client C Management Services Manager	Property Investment & Development	British	Selective 1. hardware & software maintenance 2. legacy system, & software development	1. 1993 2. 1995	1. 4 years 2. 3 years	1. £2.5mn 2. £10mn	none	1. **Confidential** 2. **Confidential**
Client D Economic Analyst	Aerospace Manufacturer	British	Total & major business process reengineering programs	Early 1996	10 years	$900mn	850	**Supplier A**
Client E MIS Executive	Motor Car Manufacturer	British	Selective 1. software development & IT operations 2. systems integration 3. global networking	1. 1992 2. 1992 3. N/A	1. 5 years 2. <3yrs 3. 3 years	1. <0.5mn 2. <0.5mn 3. £1mn	1. 12 2. none 3. none	1. **Confidential** 2. **Supplier B** 3. **Confidential**
Client F IT Coordinator	Electronics Manufacturer	Japanese	Selective legacy & operating systems	1994	5years	£2.5mn	none	**Supplier D**
Client G Corporate IT Adviser	Oil, Gas, & Nuclear Fuels	Dutch/ British	Selective & Total (Global) 1. desktop computing, networking, & others 2. Total	1. N/A 2. 1993	1. <1yr 2. 3 years	1. <20mn 2. <20mn	1. <10 2. <10	1. **Others** 2. **Supplier A**

Table 5.3   Supplier Organizations and Interviewees

Supplier company & Interviewee	Origin
Supplier A – Managing Director & Program Director	American
Supplier B – European Strategic Director	American
Supplier C – Partner	American
Supplier D – Executive Director (UK)	British/French
Supplier E – Business Director & Principal Consultant	French/British

memos, minutes of meetings, and outsourcing contracts. Tables 5.1 and 5.2 present an overview of the client and supplier organizations interviewed, which we have disguised to respect their request for confidentiality.

Data analysis

The responses from both parties were then collated and analysed into subject categories by use of broad data matrices (Miles and Huberman, 1994), which in turn represented those features of the data that identified the main areas of commonality in what interviewees found particularly important in their relationships. As Turner (1983, p. 334) elaborates: "these emerging categories and concepts, derived from the data, are then used as basic building blocks of the growing theoretical understanding of the area under study." As patterns were gradually identified during the investigation and analysis, the authors began to look for the logic behind these, for which direct and indirect links could be drawn with the dimensions and variables of the "interaction approach". The resulting "hermeneutic circle" principle in moving back and forth between the data and the theory enabled us to make sense of the large data sets. This approach thus turned out to be particularly helpful in identifying the links and promoting the development of theoretical accounts which closely reflected the interviewees' concerns.

Throughout the research process, the authors tried to address in a number of ways issues of validity and reliability. Following Yin (1989) and Kirk and Miller (1986), we used multiple sources of data including tape recorded interviews, documents, reports, newspaper articles and many others (see above). The resulting data was found to converge in various ways, assuring validity of findings. The issue of reliability of data tends to be a complex issue to address in qualitative research. One of the primary approaches to ensure reliability is to build and provide access to a research database. Following this suggestion we established a database that recorded and provided access to the data and the material that informed the observations and interpretations of the authors. In addition, we stored an overview of the classifications of the categories we used for the analysis. Together, this strategy assured a high validity and reliability of the data.

Cross case summary of the exploratory findings

The data below has been structured by using the main dimensions and constructs of the model.

The parties

Tables A and B in the Appendix present a summary of the findings concerning the client and supplier organizations. As the tables illustrate, the factors characterizing the organizations had to be interpreted and adapted to the outsourcing context, in particular the client and supplier organization. It was here that the first direct applicability limitation of the Interaction approach became apparent. Although we were able to identify supporting data that fits the different organizational factors, it was when we got to the individual dimension that no direct supporting data could be elicited. However, the identified cross-case data does present some interesting insights about the client and supplier organizations, which we found sufficient to provide an understanding and overview of the parties to the relationship.

The client organizations in this study are clearly very large organizations in terms of size, structure (i.e. employees, subsidiaries, and global location) and of course turnover. As Håkansson (1982) noted, this is likely to have a significant influence on the degree of power these organizations have in their inter-organizational relationships, due to their prestige, industry standing and reputation. Moreover, the participating client organizations all entered into the outsourcing venture (i.e. relationship) with the underlying objective to save costs and become operationally more efficient. As part of this drive, many perceived outsourcing as a means to focus on their core competencies. Of particular interest was the fact that all organizations did have prior experience with outsourcing and it could thus be expected that all of them had relationship management expertise when it came to operationalizing their outsourcing venture. The mix of IT functions outsourced ranged from outsourcing the complete IT infrastructure to outsourcing only selective functions. In four of the client organizations, legacy systems and desktop management posed as the main reason to outsource and it is likely that these were considered to be merely commodity functions. Outsourcing for the client companies evidently presented an important information management vehicle and in some defined their complete IT management approach.

Parallel to the size of the client organizations, the supplier organizations similarly were some of the largest outsourcing service companies in the global market. The participating supplier organizations all provided a complete service portfolio, ranging from technology services to strategic management consultancy – except for Supplier E who seemed primarily focused on the information technology issues. It is thus very likely that these large supplier organizations have provided services to these client organization in the past due to the range of services they offer and may thus have a track record or business history with the client organization. Another interesting point to note is the market focus of these suppliers, which for Supplier D and E is primarily Europe. Their selection may point to a cultural and operational issue that clients may have had with supplier organizations like A, B and C, which are primarily American and globally focused.

Interaction process

Products and/or services

The exchange of products and/or services formed the core interaction in the relationship. This made it essential that service and/or product requirements are carefully listed, which most clients had done in contract exhibits such as service level agreements (SLAs). Since these deliverables are key to the relationship, they tended to be very closely monitored and scrutinized. To ensure that SLAs were delivered according to expectations and the agreement, clients and vendors operated an array of hard and soft performance measurement methods. Again, depending on the outsourcing intent, customers focused their measures on cost reductions, services delivered, service improvement, specific projects, new technology, and user satisfaction. In the majority of cases clients and vendors measured a range of the former to check simultaneous business and user requirement achievement (see Table 5.4). For this, Client B tended to measure primarily service delivery according to the SLAs, step changes in performance, return on net assets, and other business issues, such as customer responsiveness, output (e.g. On

Table 5.4   Cross Case Analysis of Products and Service Exchanges

Client	Products/Services	SLA	Measures
A	All IT services excluding control over IT strategy	Detail specified over time. Flexible	SLAs & soft
B	Telecomms network, data center, software support & legacy systems, desktop systems & phones	Very Detailed	Primarily SLAs
C	hardware & software maintenance legacy system, & software development	Detailed	Primarily SLAs
D	All IT services & major business process reengineering program	Detail specified over time. Flexible	SLAs & soft
E	software development & IT operations, systems integration, global networking	Very Detailed	Primarily SLAs
F	legacy & operating systems	Detailed	Primarily SLAs
G	desktop computing, networking, & other outsourcing services	Detailed	SLAs & soft

Time In Full). In contrast Client A and Supplier D employed a scorecard scheme, that allowed them to score performances against predefined measures on a range of issues from business process impact to users perception.

In contrast, vendors explained that their performance measures involved an array of objective and soft measures, including third party auditing. The Executive Director (Supplier D) and the Partner (Supplier C) said that they measure their performance against the clients SLAs, perform a customer satisfaction survey, undertake an internal quality review of staff, and attain an external auditor's assessment of specific contracts. Contrastingly, the Business Director from Supplier E commented:

> "we have every month a service measurement report. So we have clear statements every month on at least the objective measures. That doesn't tell the whole story because it's the subjective measures which are also very important. [...] we also from time to time commission bits of research from a market research organisation who go to our customers and ask them about services, service values, and so forth."

The subjective measures were crucial as they elicited whether the services delivered satisfied the user community. Clients found that, although services were delivered according to agreement, in many situations they did not satisfy user requirements. This anomaly required rapid attention and adjustment, which in many cases vendors would not undertake without formally increasing costs. Conversely, in Client D, the supplier employed instead a measurement scheme of customer values and expectations, alongside their objective measures. The Programme Director (Supplier A) explained:

> "it isn't just a matter of asking the customer are you satisfied or not; we have to understand what his expectation is rather than what his requirement is. Then there are some quite sophisticated measurement systems that we deploy to actually take a particular user, look at all the parameters of interest to him.... So you get a picture of what he wants and then how he thinks we are measuring up against that. So that's how you measure the soft issues. And we have to do that on a continual basis across all aspects of the relationship."

Financial exchanges

For all clients interviewed, outsourcing was perceived essentially as a means to financial savings and/or benefits. In turn, the focus was on the payments to be made to the vendor and the kind of margins the vendor was likely to make. As a direct result, the financial exchanges, together with products and services exchanges, received the greatest scrutiny by both clients and suppliers. To be able to undertake such in-depth assessments, it was argued, you need complete access to the costs figures and pricing schedules of your vendor. Arrangements such as open book accounting were identified as providing such an insight. In turn, Client D – but also A and G – introduced such an arrangement following their contract revisit, in an effort to ensure greater clarity of costs. In addition, incentives were put in place for Supplier B to endeavor to further reduce costs. This arrangement was purported to result in more cost savings and service improvements.

Another means for controlling costs was through a competitive benchmarking process. As noted by a lawyer we interviewed: "benchmarking is an important contractual contingency." It protects clients against increasing prices, where the quality of services might actually be decreasing. It also allows clients to compare prices and services against competitors, and push vendors to match industry "best practice". This seemed particularly appropriate for commodity processes such as basic computing and telecomms. The Group IS Manager for Client B noted:

> "to ensure cost control you continually set your suppliers of the commodity services at each others throat, demand that they keep to a certain international standard, and request lower and lower prices the whole time."

Clearly, cost control defines the clients' main control concern, especially since the driving motivation for the vendor is increasing its margins. In turn, regular cost reporting was the norm across the client and suppliers we researched, to ensure transparency of the service costs and operations. Table 5.4 summarizes the clients' approach to ensuring cost control and clarity over financial exchanges.

Information exchanges

Information exchanges are an embedded process occurring via modern telecommunication methods in relationships, but also involve contractually agreed mechanisms such as regular meetings and report exchanges (e.g. service performance reports, accounts, payment schedules, change requests). Interestingly, both clients and vendors acknowledged the importance of communication and information exchange, but only a few addressed the criticality of this dimension in their relationship. One exception was Client B, who noted:

> "you have to get a high level of dialogue between yourself and the vendor to really ensure that you've got a supplier who is working hard to understand you and your business, what you are about and where you are heading, so they can respond constructively, and creatively."

The kind of information exchanged would often vary between informal and formal information. Client C characterized formal information as an instance where the vendor reports on the "supply of the services within the performance measures" while informal exchanges focused more on open discussions on problem areas. These different types of information exchanges often depended on the kind of meeting or setting for a meeting. In turn, discussions, and indeed meetings, could also vary between both formal and informal issues, which would then also characterize the kind of information exchanged. The Business Director from Supplier E found that:

> "meetings are a vehicle for communication. They are both formal and informal. The formal part being minuted, whereas for the informal no record is kept. [...] There will be a structure of formal meetings, as defined within the contract. We follow that structure."

Social exchange

For social exchanges to occur, closer ties had to be established. Indeed, interview participants noted that it is essential to know the person and/or people you are dealing with in the other firm. It seemed that the better client managers got to know their partnering vendor managers the better the overall relationship worked. However, client managers had to guard themselves – and this was the other extreme – against developing relations that unconsciously hindered them from possibly terminating the contract. The Manager from Client C explained:

> "in any customer-supplier relationship the customer has to reserve the right to say at some point in time I've had enough. So there is a dividing line there somewhere, I don't know where it is, it's something you can only measure when you go along. Somehow you have to get a relationship which is relatively close and friendly, but on the other hand still gives you the capability to turn your back on it if you want to."

Conversely, relations between individuals that were too close fostered the problem of dependency and opaqueness. Managers in Client A found that when you get two people who work together for too long they can become too close or too cosy and you can end up with a situation where Tom and Peter are the only two people who understand what is going on, such that, unless these managers are present, some problems cannot be resolved because nobody understands the background and the reasons behind them. The Business Support Manager (Client A) noted:

> "if you have that situation you don't necessarily have to change the people; you just might need to make it more transparent what the decision-making process is, or how the relationship works to avoid getting into a dependency situation."

In turn, a relational code of working practices, defining the degree of informality to which relations could be taken, were specified in Client A.

Clients and suppliers noted arranging social activities as a useful means to fostering these critical closer relations. The informal settings of these activities provided the kind of environment in which relations could be truly fostered:

> "It is the best way to learn to judge whether you can rely on someone because you know something about that person as a person as opposed to a supplier. I tend to think that as a supplier-customer relationship develop a limited amount of social fraternization – for want of a better word – actually adds to the relationship and makes the relationship work better because you get to know someone personally. [...] then he's going to be more disposed to help you." (Manager, Client C)

Most vendors fully endorsed this concept, as they similarly found that social gatherings helped people to form links and to get to know each other much better and faster. In part, some of these gatherings were actually aimed at winning over management, because, once management was won over, the staff tended to follow blindly (Principal Consultant, Supplier E). The inherent problem, though, was that issues were often decided at these meetings, without any actual documentation to back it up.

Long-term institutionalization and adaptation

The only direct data we found that suggested institutionalization or adaptation had occurred was the effect of the venture on organizational culture. This became evident in the operational adjustments, which were said to have occurred over time. In fact they were found to be an integral part of relations, in order to smooth operations and to minimize relational breakdowns. However, in many instances, managers reported that no matter how many adjustments clients and vendors made, even after a number of years into the contract, the cultures as such remained quite distinctive and separate. We found the comment from client A exemplary of this:

> "We tend to make decisions two weeks after the drop dead date, we tend to change our mind a lot, we tend to change a lot, we won't approve anything, or we won't invest in anything, and on Tuesday it is all right again and we will suddenly be more approachable. I suspect that can be very difficult sometimes. Whereas the Supplier B people can be very structured in their approach which is very typical of IT type people. And sometimes this clashes with [Client A]."

Regardless though of the differences, clients explained that "understanding of their business" is the only way of adjusting. A vendor has to learn to understand the client's business drivers, and where the business is heading.

Only by achieving this can suppliers become more proactive and receptive to the business needs that essentially define the clients IT requirements.

The atmosphere

A number of issues were raised that can be interpreted as characterizing the relationship's atmosphere. The most common issues managers discussed were cooperation, commitment, control, power and dependency, conflict, and trust. There was, however, no particular order in which these were discussed, as they were termed as pervading the relationship separately but also simultaneously.

Commitment

The issue of commitment arose as early as the selection of the vendor, and then became formalized with the signing of the contract. The contract generally represented the formal indication of the parties' commitment. It is essentially "drafted as a long term commitment". Thus, in the context of the relationship, commitment for the client essentially implied trying to make it work with the vendor(s) and to pay X amount for services and products delivered as contractually agreed. Conversely for the vendor, commitment meant achieving the contractually stipulated terms. The Director from Supplier D exemplified this viewpoint:

> "their commitment really is spelled out in the contract, and then when a particular piece of work comes up there is a service order, which is in itself a contractual document, and our commitment is quite clearly spelled out in that. So that's our commitment."

Although there was the contractual commitment, clients emphasized they still tried to find an extra angle somewhere, because in most cases they actually need slightly more commitment than just the contractual terms. For example, the MIS Executive from Client E highlighted that they expected their suppliers to be more proactive than just reactive as the contract suggests. This expectation of greater commitment, resultantly puts the onus and pressure on the vendor to perform. It also seemed a plausible reason for why some clients explained that following the vendors initial efforts,[4] a period of slackness took over.

Cooperation

Interestingly, the concept of cooperation was not addressed expressly by any of the client interviewees. Only some of the vendors actually highlighted that outsourcing is based on cooperation. Most perceived cooperation rather implicit to the venture, so much so that some professed that once it breaks down the overall venture failed. The principle of cooperation, however, was evident in a number of explanations of how both parties handled the deal and worked with each other. For example, the Executive Director (Supplier D) found that:

> "when you have a problem in front of you that may or may not have been created by one party or the other or may just be something that nobody could ever have predicted – that is an issue. And it's how you mutually work at that problem to get it solved to deliver a service. It's in working through a problem that you look back and say actually we were able to do that because we had a good relationship."

Therefore, in terms of co-operation in IT outsourcing, a balance needs to be struck between contractual strictness and flexibility. It is the resulting flexibility to give and take that at the end of the day often ensured that deals did not falter. In other words, inherent to the relationship was a flexibility that allowed people to make an odd mistake without penalization, and if a mistake had been made, conjoint efforts were focused on solving the problem. Without cooperation, both parties would surely pertain towards an adversarial relationship, and disputes or conflicts would be very difficult to resolve. In turn, cooperation was found implicit to relations and it was suggested that ultimately working cooperatively through difficulties and not falling out over problems may explain one important dimension of the relationships evolution over time.

Conflicts

Both parties stressed that in IT outsourcing conflicts or problems frequently arose. Nothing runs smoothly day after day. Two main problem types were identified: (A) the day-to-day problems, and (B) the operational, cultural and contractual problems. Depending on their level of impact, they were either handled by the operational managers or escalated, following contractual procedures, to senior managers.

It was generally accepted that working through conflicts and resolving problems strengthened relations at the end of the day. It was a case of cooperating through these conflict situations and finding solutions together that helped bind the relationship. A Principal Consultant for Supplier E noted:

> "I think you will reach a maturity stage following a success of going through a conflict and coming out with a satisfactory solution. It doesn't have to be a contract re-negotiation, just a very difficult problem of some sort."

Trust, i.e. closeness[5]

All interviewees stated that the relationship only really works when trust exists in some way or form. It is associated chiefly with creating vendor confidence, and enforcing openness and honesty. Interestingly, vendors were far more explicit about the criticality of trust than client companies. Some even went so far as to suggest that without it the relationship will wither and surely terminate, while others suggested the relationship can be built solely on trust. Trust in relations though, was noted to work only with the knowledge that there is a contractual relationship in place, and that is the basis on which you do business:

> "It's better that both sides understand that [contract vs. trust] fully from the start because you then both know where you are. If you pretend it's not there and you pretend everything is nice and soft and fluffy and cushy, you will get a rude awakening when someone says sorry this is what the contract says. You've got to be completely realistic about it and we refer to the contract constantly." – European Strategic Director, Supplier B

A recurring comment was that trust did not exist from the start – it was something that had to be earned over time. So, in the beginning of a deal some suggested there is mutual respect and as a track record evolves one can determine forms of trust, such as confidence and a willingness to be more open. For clients, though, trust is mainly about confidence in the vendor to deliver the stipulated contractual terms, to attend to problems, and to be fair and honest about charges.

Honesty and openness were found by interviewees to evolve primarily between the individuals handling the outsourcing deal. They were often noted as the basis upon which trust was built. Only through openness was either party going to be frank in discussions about problems and difficulties. Openness and honesty, in turn, improved the relationship's chances of success:

> "if they've got a problem they need to tell us, if we've got a problem we need to tell them. There's no point having a relationship unless we are open with each other, it's like being married quite honestly. If you think about it's very similar because two parties should be working towards a common goal and if they are not talking to each other and don't trust each other they are going to miss, whatever the contract says" – Services Manager, Client C

Honesty, on the other hand, became crucial when things went wrong and there had to be a working context that permitted admittance that there truly was an issue that required urgent attention. If this level of closeness was evident then, according to interviewees, trust was truly said to exist in the relationship:

> "trust is a critical success factor really, because you have to be very very honest because as soon as you stop being that then your ability to main-

tain the programme disappears very quickly. We have to be honest, because when one side of the operation fails then there has to be the trust and the environment in which people can honestly admit that there is something that needs to be attended to so that we all as a team sort it out" – Programme Director, Supplier A

Power and dependency

Cross case analysis further revealed the issues of control, power and dependency in outsourcing relationships as interrelated. For the client power is reflected by control, whereas control arose because of the ensuing dependency on the vendor. The crux was that they defined an ongoing concern for the client – the loss of control over the outsourced functions. Control was essentially explained as the ability to get what you want done, when you want it done, for an agreed price, and with the possibility to change your mind at a later stage. This intention determined the client's endeavors in the relationship. The Group IS Manager from Client B noted:

> "you need a very strong grasp on the steering wheel ... and you've got to have it so that it is very clear that there is an imbalance ... in the relationship that says that the business is in charge and has the capability to drive. Because it's only the business close to its marketplace and its drivers that really understands where the business must go."

To affirm control, clients relied on the contractual clauses and specified requirements. Vendors' explanations corroborated that the contract essentially defined each side's level of control.

Power conflicts arose between individuals at some stage during the relationship. These were unavoidable, but they can be managed by identifying the power sources within organizations. The Managing Director from Supplier A noted:

> "We have a term for those people [power holders] called "foxes". It's part of our methodology, the mechanism for identifying foxes and then the people that are clustered around a fox are called a power base of people that are led by that person, and represent that person's agenda to the organisation."

Awareness of the power bases then allowed the vendors to assess whether they were in conflict with outsourcing or support it, which determined the level of collaboration to expect.

Dependency, on the other hand, emerged as a by-product of outsourcing. The client managers found themselves dependent on the services delivered by the vendor, even though they did have the ultimate power to terminate the contract at any time, but high switching costs tended to prevent that option. On the other hand, the vendor found itself dependent on the client for remuneration for services rendered. The level of dependency was considered an influence on the power-control dichotomy. The Managing Director of Supplier A suggested dependency can be dealt with by trust, because, without it, no sensible organization would allow dependency to arise.

The Interaction approach: potential and limitations

The Interaction approach proved to be of sufficient breadth and depth as a classificatory framework to help us, as researchers, catch some fundamental aspects of interorganizational relationships in IT outsourcing. The findings revealed not only the complexity, but also diversity of relationship factors that pervade the client-supplier dyad in outsourcing. This may come at no surprise, except that in terms of strategic planning for such ventures the relationship generally does not warrant much attention from clients during the evaluation and vendor selection period (independent of its impact on the venture's overall success). Our initial assumption, that the Interaction approach is a useful means to explicate and delineate more holistically the IT outsourcing relationship, received considerable supported by its use here, and this use builds on the work of Cunningham and Tynan (1993) and Leek, Turnbull and Naude (2000), who had already shown the potential of the Interaction approach for making sense of IS relationships.

As researchers in the IS field have argued before us (e.g. Bensaou, 1992; Henderson, 1990; McFarlan and Nolan, 1995), knowing what defines a relationship will not only improve our understanding, but also ensures effective planning and management by enabling practitioners to focus their attention on particular dimension that are critical to the relationship. However, the preliminary findings also corroborated our analysis of Klepper's (1995) research: that it is difficult to appropriate and apply an interdisciplinary framework to the outsourcing relationship. Indeed, we found a number of limitations in respect to exploring the outsourcing relationship, even though the framework proved valuable in focusing attention on particular important relationship dimensions and management issues.

The environment

No particular findings were elicited that would support the interaction model's suggestion that the external environment needs to be explicitly considered in the management of the outsourcing relationship. It seems rational, though, to assume that the environment implicitly influences, shapes and guides the outsourcing relationship. Therefore, the interaction approach's market structure, dynamism, internationalization of the market, and social system will eventually, for example, influence those factors that determines the client's IT services needs to, for example, differentiate its products (Porter, 1985) and to compensate for uncertainty and information demands (Bensaou and Venkatraman, 1996). However, our findings emphasized that most managers involved in the outsourcing deal were too caught up with internal organizational issues, such as IT service demand, service levels, conflict resolution and relationship management to reflect on and consider environmental factors in their management tasks. The limitations of the findings, however, were that they focused primarily on managers involved in operational and day-to-day management of the outsourcing venture and did not include an external CIO/Senior IT management perspective.

Nevertheless, we stipulate that it will become necessary over the life-time of an outsourcing venture to evaluate carefully these external factors to ensure not only adequacy of IT services, but also competitiveness and comparability of services to what the market has to offer. In other words, it is ensuring that the optimal price for the sourced economies of scale is maintained. In exploring the operational factors of an outsourcing relationship the environment can be neglected, but ultimately cannot not be ignored. This is underlined by our work elsewhere on risk profiling and management in IT outsourcing relationships (Kern and Willcocks, 2001; Lacity and Willcocks, 2001; Willcocks, Lacity and Kern, 2000). Here we found that the competitive context of the client organization and its selected strategic intent greatly influenced the type of relationship and objectives that could be realistically pursued with a supplier organization. Furthermore supplier market strategies and capabilities also were big influences on supplier behaviours and objectives in a specific IT outsourcing arrangement. Mutual knowledge of strategies of parties in the dyad was also important. In the present research we surfaced that supplier organization strategies were confidential (see Appendix B). An interesting question we did not explore, but that is suggested a result of applying the Interaction approach framework, is how far did client organizations understand supplier strategies, and how far did this level of knowledge and the level of sharing influence the relationship in each case?

The parties

A serious limitation of the Interaction approach here is that it does not differentiate between the different types of data characterizing the client and supplier organization. Our research revealed clearly that for client and supplier organizations the general factors the Interaction approach suggests as defining the parties had to be interpreted and adapted differently according to the client and supplier party. In other words, unique descriptors for both client and supplier organizations had to be identified, to be able to adequately describe both parties.

Moreover, as already noted above, the individual dimension in the interaction approach could not be applied, as it identifies the individual person responsible for the relationship. In outsourcing relationships, however, it is clear that typically there are numerous managers involved at differing hierarchical levels (see Lacity and Willcocks, 2001; Willcocks and Fitzgerald, 1994) so that selecting an individual to be representative for the whole group was and generally would be very difficult. Here it would be more important to focus on the management capabilities that the client's residual IT group needs to incorporate and which the vendor has to match to ensure effective relationship management. Outsourcing practice has illustrated the detrimental effect on relationships when insufficient residual capabilities are retained and mismatched or non-existing interface points exist on the vendors side (see Feeny and Willcocks, 1998; Kern and Willcocks, 2001; Kern, *et al.*, 1999).

However, we suggest that the characteristics as interpreted and adapted provide insightful data that gave a good overview and understanding of the organizations involved in the relationship. To this extent the dimension was extremely valuable and we suggest that, if adapted as we have done, it provides a descriptive overview of the outsourcing parties.

Interaction process

The interaction approach proved particularly valuable here in identifying the core underlying exchanges in outsourcing relationships. Our findings endorsed the fact that the four short-term exchange episodes, i.e. product/ service, information, financial, and social, in some way became institutionalized over time as parties adapted to the outsourcing venture, organizational cultures and each others management style. Service levels and payments defined the key formal contractual exchanges that undergird the outsourcing relationship. The primary focus is on service levels and performance according to which either party evaluates and rates the other. In case of under-performance, the client has the penalty payment "stick", while in situations of exceeding performance the client has the bonus payment "carrot" to operationalize the deal. Payment was thus found to be the main motivator for suppliers and the main issue of control for clients. Interestingly, in situations where either service performance or payments were not up to agreement levels there was evidence that relations quickly became strained.

Information exchanges, both formal and informal, were found to pervade all interactions. For example, monthly, quarterly and yearly service performance reports were termed a formal information exchange requirement in the relationship, that may or may not be agreed to in the contract, but which essentially justifies the financial exchanges, i.e. payment or non-payment. On the other hand, informal information exchanges pervade and are an inherent part of day-to-day interactions and operations. In turn, those managers that "span the organizational boundary" and define the interface points, need to be good communicators at both the interpersonal, technical and business level (Katz and Kahn, 1966; Feeny and Willcocks, 1998). Information exchanges in fact define, according to interviewees, a key operational effectiveness measure in outsourcing relationships. It was found to be the engine that drives any relationship. To ensure good communication was not an easy process. It often needed thorough planning of an appropriate communication structure, which few actually had done.

> "One thing that we discovered early on was that we weren't doing enough to communicate with the customer right the way across the customer base. So we've now got a joint newsletter which we do with this group, and every couple of months or so this newsletter goes out right across the company to tell them about progress in IT. ... And we actually have a communications plan which we've put in place." – Business Director, Supplier E

Social exchanges are possibly the most underrated and ignored dimension by researchers who have looked at the outsourcing relationship (Kern, 1997). These exchanges were shown as those that enable the parties to adapt to the idiosyncratic working practices of each other. In some cases they described tangible and intangible investments that became necessary to ensure the relationship's ongoingness. In short, they often help sustain relationships, especially in situations of strain, dispute, and conflict. In addition, these interactions and exchanges were found to be responsible for fostering social ties between managers and ultimate contributed to forming closer relations between both parties. Key to developing these were informal and social events:

> "One of the things that I would like to do more often is some of the management meetings we have I would like to have a sandwich lunch before or afterwards when the meeting ends, because I think you get a lot of information in a short almost informal conversation and learn more about problems." – Business Support Manager, Client A

The effect of social exchange on the success of the venture was alluded to by the managers' suggestion that closer ties are critical for attaining benefits and value added, and developing a win-win scenario. In fact, endogenous to these interpersonal relations are behavioral and attitudinal factors that have been identified by Mohr and Spekman (1994) and Ring and Van de Ven (1992) to affect the success of the whole inter-firm relationship.

Atmosphere

The interaction approach was very limited in terms of what it identified as being the defining behaviours. Again we interpreted what Cunningham (1980) and Håkansson (1982) suggested for the relationship atmosphere. We found that, in addition to power-dependence, cooperation and closeness (which we interpreted to imply trust), commitment and conflict were also an integral part to defining the outsourcing relationship's "atmosphere". Of interest was cooperation which could not be clearly distinguished from how managers worked together. Even when asked explicitly to explain situations, some found it very difficult and refrained from stating that it is indistinguishable from how they work. Conflict, commitment, power, and dependency encapsulate those behavioral traits that also outline the chief concern about "loss of control" by the client. Here conflict often arose because services were not delivered to expected levels, power and dependence arose in routine issues of enforcing control, and commitment was evident primarily in the form of the underlying contract that defined the relationship. Commitment was a particularly interesting issue as it only ever emerged in discussions about the contract or the SLA. To that extent, it might be termed a very formal dimension of the atmosphere. Closeness, on the other hand, was chiefly associated with achieving a degree of trust, where clients could rely on the vendor to deliver the expected and agreed service and products. Trust went so far as defining operations. For example, when minor problems with services arose, or the vendor identified a particular service they could do better, then the client trusted the supplier to improve and/or alleviate a particular problem without having to go through the trouble of discussing and negotiating it in terms of costs and service levels.

Trust was often quoted as critical to the relationship, although it was not clear at times whether managers meant confidence or interpersonal trust, i.e. honesty and openness. Indeed, trust took time to develop and in most cases evolved with the appearance of a good track record of accomplishing stipulated terms (as Kern and Willcocks, 2001, and Lacity and Willcocks, 2000b found in other detailed case research). Building confidence seemingly preceded trust. Satisfaction also played a role, but it was not clear how it influenced the relationship. It rather seemed satisfaction was a measure concerned with evaluating the users' perception of the services, which very likely could lead to confidence in the supplier's service quality.

Further limitations of the interaction approach

Outsourcing research and experience recurrently emphasizes the importance of the contract (e.g. Kern, 1999; Lacity and Willcocks, 1998; Klepper and Jones, 1998), yet the Interaction approach largely neglects it. Contracting needs careful consideration, as it is traditionally seen as the beginning and foundation of the outsourcing relationship (Kern, 1999; Kern and

Willcocks, 1999). Past studies in turn have focused, for example, on how the contract governs the ensuing relationship, alluding to its dichotomic focus on transactions or relations (Klepper, 1994; Lacity and Willcocks, 1995). Yet, although the outsourcing relationship is contractually governed to ensure opportunistic behavior can be at any point regulated by termination, our research underlines that the contract is no panacea nor does it ensure successful relations. Instead, as one of the interviewees explained:

> the contract provides a sub-stratum, it's about getting the foundations right. But to really get the partnership working and delivering you've got to have the confidence in the personal relationships and the ways of working together and these processes of working together are very difficult to capture in the contract. But the things that you are talking about in a outsourcing partnership are more about process and relationships and common visions which are difficult things to track in a contract. – Group IS Manager, Client B

Nevertheless careful contract management is fundamental, and entails careful monitoring of services, payments and other requirements and regular revisiting of the contract for updates.

Neglected relationship management issues in outsourcing

Three additional relationship management issues were identified that neither the Interaction approach nor any of the extant IT outsourcing research has discussed explicitly in terms of relationship management. First is the management structure that needs to be in place to handle the outsourcing relationship. The findings highlighted that IT outsourcing requires active management involvement beyond what most expect when they contract out. Traditionally, clients expect that the supplier takes over and delivers the service while the client stands back and monitors. However, this is a misperception. In fact our findings here suggest that 70% of the client managers' time in post-contract management is spent on managing relations. This suggests two considerations – that also need integration into the Interaction approach. Firstly, it is critical for the client to establish an appropriately skilled management infrastructure prior to outsourcing, that it can implement during post-contract management. Secondly, the supplier needs to formalize an account team that mirrors the customer's management group. In other words, the overall contract structure should be formalized and both parties should be aware who their respective counterpart is.

The second issue focuses on the hidden management costs in outsourcing relationships. Three areas of hidden costs were identified in the present research, which receive little attention at the outset by client companies. Firstly, the significant costs involved in post-contract management are not planned for. The findings suggested that management resourcing to develop and maintain relations are generally higher than initially anticipated and expected. The split of management time on relationship management and the rest, i.e. contract management is 70–30, as noted above. Secondly, ongoing monitoring costs generally are not considered. These arise due to the client's management agenda of assuring not only that the vendor keeps its commitment to deliver the agreed services, but also to control the costs of the deal. Finally, the renegotiation or update costs involved in ensuring the contract always reflects the current statues of the IT outsourcing arrangement. This is essential to ensure, for example, that in the event of termination all service levels, technology assets, staffing are listed to simplify insourcing or vendor switch. Note that planning a contract that caters for every contingency is generally impossible in long-term business deals (Macneil, 1974; Mariti and Smiley, 1983). Hence, outsourcing contracts, like so many other long-term business contracts, suffer from an inherent incompleteness and hence necessitate updating.

The third issue is moving quickly to the institutionalization of operations and processes. It should be a key goal of client companies to move together with the supplier towards standardization of interactions and routine operations. Achieving what others have termed the state of "embeddedness" (Uzzi, 1997) holds the true benefits of outsourcing ventures for both parties. For the client it provides potential areas of where the supplier can add true value by applying its specific technological expertise, which in a number of the client organizations researched had resulted in reengineering programs and new technology investments. For the supplier it entailed potential opportunities for new business and hence increased profits. Some refer to this level of client-supplier integration as a win-win situation, where both parties benefit in their ways from the relationship. Others have explained it as the result of embeddedness, where economic actions become embedded in ongoing social ties that facilitate further exchange relations (Uzzi, 1997).

Conclusion

This chapter has argued, following a critical review, that our understanding of the operations of IT outsourcing relationships is limited at best (and that this in fact continues into 2008). To alleviate this gap, the paper presented the Nordic School's Interaction approach to explore if it enhances our understanding of IT outsourcing relationship practice. A resulting study of 12 client and supplier companies, using the Interaction approach, illustrated its potential and limitations in explaining IT outsourcing relationships. The findings presented many insights into relationship operations and allowed us to conclude that the Interaction approach presents an interesting starting point for further research into identifying IT outsourcing relationship practice.

This chapter found that relationship management in outsourcing centres primarily around the main exchange episodes of services/products, financial, information and social issues which over time become institutionalized and characterize the routine operations. Pervading these various exchanges are external factors such as market structure, dynamism, internationalization of the market, and social system and internal behavioral factors, such as power, dependency, conflict, control, commitment and trust, which together characterize the relationship. In terms of relationship management the exchange episodes and external and internal factors are those that need careful planning and management. In addition, issues influencing these will arise in the form of having an explicit management structure that comprises all the necessary capabilities in both parties to handle the deal; being aware of hidden costs that arise in form of management resources and time, ongoing monitoring costs, and regular contract renewal phases; and trying to move the routine operations, i.e. exchange episodes, towards institutionalization as soon as possible to attain access to the true value added that vendors can offer in terms of, for example, technology expertise and process improvement.

A clear limitation of this overall study was its focus on mainly client and supplier managers directly engaged in handling outsourcing relationships. It would have been interesting to investigate how senior managers that are not directly involved see the impact of external factors on the relationship. This would have allowed us to present more relevant data concerning the environment dimension, although we did not find it directly relevant in routine operations of the relationship. However, we acknowledge that there are difficulties here for analysis where the full context is not elaborated – and indeed a strength of the Interaction approach is its ability to focus researcher attention on a much broader context for study.

The research revealed a number of avenues for further research, in particular undertaking a more extensive and longitudinal study to investigate the Interaction approach not only across a number of relationships, but also to learn more about how institutionalization and adaptation occurs. In fact, it would be useful to take each of the main dimensions of the Interaction approach and research these in greater depth. In other words, what are the external impact factors on relationship operations, what are the characteristics of each of the exchanges, how does the atmosphere evolve and what are the various behaviours impact on the relationship? Finally, do these various dimensions evolve over time? Our own view is that the Interaction approach's focus on exchange issues is highly pertinent to the study of IT outsourcing relationships, but that it further needs to be combined with contract and transaction cost perspectives, as we attempted to achieve in further parallel work on the theorisation of IT outsourcing relationships (Kern and Willcocks, 2001).

Notes

1 The area was investigated over a four year period leading to a DPhil at Oxford University.
2 This view is commonly informed by approaches such as transaction cost theory (TCT) or agency cost theory (see Alpar and Saharia, 1995; Aubert, *et al.*, 1996; Earl, 1991; Cronk and Sharp, 1998; Grover *et al.*, 1995; Lacity and Hirschheim, 1993; Lacity and Willcocks, 1995; Rao, *et al.*, 1994 & 1996).
3 This view argues that the long-term nature of outsourcing and the uncertainty surrounding these ventures, demands a relationship that provides the flexibility and collaborative benefit of a partnership (McFarlan and Nolan, 1995; Davis, 1996). Therefore, this view commonly tends to focus on the behavioral and socio-logical issues involved in developing and maintaining a relationship (Auwers and Deschoolmeester, 1993; Davis, 1996; Klepper, 1994 & 1995).
4 The honeymoon phase or first year of an outsourcing venture.
5 We found trust in the context of outsourcing relationships to determine close-ness, which also defines a more precise descriptor of closeness.

References

Alpar, P. and A.N. Saharia (1995) "Outsourcing Information System Functions: An Organization Economics Perspective," *Journal of Organizational Computing* 5(3): 197–219.

Anderson, J.C. and J.A. Narus (1990) "A Model of Distributor Firm and Manufacturer Firm Working Partnerships." *Journal of Marketing* 54(1): 42–58.

Aubert, B.A., S. Rivard and M. Patry (1996) "A Transaction Cost Approach to Out-sourcing Behaviour: Some Empirical Evidence." *Information and Management* 30: 51–64.

Auwers, T. and D. Deschoolmeester (1993) The Dynamics of an Outsourcing Rela-tionship: A Case in the Belgian Food Industry. *Working Paper, De Vlerick School voor Management, University of Gent*: pp. 1–25.

Axelrod, R. M. (1984) *The Evolution of Cooperation*, New York: Basic Books.

Bensaou, M. (1992) Interorganisational Coordination: Structure, Process, Information Technology: An Empirical Study of Buyer-supplier Relationships in the US/Japanese Automobile Industries. Working Paper 165, *Massachusetts Institute of Technology, Boston*.

Bensaou, M. and N. Venkatraman (1996) "Inter-Organizational Relationships and Information Technology: a Conceptual Synthesis and a Research Framework." *European Journal of Information Systems* 5(2): 84–91.

Bravard, J.L. and Morgan, R. (2006) *Smarter Outsourcing*. London: FT/Prentice Hall

Child, J. and D. Faulkner (1998) *Strategies of Co-operation: Managing Alliances, Networks, and Joint Ventures*. Oxford: Oxford University Press.

Cronk, J. and J. Sharp (1997) A Framework for IS Outsourcing Strategy in Private and Public Sector Contexts. *Strategic Sourcing of Information Systems*. Willcocks, L.P. and M.C. Lacity. Wiley, Chichester, pp. 164–185.

Cross, J. (1995) "IT Outsourcing: British Petroleum's Competitive Approach." *Harvard Business Review* (May–June): 94–102.

Cunningham, C. and C. Tynan (1993) "Electronic Trading, Interorganizational Systems and the Nature of Buyer-Seller Relationships: The Need for a Network Perspective." *International Journal of Information Management* 13(1): 3–28.

Cunningham, M.T. (1980) "International Marketing and Purchasing of Industrial Goods – Features of a European Research Project." *European Journal of Marketing* 14(5/6): 322–338.

Davis, K.J. (1996) IT Outsourcing Relationships: An Exploratory Study of Inter-organizational Control Mechanisms. *Graduate School of Business Administration.* Boston, USA, Harvard University: 310.

Dwyer, F.R., P.H. Schurr, *et al.* (1987) "Developing Buyer-Seller Relationships." *Journal of Marketing* 51: 11–27.

Earl, M.J. (1991) "Outsourcing Information Services." *Public Money and Management* 11(3): 17–21.

Emerson, R.M. (1962) "Power-Dependence Relations." *American Sociological Review* 27(1): 31–41.

Feeny, D. and L. Willcocks (1998) "Core IS Capabilities for Exploiting IT." *Sloan Management Review* 39(3): 1–26.

Fitzgerald, G. and L. Willcocks (1994) "Contracts and Partnerships in the Outsourcing of IT", in (eds), *Proceedings of the 15th International Conference on Information Systems,* Vancouver, Canada, ICIS: 91–98.

Ford, D. (ed.) (1990) *Understanding Business Markets: Interaction, Relationships, Networks.* London: Academic Press Limited.

Granovetter, M. (1985) "Economic Action and Social Structure: The Problem of Embeddedness." *American Journal of Sociology* 91(November): 481–510.

Grover, V., M.J. Cheon, *et al.* (1995) "Theoretical Perspectives on the Outsourcing of Information Systems", Working Paper *Columbia, Management of Science Department,* pp. 1–27, University of South Carolina.

Håkansson, H. (1982) *International Marketing and Purchasing of Industrial Goods: An Interaction Approach,* Chichester: Wiley.

Halvey, J.K. and B. Murphy Melby (1996) *Information Technology Outsourcing Transactions: Process, Strategies, and Contracts.* Wiley, New York.

Henderson, J.C. (1990) "Plugging into Strategic Partnerships: The Critical IS Connection." *Sloan Management Review* (Spring): pp. 7–18.

Johnson, M. (1997) *Outsourcing...In Brief.* Oxford: Butterworth-Heinemann.

Katz, D. and L.K. Kahn (1966) *The Social Psychology of Organizations.* New York: Wiley.

Kern, T. (1997) The Gestalt of an Information Technology Outsourcing Relationship: an Exploratory Analysis. *Proceedings of the 18th International Conference on Information Systems,* Atlanta, Georgia, December.

Kern, T. (1999) *Relationships in Information Technology Outsourcing: An Exploratory Research Study of a Conceptual Framework.* Unpublished DPhil Thesis, Christ Church. Oxford: University of Oxford.

Kern, T. and L. Silva (1998) "Mapping the Areas of Potential Conflict in the Management of Information Technology Outsourcing", in *Proceedings of The 6th European Conference on Information Systems,* Aix-En-Provence, France, June.

Kern, T. and L.P. Willcocks (1999) "Contracts, Control, and Presentation in IT Outsourcing: Research in Thirteen UK Organisations," in *Proceedings of the 7th European Conference on Information Systems,* Copenhagen, Denmark, June

Kern, T., L.P. Willcocks and E.V. Heck (1999) "Relational Trauma: Evidence of a Winner's Curse in ICT Outsourcing," *Management Report No. 50,* Rotterdam School of Management, Erasmus University Rotterdam.

Kern, T. and K. Blois (2000) "Norm development an essential ingredient to outsourcing relationships", *Proceedings of The 16th Annual IMP Conference,* Bath, United Kingdom, April.

Kern, T. and L.P. Willcocks (2000) "Cooperative Relationships Strategy in Global Information Technology Outsourcing: The Case of Xerox Corporation", in D. Faulkner and M. De Rond (ed.), *Perspectives on Cooperation*, Oxford: Oxford University Press.

Kern, T. and L.P. Willcocks (2001) *The Relationship Advantage: Sourcing, Technologies, Management*, Oxford: Oxford University Press.

Kirk, J. and M.L. Miller (1986) *Reliability and Validity in Qualitative Research*. Sage, Beverly Hills.

Klepper, R. (1994) "Outsourcing Relationships," in *Managing Information Technology with Outsourcing*, Khosrowpour, M. (ed.), Harrisbury: Idea Group Publishing.

Klepper, R. (1995) "The Management of Partnering Development in IS Outsourcing," *Journal of Information Technology* 10(4): pp. 249–258.

Klepper, R.W. and W.O. Jones (1998) *Outsourcing Information Technology, Systems and Services*. Prentice Hall, New Jersey.

Lacity, M.C. and R. Hirschheim (1993) *Information Systems Outsourcing: Myths, Metaphors and Realities*, Wiley, Chichester.

Lacity, M. C. and L. P. Willcocks (1995) "Interpreting Information Technology Outsourcing Decision from a Transaction Cost Perspective: Findings and Critique." *Accounting, Management and Information Technology* 5(3): 203–244.

Lacity, M.C. and L.P. Willcocks (1998) "An Empirical Investigation of Information Technology Sourcing Practices: Lessons from Experience." *MIS Quarterly* 22(3): pp. 363–408.

Lacity, M.C. and L.P. Willcocks (2000) *Inside IT Outsourcing: A State-Of-Art Report*. Templeton College, Oxford, March.

Lacity, M.C. and L.P. Willcocks (2000b) "Survey of IT Outsourcing Experiences in US and UK Organizations", *Journal of Global Information Management*, Vol. 8, 2, pp. 5–23.

Lacity, M.C. and L.P. Willcocks (2001) *Global Information Technology Outsourcing: In Search Of Business Advantage*. Wiley, Chichester.

Leek, S., P.W. Turnbull and P. Naude (2000) "Is the Interaction Approach of Any Relevance in an IT/e-commerce Driven World?", in (eds), *Proceedings of the 16th Annual International Marketing and Purchasing Conference*, University of Bath, UK.

Loh, L. and N. Venkatraman (1992) "Diffusion of Information Technology Outsourcing: Influence Sources and the Kodak Effect." *Information Systems Research* 4(3): pp. 334–358.

Macneil, I.R. (1974) "The Many Futures of Contracts." *Southern California Law Review*, 47: pp. 691–816.

Mariti, P. and R.H. Smiley (1983) "Cooperative Agreements and the Organization of Industry." *The Journal of Industrial Economics* 31(4): 437–451.

McFarlan, F.W. and R.L. Nolan (1995) "How to Manage an IT Outsourcing Alliance." *Sloan Management Review* (Winter): pp. 9–23.

Miles, M.B. and A.M. Huberman (1994) *Qualitative Data Analysis*, 2nd edn, Sage, California.

Mohr, J.J. and R.E. Spekman (1994) "Characteristics of Partnership Success: Partnership Attributes, Communication Behaviour, and Conflict Resolution Techniques." *Strategic Management Journal* 15(2), pp. 135–152.

Mylott, T.R. (1995) *Computer Outsourcing: Managing the Transfer of Information Systems*. Prentice Hall, New Jersey.

Oshri, I., Kotlarsky, J. and Willcocks, L. (eds) (2008) *Outsourcing Global Services: Relationships, Social Capital and Knowledge*. Palgrave, London.

Parkhe, A. (1993) "'Messy' Research, Methodological Predispositions, and Theory Development in International Joint Ventures." *Academy of Management* 18(2), pp. 227–268.

Porter, M. (1985) *Competitive Advantage Creating and Sustaining Superior Performance.* The Free Press, New York.

Rao, H.R., K. Nam, A. Chaudhury and S. Rajagopalan (1994) Dimensions of Outsourcing: Transaction Cost Framework. *Managing Information Technology with Outsourcing.* Khosrowpour, M. Harrisbury, PA., Idea Group Publishing: pp. 104–127.

Rao, H.R., K. Nam, A. Chaudhury and S. Rajagopalan (1996) "A Two-Level Investigation of Information Systems Outsourcing." *Communications of the ACM* 39(7): pp. 36–44.

Ring, P.S. and A.H. Van de Ven (1992) "Structuring Cooperative Relationships Between Organizations." *Strategic Management Journal* 13: pp. 483–498.

Turner, B.A. (1983) "The Use of Grounded Theory for the Qualitative Analysis of Organizational Behaviour." *Journal of Management Studies* 20(3): pp. 333–348.

Uzzi, B. (1997) "Social Structure and Competition in Interfirm Networks: The Paradox of Embeddedness." *Administrative Science Quarterly* 42: pp. 35–67.

Walsham, G. (1995) "The Emergence of Interpretivism in IS Research." *Information Systems Research,* 6(4): pp. 376–394.

Willcocks, L. and C.J. Choi (1995) "Co-operative Partnership and Total IT Outsourcing: From Contractual Obligation to Strategic Alliance." *European Management Journal* 13(1): pp. 67–78.

Willcocks, L. and Cullen, S. (2005) *The Outsourcing Enterprise 2: The Power of Relationships.* LogicaCMG, London.

Willcocks, L. and T. Kern (1998) "IT Outsourcing as Strategic Partnering: The Case of the UK Inland Revenue." *European Journal of Information Systems* 7: 29–45.

Willcocks, L. and C.M. Lacity (eds) (1998) *Strategic Sourcing of Information Systems: Perspectives and Practices.* Wiley Series in Information Systems. Wiley, New York.

Willcocks, L. and G. Fitzgerald (1994) "IT Outsourcing and the Changing Shape of the Information Systems Function: Recent Research Findings", *Working Paper, Oxford Institute of Information Management,* Templeton College, Oxford pp. 1–24.

Willcocks, L., G. Fitzgerald, and Lacity, M. (1996) "To outsource IT or not?: Recent Research on Economics and Evaluation Practice" *European Journal of Information Systems,* 5, pp. 143–160.

Willcocks, l. and Lacity, M. (2006) *Global Sourcing of Business and IT Services,* London: Palgrave.

Willcocks, L., Lacity, M. and Kern, T. (2000) Risk In IT Outsourcing Strategy Revisited: Longitudinal Case Research At LISA. *Journal Of Strategic Information Systems,* April.

Yin, R.K. (1989) *Case Study Research: Design and Methods,* 2nd edn, Sage, Newbury Park, California.

Appendix – An Overview Table of the Parties according to the Interaction Model

A. Client Organizations

Organisations	Client A	Client B	Client C	Client D	Client E	Client F (UK)	Client G
Technology[1]	• 3 Data centres • 40 Local area networks • 120 Staff • 1,000 desktop computers	• telecomms & networks • data centres • software support • Legacy systems • Desktop systems	• Desktop management • Software maintenance & development • Legacy systems	• Systems integration • Day-to-day IT operations • Legacy systems • Data centres • Software & hardware	• Software development • Desktop management • Systems integration • Global networking	• Legacy systems • Desktop management	• Desktop computing • Networking • Software development
Structure[2]	• Flat hierarchy • Decentralised	• Hierarchical • Numerous divisions & subsidiaries • Global organization	• Hierarchical • Centralized	• Hierarchical • Centralized	• Hierarchical • Centralized • A division of a defence & technology firm	• No data available	• Hierarchical • Combination of centralised & decentralised operations
Experience[3]	Yes	Yes	Yes	Yes	Yes	Yes	Yes
Resource[4]	• 135 Stores • 14,000 Staff • £780m turnover (1995)	• 55,600 employees • £11bn turnover (1998)	• £240m turnover (1996) • £5.7bn assets • 580 employees	• £4bn turnover (1996) • 43,000 employees • £7bn order book (1996)	• £397 turnover (1995) (includes other subsidiaries)	• £263m turnover (1995, UK) • 1,413 employees	• £23.7bn turnover (1995) • 106,000 employees
Strategy[5]	• Company restructuring • Lean management • Reduce costs • Sale of subsidiaries	• Restructuring • Sale of non core commodity divisions • Operational efficiency	• Operational efficiency • Focus on core operations	• Focus on core business • Operational efficiency • Re-engineering of business processes	• Restructuring • Operational efficiency • Cost reduction	• Operational efficiency focused	• Operational efficiency

Note: Data presented in the table was drawn from multiple sources including interviews and secondary documentation.

B. Supplier Organisations

Organisations	Supplier A	Supplier B	Supplier C	Supplier D	Supplier E
Technology[6]	• Management consulting • Systems & technology services • Business process management • Electronic business	• Management consulting • Professional services • Systems integration • Outsourcing services • Business process management	• Management consulting • Outsourcing services • Business process management • Change & strategic management	• Management consulting • Process management • IT outsourcing services • Project services • Education & training	• IT consulting • Systems integration • Data management • Technology products • Outsourcing services
Structure[7]	• Hierarchical • Centralized organisation	• Hierarchical • Centralized • Structured around centers of excellence	• Flat hierarchies • Autonomous global groups • Decentralized	• Hierarchical • Centralized	• Hierarchical • Centralized
Experience[8]	Leader (one of the largest American suppliers in the market, with global competencies and resources)	Leader (one of the largest American suppliers in the market, with strong American and European competencies and resources)	Leader (one of the largest American suppliers in the market, with global competencies and resources)	Medium-sized European player with strong European resources and competencies	Medium-sized European player with strong European resources and competencies and a presence in the Americas
Resource[9]	• $16.8bn turnover (1998) • 120,000 employees • Operations in 47 countries	• $6.6bn turnover (1998) • 50,000 employees	• $6.5bn turnover (1998) • 53,426 employees	• £1.8bn turnover (1996) • 27,000 employees (1996)	• £1.2bn turnover (1998) • 18,200 employees (1998)
Strategy[10]	• Confidential	• Confidential	• Confidential	• Confidential	• Confidential

Note: Data presented in the table was drawn from multiple sources including interviews and secondary documentation.

182

B. Supplier Organisations – *continued*

Organisations	Supplier A	Supplier B	Supplier C	Supplier D	Supplier E

[1] Technology refers to functions outsourced, as these outlined the product processes for which the companies entered into the relationship

[2] Describes the current state and objective of the organization for the company structure. Often we found outsourcing was to facilitate or contribute in part to the reorganization.

[3] Refers to previous outsourcing and procurement experience.

[4] Outlines vital company statistics and provides an overview of the size of the organization

[5] Explains key strategic initiatives for the company, in particular those which where seen in conjunction with outsourcing

[6] Technology in the supplier organizations refers to their core service portfolio.

[7] Describes the current state and objective of the organization for the company structure.

[8] Refers to their market share according to whether they are a leader (largest outsourcing service organizations), medium sized or niche supplier

[9] Outlines vital company statistics and provides an overview of the size of the organization

[10] Explains key strategic initiatives for the company, in particular those which where seen in conjunction with outsourcing

Part III
Studies of Practice

6
Outsourcing Myths and Contracting Realities

Mary C. Lacity and Rudy Hirschheim

Introduction

This chapter is based on one of the first articles we published for practitioners (Lacity and Hirschheim, 1993). At that time, very little research had been conducted on what actually happens in client organizations when they outsourced IT. Based on 14 case studies in US organizations, the article examined three myths about outsourcing and proposed that clients need to sign much better contracts. Since its initial publication, clients and suppliers have indeed become much better at contracting. Defining services, setting prices, and creating a flexible framework to adapt to business and technical changes are now norms in ITO contracts. Although our research focus soon evolved from contractual issues to decision strategy and relationship management, it is certainly interesting to reflect back on this early contribution. It is also interesting to see how IT sourcing practices changed as the overall perception as to the role of IT changed.

During the 1980s, executives were advised of the strategic role that information technology could provide to organizations. Through IT, companies could squelch competition, secure suppliers, obtain customer loyalty, and reduce the threat of new entrants (Porter and Millar, 1985). Executives were offered the IT victory stories of American Airlines, American Hospital Supply, and Merrill Lynch as evidence to the success of exploiting information systems. Many executives followed this advice by applying strategic IT models to their own organizations.

As we entered the 1990s, the advice shifted as many companies pursued a core competency strategy (Prahalad and Hamel, 1990). Executives were advised to focus on their core competencies to increase revenues and outsource their non-core companies to reduce costs. For many corporations, much of IT was deemed non-core, along with their cafeteria, mail delivery, and custodial services. By acquiescing many or all of their information services, executives were promised savings of 10% to 50% off their IT expenditures (Greenbaum, 1992; Krass, 1990; Rochester and Douglass, 1990; Hamilton, 1989; Anthes,

1991; Wilder, 1991; Huff, 1991). Prudent companies were advised to follow suit behind Eastman Kodak, American Bankshares, Enron, Southeast, Continental, and others. Many companies heeded this advice, as evidenced by the tremendous growth in ITO markets during the 1990s. During this time, we asked the question:

When did IT become a commodity?

So what happened to the IT function in the past few years? Has IT suddenly become a commodity service that is best managed by a large supplier? Several practitioners believed so:

> Pfendt, Director of Information Technology at Kodak, claimed outsourcing came down to one question: "Do you want to manage commodities?" (Kass and Caldwell, 1990, p.14)

> McNeil, Southland's MIS Manager: "It's like the electric company; you use less, you pay less." (Ambrosio, 1991)

> Gardner, in a commentary on IT outsourcing in the health care industry: "Outsourcing takes over all information systems functions, much the way an outside company would manage food service or laundry." (Gardner, 1991, p. 35)

> Ward, editor of Sky magazine, described IT outsourcing: "Like shoppers at a fruit stand, companies are picking an apple here or an orange there until they have selected a menu of outsourcing services." (Ward, 1991, p. 40)

Were electric utilities, fruit stands, and laundry services reasonable metaphors for IT? A strong argument for the IT as utility metaphor was that *information*, rather than *information systems*, creates a competitive advantage. Hopper, Senior Vice President for American Airlines, noted that it was "dangerous still to believe that on its own, an information system can provide an enduring business advantage. The old models no longer apply" (Hopper, 1990, p. 119). Instead, Hopper and other executives argued that competitive firms should shift their attention from *systems* to *information* (Huber, 1993).

Once IT was viewed as a utility, executives shifted their efforts from harnessing IT as a competitive weapon to providing IT services at the lowest possible cost. Under the theory of economies of scale, these executives would argue, mass production and specialized labor allow large vendors to provide utilities at the lowest possible cost. By letting the technology vendors provide the IT utility, executives can focus energies on nurturing their company's core competencies.

The notion that IT became a utility and was therefore most efficiently provided through outsourcing was reinforced by many trade reports. *Computerworld* and *InformationWeek*, for example, tracked outsourcing arrangements in which customers reported savings of 10 to 50%. Many companies, in their exuberance to duplicate savings advertised in these reports, jumped on the IT outsourcing bandwagon. Press reports, however, portrayed an overly optimistic view of outsourcing because reports were made during the honeymoon period when a customer and vendor first signed a contract. At that point, the reported savings were only projected, not actual savings. In addition, outsourcing failures were under-represented in the press. This simply may be a characteristic of human nature. After all, no organization wishes to offer a failure for public scrutiny.

Thus, the outsourcing phenomenon could be explained by at least two trends. First, many executives believed that IT was quickly evolving into a utility. As such, utility services are more efficiently acquired through specialized vendors that achieve economies of scale. Second, a significant bandwagon effect was noted (Loh and Venkatraman, 1992c); the success of Kodak's outsourcing arrangement as well as other outsourcing successes reported in the trade press prompted many executives to outsource without due consideration of the potential consequences.

Sure, outsourcing successes existed, but there were also outsourcing failures. The ultimate goal remains "smart-sourcing" – companies retain strategic applications while farming out only those services that vendors can provide more efficiently. Some companies find, however, that even so-called "utility" services, such as data center operations, are often most efficiently managed internally. In this article, we questioned the blanket endorsement of outsourcing and exposed several outsourcing myths generated by press reports. We also advised customers to follow the contract negotiation strategies presented in this article.

Information technology outsourcing from the 1960s to early 1990s

Outsourcing, in its most basic form, can be conceived of as the purchase of a good or service that was previously provided internally. Information technology outsourcing options have existed since the dawn of data processing. As early as 1963, Perot's Electronic Data Systems (EDS) handled data processing services for Frito-Lay and Blue Cross. Other outsourcing options, such as the use of contract programmers, timesharing, and purchase of packaged software have been exercised for decades. What renewed interest in IT outsourcing and demanded our attention in 1993 was the dramatic change in scope. Early forms of IT outsourcing typically dealt with single-system contracts comprising a small portion of the IT budget. "In the past, outsourcing was available in the form of such specialty applications as payroll, insurance processing, credit cards, and mailing lists" (Hammersmith,

1989). Outsourcing grew to span multiple-systems and represented a significant transfer of assets, leases, licenses, and staff to a vendor that assumed profit and loss responsibility. Enron's 750 million dollar, ten-year contract with EDS provided a typical example of the increased scope of IT outsourcing. The phrase "keys to the kingdom" could be applied to these outsourcing arrangements where vendors actually operated, managed, and controlled IT services. It was this type of outsourcing arrangement that warranted our attention and concern.

The "keys to the kingdom" outsourcing arrangement worked as follows. The vendor typically charged a fixed fee for a pre-specified number of services, known as the "baseline." The customer was guaranteed that their IT costs for this baseline would be fixed over the contract duration, typically five to ten years. During the contract period, services not included in the baseline could be purchased from the vendor for an excess fee. Deals were often sweetened with financial incentives, such as stock purchases, loans at low interest rates, and postponed payments. At the outset, these deals were extremely attractive, especially to an organization that suffered financially. But what happened in the long term? This question provided the motivation for this research. Given the considerable hype associated with IT outsourcing, it was time to research the topic with the intention of separating the facts from the myths.

The study

The insights from this research were based on an in-depth, multiple case analysis of 14 *Fortune 500* service or manufacturing companies that faced outsourcing decisions. Individuals who were directly involved in the outsourcing decision on behalf of the organization or outsourcing vendor were interviewed for one to three hours. Participants included Chief Financial Officers, Controllers, Treasurers, IT Directors, Account Managers, and Consultants hired to assist customers. In addition, members of the information systems staff responsible for gathering technical and financial details were interviewed.

During the interviews, participants were first asked to relay their outsourcing story in their own words. This way, participants could discuss what they thought was the "essence" of the outsourcing decision as well as to provide contextual information that they felt was relevant to their company's decision. Participants took between 20 and 25 minutes to relay their stories. After they finished, participants were asked semi-structured questions about the financial, historical, and political details that may have been absent from their previous recollections. In addition to the interviews, the participants were given a structured questionnaire to gather demographic and other vital information. Significant documentation was also gathered, including request for proposals, outsourcing bids, outsourcing contracts, efficiency assessments, annual reports and organizational charts.

Table 6.1   Outcome and Scope of Outsourcing Decisions

#	Fortune's Taxonomy*	Decision Outcome**	Functions Considered for Outsourcing	Year Contract Began	Initiator of the Decision
1	Chemical Manufacturer	No/No	Data Center	n/a	IT Manager (both decisions)
2	Diversified Services Company	No	Data Center	n/a	IT Manager
3	Petroleum Refining	No	All	n/a	Senior Manager
4	Petroleum Refining	No	Data Center	n/a	Senior Manager
5	Petroleum Refining	No	Data Center	n/a	IT Manager
6	Commercial Bank	Yes	Data Center, Telecommunications	1990	Senior Manager
7	Diversified Services Company (Energy Related)	No/Yes	All	1988	IT Manager (1st decision) Senior Manager (2nd decision)
8	Petroleum Refining	Yes	Data Center, Telecommunications	1991	IT Manager
9	Metals	Yes	All functions except strategic systems	1990	IT Manager
10	Transportation Services	Yes	All	1991	Senior Manager
11	Mining	Yes	All	1991	Senior Manager
12	Aerospace	Yes	All	1993	Senior Manager
13	Chemical Manufacturer	Yes/No	All	1984	Senior Manager (1st decision) IT Manager (2nd decision)
14	Rubber & Plastics (Industrial Equipment Manufacturer)	Yes/No	All	1987	Senior Manager (1st decision) IT Manager (2nd decision)

* Companies are only identified by industry since participants were guaranteed confidentiality.
** Four companies evaluated outsourcing on two occasions yielding a total of 18 outsourcing decisions

The documentation was used to corroborate statements made during the interviews and was helpful in analyzing contract specifics.

Of these 14 companies, six limited the outsourcing domain to data center operations and/or telecommunications (see Table 6.1). Seven considered outsourcing the entire IT department – data processing, applications support, applications development, end user computing, training, etc. Five companies decided against outsourcing (cases 1–5) and nine decided to outsource (cases 6–14). Two of these companies suffered such severe service degradation that they prematurely terminated their contracts, erected new data centers, and populated new IT departments (cases 13 and 14).

This study tempered the press's optimistic claims by examining (1) some outsourcing arrangements three to seven years into the contract (2) several outsourcing failures as well as successes, and (3) organizations that decided they could duplicate vendor savings without outsourcing. Although the research was not a random sample, it provided some alternative views absent from the trade press. In particular, the look at organizations that decided not to outsource provided a control group absent from other studies. These cases provided some support for the argument that "there is nothing that vendors can do that you can't do for yourself" (Radding, 1990, p. 70).

The 1993 information systems outsourcing myths

Although considerable variation in the nature, style and outcome of the outsourcing decision of these companies was expected, a surprising number of common themes were apparent across the companies. In particular, three outsourcing myths surfaced.

Myth: Outsourcing vendors are strategic partners.
Fact: Outsourcing vendors are not partners because the profit motive is not shared.

The idea that outsourcing vendors are "strategic partners" may be attributed to Eastman Kodak. In 1987, Eastman Kodak outsourced almost its entire IT operations to IBM, Businessland and DEC. Vaughn Hovey (1991), Director of Data Center Services for Kodak, told an audience of practitioners, "We think of our strategic alliances as 'partnerships' because of their cooperative and long-term qualities." Kodak sealed these partnerships with little more than a gentleman's agreement. According to Hovey, Kodak rarely refers to their "six or seven page contract." The importance of Kodak's success cannot be underscored; statistical analysis suggests that the outsourcing trend can be explained as "imitative behavior" of Kodak's decision (Loh and Venkatraman, 1992c). Kodak made it acceptable for large organizations to outsource and popularized the notion that outsourcing vendors are strategic partners; therefore loose agreements could serve as acceptable contracts. What worked for Kodak, however, did not work for others (Radding, 1990). In the case of Kodak, an outsourcing consultant who participated in the study speculated that IBM used the arrangement as a loss-leader to get a foothold in the outsourcing market. The enormous press which went along with the outsourcing agreement suggests that IBM accomplished its objective (see Applegate and Montealegre, 1992 for a full description of the Kodak outsourcing decision).

The term "strategic partner" is unsuitable to characterize the relationship between an outsourcing vendor and their customer when the profit motive is not shared. (See Henderson, 1990 for circumstances in which the term "partnership" is applicable.) Account managers at outsourcing providers are rewarded for maximizing profits, primarily by charging customers additional fees for services that extend beyond the contract (in the outsourcing parlance, these are called "excess fees"). When a customer's costs increase, so do the vendor's profits. How, then, can an outsourcing vendor be conceived of as a partner? Claiming that vendors are partners is like claiming that Chrysler is a partner just because you purchase a LeBaron. The term "customer" is more appropriate.

The danger in viewing the outsourcing vendor as a partner was that the customer often signed a very loose agreement. After the agreement went in effect, the vendor may not provide the level of service the customer expected. Instead, the vendor often referred to the written contract as the only source of obligation. Customers subsequently were charged excess fees for services that they assumed were in the contract. One petroleum company was charged almost $500,000 in excess fees the first month into the contact. These were for services they assumed were covered in the agreement. The vendor rightfully retorted that services not documented in the contract were above baseline and subject to excess fees. This does not imply that outsourcing vendors were opportunistic; more likely, the outsourcing customers and vendor representatives miscommunicated the full scope of the agreement. Customers in this situation had little recourse since the vendor possessed a significant amount of power over the relationship. What other information alternatives were available to the dissatisfied customer? They sold their assets and transferred leases, licenses, and employees in order to enter into the arrangement.

Myth: Outsourcing vendors are inherently more efficient than internal IT departments
Fact: Internal IT departments can be cost competitive.

Proponents of outsourcing, such as Biddle of American Standard, claimed that outsourcing vendors are more efficient due to economies of scale (Krass, 1990; Livingston, 1990; Radding, 1990; Huff, 1991). A review of the theory of economic efficiency, however, exposes several myths about its blanket applicability to IT outsourcing.

The theoretical basis of economies of scale is that large-sized companies have lower average costs than small-sized companies due to mass production and labor specialization efficiencies. Mass production is presumed to reduce average costs by allocating fixed costs over more units of output and by receiving volume discounts on inputs. Labor specialization is presumed to reduce costs by allowing workers to focus on tasks at which they are most adept.

Applying the economic theory of efficiency to IT outsourcing is a messy proposition. For one, the inherent problems of measuring efficiency surfaces. How do we know a vendor is inherently more efficient than the internal IT department? The only area of efficiency that has been adequately measured is data processing, in particular, cost per millions of instructions per second (MIPS) (Barron, 1992). Most of the efficiency arguments, however, are more esoteric. For example, vendors are assumed to have lower average hardware and software costs due to volume discounts and the sharing of software lease costs over multiple customers. On the labor specialization side, outsourcing vendors are assumed to be information systems specialists. They can allegedly design, develop, and maintain systems more efficiently because of their expertise. These arguments are, however, largely fallacious.

Very small companies may pursue hardware strategies that enable them to achieve average costs comparable to an outsourcing vendor. Industry experts reported that data processing shops achieve economies of scale around 150 MIPS (Krass, 1990). Real Decisions, for example, documented that costs per CPU minute were lowest for data centers in the 135–200 MIP range. Their analysis was based on data gathered and normalized from hundreds of their customers. Their evidence seemed compelling: large IT shops were more efficient than smaller IT shops. However, several examples from our research suggested that small shops were as efficient than large shops.

Smaller companies can be more efficient through lower wages and tight operating procedures as well as by using older technology. Smaller companies are often able to negotiate dirt cheap hardware leases by using older technology. The IT Manager at a petroleum company, for example, leased an IBM 3081K for only $4,000/month. He felt that smaller IT shops can contain hardware costs by renegotiating leases on dated equipment:

> "And I said as long as we stay on the trailing edge of technology – and I've been pushing this concept to senior management – we have an opportunity to capitalize on cheaper computing costs."

A vendor's volume discounts were often negligible. Economic theory purports that large companies have lower average costs than small companies partly because they receive volume discounts on inputs. The volume discount theory presumes that large companies buy in bulk and therefore receive quantity discounts. This argument extends to the outsourcing arena by assuming that outsourcing vendors buy hardware for less (Friedberg and Yarberry, 1991). Many internally-managed companies, however, receive discounts similar to outsourcing vendors. One prominent outsourcing consultant offered the following example:

> "Can an outsourcing vendor buy a machine for less than Enron? Sure they can. I'll give you numbers that aren't exactly accurate, but a large IBM 3090 probably is in the $15 million dollar list range. An outsourcing vendor could probably get it for $11 million. Enron or First City could probably get it for about $11.5 or $12 million. Now, over a five-year period, there is not a whole lot of money being saved."

This finding was corroborated by a *Datamation* (1988) survey which reported that the major hardware vendors typically sell equipment at 9 to 17% below list price.

Changes in software licensing agreements greatly reduced a vendor's advantage. The assumption that average costs decrease when fixed costs are spread over more units of output has been applied to software costs (Friedberg and Yarberry, 1991). The argument was that outsourcing vendors spread software licensing fees over multiple customers. This argument, however, was no longer valid for two reasons. First, software companies changed the structure of their software licensing fees in response to outsourcing. Second, software companies charged customers excessive fees to transfer licenses to an outsourcing vendor.

Before outsourcing came into vogue, software houses issued site licenses to customers. This meant that a company paid a fixed fee for one copy of a software package used at a single data center site. It followed that the average cost per transaction was lower for an outsourcer than for an internally-operated IT shop because the outsourcer spread the site licensing fee over more transactions. Software houses, however, changed the structure of site licensing fees in reaction to outsourcing. Rather than charge customers a fixed fee for every site, the software vendor charged a fee based on the size of the hardware. With these group licenses, customers with bigger machines got charged more money.

The change to group licenses seriously curtailed the outsourcing vendors' profitability. An account manager for a mining customer explained the impact on an outsourcing vendor's costs:

> "Computer Associates is thinking, 'All the times these deals are signed, the outsourcer can channel everything into one box, use one copy of the software. Therefore, we are going to lose money.' And from a business

perspective, I suppose that makes sense. So what the software vendors have done is gone to group pricing. And of course, the outsourcer operates a larger box than [the mining company], so they pay more fees...This has dire consequences for outsourcing deals."

In addition to the structural change, many software houses charged transfer fees to their customers who outsourced. At a large commercial bank, for example, a software house sued them for $500,000 for transferring the software license to an outsourcing vendor. From the software house's perspective – outsourcing reduced their revenue; the transfer fee was their way of seeking compensation.

In "keys to the kingdom" deals, access to technical talent was limited since customers were supported by their previous staff. The labor specialization myth was based the fact that the outsourcing vendor typically hired the entire previous IT staff, so the level of expertise remained comparable. Many companies outsourced to access the vendor's pool of technical talent only to find (a) they were supported by the same staff and (b) additional vendor expertise was expensive.

One industrial equipment manufacturer outsourced because they felt their IT staff did not have the technical skills to implement a new computer architecture. The conversion (not to mention the whole outsourcing arrangement) failed because the same people (now vendor employees) performed the installation. The company's IT Director noted:

> "They (the vendor) took over all the people as they usually do, so what happens in that environment is your unqualified IT people that you had become unqualified (vendor) people."

One mining company outsourced largely to acquire vendor expertise. In this case, only half of the company's IT Department transferred. Since the company informed employees of the outsourcing decision early in the process, many found positions elsewhere. The vendor, however, was able to replace the missing staff. However, this new talent was expensive. A Purchasing Manager from the company noted:

> "None of it is cheap. I guess there is a perception that once you have (a vendor) locked in that you have a conduit to all this expertise, but you pay."

Access to business talent was questionable. Many participants who outsourced felt a real loss of business expertise. The problem was that vendors often siphon talented employees to woo other accounts in the industry. In addition, customers claimed outsourcing vendors preferred specific directions and rarely initiated business strategies.

An IT manager at an industrial chemicals manufacturer believed that outsourcing reduced the business expertise of the IT staff. He claimed talented business people often transferred to new accounts:

> "You pay for them to learn your business, then they move those people to court other companies in your industry. They transfer skills to get new business, now the learning curve is yours to pay for again."

A vice president of liquid fuels at a diversified services company concurred. He claimed that the vendor not only transferred the best employees to other accounts, they retrained the remaining staff to be more technical:

> "But of the managers that we had, we lost the three best managers that were transferred. Has the caliber improved or changed radically? The nature of the people has changed. They are more technical, less user-oriented, they are more technically-oriented and less functionally-oriented, less industry-oriented. So if you were to grade them overall, I lost."

Many vendors did not pass savings onto their customers. If a vendor submits a bid that undercuts current IT costs, the potential customer should determine how the vendor proposes to reduce costs. The vendor may inherently be more efficient, but this should not be accepted without scrutiny. Furthermore, a natural cost advantage must be significant to cover a vendor's profit margin. The IT manager at an equipment manufacturer warned:

> "Let's just assume that they have a certain amount of cost (that is lower). But those guys look for a gross margin of 50–60%. So how can they do it cheaper?"

In 1992, he stated that the average cost of a CPU minute was $6.00. Vendors, however, often charged their customers $10 or more dollars per CPU minute. Also, customers should investigate what costs are included in the calculation. If cost per MIP is low, vendors may charge excess for other resources such as tape mounts or disk space.

If the vendor does not have inherent efficiencies of scale, the potential customer may decide to reduce costs on their own.

Myth: Savings of 10 to 50% can only be achieved through outsourcing. Fact: Many internal IT departments can achieve similar results without vendor assistance.

If outsourcing vendors did not possess inherent cost efficiencies, how then did they propose to reduce IT costs? Three answers were evident. First, the vendor may have offered a purely financial package that was independent of IT management issues. Second, vendors may have exploited price/ performance improvements. Third, the vendor may have initiated cost saving practices that the customer could have implemented on their own.

Some outsourcing vendors underbid current IT costs by offering an attractive financial package. Some vendors offered a financial package whose net present value was extremely attractive to the prospective customer. Cash infusions for information assets, postponing payments until the end of the contract, and even purchases of the customer's stock rendered outsourcing desirable. These outsourcing arrangements were not based on sound IT management decisions, but rather were solely a monetary arrangement.

The First City and EDS outsourcing arrangement provides an example of the cash an outsourcer can bring to a faltering organization. EDS provided a much needed cash infusion by purchasing First City's information systems assets. EDS also hired their IT staff. In addition, EDS purchased $20 million in First City's preferred stock. "Both companies insist the transactions are unrelated, but the facts are that EDS landed a $550 million dollar account, and the bank completed a badly needed recapitalization" (Mason, 1990, p. 287). An interview with an EDS manager on the First City account stated, "Currently, the whole banking industry is scaling back and systems fall low on the list of the bank's priorities."

In essence, outsourcing was used to salvage a losing enterprise. Is it sound business practice to liquidate the IT department to rescue a firm? Many shareholders believed so–stock prices systematically rose just after an outsourcing announcement (Loh and Venkatraman, 1992b).

Outsourcing vendors exploited price/performance improvements. Outsourcing vendors could often achieve savings simply by taking advantage of improvements in price/performance ratios. The improvement in price/performance is still significant; a unit of today's computing resources will cost 20 to 30% less next year. For example, one mainframe MIP cost $1 million in 1965 and cost less than $30,000 in 1993 (Benjamin and Blunt, 1992). Outsourcers knew that cost per resource unit significantly falls over time. They could take over a data center, offer 10% savings over a ten-year period, and enjoy the profits generated by riding the price/performance curve.

Proposed vendor savings may be achieved internally. Many participants felt that cost savings achieved by vendors could be produced internally. In particular, companies were able to reduce costs in a number of ways by consolidating data centers, optimizing current resource use, and implementing more controls.

One reason why vendors offered lower costs was because they ran their customer's information systems through one data center. Prior to outsourcing, customers ran multiple data centers, each having excess capacity. Since the overhead costs were excessive, vendors consolidated data centers to reduce costs. The question remained, however, whether customers could have consolidated data centers without outsourcing. The corporate culture may resist consolidation without considerable upper management support. One large petroleum company tried and failed to consolidate because the IT department could not convince the powerful operating divisions to consolidate the six data centers into one. Not until senior management threatened divisions with outsourcing were they willing to consolidate. This company subsequently reduced costs by $22 million dollars – without vendor assistance.

Companies may also be able to reduce costs by optimizing current resource use. One outsourcing consultant said that IT Managers should occasionally "spring clean" operations:

"Across the board, if I were to look at hardware, there is probably some old hardware that is around that I am paying maintenance on that we inherited from someone else, some other acquisition that we did, that we can turn around and say, "get that out of here." Software that nobody is using anymore. DASD [direct access storage device] space that is sitting out with files on it that haven't been used in a year and a half."

Typically, however, a formal efficiency audit is needed to supplement "spring cleaning". A number of reputable consultants helped their customers "in-source" – that is, use the current IT department to achieve savings similar to those of a vendor. These consultants recommended improvements to resource usage, controls, hardware and software purchasing practices.

IT departments can decrease costs by implementing cost controls such as chargeback systems, monthly software releases, or user request prioritization. Surprisingly, many participants did not employ these rudimentary controls. Without these controls, users simply viewed IT resources as "free". With no demand restrictions, users requested many services that simply were not cost-justified.

In an 1993 article, Huber of Continental Bank argued that the outsourcing culture in his organization gained momentum partly because outsourcing tied real dollar costs to support services. For example, before Continental Bank outsourced legal services, users routinely sent standard documents to the legal department.

"Perhaps half of Continental's problems with in-house services stemmed from overuse. For instance, the most routine documents were always sent to the legal department for review. "Better safe than sorry," people would say, while thinking, "and besides, it's just an internal cost, not real dollars" (Huber, 1993, pp. 122–123)."

With the outsourcing of legal, peripheral, and information services, Continental Bank was able to reduce costs. The question remained, however, whether Continental Bank could have implemented chargeback systems and other control methods without vendor assistance. One outsourcing consultant who participated in our study stated that customers could achieve the same savings as vendors by implementing chargeback systems:

> "A chargeback system is typically the best run-time improvement there is. With a chargeback system you get a bill that shows you here's everything that you ran for that month. And if you were wasting resources, and the bill jumps as a result of that, you'd be amazed how much people reduce their costs the minute a chargeback system is implemented."

At another large petroleum company, for example, users would run production systems two or three times due to sloppy procedures. With a chargeback system implemented by the vendor, they postpone execution until input data was validated.

Another cost saving measure was to implement monthly releases. At a large international bank, for example, users told analysts to change production code daily. Once the bank outsourced, the vendor tightened controls so that changes were only migrated to production every two months. The bank's outsourcing consultant explained:

> [The bank] is an example where people made changes to production at least once a week. And they make changes to production every time the user calls and says "I need this fixed, I want the screen changed." There is a tremendous amount of money to be burned up in doing that.

Another cost saving measure was to have users prioritize work requests. In many companies, the "squeaky wheel got greased" syndrome existed where some users acquired the greatest share of IT resources by virtue of their lung-power. By requiring user managers to prioritize requests for their departments, IT only addressed the most pertinent issues. In addition, users were less likely to request cosmetic or non-essential changes when they knew their managers would scrutinize work requests.

Returning to Continental Bank, after it outsourced, Huber organized a technical oversight group (TOG) comprised of user representatives from the business units:

> "The TOG…balances the technological requirements of individual units with the bank as a whole and decides which projects we will contract

out and which must wait. Individual fiefdoms used to stake out priorities. Now they must submit IT proposals to the TOG for evaluation, which ranks them on a bank-wide scale of priorities (Huber, 1993, p. 129)."

In summary, the cost saving strategies mentioned here could all be achievable by an internal IT department. If the vendor does not enjoy an inherent efficiency advantage, "in-sourcing" may be more prudent since an internal IT department does not have to turn a profit. Some companies, however, may still wish to outsource for a number of reasons: the political climate of the organization's culture may prevent the IT department from initiating cost-savings, the company may prefer to focus energies on more strategic issues than information systems, or the company may need the cash generated by the sale of information assets. If companies decide to outsource for one or more of these reasons, they need to protect their interests. The next section addresses fourteen negotiation strategies designed to balance the power between the outsourcing customer and the outsourcing vendor.

Negotiation strategies to ensure that outsourcing expectations are realized

Once potential outsourcing customers realize that vendors are running businesses and are therefore motivated to maximize profits, they can ensure that outsourcing expectations are realized by signing sound contracts. Sound contracts establish a balance of power in the outsourcing relationship. Every person spoken to in this research who decided to outsource stated that the contract is the number one key to a successful outsourcing relationship. In this study, the companies most dissatisfied with outsourcing all signed contracts that dramatically favored the vendor. These contracts merely stipulated that the vendor would provide the same level of service that the company received prior to outsourcing. However, the service levels in the base year were poorly documented, so customers were subjected to costly excess fees for services they presumed were included. In contrast, participants most pleased with their outsourcing arrangements, found that rigorous contracts reduce the threat of opportunism. When service levels, cost structures, and penalties for non-performance are specified in the contract, the vendor becomes legally obligated to accommodate.

The following lessons provided advice on how customers should negotiate contracts with outsourcing vendors. Although the lessons seemed to favor the customer over the vendor, the true motive was to establish a balance of power that benefited both parties. Since the initial position favored the vendor (they were typically the experts at negotiation and had experience in outsourcing, unlike the customer), the customer needed

Table 6.2   Lessons in Contract Negotiations

1. Discard the vendor's standard contract.
2. Do not sign incomplete contracts.
3. Hire outsourcing experts.
4. Measure everything during the baseline period.
5. Develop service level measures.
6. Develop service level reports.
7. Specify escalation procedures.
8. Include penalties for non-performance.
9. Determine growth.
10. Adjust charges to changes in business volume.
11. Select your account manager.
12. Include a termination clause.
13. Beware of "change of character" clauses.
14. Take care of your people

to leverage their position by attending to the major lessons presented in Table 6.2.

Discard the vendor's standard contract. In the early 1990s, vendors paraded their standard contract in front of their prospective customers. The vice president and director of IT for a commercial bank that outsourced IT, noted that vendor contracts should be immediately discarded. She, as well as other participants, felt that the key to successful outsourcing arrangements is building a site-specific contract:

> "One thing for sure: you can not use the vendor's contract. It is too one-sided. I mean I tell people – the vendor gave us a generic contract, but we didn't use it. The problem is that all deals are so different."

The vendor's standard contract typically obligated the vendor to perform the same level of service that the company's internal IT department provided during a baseline period. These contracts did not, however, set performance standards or include penalty clauses if the vendor failed to meet requirements.

The payment schedules in these standard contracts also favored the vendor. For example, an outsourcing vendor for a metals company wanted them to sign their standard contract. This contract required the metals company to pay the bill on the first day of the month, prior to service delivery. The IT consultant who assisted the metals company with their contract negotiations, explained the impact of the vendor's proposed payment schedule:

> "[the outsourcing vendor] wanted it day one net 15. We got it to in arrears net 45. There was a difference in a ten-year contract, there was a

difference of $8 million. So [the outsourcing vendor], they play those games."

Do not sign incomplete contracts. Since both parties were often anxious for the relationship to begin, the temptation to close negotiations swiftly was strong. The outsourcing vendor, in particular, tried to convince their customers to sign the contract before items were clearly specified. They assured their customers, "we'll take care of the details later." But since the vendor was not legally bound to alter the contract a posteriori, they may never have agreed to supplement the original contract.

At a diversified service company, for example, the CEO signed an incomplete outsourcing contract in January of 1989. The vendor promised to define services, service level measures and service level reports within the first six months. As of June 1992, these items remained incomplete, primarily because of the discrepancies over the contents of the baseline bundle. Managers at the company argued that certain services were understood to be covered in the contract. The vendor argued that if they were not already in the contract, then those services were subject to excess fees. This major problem could have been avoided if the commencement date was postponed in order to complete the contract.

Hire outsourcing experts. During negotiations, the vendor used a host of technical and legal experts to represent their interests. These experts thoroughly understood the way to measure information services and how to protect their interests. In order to counterbalance the vendor's advantage, the customer should hire experts to represent their interests. Participants in our study noted that experts were a critical success factor in negotiating an equitable contract. Although participants admitted that outsourcing experts were expensive, they believed experts helped to prevent excessive above-baseline charges.

Two types of outsourcing experts are recommended – a technical expert and a legal expert. A technical expert was particularly helpful when measuring baseline services. They not only created technical measures of the customer's information resources, they converted these measures to the technical idiosyncrasies of the vendor's environment. In simpler terms, technical experts converted the customer's apples to the vendor's oranges – a crucial skill that many customers did not possess. In addition, customers felt wary about using their in-house technical staff to assist in baseline measures because many of these people were affected by the outsourcing contract.

A legal expert familiar with outsourcing contracts is also recommended. These legal experts, who typically worked in conjunction with the customer's internal legal department, ensured that the customer's wishes were adequately documented in the contract. Together, the legal expert and internal lawyer posed a formidable negotiation team.

Measure EVERYTHING during the baseline period. During contract negotiations, the customer's current information services were documented during the baseline period. The baseline period became the yardstick that determined what services the vendor was obligated to provide to the customer. The outsourcing vendor charged a fixed fee for delivering this bundle of services, but charged an excess fee for services above and beyond the baseline. Therefore, customers needed to measure every service during the baseline period to ensure that these services were included under the fixed fee obligation.

When the outsourcing arrangement encompassed the entire IT department, customers needed to measure data processing, telecommunications, applications development, applications support, and residual services. Residual services included any services that weren't captured in the other categories such as user consultation, training, report distribution, and office moves. Each of these areas is briefly discussed below.

Data Processing and Telecommunication Services. Of all the IT service areas, participants felt that data processing and telecommunications were the easiest to measure. Most participants used the system's monitoring facilities (SMF) to capture resource usage during the baseline period. In IBM environments, for example, SMF data was typically used to assess baseline data processing activity. Monitoring facilities track the number of jobs submitted, the resources used for each job (tape mounts, data storage, computer minutes), turnaround time for jobs, on-line response time, and system availability. Similar reports were generated by network management systems for telecommunications.

During the baseline period, participants felt confident that their monitoring systems adequately captured their current level of processing. Resource requirements, however, vary based on the machine. Thus, a company's systems may perform significantly different on a vendor's machine. Care must be taken to convert the company's baseline activity to a comparable load on the vendor's machine. Vendors typically developed a conversion model based on a sample set of test transactions run on their test machine. One technical expert we spoke to advised customers to discard the vendor's conversion model because a vendor's test environment may vary significantly from their operating environment. The customer ran the risk of being charged excess fees if the vendor under-estimated the resources required to run the customer's systems. To avoid this risk, some customers stipulated in the contract that the conversion model be updated after the customer's systems were run at the vendor site.

Applications Development and Support. These labor-intensive services were difficult to measure. Participants in the study typically decided to use headcount as the baseline measure. Thus, if 200 analysts and programmers worked in applications prior to outsourcing, the customer became entitled to 200 Full-Time-Equivalents (FTEs). Two-hundred FTEs typically equated to 8,000 hours worth of work a week (200 people times a 40 hour work week).

Participants, however, cited four problems with this measure. First, some vendors eliminated people and made the remaining staff work excessive hours. The IT manager at an industrial chemicals manufacturer, explained the problem when the vendor reduced staff:

> They (the remaining staff) pick up the slack so I still get my 1,000 hours so contractually I couldn't do anything about it. The programmers, so they have to pick up more hours, they are tired, sick. They make mistakes.

Second, several participants complained that the quality of the analysts and programmers diminished. Vendors siphoned their best employees from the account to attract other customers. Third, non-productive hours were included in the FTE hours such as vendor group meetings and analyst training. Fourth, the FTE did not provide a measure of productivity, merely hours worked. Since the vendor charged for hours that exceeded the FTE, customers feared that they had no way to detect if vendors exaggerated project estimates. These service problems, however, could not be blamed on the vendor. They were free to hire, fire, and assign staff any way they saw fit. If the customer wanted control over headcounts, hours worked, project estimates, and staff quality, perhaps they should not have outsourced applications. (See Richard and Whinston, 1992 for more details on IT development contracts.)

Residual Services. In full blown outsourcing arrangements, companies often neglected to measure many services because (a) they were not reflected in IT budgets (b) they were not monitored or measured, and/or (c) customers assumed they fell within other service areas. For example, many times users ask in-house analysts to help them set up their printers, verify spreadsheets, recommend products, etc. The analysts usually respond without documenting or charging users for these favors. However, if the customer did not document and measure these services, the vendor did not include them in the baseline.

Residual services included such items as disaster recovery testing, environmental scanning for new hardware and software, microcomputer support (purchase decisions, installation, training repair), office relocation services such as rewiring and node changes, storage management to balance cost and performance trade-offs, teleconferencing support, etc. As evidenced by these examples, many residual services were difficult to measure. How do you measure intangible items such as advice, courteous service, and environmental scanning? In most cases, these services could only be measured during the baseline period by maintaining service logs. Since outsourcing decisions often caused a degradation in morale, management feared that IT employees ignored or sabotaged the measurement effort.

Therefore, some companies assigned their users to maintain the service logs during the base period.

The consequences of not measuring services were readily apparent in this study. Participants that neglected this phase all suffered serious service problems and excess charges because they failed to measure all information services during the baseline period. Some participants assumed that their request for proposals (RPFs) documented their service needs, but RPFs were only high level descriptions of service requirements. Baseline measures must be monotonously detailed.

The length of the baseline period was also an important consideration. Since service volumes typically fluctuate with the tax season, seasonal business oscillations, and end-of-year processing, a baseline period of six months was needed. Typically, measures were calculated once a month for each service. For example, during March the customer may use X hours of a computer resource. During April, volumes may decrease or increase. At the end of the baseline period, six observations exist for each service. The customer and vendor must then establish an algorithm to determine the baseline number. Vendors often suggested averaging monthly measures, but this resulted in the customer exceeding baseline services 50% of the time. A more equitable solution was to create a volume variance for each service level. The customer was not charged an excess fee as long as volumes remained within specified ranges.

Develop service level measures. Some may question why service level measures need to be developed since the baseline period allegedly covered this issue. The answer is simple: the customer or vendor may wish to add, combine, improve, or delete measures. Thus, baseline measures merely provided a yardstick for what the vendor's obligations would be during the arrangement. For every service that the vendor is expected to provide, a service level measure should unequivocally express the level of required service.

During this phase of contract negotiations, participants warned that vendors tried to manipulate measures in their favor. At a diversified services company, for example, the vendor attempted to dilute measures in two ways. First, they tried to dodge accounting for 100% of services. Second, the vendor tried to manipulate the laws of probability in their favor. Both these issues are discussed below.

Specify 100% service accountability. Measures typically required vendors to deliver a certain amount of work in a certain period of time. For example, vendors may agree to process 90% of all service requests within three days. The customer, however, may never know what happens to the remaining 10% of the service. This 10% may be serviced very late or never at all. Despite the fact that 10% of the work may never be accounted for, vendors technically meet their service level requirements.

The best way to avoid services from falling through the proverbial cracks is to specify 100% service accountability. For example, if the vendor agree to process 90% of all service requests in three days, then make an additional requirement that specifies the remaining 10% must be completed within five days. The customer should require that exceptions be fully documented and reported.

Know the basic laws of probability. Vendors also diluted measures by exploiting some simple laws of probability. Returning to the outsourcing experiences of the diversified services company, the vendor finally agreed to deliver 95% of a particular service within the agreed upon time frame. The customer agreed to the measure, as long as the service was delivered correctly. The vendor countered with a proposal to implement two measures. The first measure specified that 95% of the service requests be completed by the target date. The second measure specified that 95% of the service requests be completed accurately. By proposing two measures, the vendor attempted to dilute the service level since the probability of the service being delivered on time and accurate is only 90%.

Develop service level reports. During outsourcing negotiations, companies may spend a significant amount of time developing measures, then fail to require the vendor to report on these measures. Vendors may tell their customers that their standard reports address their measures, but several participants found this assertion untrue.

One participant, for example, complained that the vendor's standard reports only indicate the volume of service performed. For instance, the vendor's security request report indicated "100 security requests were implemented this month." This report does not specify how many security requests were submitted or the average turnaround time for the requests. According to the contract, the vendor was meeting service levels. Users, however, complained that requests took an excessive time to process:

"We have, at one time, in excess of seventeen working days to get somebody through security. We have a big problem with that."

Service level reports should document the agreed upon service level, the service performance for the current time period, exception reporting for missed measures, and a trend analysis of the performance from previous reporting periods. Customers were often charged for the creation of these reports. The investment was well worth it – how could service level measures be monitored without service level reports?

Specify escalation procedures. Customers realized that IT was often times a volatile business – there were bound to be occasional events that prevented the vendor from meeting a service level measure. In many instances, the customer was even at fault. Thus, in addition to the service level reports, the customer and vendor needed to agree upon problem escalation procedures.

Typically, the vendor requested that fault (customer or vendor) be determined for each missed measure. This protected the vendor's interests – since they are contractually bound to meet measures, they should not be punished for customer errors. Granted, this task was repulsive to most; as professionals we want to fix problems, not fix blame. However, the reality was that dollars may be exchanged as a result of nonperformance.

Services may be divided into critical versus non-critical categories to prevent micro-management. For non-critical measures, such as analyst training hours, perhaps the vendor may miss this measure once or twice a year. For critical services, such as on-line availability, the customer may require immediate reporting, problem resolution within a specified period of time, and perhaps even a cash penalty.

Include cash penalties for non-performance. In cases of severe service degradation, the customer may insist on cash compensation. At a commercial bank, for example, there were penalty charges for failure to meet end user response time, system availability, and batch delivery deadlines for critical systems. Customers also escalated cash penalty amounts with frequency. For example, the first occurrence resulted in a penalty of $25,000. Another occurrence for the same service within a specified time period cost the vendor $50,000.

Participants that specified cash penalties in their contracts hoped that they would never need to enact the penalty clause. The CFO at a transportation services company noted that penalty clauses did not fully compensate the customer. Rather, the purpose of penalty clauses was to ensure that the vendor's senior management would attend to service level problems:

> "You don't get total reimbursement for your lost profit and your lost cash. But you do have a penalty that is significant to [the outsourcing vendor] and gets their attention. Our penalty is in the $100,000 range up to $1 million. So it's not enough to compensate us for the downtime, but it will certainly get their attention. It will get somebody fired. You know it will get to the top layers within [the outsourcing vendor]."

Determine growth rates. Most outsourcing contracts included a growth rate where the customer got a certain amount of growth for free. The reasoning was that the cost of a unit of processing decreases every year, so the customer deserves to share the benefits of price/performance improvements. The problem, however, was that the vendor understood growth rates much better than the customer. The customer was warned that the vendor may under-estimate growth so that they may charge excess fees in the future.

The following example illustrates the problem. The vendor may convince the customer that their growth rate is 5%–6% per year, based on IT budget increases. The vendor then offers to provide a 6% increase in resource requirements (MIPS, storage, tapes) free of charge. To a customer unfamiliar with the intricacies of IT, this deal seems appealing. However, in actuality, the resource requirements may be growing at 10% to 20% since the IT department is able exploit price/performance improvements discussed before. During the outsourcing arrangement, the customer will either pay extra for resource growth above 6% or they will curtail growth.

Adjust charges to changes in business. Customers should also include a clause for severe volume fluctuations caused by acquisitions, mergers or sale of business units. In cases of a sale of a business unit, the customer may specify a major reduction in the fixed fee expense. The vendor, however, may insist on several months notice to allow ample time to re-direct resources. The customer may also want the *vendor* to promptly accommodate mergers or acquisitions. The vendor may insist, again, on advanced notice. In addition, the vendor may insist on charging the customer a transition fee for the volume adjustment.

Select your account manager. At a mining company, the controller specified the name of the account manager in the contract. The controller had so much faith in this particular individual, one of the vendor's account managers, that he required him to manage the arrangement. This account manager was indeed a special character; as a previous outsourcing customer, he was once the vendor's most vocal critic, often complaining about services and fees. The vendor finally hired him "to shut him up". The controller felt that the account manager's background as a former outsourcing customer minimized the threat of opportunism. His choice was wise; after one and one half years with the vendor, the mining company had never contested the vendor's bills or services. Although the contract seemed weak in other areas (lack of service measures, penalty clauses), the controller's utter trust in the account manager compensated for any legal loopholes.

Include a termination clause. Most lawyers will insist that a termination clause be included in the contract. This clause protects both parties, since the desire to terminate by one party will severely affect the other party. Either party may need to terminate because of bankruptcy or sale of the company. In addition, the customer may wish to terminate because of failure to provide services. Most contracts require either party to notify the other within a specified time period, such as three months. Failure to give adequate notice may result in a severe penalty charge.

The customer, however, will typically need more than three months to find an alternative supplier. Negotiation with another vendor may require six months; Re-building an internal IT department may require a year or more. In addition, the customer needs the vendor's assistance to trans-fer systems to an alternative site. Therefore, vendor assistance should be specified as a requirement for termination – regardless of the initiating party.

Watch out for "change of character" clauses. Another weakness of several outsourcing contracts was the "change of character" clause. This provision stated that the customer would be charged for any changes in functionality. This clause triggered several disputes. At a diversified services company, for example, the vendor wanted to charge for changing their word processing software. The vendor argued that this represented a change of character since the new product was not supported during the baseline period. The customer argued that this was not a change of character since the function – word processing – had not changed, only the software.

Personal computers was another point of contention. Their contract said that the vendor would service all personal computers for a fixed price. However, the number of computers doubled since 1989, and many PCs were now connected to LANs. The vendor claimed that LAN technology was a "change in character", whereas the customer claimed it's only a difference in technology. In addition, the outsourcing vendor wanted to charge a particular dollar amount for each additional PC supported. The customer contended that "volumes do not equal costs". In other words, doubling the number of PCs did not double the cost to support them.

Take care of your people. The discussion so far has concentrated on protecting the interests of the customer. (We have assumed the vendor is capable of protecting their own interests). The collective term "customer", however, excludes many of the organization's people. In particular, the IT employees were dramatically affected by the outsourcing decision. Companies have a social responsibility to treat these people fairly; that includes informing them of the final decision as soon as possible and helping them secure positions elsewhere if necessary.

In typical outsourcing arrangements we studied, the vendor hired the majority of IT employees for a one-year trial basis. This allowed the employees to prove themselves to the vendor before the vendor committed to permanent employment. The vendor also requested performance ratings for each analyst from the customer. If the customer views outsourcing as an opportunity to eliminate low-performers, they may be tempted to share this information. However, the customer may be pleasantly surprised to find that low performers in one culture may thrive in another culture.

Conclusions from a 2008 perspective

Looking back over this early contribution, we note a number of things about the maturation of the ITO market. First, clients have become immensely wiser. Very few client firms today have the naïve assumptions about outsourcing that client organizations had back then. Experience proved the best teacher, and clients quickly learned from their own mistakes as well as from the mistakes of others. Second, we no longer call the client's contracting partner a "vendor" but rather a "supplier" or "provider". The term "vendor" connotes the same "commodity" type rhetoric we criticized back in 1993 – we buy hotdogs from a *vendor*, but services from a *supplier*. Third, since this study, the number of supplier options has exploded. Back in 1993, all large scale ITO contracts were essentially domestic contracts between US-based or UK-based clients and a handful of firms like IBM, EDS, CSC, and Andersen Consulting (now Accenture). The small number of suppliers certainly limited the client's power back in 1993. But to their credit, these large suppliers reinvented themselves many times in response to customer complaints and increased global competition from firms we barely knew back in 1993, such as Wipro, Infosys, and Tata. The explosion of the Internet has also enabled smaller suppliers to scale quickly and offer IT products and services in hosted environments undreamed of in 1993.

And what about those contracts, which were our main prescription in 1993? We believe the contract is still the major governing mechanism of client-supplier relationships. And nearly all the advice we recommended in 1993 is now standard in large contracts, thanks to the major consulting firms like Technology Partners International, Shaw Pittman, and the Everest Group who helped client organizations sign sound contracts. We now know that the main value derived from contract negotiations is a shared understanding of the mutual obligations of both parties. Suppliers simply cannot execute an ITO contract without good client-side support.

As we are now in 2008, the role of IT is no longer perceived as either the 1980s strategic enabler *or* the 1990s commodity support function (despite what Carr writes). Rather, nearly every informed practitioner considers IT as a portfolio of services that provide various technical, operational, and strategic value to organizations. Subsequently, the IT sourcing portfolio mirrors the IT value portfolio. Companies no longer ask whether to outsource IT, but rather how to best source different portions of the IT portfolio. Cost considerations remain important in ITO decisions, but this reasoning is supplemented with the need for faster delivery speed, ability to focus in-house IT staff on more higher-value work, access to supplier resources and capabilities, and process improvement. Many clients simply must source IT globally, as local talent is expensive and in short supply. Today's sourcing questions focus on sourcing locations (offshore, onshore, nearshore), engagement models (fee-for-service, application service provision, joint ventures, captive centers), and managing relationships among a global network of suppliers. We tackle many of these contemporary issues in subsequent chapters.

References

Ambrosio, J. (1991) "Outsourcing at Southland: Best of Times, Worst of Times," *Computerworld*, Vol. 25, p. 12.

Anthes, G. (1991) "Perot wins 10-year Outsourcing Deal," *Computerworld*, Vol. 25, 14, p. 96.

Applegate, L. and Montealegre, R. (1991) "Eastman Kodak Co: Managing Information Systems Through Strategic Alliances," Harvard Business School Case 9–192–030.

Barron, T. (1992) "Some New Results in Testing for Economies of Scale in Computing," *Decision Support Systems*, Vol. 8, pp. 405–429.

Benjamin, R. and Blunt, J. (1992) "Critical IT Issues: The Next Ten Years," *Sloan Management Review*, Vol. 33, 4, pp. 7–19.

Datamation (1988) "Large-Scale Systems Survey", May 15, p. 60.

Friedberg, A. and Yarberry, W. (1991) "Audit Rights in An Outsourcing Environment," *Internal Auditor*, August, pp. 53–59.

Gardner, E. (1991) "Going On-line with Outsiders," *Modern Healthcare*, July 15, pp. 35–47.

Greenbaum, J. (1992) "Planning for Pan-European Outsourcing," *InformationWeek*, June 22, 1992, pp. 40–48.

Hamilton, R. (1989) "Kendall Outsources IT Chief," *Computerworld*, Vol. 23, 46, pp. 1, 4.

Hammersmith, A. (1989) "Slaying the IT Dragon with Outsourcery," *Computerworld*, Vol. 23, 38, pp. 1, 4.

Henderson, J. (1990) "Plugging into Strategic Partnerships: The Critical IT Connection," *Sloan Management Review*, Vol. 31, 3, 1990, pp. 7–18.

Hopper, M. (1990) "Rattling SABRE – New Ways to Compete on Information," *Harvard Business Review*, Vol. 68, 3, pp. 118–125.

Hovey, V. (1991) Presentation to the University of Houston's Information Systems Research Center, January 22.

Huber, R. (1993) "How Continental Bank Outsourced Its 'Crown Jewels'", *Harvard Business Review*, Vol. 71, 1, pp. 121–129.

Huff, S. (1991) "Outsourcing of Information Services," *Business Quarterly*, Vol. 55, 4, pp. 62–65.

Kass, E. and Caldwell, B. (1990) "Outsource Ins, Outs,: *Information Week*, Issue 260, p. 14.

Krass, P. (1990) "The Dollars and Sense of Outsourcing," *Information Week*, Issue 259, pp. 26–31.

Mason, T. (1990) *Perot*, Dow Jones-Irwin, Homewood, Illinois.

Lacity, M. and Hirschheim, R. (1993) "The Information Systems Outsourcing Bandwagon," *Sloan Management Review*, Vol. 35, 1, pp. 73–86.

Livingston, D. (1990) "Take My System – Please!" *Systems Integration*, Vol. 23, 12, pp. 40–44.

Loh, L. and Venkatraman, N. (1992a) "Determinants of Information Technology Outsourcing: A Cross-Sectional Analysis, *Journal of Management Information Systems*, Vol. 9, 1, pp. 7–24.

Loh, L. and N. Venkatraman (1992b) "Stock Market Reaction to Information Technology Outsourcing: An Event Study," Working Paper No. 3499–92BPS, Sloan School of Management, November 1992.

Loh, L. and Venkatraman, N. (1992c) "Diffusion of Information Technology Outsourcing: Influence Sources and the Kodak Effect," *Information Systems Research*, Vol. 3, No. 4, pp. 334–358.

Network World (1992) February 17, pp. 1, 31–36.

Porter, M. and Millar, V. (1985) "How Information Gives You a Competitive Advantage," *Harvard Business Review*, Vol. 63, 4, pp. 149–160.

Prahalad, C.K. and Hamel, G. (1990) "The Core Competence of the Corporation", *Harvard Business Review*, Vol. 33, pp. 79–91.

Radding, A. (1990) "The Ride is no Bargain if You Can't Steer," *Computerworld*, Vol. 24, 2, pp. 67, 70–72.

Richard, W. and Whinston, A. (1992) "Incomplete Contracting Issues in Information Systems Development Outsourcing," *Decision Support Systems*, Vol. 8, pp. 459–477.

Rochester, J. and Douglass, D. (eds) (1990). "Taking An Objective Look at Outsourcing," *I/S Analyzer*, Vol. 28, 8, pp. 1–16.

Ward, B. (1991) "Hiring Out: Outsourcing is the New Buzzword in the Management of Information Systems," *Sky Magazine*, Vol. 20, 8, pp. 37–45.

Wilder, C. (1991) "Bend Me, Shape Me," *Computerworld*, Vol. 24, 52–53, December 24, 1991–January 1, p. 14.

7
Making the Outsourcing Decision

Mary C. Lacity, Leslie P. Willcocks and David Feeny

Introduction

In this chapter, we present our ITO decision framework which guides practitioners to consider business, economic, and technical factors. Originally published as Lacity, Willcocks, and Feeny (1996), this framework is still remarkably relevant. When discussing business factors, we dismiss the traditional "core versus non-core" criterion because we found it was difficult for practitioners to differentiate IT activities on this basis. Instead, we guide practitioners to consider an IT activity's contribution to competitive advantage as well as to its critical support of daily business operations. In the discussion of economic factors, we challenge practitioners to examine the *practices* that lead to economic efficiency rather than just economies of scale. Surely, suppliers operate on a larger scale than internal IT departments, but economic efficiency depends more on practices such as standardization, centralization, and tight controls than *size*. In the discussion of technical issues, we discuss a technology's maturity (stability, measurability, and requirements certainty) and technology's integration with other business functions as the most important technical criteria to consider. This framework continues to be used by practitioners and is still widely cited by academics.

As we have noted several times, IT is outsourced for many reasons, ranging from a bandwagon effect from the subject's high profile to cost pressures due to competition and economic recession (Lacity, Hirschheim and Willcocks, 1994; Lacity and Rottman, 2008). One major driver of the growth of the IT outsourcing market was the major shift in business strategy. During the 1990s, many companies abandoned their diversification strategies – once pursued to mediate risk – to focus on core competencies. Senior executives have come to believe that the most important sustainable competitive advantage is concentrating on what an organization does better than anyone else and outsourcing the rest (Prahalad and Hamel, 1991). As a result of the focus strategy, IT came under scrutiny: is IT a competitive weapon or merely a utility? Senior executives frequently view much of the IT function as a non-core activity, and reason that IT service suppliers possess economies of scale and technical expertise to provide IT services more efficiently than internal IT departments (Lacity and Hirschheim, 1993; 1995).

Among our case studies, most of the successful ITO experiences were associated with a reasoned, incremental, and selective approach to outsourcing, which is increasingly reflected in the structure of the market. The practice of outsourcing select IT applications to suppliers while retaining other IT applications in-house has been variously referred to as "smartsourcing" and "rightsourcing". This practice eschews the all-or-nothing approach to outsourcing in favor of a more flexible and modular approach. But while selective outsourcing provides managers with a greater array of options, it is also more confusing – managers may make wrong decisions about what IT services to outsource and what services to retain in-house, neglect the technical issues involved in outsourcing, and miscalculate the long-term economic consequences. Based on the successful (as well as unsuccessful) experiences of our case companies, we have developed a selective sourcing framework for working through the complex issues and assumptions associated with information technology sourcing decisions.

The scope of sourcing decisions

Our case studies represent a variety of sourcing decisions, with many options ranging from ten year contracts for the provision of all IT services to providing almost all IT services through the internal IT staff. In addition to 'outsourcing' contracts, there were many examples of 'insourcing' – where companies were using external staff and resources within IT activities that remained under in-house management. For the purpose of analysis we grouped the decisions of our case study participants into four cat-egories:

Total outsourcing: the decision to transfer IT assets, leases, staff, and management responsibility for delivery of IT services from internal IT functions to third party suppliers which represents at least 80% of the IT budget.

Total insourcing: the decision to retain the *management* and *provision* of at least 80% of the IT budget internally after evaluating the IT services market. Included in our definition of insourcing is the buying-in of supplier resources to meet a temporary resource need, such as the need for programmers in the latter stages of a new development project or the use of management consultants to facilitate a strategic planning process. In these cases, the customer retains responsibility for the delivery of IT services – supplier resources are brought in to supplement internally-managed teams.

Selective sourcing: the decision to source selected IT functions from external providers while still providing between 20 and 80% (typically 24%) of the IT budget. The supplier becomes responsible for delivering the result of the selectively outsourced IT activities, while the customer remains responsible for delivering the result of the insourced IT activities.

De facto insourcing: the exclusive use of internal IT departments to provide IT products and services which arise from historical precedent, rather than a reasoned evaluation of the IT services market.

The problems with all-or-nothing outsourcing

The first insight from our study is that total outsourcing, characterized by long-term mega-deals, can lead to trouble a few years into the contract (Lacity and Willcocks, 2001; Rossetti and Choi, 2005). After the initial honeymoon period, many companies complain of a loss of alignment between business strategy and IT, failed promises to access new technologies, and contractual costs which are significantly greater than current market prices. Although several of the companies in our study involved in mega-deals wish to terminate their contracts, senior executives often find it prohibitively expensive to switch suppliers or bring IT back in-house when "strategic partnerships" fail. Some companies, like the one described below, have bitten the bullet and actually brought IT back in-house.

Case example: US chemical company

The experiences of this company, which are by no means atypical, challenge the concept of total outsourcing. Here the senior executives who signed a seven-year, total outsourcing contract saw the entire IT function as a commodity. They selected a particular supplier partly because its representatives promised access to the industry-specific systems that other chemical customers used. Because the representatives presented themselves as 'partners', senior executives from the chemicals company neglected contract negotiations and hastily signed the supplier's generic contract. They failed to analyze the economics of the deal or question how the supplier would cut costs or whether the internal IT department could implement practices to reduce costs on its own. They merely assumed that the supplier was more efficient because of its size.

After the first month, the supplier's excess charges for items missing from the contract exceeded the fixed monthly price. As time went on, promises of access to additional software disappeared, and, instead, the chemical company paid the supplier to build new systems. When these systems were late and over-priced, users purchased cheaper desktop solutions, funded by discretionary money. Rather than continue the partnership with the outsourcing supplier, senior executives paid a stiff penalty to terminate the contract, purchased hardware and software, and hired a new IT staff of 40 people.

Total insourcing

Although such total outsourcing "war stories" discourage total outsourcing, they do not suggest that exclusive sourcing by an internal IT department is the answer. Our research strongly indicates that internal IT "monopolies" promote complacency and erect organizational obstacles against continuous improvement. Many IT managers in our study exploited total outsourcing failures and have adamantly refused to deal with outsourcing suppliers. These IT managers have met personal misfortune when their own organizations have failed to demonstrate value for money. For example, the vice president of IS at a waste management company tried to deflect his CEO's interest in outsourcing by producing a white paper highlighting outsourcing failures. His CEO eventually dismissed the white paper and signed an outsourcing contract for all applications development and support.

More commonly, de facto policies of exclusive insourcing create organizational obstacles against improvement because internal users resist cost reduction tactics proposed by IT managers. Because IT typically lacks the clout to implement the unpopular tactics practiced by outsourcing suppliers – such as data center consolidation or software standardization – unbridled users can significantly drive up IT costs. For example, at an American food manufacturer, users resisted the IT Director's attempts to cut costs by standardizing software. Despite the IT department's efforts, users insisted on their own operating systems, utilities, report generators, statistical packages, spreadsheets, and electronic mail. It was not until senior executives threatened the organization with outsourc-ing that the IT Director was empowered to behave like outsourcing suppliers. Users agreed to allow him to standardize software rather than have an external supplier do it for them. IT software costs subsequently dropped by 45%. We saw similar results with nine other insourcing decisions-insourcing led to lower costs *after* formal evaluation of market capabilities enable internal IT managers to behave like suppliers.

The distinctiveness of IT

We believe the problems with all-or-nothing outsourcing stem from the distinctive nature of IT (see also Chapter 2 for how this could affect the applicability of a Transaction Cost Economics perspective on IT outsourcing). Although many senior executives approach IT outsourcing like any other make or buy decision, this can be a mistake. Unlike other functions – such as mailrooms, cafeterias, legal departments, manufacturing, distribution, and advertising – IT cannot be easily handed over to a supplier. IT is different in a number of ways.

- *Information technology is not a homogeneous function, but comprises a wide variety of IT activities.*

Some IT applications enable business operations and management pro-cesses in a unique way. Other IT activities, such as accounting systems, may appear less critical, but closer scrutiny often reveals that the value of such systems lies in the cross-functional integration of business processes. In many organizations, information technology integrates product design, material purchases, manufacturing processes, sales, and customer service. The ubiquitous penetration of many IT appli-cations across business functions hinders outsourcing because IT can-not easily be isolated, unlike other commonly outsourced functions such as legal departments. Outsourcing such activities can hinder busi-ness performance because suppliers lack an understanding of the impli-cations IT has on other business processes. For example, a UK food manufacturer outsourced the development of its factory automation system, only to discover that the supplier did not understand the critical interfaces with other business units such as purchasing and inventory control. The system was delivered two years late and was twice as expensive as the company expected. This and other examples strongly suggest the need for a selective rationale for outsourcing – while some acti-vities can be outsourced, many others require management's atten-tion, protection, and nurturing to ensure current and future business success.

- *IT capabilities continue to evolve at a dizzying pace; thus, predicting IT needs past a three-year horizon is wrought with uncertainty.*

Although companies initially perceived that suppliers would provide access to new technologies, mega-deals are usually contracted around current technologies with only vague references to future techno-logies. Most companies find that by the third year into an outsourcing deal, the original contract actually hinders their adoption of new tech-nologies. For example, when a US petrochemical company signed a ten-year total outsourcing contract, the majority of the company's systems were running on mainframe technology. With the advent of client-server technology, the company wanted to migrate to the smaller platform, but found their outsourcing contract erected signi-ficant obstacles. In the end, business unit managers were forced to use discretionary funds to build client-server systems, while still meeting their contractual obligations for the increasingly obsolescent mainframe.

- *There is no simple basis for gauging the economics of IT activity.*

Although price/performance improvements occur in every industry, in few industries do the underlying economics shift as fast as IT. Today's computing resources may well cost 20 to 30% less next year. The rapid change in the underlying economics makes it extremely difficult for senior executives to evaluate the long-term costs of outsourcing. While a 20% reduction of current IT costs for the next ten years may be appealing to a senior executive today, a few years into the contract he or she may be paying the supplier above-market prices for computer resources.

- *Economic efficiency has more to do with IT practices than inherent economies of scale.*

Although there are indeed economies of scale in some aspects of IT, they occur at a size achievable by many medium-sized and most large-sized companies. Our research suggests that supplier bids are based more on management practices than inherent economies of scale. For example, suppliers may cut costs through chargeout mechanisms which motivate business users to manage demand, by consolidating data centers from multiple sites to one site, or by standardizing software. From our experiences, IT managers can often duplicate these cost reduction tactics if empowered by senior executives to overcome user resistance. For example, IT costs at an American shoe manufacturer/retailer were high because users refused to let IT managers consolidate their data centers. Once senior management threatened users by inviting outsourcing bids, users acquiesced and agreed to let IT managers consolidate. IT costs subsequently dropped by 54%.

- *Most distinctively of all, large switching costs are associated with IT sourcing decisions.*

In most business operations, management can protect itself against poor sourcing decisions in a number of ways, for example by dual sourcing of component supply or annual reviews of an advertising agency contract. These techniques are often inapplicable or ineffective for IT outsourcing, particularly when a total outsourcing approach is taken. The CFO from a US airline who signed a ten-year total outsourcing contract, perceives that switching costs pose a major risk:

> Once you sign with a supplier, you have no options other than onerous contract terms, so when you get into that situation it's a lose/lose for

both parties. What are you going to do? Sue them? Fire them? Stop buying services? There is nobody else, in a short period of time, who you can buy services from.

Those who approach outsourcing in all-or-nothing terms either incur the great risks involved in total outsourcing or forego the potentially considerable benefits of selective sourcing by committing to a policy of total insourcing.

Beyond all–or-nothing: selective outsourcing

We believe that the debate about all-or-nothing outsourcing has obscured the real issue. The key question is not, 'Should we outsource or insource IT?', but rather 'Where and how can we take advantage of the developing market for IT services?' Based upon our research, successful organizations carefully select which IT activities to outsource, rigorously evaluate suppliers, tailor the terms of the contract, and carefully manage the supplier. From the rich variety of case experiences studied we have been able to build a set of frameworks for thinking through sourcing decisions. These frameworks embody a logic of firstly clarifying the sourcing options, then considering the critical business, economic and technical factors influencing the effectiveness of sourcing decisions.

IT sourcing options

A first stage is to clarify the different ways in which IT can be delivered to the business. Our case study organizations expressed some frustrations over the terms 'outsourcing' and 'insourcing'. In many ways 'outsourcing' is not a new concept. External providers such as service bureaux, facilities management companies, contract programmers and consulting firms have been used since the early days of data processing. Equally confusing was the term 'insourcing' which was used to describe a variety of sourcing options, such as managing and delivering IT services solely through the in-house function, bringing previously outsourced activities back in-house, or buying in supplier resources but managing them internally. Figure 7.1 provides a consistent set of concepts for thinking through the IT sourcing options. It suggests that a wide variety of contracting strategies can be used to manage suppliers, from buying in resources as part of an in-house team, to contracting out the entire delivery of an IT activity. In general participants' contracts can be categorized based on two dimensions: purchasing style and purchasing focus. We identify two purchasing styles: transaction or relationship. The transaction style involves one-off contracts with enough detail to serve as the original reference document. The relationship style involves less detailed, incentive-based contracts based on the expectation that customer and supplier will do business over many years.

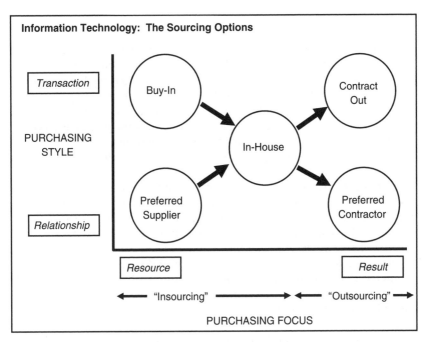

Figure 7.1   Information Technology: The Sourcing Options

We identify two purchasing focus options: resource or result. With a resource option, companies buy-in supplier resources, such as hardware, software, or expertise, but self-manage the delivery of the IT activity. With a result option, suppliers manage the delivery of the IT activity to provide the company with the specified results.

Combining purchasing style and focus, four distinct ways of using the external IT market emerge, which we label 'buy-in', 'contract-out', 'preferred supplier', and 'preferred contractor'.

With a buy-in strategy, companies buy supplier resources to meet a temporary resource need, such as the need for programmers in the latter stages of a new development project. In these cases, companies are often unsure of the exact hours needed to complete the coding, so they sign contracts that specify the skills required and per diem cost per person.

With a contract-out strategy, the supplier becomes responsible for delivering the result of the IT activity. This strategy is most successful when the companies can clearly define their needs in an air-tight contract. The contract must be complete because it will serve as original reference to manage the supplier. For example, companies often use a contract-out strategy to outsource data center operations. In these contracts, precise service levels, escalation procedures for missed measures, cash penalties for non-performance, adjustments for volume increases or decreases, and termination clauses, are specified.

With a preferred supplier strategy, companies intend to develop a close relationship with a supplier in order to access their resources for on-going IT activities. The relationship is managed with an incentive-based contract that defines complementary goals. For example, one company engaged a preferred supplier to provide contract programmers whenever they were needed. The contract ensured complementary goals – the participant received a volume discount in exchange for not going out to tender when programmers were needed. The supplier was motivated to perform because they relied on a steady stream of revenue.

With a preferred contractor strategy, companies intend to engage in a relationship with a supplier to help mediate risk. The supplier is responsible for the management and delivery of an IT activity. To ensure supplier performance, the company tries to construct an incentive-based contract that ensures shared goals. For example, when one company decided to reduce costs by outsourcing data center operations and support of existing, they mediated risk by entering into a joint venture with a software house. By establishing a jointly-owned company they created shared goals and prevented supplier opportunism.

There remains, in Figure 7.1, the in-house arrangement. We found this option having a critical role to play even when organizations were spending over 80% of the IT budget on contracting out or on preferred contractors. All forms of contract run larger risks if certain capabilities are not retained in-house (see also Chapter 15):

- ability to track, assess, and interpret changing IT capability, and relate this to the needs of the organization;
- ability to work with business management to define the IT requirements successfully over time;
- ability to identify the appropriate ways to use the market, to help specify and manage IT sourcing and to monitor and manage contractual relations.

We refer to the 'buy-in', 'preferred supplier' and 'in-house' options collectively as 'insourcing' options because in all of them in-house management retains full visibility, and control of the IT activity. We refer to the 'contract-out' and 'preferred contractor' options as 'outsourcing' options because in each of them in-house management pass control of the IT activity to the external supplier.

Having clarified the sourcing options we now present a decision matrix for each of the key sets of business, economic and technical factors. These matrices seek to capture the key learning from our research case studies. They aim to represent a structure for management discussion and decision, not a mechanistic methodology. In practice managers will need to choose between a range of trade-offs that will arise during the debate. Political issues and interests will also be integral to the decision-making process. However, we have found that where business and IT executives can agree how to map their IT activities onto these matrices, the frameworks will provide a strong guide towards an effective strategy.

Being selective: business considerations

Selecting which IT activities to outsource and which to retain in-house requires treating IT as a portfolio. Successful sourcing begins with an analysis of the business contribution of various IT activities. Conventional wisdom has it that "commodity" IT functions, such as payroll or data center operations, are potential outsourcing fodder, while "strategic" functions, such as on-line reservation systems, should be retained in-house (McFarlan and Nolan, 1995). Our study indicates that this delineation is too simplistic for two reasons. First, generalizations about which IT activities are "commodities" or "strategic" are often fallacious. For some companies, alleged IT commodities such as payroll, accounting systems and data center operations actually serve to critically differentiate them from competitors. For example, in one security guard firm, payroll is a strategic application because on-time payment attracts a better quality of staff, leading to superior customer service. Also, applications often migrate from "strategic" to "commodity" within each industry as competition ebbs and flows. For example, while early adoption of automated teller machines (ATMs) once represented a strategic advantage by attracting more customers, universal adoption has delegated ATMs to mere commodities, as we found in our banking cases. Thus, each company must analyze the delineation of IT activities in its own business context, rather than accept generalities.

Second, many companies do not operate highly visible competitive systems, so senior executives may mistakenly classify all IT activities as commodities. In many cases, the business contribution of IT may be masked by accounting for IT as an overhead, which serves to highlight only the costs of IT. In a US petroleum company the CEO continually asked his CIO why IT costs were rising when other departments had managed to cut costs. The CIO explained that other departments primarily reduced costs through IT. Transportation costs were cut when IT automated 16 truck terminals, and market costs were reduced when IT implemented a new credit card system. By abandoning the view of IT as a cost to be minimized, this CEO realized IT's business contribution and he subsequently rejected an outsourcing supplier's request to bid.

We have found that companies that consistently succeed in their selection of what can be outsourced to advantage use a richer vocabulary. They distinguish between the contribution that an IT activity makes to business operations, and its impact on competitive positioning. These dimensions, which are depicted in Figure 7.2, are further explored below.

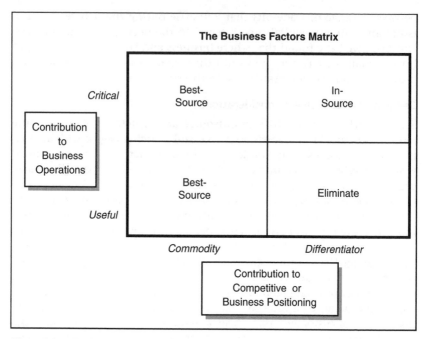

Figure 7.2   The Business Factors Matrix

Some IT activities can differentiate a company from its competitors while other IT activities merely provide necessary functions. Some well publicized examples of IT products that have successfully differentiated companies from their competitors include American Airline's SABRE, Wal-Mart's IT-enabled supply chain, American Hospital Supply's Order Entry System (subsequently acquired by Baxter), and Merrill Lynch's Cash Management System (Clemons and Row, 1988; Copeland and McKenney, 1988; Niederman *et al.*, 2007; Venkatraman and Short, 1990). These systems created barriers to entry, increased switching costs, and changed the nature of competition. Most IT activities, however, are viewed as commodities. Although IT commodities do not distinguish a company from its competitors in business offering and performance terms, these types of activities need to be performed competently. Examples of IT commodities, depending on the specific company, may include IT products such as accounting systems or IT services such as data processing centers.

Some IT activities are viewed as critical contributors to business operations, whereas other IT activities are viewed as merely useful because they only make incremental contributions to the bottom line. For example, a US petrol refiner views an information system which monitors the refining process as a critical contributor because it prevents fires and ensures product quality. Conversely, the company views an employee scheduling system as a useful contributor to business operations, but not a critical contributor.

After mapping an IT activity's contribution to business positioning and business operations, four categories of potential outsourcing candidates emerge:

1. *'Critical-Differentiators' – IT activities which are not only critical to business operations, but also help to distinguish the business from its competitors.* A European ferry company considered its reservation and check-in systems to be 'critical differentiators'. The company had ships similar to those of its main rival, and operated them from the same major ports across the Channel between Britain and France. Its competitive strategy was to differentiate through service, including the speed and ease with which passengers and their cars complete the boarding process. It is constantly making innovations in this respect, and the systems are instrumental in achieving this. Even though the company outsources a number of its IT activities, the reservation and check-in systems are retained in-house. This protects their ideas, expertise, and continuing ability to rapidly innovate.

As three examples, we found similar "critical-differentiators" in a comprehensive customer management system at a UK insurance company, a product development support system at a UK chemical manufacturer, and a foreign exchange system in a US commercial bank. Although such systems should be managed internally, we have seen organizations boost their in-house IT capability by bringing in specialists from an external supplier. However, these outsiders work alongside in-house people, under the company's own management.

2. *'Critical-Commodities' – IT activities that are critical to business operations but fail to distinguish the business from its competitors.* A major British airline views its IT systems which support aircraft maintenance as critical-commodities. Like its rivals, the airline must obviously maintain its fleet to specification or face very serious consequences. However, the maintenance activity and supporting systems respond to the mandated requirements of the manufacturers and regulatory authorities. There is no benefit from over-performance. Although the airline has not yet outsourced these systems, it is in principle prepared to do so. Because of the risks involved for the business, such a decision would be based on clear evidence that an external supplier could meet stringent requirements for quality and responsiveness, as well as offer a low price. The policy is "best source", not "cheapest source". A more standard critical-commodity – the provision of an emergency/standby computer centre – is commonly outsourced by businesses because a number of high-quality suppliers are available.

3. *'Useful-Commodities' – the myriad IT activities that provide incremental benefits to the business, but fail to distinguish it from its competitors.* In our experience, payroll, benefit, and accounting systems are the first examples

of useful-commodities volunteered by most businesses. But sweeping generalizations cannot be made, even within industries, as we have noted with the security guard firm. Useful-commodities are the prime candidates for outsourcing. We found many such examples in the cases, such as desktop computer support at a US chemical manufacturer, accounting services at UK oil company, and mainframe operations at a US commercial bank. External suppliers are likely to have achieved low costs and prices through standardization. The business makes further gains if it can free up internal management time to focus on more critical activities. But the expectation of outsourcing must be validated through analysis of economic considerations.

4. *'Useful-Differentiators' – IT activities that differentiate the business from its competitors, but in a way that is not critical to business success.* Useful-differentiators should not exist, but we have found that they frequently do. One reason is that the IT function is sometimes relatively isolated from the business and subsequently pursues its own agenda. For example, the IT department at a European paint manufacturer, created a system that precisely matched a paint formulation to a customer's color sample. IT managers envisioned that the system would create competitive advantage by meeting customers' wishes that paint should match their home furnishings. However, senior management had established the company's strategy as color innovation. They failed to market the system because it ran counter to their strategy, and the system became an expensive and ineffective distraction. The system was eventually eliminated.

A more common reason for the creation of useful-differentiators is that a potential commodity has been extensively reworked to reflect 'how we are different' or to incorporate the 'nice-to-haves'. This was an extensive phenomenon at a Dutch electronics company, resulting in very problematic and high cost software maintenance. The CIO of the company has now implemented a policy requiring that all needs for useful systems be met through standard software packages, with strict limits to customization. Useful-differentiators need to be eliminated from or migrated within an IT portfolio, but never outsourced merely to reduce their costs.

In summary, treating IT as a portfolio helps to identify outsourcing candidates by analyzing not only an IT activity's contribution to competitive strategy, but also its contribution to business operations. Through these two dimensions, senior executives more easily identify the value of IT. In addition to business contribution, economic considerations, which are often prematurely assumed to favor the supplier, are an important consideration in confirming the viability of IT outsourcing candidates.

Economic issues: comparing supplier offerings with in-house capabilities

Many senior executives may assume that a supplier can reduce their IT costs because suppliers possess inherent economies of scale that elude internal IT departments. But we have noted that a distinctive feature of IT is that economies of scale occur at a size achievable by many medium to large organizations. If this is true, how can a supplier under-bid current IT costs? Often, the answer is that suppliers implement efficient managerial practices that may be replicated by internal IT departments if empowered to do so (see also chapter 6). Successful companies we studied compare supplier bids not against current IT offerings, but against a newly-submitted bid prepared by internal IT managers.

As previously noted, many IT managers possess a plethora of ideas to reduce costs, but internal user resistance, or even outright user sabotage, may have hindered their efforts in the past. The problem stems from stakeholders within organizations who have different performance expectations for IT. Senior executives, who typically write the cheque for IT every year, often set cost minimization as the performance expectation for IT. Business units and users – who actually consume computer resources – often demand service excellence as their primary performance expectation. These expectations are in conflict because service excellence drives up IT costs. For example, users perceive software customization, local data centers, fast response time, and 24-hour help-lines as elements of service excellence – practices that drive up IT costs. IT managers are left to resolve the dilemma: provide a Rolls Royce service at a Chevrolet price.

Senior management's threat of outsourcing often serves to align IT performance expectations, typically with the cost minimization agenda. IT managers are then free to prepare bids which include cost reduction tactics practised by suppliers. These practices include chargeback systems to curtail user demand, employee empowerment to reduce supervision costs, consolidation of data centers to one physical site, standardization of software, automation of data center operations, and archival of inactive data. Users understand that if their internal IT managers, who are at least familiar to them, do not implement these practices, a hoard of supplier employees will.

We studied a number of turnaround cases where previous attempts by IT managers to reduce costs failed until senior management invited external and internal bids. To ensure fair play, internal bid teams are removed from the organization – in the case of a US petrochemicals company from Tulsa offices to a Dallas bunker – and treated with the same formality as suppliers. For example, all bidders submit questions in writing and responses are distributed to all parties. In these companies, the internal bids not only beat current IT costs, but significantly beat supplier bids. After insourcing, IT managers from an American food manufacturer reduced costs by 45% through software standardization. A US university reduced costs by 20% by reorganizing the IT department and eliminating redundant staff. An American petroleum company reduced costs by 43% by consolidating three data centers into one.

Case example: the outsourcing threat

Prior to the outsourcing threat, users in all these companies had resisted cost reduction practices. At a US telecommunications company, however, an outsourcing threat served to mobilize a more formidable opponent than users, namely an IT trade union. They rightfully perceived that the internal IT department was not cost competitive due to a strong IT labor union that promoted inefficient work practices. In particular, the union specified narrow job descriptions that created excessive staffing. For example, it forbade data center managers to touch the hardware and software, required a union manager on every shift, and called for both a manager and a worker in emergencies. Although the IT manager had tried many times to negotiate better terms, the strong labor union resisted. Only after the request for proposal attracted two external bids did the labor union agree to allow the internal IT department to include revised union rules in their internal bid. The union had to either succumb or risk losing the entire work site. The internal IT department subsequently reduced headcount by 45%.

Decision-making matrix

We have incorporated these two economic considerations – in-house economies of scale and adoption of leading practices – into a matrix to

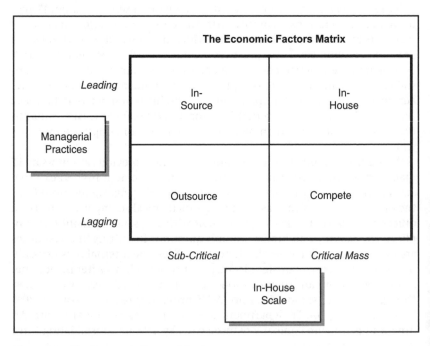

Figure 7.3   The Economic Factors Matrix

guide senior executives through these issues (see Figure 7.3). If the internal IT department has reached critical mass and has adopted leading management practices, it is unlikely a supplier will be able to reduce costs further because suppliers have to earn a profit, whereas internal IT departments merely need to cover costs. If the in-house IT department possesses theoretical economies of scale but has failed to implement efficient managerial practices, senior executives should allow internal IT managers to compete against supplier bids. As we have seen in the previous cases, competition serves to empower IT managers to overcome user resistance to the idea of reducing costs. If the internal IT department is of sub-critical mass but has adopted efficient practices, it is quite possible that a supplier's size advantage may be negated by their need to generate a profit. We recommend best source in these cases, that is, test the market to determine the economic validity of outsourcing. Finally, if the internal IT department is of sub-critical mass and has failed to adopt efficient practices, there is a strong economic justification for outsourcing. But even companies that fall in this quadrant may wish to empower IT to implement what practices they can before outsourcing to avoid giving the supplier the large share of easy savings.

But what happens when external supplier bids beat internal bids? Prudent managers question where and how the supplier proposes to earn a profit while still meeting the bid. In the most desirable scenario, suppliers clearly out-bid internal IT departments based on a number of valid reasons – superior management practices which could not be replicated by the internal staff, inherent economies of scale, or superior technical expertise. But in many cases, supplier bids may be based on "voodoo" economics, i.e. customers are offered long-term, fixed prices which are attractive in year one but will be out of step with price/performance improvements a few years into the contract. Or the supplier may be trying to buy market share in a fiercely competitive market. Once the contract is signed, the supplier may recoup losses by charging exorbitant excess fees for any change, realizing that customers are captive. Supplier bids may contain hidden costs. For example, a US commercial bank failed to question a software transfer fee license clause that ended up costing the bank half a million dollars.

Of particular note, some companies may actually seek a purely economic package based on financial manipulations rather than inherent best practices or efficiency. Two of our case studies – a US transportation company and a US aerospace company – used outsourcing to escape financial peril. The CFO from the transportation company signed a ten-year outsourcing contract when his company went bankrupt. Senior executives from the aerospace company signed a ten-year contract after several years of negative profits. These arrangements bought in multi-million dollar cash infusions when the supplier purchased IT assets, transferred 2,000 employees in one case and 1,600 employees in the other to a more stable supplier, and postponed fixed-fees until the later portion of the contract.

Technical issues: selecting an appropriate contract

Regardless of the impetus for outsourcing, once senior executives are convinced of the validity of supplier bids, the process continues by selecting appropriate contracting options. In practice, appropriate contracting depends on several important technical considerations. The danger in ignoring technical considerations is that senior executives may sign flimsy contracts which strongly favor suppliers. Suppliers negotiate many deals each month and understand the technical implications of contracting, while the customer company may have little or no experience with outsourcing. To counter-balance supplier negotiating power, senior executives must have a sound understanding of the specific service requirements associated with the outsourced technology. We have determined from our research that the degree of technology maturity and the degree of technology integration are two key technical considerations.

Technical maturity

The degree of technical maturity determines a company's ability to precisely define their requirements to suppliers. We describe an IT activity as having low technology maturity when the technology itself is new and unstable, when the business has little experience with a technology that may be better established elsewhere, and/or when the business is embarked on a radically new use of a familiar technology. Examples include an organization's first venture into imaging or wireless technologies, or the development of a major network to support a new business direction of globalization. In these instances, all that senior executives know for sure is that requirements will change over time, based on experience and the availability of new options.

Outsourcing technically immature activities engenders significant risk. Ironically, these are precisely the IT activities many senior executives wish to outsource, reasoning that suppliers possess the technical expertise lacking in-house. This practice often proves disastrous because companies are in no position to negotiate sound contracts. In addition, such companies lose a valuable learning opportunity which leaves them dependent on the supplier after implementation.

Consider the experiences of a US retailer. For all of Retail's history, local store managers decided which products to stock. Each store manager would look at Retail's product offerings and decide which products, colors, sizes, and quantities they wanted in their stores. In about 2000, Retail's senior leaders decided to centralize assortment. Retail needed a centralized assortment IT system to enable the change in business strategy. They offshore outsourced, with great success, the development of a centralized assortment program. The supplier built the application using a newer programming language. However, one negative consequence of the project was that Retail's internal team did not learn enough about the application to support it in production. The offshore supplier was given the maintenance contract. A Development Director at the retailer said, "If something happens to the [the supplier], God forbid, we'd be at a complete standstill" (Lacity and Rottman, 2008).

The important lesson from this case history is that the company lost a learning opportunity by completely outsourcing the new development of a strategic application. On the other hand, companies in this position may well benefit from an injection of external expertise to support their voyage of discovery. The recommendation is to 'buy-in' this expertise, but to integrate external resources into an internally-managed team. The business retains full management control and visibility of the project, capturing as much learning as possible about the technology and its application.

In contrast to the risks of outsourcing low technology maturity, there is significantly less risk in outsourcing activities characterized as technically mature. We can describe an IT activity as having high technology maturity when it represents well-established use of familiar technology. Data center operations and accounting systems were highly mature activities for many of our case companies. In these cases, the business has conquered the learning curve and reached a point where its requirements are well-specified and reasonably stable.

Outsourcing technically mature activities provides less risk to organizations because they can precisely define their requirements. For example, a US commercial bank outsourced its mainframe operations to a supplier. The CIO was able to negotiate an air-tight contract because of her experience and understanding of the requirements and costs of her mainframe operations. In the contract, she fully specified the service levels required, such as response time and availability, service level measures, cash penalties for non-performance, and adjustments to changes in business volumes. After three years into the contract, she achieved the anticipated savings of 10%.

Degree of integration

A second important technical consideration is the degree of integration with other business processes. In the simplest case, an IT activity is easily separated out and handed over to suppliers. For example, a US chemicals company successfully contracted out support for desktop computers. The CIO wanted to outsource desktop support because the growing demand forced him into regular and poorly received requests for additional headcount. Through his two-year outsourcing contract, he reduced costs and avoided further requests for staffing.

In cases where technical integration with other business processes is high, the risks of outsourcing increase. For example, when a UK food manufacturer outsourced the development of factory automation, managers soon realized that the new system had profound implications for almost every business unit in the company. Although the supplier was an expert in factory automation software, it lacked an understanding of business interfaces. The system took four years to develop instead of two.

In contrast, one financial services company – outside our research but widely documented – successfully outsourced the development of a highly integrated system using a preferred supplier model. This company invested in imaging technology to replace paper records (such as customer letters) with an electronic file. The company first explored the technology through a discrete research and development project. Senior executives reached a point at which they were convinced of the benefits of large scale adoption but realized that many of their existing systems would now be affected. At this stage, the company turned to its preferred IT supplier, a supplier with a very broad product line, with whom it had worked for many years. Resisting the supplier's instinct to develop a detailed fixed-price agreement, the company set up an enabling, resource-based contract. The project was completed successfully, providing competitive advantage for both the business and its supplier, which had established a reference site for its own imaging products.

Technical considerations – the degree of technical maturity and degree of integration – strongly suggest the need to limit the length of contracts. A typical respondent view from our research is that three years is the maximum period for which one could assume requirements would be stable.

Making technical decisions

We have mapped the two technical considerations – technology maturity and integration- in Figure 7.4. Of particular note is the absence of the term "strategic partnership" from the contracting options. The strategic partnership contracting model has been widely recommended as the preferred governor of outsourcing contracts (DiRomualdo and Gurbaxani, 1998; Henderson, 1990; McFarlan and Nolan, 1995). But we have seen the rhetoric of strategic partnership used as an excuse to sign poorly constructed contracts and lead to failure in five of our total outsourcing cases. We argue that strategic partnerships require shared – or at least complementary – risks and rewards (Willcocks and Lacity, 2006). In the five total outsourcing failures, this requirement was missing. Instead, every dollar out of the customer's pocket in terms of excess fees or hidden contractual costs went directly into the supplier's pocket.

Instead of the term 'strategic partnership', we have labeled relationships based on shared or complementary goals as 'preferred contractors'. With a preferred contractor strategy, companies engage in a relationship with the supplier to help mediate risk. This strategy worked best for technically

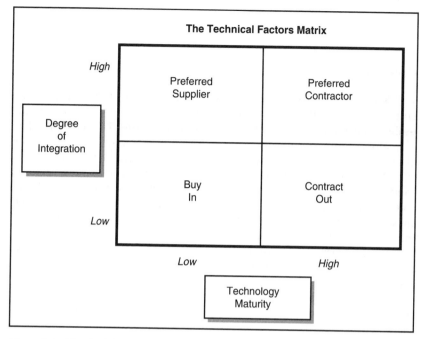

Figure 7.4 The Technical Factors Matrix

mature and highly integrated IT activities. Because of technical maturity, companies can negotiate a detailed contract in which the supplier is responsible for the management and delivery of an IT activity. Because of the high integration with other business processes, companies must develop a close relationship to maintain the integrity of interfaces. To ensure supplier performance, the company tries to construct an incentive-based contract that ensures shared goals. For example, when a Dutch electronics company decided to reduce costs by outsourcing data center operations and support of existing systems, it mediated risk by entering into a joint venture with a software house. By establishing a jointly-owned company, it created shared goals that prevented supplier opportunism. In another example, a large British clothing and household products company set up such an arrangement with one of the biggest outsourcing suppliers. In a ten-year deal, the supplier will provide almost all the company's IT services. In addition, the retailer and the supplier will share profits from exploitation elsewhere of the retailers existing and future systems. For example, the supplier has already proposed to market the retailer's data models, which will generate profits for both parties. In the words of one of the Directors of the retail business: "We believe, as they do, that we are working together to make the profit pie bigger rather than just arguing over who gets the biggest piece."

The success of the deal depends on these attitudes being maintained, and on achieving a bigger profit pie.

Conclusions

The frameworks we have described have a number of strengths. They are empirically derived, focus attention on the critical factors, and provide usable tools for a variety of decision-making processes. To our knowledge, 11 major corporations have actively employed these frameworks in arriving at an effective IT sourcing strategy. For example, Grand Metropolitan, a US$14 billion global corporation, that manufactures and markets branded foods and drinks, used the decision-making framework to review its IT sourcing strategy. The analysis structured IT into ten major activities. Of these, five were potential candidates for outsourcing. The company determined that the market was not yet sufficiently mature for two other functions; it is waiting to outsource those, while improving current in-house performance. It is benchmarking the three remaining activities. The process resulted in clear identification of the candidates for outsourcing together with a planned program of formal benchmarking to assess the ongoing in-house performance against opportunities in the IT services market. The director of IS Planning, Berwick Mitchell, commented: 'The frameworks and process allowed us to clearly identify and assess the factors that were most important for GrandMet in making IS sourcing decisions. We were able to involve both senior business executives and technical staff in the review process in a structured way, and were able to reach rational conclusions that now have support across the organization'.

Such experiences, and those of our case study organizations suggest a number of final points. The outsourcing market is changing in the customer's favor. Once dominated by a few big US-based players – EDS, CSC and IBM – the IT outsourcing market has since dramatically grown with other global players like CGI based in Canada, Cap Gemini based in France, and Wipro and Infosys based in India. In addition, tens of thousands of smaller suppliers offer niche services. As competition in the outsourcing market increases, companies have more power to bargain for shorter contracts, more select services, and better financial packages. Also in the customer's favor is a growing experience base with IT outsourcing, which allows customers to intelligently evaluate and negotiate outsourcing deals. In fact many of our respondent companies adopted incremental outsourcing precisely to mitigate risk and develop in-house learning from outsourcing over time. Our evidence points to long-term total outsourcing as a possible option only for those highly experienced in IT outsourcing contracts and in managing major, long-term relationships with suppliers (Kaiser and Hawk, 2004).

More importantly, juxtaposed with the growing evidence, including our own, of the problems with an all-or-nothing approach to IT outsourcing are the benefits of selective sourcing. When companies properly select and contract for specific IT activities by treating IT as a dynamic portfolio, companies maintain management and control of core IT activities – such as strategic planning, scanning the environment for new technologies applicable to business needs, development of business-specific applications, and support of critical systems – while still accessing supplier expertise and economies of scale for well-defined, isolated, or mature IT acti-vities. We believe, based on good evidence, that strong in-house capabilities empowers a company to better engage outsourcing suppliers (see Chapter 15).

References

Clemons, E. and Row, M. (1988) "McKesson Drug Company," *Journal of Management Information Systems*, Vol. 5, 1, Summer pp. 36–50.

Copeland, D. and McKenney, J. (1988) "Airline Reservation Systems: Lessons From History," *MIS Quarterly*, Vol. 12, 3, pp. 353–370.

DiRomualdo, A. and Gurbaxani, V. (1998) "Strategic Intent for IT Outsourcing," *Sloan Management Review*, Vol. 39, 4, pp. 67–80.

Henderson, J. (1990) "Plugging into Strategic Partnerships: The Critical IS Connection," *Sloan Management Review*, Vol. 31, 3, pp. 7–18.

Kaiser, K. and Hawk, S. (2004) "Evolution of Offshore Software Development: From Outsourcing to Co-Sourcing," *MIS Quarterly Executive*, Vol. 3, 2, pp. 69–81.

Lacity, M. and Rottman, J. (2008) *Offshore Outsourcing of IT Work*, United Kingdom: Palgrave.

Lacity, M. and Hirschheim, R. (1993) *Information Systems Outsourcing: Myths, Metaphors and Realities*, Chichester: Wiley.

Lacity, M. and Hirschheim, R. (1995) *Beyond The Information Systems Outsourcing Bandwagon*, Chichester: Wiley.

Lacity, M., Hirschheim, R. and Willcocks, L. (1994) "Realizing Outsourcing Expectations: Incredible Expectations, Credible Outcomes," *Journal of Information Systems Management*, Vol. 11, 4, pp. 7–18.

Lacity, M. and Willcocks, L. (2001) *Global Information Technology Outsourcing: In Search of Business Advantage*, Chichester: Wiley.

Lacity, M., Willcocks, L. and Feeny, D. (1995) "IT Outsourcing – Maximize Flexibility and Control," *Harvard Business Review*, 73, 3, May–June, pp. 84–93.

Lacity, M., Willcocks, L. and Feeny, D. (1996) "The Value of Selective IT Sourcing," *Sloan Management Review*, Vol. 37, 3, p. 13–25.

McFarlan, F.W. and Nolan, R. (1995) "How to Manage an IT Outsourcing Alliance," *Sloan Management Review*, Vol. 36, 2, pp. 9–23.

Niederman, F., Mathieu, R., Morley, R. and Kwon, I. (2007) "Examining RFID Applications in Supply Chain," *Communications of the ACM*, Vol. 50, 7, p. 92–101.

Prahalad, C. and Hamel, G. (1991) "The Core Competence of the Corporation," *Harvard Business Review*, Vol. 63, 3, pp. 79–91.

Rossetti, C. and Choi, T. (2005) "On the Dark Side of Strategic Sourcing: Experiences from the Aerospace Industry," *The Academy of Management Executive*, Vol. 19, 1, pp. 46.

Venkatraman, N. and Short, J. (1990) *Strategies for Electronic Integration: From Order-Entry to Value-Added Partnerships at Baxter.* MIT Working Paper, Sloan School of Management, Massachusetts.

Willcocks, L. and Lacity, M. (2006) *Global Sourcing of Business and IT Services*, London: Palgrave.

8
Taking a Knowledge Perspective on IT and Business Process Outsourcing

Leslie P. Willcocks, John Hindle, David Feeny and Mary C. Lacity

Introduction

Even in semi-recessionary times, in the developed economies IT and business process outsourcing have been some of the biggest business trends and highest growth sectors. For example on our figures IT outsourcing global revenues moved from US\$ 154 billion to over US\$ 200 billion across the 2002–5 period. Business process outsourcing (BPO) grew more than 25% per annum across 2002–3 in the UK. In Europe, across 2002–5 BPO revenues increased from 43 billion to 72 billion Euros. The USA also experienced noteworthy BPO growth throughout the 2000–2008 period. These figures are likely to increase by at least 7% (ITO) and 10% (BPO) per annum over the 2005–12 period (Willcocks and Cullen, 2005; Oshri *et al.*, 2008) But despite outsourcing's rise to become a perennial, if not yet routine way of managing IT and business processes, it is surprising that its knowledge management implications have received so little attention, something, we predict, will continue over the next five years Willcocks and Craig, 2007).

One view, supported by a number of our case studies, is that, most typically, organizations simply lack the means and experiential research to assign value to the knowledge they are transferring and receiving, and no real understanding of how new knowledge can be created in outsourcing situations, let alone exploited. Nor are they inclined to assign that much importance to what is after all pre-defined as a 'non-core' set of outsourced activities But whatever the cause, lack of focus on what happens to knowledge when an organization outsources is a serious gap in practice, and one that deserves serious study and analysis. An analogy may help to make this point. People who suffer the loss of a limb frequently report they continue to feel its presence long afterwards. "Phantom limb sensation" affects some 80% of amputees, and arises when the brain remaps neural signals inputs from other areas of the body to adapt to the loss of sensory information – crossing the wires, as it were, to compensate. Many organizations report similar effects when they outsource key functions – cut off from knowledge and skills of former employees, the *corps commercial* struggles to adjust. And for the severed population, grafted onto a new body, the shift in identity, direction, and authority results in aimless motion and misspent energy.

We proceed to investigate knowledge issues in outsourcing by first describing intellectual capital, and how, by harnessing social capital, it can be developed and leveraged. We then apply these ideas to five major sourcing arrangements to show how intellectual capital can be missed or evolved and leveraged. In particular we focus on a detailed case of "enterprise partnering" that establishes a highly pertinent benchmark for those assessing how to use outsourcing to create and exploit knowledge. We compare the enterprise partnering case with two others of more conventional ITO and BPO arrangements and draw a number of conclusions for practice.

Developing intellectual capital

Most students and practitioners of knowledge management are familiar with the formulation adopted by Stewart (2001) and others to describe the essential elements or assets that contribute to the development of intellectual capital:

- *structural capital*, representing "the codified bodies of semi-permanent knowledge that can be transferred" and "the tools that augment the body of knowledge by bringing relevant data or expertise to people"
- *human capital*, or "the capabilities of the individuals required to provide solutions to customers"
- *customer capital*, or "the value of an organization's relationships with the people with whom it does business – shared knowledge"

While there are specific investments and activities that can strengthen each of these elements, Stewart (2001) argues that creating intellectual capital is more complicated than simply hiring bright people or buying a knowledge management software programme: "...intellectual capital is not created from discrete wads of human, structural, and customer capital, but from the *interplay* among them." How, then, can organizations create the conditions, structures, and policies that encourage "interplay?" What specific actions can they take to maximize knowledge exchange and combination? We suggest there are intentional ways of creating a fourth kind of capital – social capital – which facilitates the development of trusted knowledge paths.

From a sociologist's perspective, social capital is the value of the social network individuals belong to and their inclination to do things for each other because of that network. Somewhat more simply, it is the value suggested by the motto from Cheers, "where everybody knows your name." It is the value represented by trust, loyalty and reciprocity within a community. Nahapiet and Ghoshal (1998) have examined the catalyst role of social capital in developing intellectual capital. They identify three specific dimensions of social capital that facilitate the "interplay" that Stewart speaks of:

- the *structural dimension*, which involves the network ties and configuration and "appropriable" organization that facilitate access to people and resources, thus promoting the combining and exchange of intellectual capital
- the *cognitive dimension*, which involves the shared "cultural" context of the organization – the language, codes, and narratives that provide ways of knowing and create meaning
- the *relational dimension*, which involves trust and group identity (norms, obligations, identification), creating a sense of common motivation, purpose and benefit.

Their research then maps the requirements for productive "interplay" – the ingredients for successful knowledge combination and exchange – against these three dimensions. Because these conditions are difficult, if not impossible, to achieve in pure market transactions, Nahapiet and Ghoshal argue that organizations have a special advantage over markets in creating new intellectual capital. Moreover, they argue, the process of what Stewart calls "interplay" is recursive: social capital facilitates the development of new intellectual capital, which in turn strengthens social capital. So we face an apparent conundrum: if membership in the organization conveys such a powerful advantage in creating intellectual capital, how can outsourcing, which involves the externalisation of huge swathes of people, systems, and institutional knowledge, possibly create greater advantage? Let us examine the knowledge implications of the major in-house and external sourcing options.

Back office improvement: from in-house to partnering

In this section we review our research base of over 450 case studies of back office initiatives (Cullen and Willcocks, 2003; Feeny, Willcocks and Lacity, 2003, 2005; Lacity and Willcocks, 2001; Willcocks and Currie, 1997; Willcocks and Griffiths, 1997; Willcocks, Petherbridge and Olson, 2002) covering five different options used in practice (see Figure 8.1). All five make considerable assumptions about what will happen to knowledge, assumptions that are often belied by what happens in practice. We list the potential benefits and risks identified during our research. The main focus below will be on outsourcing but let us look briefly at the "Do-It-Yourself" (DIY) and "Management Consultancy" options.

On "DIY", the case studies of Willcocks and Currie (1997) and Willcocks and Griffiths (1997) show that, in principle, this should be a strong option

Back-Office Performance Improvement

	'DIY'	'MANAGEMENT CONSULTANCY'	'OUTSOURCING I.T. OPERATIONS'	'FEE-FOR-SERVICE BPO'	'ENTERPRISE PARTNERING'
EXAMPLES	• Efficiency drives • Internal re-engineering • Technology solutions	• Analysis work • ERP • BPR • Major change initiatives	• Selective/total • Data centre/Networks • Desk-tops • Development	• Accounting • Human Resources • Call centres	– HR Transactions – Insurance Settlement/Claims – Procurement
POTENTIAL BENEFITS	– Gains accrued internally – Under in-house control/ownership – Easier to sustain gains made	– Infusion of external energy, skills – By-passing political resistance – Scale to handle work	– Hand over legacy – Reforms in-house systems development – Improves Management Practices – Cost savings	– Hand over non-core processes – Cost and efficiency gains – Access to skills and scale – Leverage off-shore advantages	– Cost and quality gains – Technology investment – Continuous improvement through (a) generic competencies (b) risk-reward – Securing new customers – Retaining/developing superior management and knowledge
RISKS	– Inertia of Legacy • Systems • Processes • Culture – Political issues e.g. over service standardization – Lack of skills, focus, investment	– Skills not transferred – Change doesn't 'stick' – Cost escalation – Little ownership of outcomes	– Lack of innovation – Technology investment not sustained – Cost-service trade-offs – Cost of add-on services – Loss of know-how	– Motivation to invest/innovate? – One-off gains – Cost-service trade-offs – Add-on services? – Loss of know-how	

Copyright (C) Feeny, Willcocks, Lacity (2003.)

Figure 8.1 Back Office Improvement: Five Options

from a knowledge perspective. In theory social capital should be strong, while structural, human and customer capital may be more variable, depending on past knowledge management practices and size of organization. However, the initiative, if set up well, offers large scope for knowledge assimilation and creation, with a view to subsequent exploitation. In practice, especially with back office initiatives, we found legacy systems, processes and culture, and political issues often creating barriers, or a lower level ambition on improvement, and knowledge creation. Moreover, back office improvement often did not attract prioritization on skills, sustained focus and the necessary technical and financial investments.

As a result, many of the organizations got attracted into the "Management Consultancy" route, looking for an infusion of human capital in the form of new skills, energy and knowledge, and structural capital in the form of knowledge bases and best practices that could be offered as a result of the scale and specialist expertise consultancy firms could offer. While in many cases this approach paid off, the risks all too often materializing were that skills and knowledge – structural and human capital – were not transferred to the client, change did not "stick" and there was little internal learning or ownership of outcomes. Clients often complained of paying for the consultant's learning, while learning little themselves. Such initiatives lacked the "glue" or knowledge transfer vehicle of social capital. New knowledge was rarely created for and internalized by the client, who rarely leveraged intellectual capital inherent in the initiative subsequently.

Knowledge in IT outsourcing: a missed opportunity

If we move to the third option, the promise from IT outsourcing is to leverage the supplier's superior management practices (structural capital) and skills (human capital), as well as plug into its scale economies arising from using a specialist IT service provider. But our own research into IT outsourcing has shown consistently over the last decade that prospects have been disappointing for meaningful knowledge management, and value creation therefrom (Cullen and Willcocks, 2003; Willcocks and Lacity, 2009). Most clients report their frustration with endless cost-service debates, and sometimes significant loss of control over their IT destiny and knowledge base. Most vendors find it difficult to deliver on their promises of innovation and value added, not least hampered by their lack of knowledge about the client's long-term business strategy (Feeny, Willcocks and Lacity, 2003).

The outsourcing promise is regularly made of superior technical know-how, superior management practices, economies of scale and, increasingly, access to strategic and business advice enabling the client to refocus on strategic, core capability and knowledge areas. More typically, even on the very big, long-term deals considered strategic relationships by their participants, our research has shown that the supplier offers technical know-how for routine solutions, with high performers in short supply. There is little influx of new technical/managerial talent, and disappointing access to the supplier's global capability and knowledge bases. Meanwhile the client does not think through thoroughly the issues of core capability and retained knowledge. As a result the client spends much time fire-fighting, and experiences little value-added or technical/business innovation. Over time, the client loses control over its IT or business process destiny as knowledge assymmetries develop in favour of the vendor (Cullen and Willcocks, 2003; Willcocks and Lacity, 2009).

The loss of information and knowledge can be traumatic for both outsourcing parties unless specific and purposeful steps are undertaken to develop and sustain new information pathways and mechanisms. One route we have advocated is the retention of nine core capabilities (Feeny and Willcocks, 1998). These ensure the elicitation and delivery of business requirements, the development of technical/business architecture, the managing of external supply, and the coordination and governance of these tasks. In practice, we have found all too many client organizations inadequately making these critical, initial, knowledge investments (see also Chapter 15 of the present volume).

Thus in two studies of major deals (Kern and Willcocks, 2001; Lacity and Willcocks, 2001), we found a more frequent pattern of clients focusing on contract monitoring and management, and of understaffing business facing and technology facing activities. In particular, the belief was that "technical architecture" and 'making technology work' were prime outsourcing targets. But, for example, after several years both DuPont in its 1997 CSC/ Andersen Consulting deal and Commonwealth Bank in its 1996 10-year EDS arrangement, discovered the vital need to rebuild their technical architecture capability and so retain more control over their IT destiny. Client organizations also routinely underestimate the degree of high performing technical "doing" capability they need to retain to deal with idiosyncratic business systems, non-routine problems, and the historically derived complexities of the technical infrastructure – all areas where suppliers do not play from a position of knowledge strength.

Typically, in managing external suppliers, client organizations also under-invest initially in the knowledge areas of informed buying and vendor development. They also inadequately secure ways in which to build shared knowledge from relationships and interchanges back into the business – through relationship building and business systems thinking capabilities (Reynolds *et al.*, 2007). We find that, in failing to make these knowledge investments, client organizations invariably run into a range of problems, which, together with a rising awareness of over-dependence on the supplier, leads to belated re-insourcing of these capabilities. One of the most obvious candidates we have seen here is the technical "doing" capability associated with applications development. The alternative is increasing problems as the client organization loses knowledge, control over its IT destiny, and the ability to leverage IT for business value.

Knowledge in business process outsourcing: an IT replay?

But this approach to outsourcing restricts creation and leveraging of knowledge only to one specialist area – IT operations. Much bigger gains can arise if whole functions or processes that include IT are outsourced. This is the premise of the dramatic growth in business process outsourcing (BPO) from 2001. BPO suppliers come in many forms – as pure plays (e.g. Xchanging, Exult), specialist providers (e.g. in logistics Ryder, UPS; in customer care Convergys; in finance and accounting (e.g. Core3), as IT outsourcers extending their range (e.g. EDS, CSC), consultants moving further into the market (e.g. Accenture, PwC), vertical specialists (e.g. McKesson in Healthcare) business service providers (e.g. Employease in HR) software providers (e.g. Genesys) or offshore providers (e.g. Wipro, Infosys).

Most of these services are offered on a fee-for-service basis. The knowledge contract is to outsource non-core (though often critical), largely back-office commodities to suppliers with superior structural and human capital in the areas of business process and specific expertise. Some deals recognize the need also for closer partnering in order to get closer to the customer (to create and leverage customer capital to both parties' advantage, and also create and leverage social capital across client and service provider.

In practice, while BPO is often handled much like classic fee-for-service IT outsourcing, such deals lie much closer to the business and the knowledge implications are even greater, though, in our experience, just as neglected. One fear is that the emergent BPO market players and their clients will repeat many of the knowledge and capability mistakes made during the early 1990s IT outsourcing boom years. The potential dangers we notice here are loss of internal business process know-how, need to create requisite capability to manage the supplier, will the supplier be sufficiently motivated to invest knowledge and innovate in a sustained way, or will there be only one-off gains, additional service charges, and interminable cost-service wrangles, basically over the price of knowledge and capability supplied. That said, these knowledge affects may well be disguised for a time by real cost and service improvements, simply because so many back-office business processes inherited by suppliers are, in our experience, so inefficient.

Enterprise partnership as a knowledge benchmark: the London insurance markets

A fifth option we have researched is that of establishing a risk-reward partnership between the client and supplier (Feeny, Willcocks and Lacity, 2003).

This can be applied to both IT and business process operations and improvement. So far we have seen few such deals in operation. The ones we have researched suggest the promise of significant cost and quality gains and technology investment. Additionally, there is a stronger emphasis on continuous improvement through the application of generic rather than specialist competencies on the part of the supplier. Even more significant (and distinctive) is the risk-reward and joint ownership arrangement that lies at the centre of such a deal, and the implications these features have for how knowledge is applied, created and exploited. Let us look at one such deal in the London insurance markets.

In May 2001 Lloyds of London/Insurance Underwriters' Association outsourced the back office policy and claims settlement systems for the London insurance markets to Xchanging. Learning from outsourcing history, the Xchanging approach introduces three key innovations. Firstly, the Enterprise Partnership business model (see Figure 8.2). Xchanging Insurance Services (XIS) was set up to serve as the Lloyd's of London and IUA back-office. Xchanging created a new service-providing organization that is jointly owned by client and vendor, who both share in its cost savings and profits. By assuming full responsibility for all transferred employees, moreover, Xchanging preserves transferred knowledge, service and relationships, and

The Enterprise Partnership: Business Model

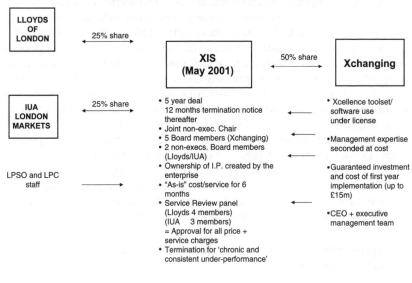

Copyright (C) Feeny, Willcocks, Lacity (2003.)

Figure 8.2   Xchanging Insure Services: Business Model

establishes an organization capable of delivering service seamlessly on an "As-Is" basis.

The Enterprise Partnership model entails multiple joint governance bodies: a Board of Directors, a Service Review Board, and a Technology Review Board. These governance mechanisms formally engage both client and vendor in a continuous process of joint planning and decision-making, ensuring that business strategies are understood and decisions taken with full knowledge, in the best interests of the enterprise partnership rather than for the sole or lopsided benefit of one or the other party. A side benefit of this knowledge-sharing governance system is the creation of trust and mutual obligation, which reinforces the institutional relationship.

In Stewart's terms one can see clearly elements of "customer capital" being created here. But in the deeper context of Nahapiet and Ghoshal's social capital research, the Enterprise Partnership business model creates a robust *structural dimension*, with a formal governance network and a jointly held organization that can be "appropriated" to develop new intellectual capital and value. It also creates the necessary anticipation of value that can arise from joining Xchanging's transformational expertise with the domain-specific knowledge being transferred.

The second innovation is an Xcellence Competency model which defines seven knowledge-based capabilities used to transform the legacy back office into a profitable Enterprise Partnership: Service, People, Process, Technology, Environment, Sourcing, and Implementation. Each competency is headed up by a highly experienced Practice Director (an example of Stewart's "human capital"), who is responsible for establishing and maintaining the competency's explicit knowledge capital in the form of a detailed competency Manual, representing, in Stewart's terms, "structural capital". Further, the Practice Director is responsible for establishing the competency in each Enterprise Partnership using mainly transferred staff. This requirement ultimately builds a community of practice at the Xchanging level across all the Enterprise Partnerships, thus promoting development and sharing of tacit knowledge and its conversion to explicit knowledge. These practice communities meet regularly, communicate online, and network with other practitioners inside and outside their organizations.

In the context of Nahapiet and Ghoshal's social capital model, the Xcellence competencies establish a shared *cognitive dimension*. They employ distinctive languages and "codes" that facilitate business transformation and knowledge exchange – the practice communities are rich environments for shared narratives. Further, the Xcellence platform facilitates access amongst practitioners, reinforces their expectation that they create value by sharing knowledge, and offers the ability to combine accumulated knowledge from across all the Enterprises.

The final key element of the Xchanging approach that creates significant social capital is its four-phased Implementation model: Preparation,

Realignment, Streamlining, and Continuous Improvement. The purpose of the implementation model is to synchronize the significant changes that take place within the former employee population and the now-client community, and to establish and manage expectations between the partners.

This innovation contributes significantly to creating the ***relational dimension*** of social capital. Recognizing that staff will initially feel powerless and resentful in an outsourcing situation, and that it takes considerable time for them to re-orient themselves to new circumstances, Xchanging's implementation approach carefully stages business transformation activity to their readiness to accept and support it.

As mentioned earlier, all employees are transferred to the Enterprise Partnership on day one, and go through an intensive change programme that lasts up to two years. Led by the People Competency, the process focuses on the Tuckman developmental cycle of Mourning, Forming, Storming, Norming, and Performing. The net result is the deliberate creation of a new culture – that of a dynamic, profitable business – to supplant the previous neglected-cost-center mindset. The process is not without cost, both direct cost in creating time for employees to make the transition, and indirect cost in deferring gains until staff are fully prepared. But this effort to build group identity and trust, establish norms of behavior and performance, and instil a sense of mutual obligation yields enormous benefits in the exchange and combination of knowledge.

As at beginning of 2004 the Lloyds of London/IUA/XIS deal was well into its third year and was adjudged very successful by all participants. XIS was achieving substantial performance improvements and cost reductions for the back office of the London Insurance markets. Partly this was because it had so many major generic competencies to apply to the cause of continuous improvement. The parties were making good profits, not least because XIS was regularly securing additional clients, and in 2003 Xchanging also won an innovator of the year award for its work at Lloyds of London and for the IUA. At the same time some risks should be noted. Internal success does not guarantee competitiveness in the open market, nor additional external customers. (In this case by 2008 Xchanging had attracted additional customers for its insurance services entity; however the human resource entity it established with BAE Systems had failed to find another customer). Conflicts can arise between maximizing the enterprise partnership's profits, and minimizing the client's costs. The governance structure does rely on both sides investing the necessary effort and resources in long-term joint customer and supplier participation, decision-making and participation.

Discussion: two comparisons

The enterprise partnership is just one, if distinctive, way of contracting for knowledge in outsourcing. However, in our view it acts as a key benchmark as to what is possible, and what needs to be in place to make knowledge creation and use happen. A useful comparison can be made with two other approaches that would also claim to be making investments in knowledge. One is a self-acknowledged strategic relationship signalled by taking shares in the supplier. The other considers itself a closer partnering arrangement than many. We critically evaluate these and their knowledge implications below.

Commonwealth Bank Australia

More details of this case appears in Chapter 15. Here we focus primarily on the knowledge issues. In 1997 Commonwealth Bank Australia (CBA) signed a 10-year preferred supplier, sole source contract with EDS for improving the IT contribution to the business. Knowledge capital was provided in the form of technical expertise and new management processes were provided as well as business advisory and consulting skills. CBA also took a 33% minority share interest in EDS Australia to bind client and supplier closer together and create social capital, though this tended not be created at lower, operational levels. From 1997–2001 CBA achieved its objectives in relation to IT cost reduction as a proportion of the bank's overall non-interest expense, while IT services were maintained largely to agreed service levels.

However, by 2000–1 CBA felt that knowledge and capability asymmetries had developed in favour of the vendor, and that the bank was losing control of its IT destiny. Nor did it always feel that it was getting the knowledge influx it required from the supplier, though it was not always in the best position to make such judgements. As a result, over the next 18 months, under its CIO Bob McKinnon, the IT function went about building up its internal capabilities, especially in the areas of technical architecture, service delivery, planning, contract monitoring, informed buying and governance. In knowledge terms these were attempts to build the necessary structural, human and customer capital (the customers being CBA business units) needed to leverage supplier and IT performance. Late into this process, the IT function also added business thinking and relationship building capabilities to align with business requirements and help business units identify and deliver on the potential business value of IT. Through all this the CIO emphasized the need to operate in a teaming manner both within the IT function, as well as in relationships with user staff in the business units. In this respect this was creating social capital by which knowledge could be transferred between the parties created, and exploited. By 2003 business units, central strategy group and the IT function were actively designing new governance mechanisms for planning for and exploiting IT. It can be seen here that a knowledge capital strategy has been put in place, but it largely treats the supplier as a bought resource, assuming little knowledge interchange, or mutual knowledge creation. By 2005, however, CBA had set about rebuilding its internal capability and knowledge base, and this issue is pursued further in Chapter 15.

Bank of America

In late 2000 Bank of America (BoA) outsourced its commodity human resource processes and services to Exult on a ten-year $1.7 billion contract. Benefits included guaranteed cost savings (plus 10% on process, plus 40% for systems integration and HR self-service investment) and qualitative improvements, e.g. speed of error rectification). Exult's job is to manage the HR back office to Six Sigma standards, and improve the shared HR service organization's performance and headcount by applying Exult's scale, expertise and volume. Over 600 employees were transferred to Exult, representing a considerable knowledge transfer. Exult took over the banks service centre in Charlotte North Carolina in exchange for Exult stock worth $50 million. The bank and Exult are also web portal partners, with bank employees using portal to handle HR issues, while the plan is for the bank to become the preferred provider of financial services and banking products to employees of other Exult clients. Another aspect of closer partnering is that the bank stands to gain a 3–10% share of revenues from third party use of the HR service run by Exult for BoA.

Classically, as for IT, the deal outsources commodity activities to enable the bank to focus on core competencies in HR and the rest of the business. There is a large knowledge transfer of employees to Exult, who are then hired back to the bank. Exult brings to bear their superior knowledge and skills in the HR area, their process expertise and their superior web-based technologies to reduce the need for the bank to make future technology and infrastructure investments. The promise is that their HR scale and specialization will bring to bear the capability to reduce HR costs by over 10% per annum while driving innovation and improvements in HR service. By late 2003 the bank reported being very satisfied with progress on all its goals as a result of outsourcing.

The risks, however do remain as for the earlier large-scale, mainly fee-for-service IT outsourcing deals recorded above. From a knowledge perspective the bank could see an erosion of its ability to understand, have an informed dialogue with and manage the supplier over HR activities and processes. Lack of in-house structural and human capital in this area could be risky, given that HR processes touch every employee. It is also not clear whether the partnering mechanisms go deep and far enough to create the social capital which will really prompt knowledge transfer, creation and exploitation across the two organizations. Also, will Exult staff continue to build customer capital and leverage this to make improvements in the customer's experience, or will improvements be restricted only to what has been contracted for? The client also becomes very reliant on Exult's willingness over a long time period to provide its best managers, knowledge bases and practices to the account. On the other hand, if, as we find in many other cases, the Bank of America HR services were not particularly efficient before they were outsourced, it may well be the case cost reduction and improvements in HR service can be made for quite some time without much new knowledge being created or applied.

Conclusion: competing on knowledge

Our judgement is that increasingly, under rising pressure to cut costs, compete and deliver, both clients and suppliers need to become much more aware of the role of knowledge assimilation, creation and application in achieving back-office improvements. As such the focus will increasingly need to move to understanding in a more fine-grained way what knowledge needs to be retained, and how to guarantee a supplier will posses, create and leverage the structural, human and customer capital needed to deliver on ambitious outsourcing objectives and claims. The further development suggested by the Xchanging example, compared to the Commonwealth Bank and Bank of America cases, is the advantages in creating social capital as the glue that converts intellectual capital into transferred and applied knowledge for business improvement.

A knowledge-based perspective does reveal that if undertaking fee-for-service outsourcing, there are limits to what can be achieved. Our prescriptions for fee-for-service outsourcing deals have been arrived at through exhaustive research. The advice remains: write complete, detailed contracts; carry out due diligence ahead of signing the contract, retain core in-house capabilities; ensure that you and the supplier have a cultural fit; be sure the supplier has sector and domain knowledge and experience; don't outsource a "mess"; and write short-term (3–5 year) contracts because the circumstances and technologies will change fast. Knowledge can be created and leveraged following this advice, but, we would contend, only to a limited extent. Both sides still bring to the party an unnecessarily constrained focus on knowledge.

But these prescriptions partly arise because knowledge assumptions and contracts between customer and supplier are often flawed, and because all too often this inhibits investment in requisite supplier and client knowledge capabilities. Changing the business, governance and implementation models allows knowledge strategy a more central, leveraging role in outsourcing. Xchanging's innovations are interesting because they support development of intellectual and social capital essential to the sharing, creation and exploitation of new knowledge. Instead of false signals and misdirected energy, the model actively incents and supports the creation and exploitation of new intellectual property.

At the same time, adopting something like an Xchanging enterprise partnership framework does require a new, different set of assumptions. For example: sign short, incomplete contracts for five years or more. Carry out diligence after contract signing. Let the supplier clean up your back-office mess. Create a clash of cultures if you want to see real back-office improvement. Hire a supplier with generic rather than domain-specific competencies. Given the history of outsourcing these modes of operating may well feel too counter-intuitive. Many may well see adopting these assumptions as too big a cultural step and too risky. At the same time, these changes in management practice on the part of both client and supplier may well be the only real way to release the knowledge potential inherent in the practice of IT and business process outsourcing. And in an ever commoditizing outsourcing market, with ever more demanding customers, it may well be that competing on knowledge becomes the new game in town, and one of the few real ways in which suppliers will be able to differentiate their services.

References

Cullen, S. and Willcocks, L. (2003) *Intelligent IT Outsourcing: Eight Building Blocks To Success*. Oxford: Butterworth.

Feeny, D. and Willcocks, L. (1998) Core IS Capabilities for exploiting Information Technology, *Sloan Management Review*, Vol. 39, Spring, 1998, pp. 9–21.

Feeny, D., Willcocks, L. and Lacity, M. (2003) *Business Process Outsourcing: The Promise Of Enterprise Partnership*. Templeton Executive Briefing. Oxford: Templeton College.

Feeny, D., Willcocks, L. and Lacity, M. (2005) "Taking the Measure of Outsourcing Providers," *Sloan Management Review*, Vol. 46, 3, pp. 41–48.

Kern, T. and Willcocks, L. (2001) *The Relationship Advantage: Information Technology, Sourcing and Management*. Oxford: Oxford University Press.

Lacity, M. and Willcocks, L. (2001) *Global Information Technology Outsourcing: Search For Business Advantage*. Chichester: Wiley.

Nahapiet, J. and Ghoshal, S. (1998) Social Capital, Intellectual Capital and The Organizational Advantage. *Academy Of Management Review*, 23, 2, pp. 242–266.

Oshri, I., Kotlarsky, J. and Willcocks, L. (eds) (2008) *Outsourcing Global Services: Relationships, Social Capital and Knowledge*. London: Palgrave.

Reynolds, P., Willcocks, L. and Feeny, D. (2007) Implementing Core IS Capabilities. *MISQ Executive*, December.

Stewart, T. (2001) *The Wealth Of Knowledge: Intellectual Capital and The Twenty-First Century Organization*. London: Nicholas Brealey.

Willcocks, L. and Craig, A. (2007) *The Outsourcing Enterprise 4: Retained Core Capabilities*. London: LogicaCMG.

Willcocks, L. and Cullen, S. (2005) *The Outsourcing Enterprise 1: The CEO Role in Delivering Strategic Advantage*. London: LogicaCMG.

Willcocks, L. and Currie, W. (1997) Does Radical Reengineering Really Work? In Willcocks, L., Feeny, D. and Islei, G. (eds) (1997) *Managing IT As A Strategic Resource*. Maidenhead: McGraw Hill.

Willcocks, L. and Lacity, M. (2009) *Studies In Outsourcing: From ITO to BPO and Offshoring*. London: Palgrave – forthcoming.

Willcocks, L. and Griffiths, C. (1997) "Management and Risk in Major IT Projects. In Willcocks, L., Feeny, D. and Islei, G. (eds) *Managing IT As A Strategic Resource*. Maidenhead: McGraw Hill.

Willcocks, L., Petherbridge, P. and Olson, N. (2002) *Making IT Count: Strategy, Delivery, Infrastructure*. Oxford: Butterworth.

9
Knowledge Transfer in Offshore Outsourcing
Joseph W. Rottman and Mary C. Lacity

Introduction

Today, nearly every manager calls their outsourcing deals "strategic." In reality, much of outsourcing is still about cost reduction in back-office services. For us, the term "strategic outsourcing" is restricted to circumstances for which suppliers play a key role in helping clients deliver innovative products to the market faster and cheaper than competitors.

Based on 160 interviews with US clients and their Indian suppliers, we found that the main impediment to strategic sourcing is knowledge transfer (see also supporting evidence in Chapters 8 and 14). At the outset, both parties realize that strategic outsourcing requires the supplier to deeply understand the client's business and technical domain. But there is often a disconnect between what each party means by "domain expertise." To the supplier, domain expertise means understanding the client's industry.

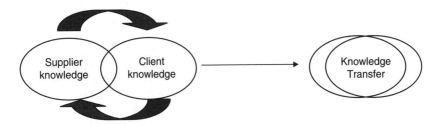

Figure 9.1   What is the Knowledge Gap & How & Who will Fill it?

Table 9.1   Effective Knowledge Transfer Practices

Practices to transfer knowledge	1. Motivate in-house staff to share knowledge with suppliers. 2. Train the supplier's employees as if they were internal employees. 3. Integrate the supplier employees fully into the development team.
Practices to protect the knowledge transfer investment	4. Require suppliers to have shadows for key onsite supplier roles to protect knowledge transfer investments. 5. Protect intellectual property by unitizing projects into small segments of work and dispersing work among multiple suppliers.

To the client, domain expertise means understanding *the clients* particular business, technology, products, markets and processes. (See Figure 9.1)

The key to strategic outsourcing is understanding the knowledge gap and how to fill it. Knowledge transfer entails balancing costs (such as supplier training) against risks (such as loss of intellectual property.) Our research uncovered five lessons on effective knowledge transfer (see Table 9.1). Three of these lessons help clients transfer knowledge to the supplier. Two lessons help clients protect their knowledge transfer investments. We illustrate these lessons by profiling one *Fortune 500* US manufacturing company.

Knowledge transfer: a US manufacturing case study

A large industrial equipment manufacturing company we shall call US Manufacturing,[1] illustrates the challenges of transferring knowledge to suppliers. This company sells heavy-duty industrial equipment that relies extensively on embedded software to operate. Executives at this company had the vision to use offshore suppliers to more quickly and more cheaply develop innovative software that is embedded in their core products. This company did not achieve their outsourcing vision until a second round of implementation. During the first attempt offshore, project costs exceeded budgets, software quality lessened and some projects were never finished. Much of the failure was attributed to the suppliers' lack of client-specific knowledge. Instead of abandoning the vision, senior executives used the experience to develop five knowledge transfer practices. In its second attempt, these practices helped to drop development costs by 10 to 15% and shorten product delivery times when compared to onshore. US Manufacturing can now declare with confidence that "our outsourcing deals are *strategic*."

The successful knowledge transfer practices highlighted in this article are centered within US Manufacturing's Six Sigma certified Software Center of Excellence (SCE). The SCE employs approximately 150 people and has an annual development spend of $32 million. The members of the SCE are tasked with the development and deployment of embedded software systems that are highly integrated into the manufacturing and operation of core products.

Recognizing the need for better knowledge transfer

The Software Center of Excellence began its journey in late 2000 when several projects were sourced offshore. As an example, one project required a new Global Positioning System (GPS) steering system to be integrated into one of the larger product lines currently in production. US Manufacturing chose a large Indian supplier for this project. The client delegated the design and creation of the integration project to the offshore supplier. They believed that the supplier had the sufficient domain knowledge because it had prior experience in this industry. This project failed to produce any of the deliverables outlined in the statement of work and was ultimately pulled back in house and completed well behind schedule and over budget.

US Manufacturing experienced similar failures with other offshore projects. Each work product delivered from the offshore suppliers needed extensive rework to correct inaccurate and incomplete application development. Looking back, the manager of the SCE and his staff underestimated the need for extensive domain knowledge transfer (product, process and market) as well as their own expertise in managing offshore projects.

Despite the failures, the SCE saw promise in some aspects of the original offshore engagements. For example, as the offshore employees became more experienced with embedded software and how the SCE interacted with business units, the members of SCE noticed that the quality of code improved and delivery times shortened. These improvements helped the management of the SCE convey a sense of optimism about offshore to the senior management. As one SCE manager noted:

> "We had to realize that our Indian suppliers did not understand embedded software or even the equipment we manufacture. They didn't even know what our product looked like! Now we are spending considerable time on domain knowledge transfer and training."

The SCE used the lessons it learned and re-launched its offshore effort in January, 2004. SCE managers' second attempt at offshore focused obsessively on knowledge transfer, adhering to the five practices discussed below.

Practice 1 – Motivate in-house staff to share knowledge with suppliers

Like all of the US clients we studied, staff employees at the SCE were initially reticent to share their knowledge with suppliers. Would they be helping to build their own guillotines? Managers at the SCE addressed this issue head-on by sharing the vision of strategic outsourcing and the staff's role within the vision. The SCE staff was motivated to share knowledge with suppliers because they were promised the following benefits:

- Job security because strategic outsourcing would be used to reduce the immense backlog, not internal headcount
- Reduction of the staff's 60–hour workweeks
- More interesting career paths

The SCE had a three-year backlog combined with a flat staffing forecast. According to the manager of the SCE:

> "My people were tired of working 60-hour weeks. We communicated that offshore was a way to better manage our project pipeline since we were not going to add a bunch of expensive North American resources to meet the demand and then lay them off later. And so they are not worried about losing their job. They just see this as a way of getting back to some kind of normal 40 to 50-hour workweek, and even more importantly, as a way for them to move up in their level of responsibility."

Considering the application development backlog facing SCE and the over-utilization of the internal staff, the SCE viewed offshore as way to better utilize their internal staff and move them into higher level tasks. As the engineering supervisor at the SCE stated:

> "Many of our junior to mid-level people were wanting and ready to move up, but they were so busy with low-level tasks, they were not able to learn the necessary skills, or have exposure to the high profile projects. Once we got offshore working properly, our junior people were freed up to begin taking on tasks with greater responsibilities."

Roles with greater responsibilities included subject-matter experts, project managers, and architects. The SCE involved Human Resources to help map exciting future career paths for the SCE staff. Through these benefits, the SCE motivated their staff to share their knowledge with offshore suppliers.

Practice 2 – Train the supplier's employees as if they were internal employees

Many CIOs would never co-train their internal employees with external supplier employees because of the high cost as well as concerns over the protection of intellectual property. The SCE, however, had little choice. The suppliers needed to deeply understand the internal functions of not only the manufacturing equipment, but of the entire company. Managers at the SCE decided that key supplier employees needed to undergo the same series of training sessions as internal employees.

The SCE provided the key supplier employees with facility tours and training classes on engine architecture, production software, equipment simulation products, operating guides for various lines of equipment, quality assurance processes and an overview of all of the various manufacturing products and platforms. They were introduced to various software development tools, the development environment and embedded development tools.

These classes were delivered on site and in person to the suppliers' onsite employees. The SCE paid the supplier employees for the time spent in training, but it only paid offshore (versus the much higher onshore) rates.

For the offshore employees, the classes were recorded and streamed offshore. According to the manager of the SCE:

> "We couldn't ship an engine or a piece of large equipment over to India, so we did the next best thing: we videotaped many equipment pieces in action and showed what the ECUs (Electronic Control Units) were designed to do."

In addition, the SCE invited most of the employees of the offshore suppliers to spend some time onsite prior to working on the outsourced projects. According to the Manager of the SCE:

> "What we saw was the benefit and real value of actually bringing those people here for a short time to bring them up to speed. Let them see how an application works and work right next to the team doing the development."

Practice 3 – Fully integrate the supplier employees into the development team

Beyond formal training, knowledge is exchanged socially among members of a group with close proximity, trust, and solidarity. To promote social exchange of knowledge, the SCE made a concerted effort to encourage and facilitate unified teams. For example, supplier employees were invited to birthday parties and happy hours. The line between "us and them" blurred and the supplier's employees (both on and offshore) were viewed by US Manufacturing's employees as team members. They all shared in the successes and challenges of the projects.

Besides the obvious benefit of knowledge sharing, the business users at US Manufacturing had higher levels of customer satisfaction. According to the Group Project Manager at one of the SCE's large Indian suppliers:

> "Of all of our embedded systems clients, the SCE at US Manufacturing has worked the hardest to make our employees feel very much part of the team. Our C-Sat (customer satisfaction ratings) from the client show

the value of this integration. Our employees have internalized the mission and values of [US Manufacturing]. It is a highly coveted assignment to work on the [US Manufacturing] account."

While the lessons so far have appeared "warm and fuzzy," the SCE was aware of two significant risks associated with such expensive and extensive knowledge sharing: high costs of training and loss of intellectual property. The next two practices address these issues.

Practice 4 – Require suppliers to have shadows for key onsite supplier roles to protect knowledge transfer investments

The SCE incurred significant training costs to transfer knowledge to the suppliers. To reap the rewards of this investment, the SCE had to protect against supplier turnover. (Unwanted supplier employee turnover was as high as 75% in some of the companies we studied.) The SCE required that trained supplier employees remain on the account for at least one year after training or the supplier would incur the costs of training a replacement.

For key supplier roles, the SCE went one step further. It required suppliers to provide shadow managers for key onsite supplier roles. Depending on the role, the required shadowing period was three to six months. This overlap period had two major benefits. First, the knowledge transfer was done predominately between the supplier's employees, thus freeing up the SCE's valuable architects and leads. Second, the incumbents were able to introduce their replacements to US Manufacturing's business units and staff. This helped to maintain the social contacts and connections that were created during the engagement. According to the engineering supervisor:

> "Once we started overlapping the liaisons, our customers felt much better about rolling people off the project. The outgoing liaisons made our job much easier since they took their initial training and subsequent learning and were able to convey it to their replacement much, much better than we can."

Practice 5 – Protect intellectual property by unitizing projects into small segments of work and disperse work among multiple suppliers

Besides protecting the knowledge transfer investment against turnover, the SCE also wanted to protect its intellectual property. This might seem to contradict the previous lessons of generous knowledge sharing, but it does not. Training focuses on products that are already in the market. The SCE's main concern was protecting the new innovations the suppliers were helping to build.

To mitigate this risk, the SCE (1) unitized projects into small segments of work and (2) dispensed these segments among three offshore suppliers to effectively distribute the intellectual property. They viewed their intel-

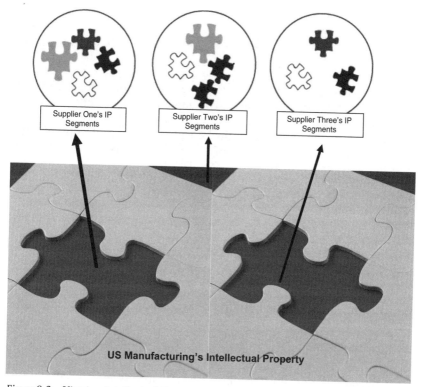

Figure 9.2 Viewing Intellectual Property as a Puzzle

lectual property as a puzzle. By distributing small pieces among three suppliers, no one supplier can assemble the puzzle on their own (See Figure 9.2).

The first part of the strategy involved the unitization of tasks to be sourced. These tasks were typically 5 to 7 business day activities that had clearly defined objectives and requirements. The statements of work (SOWs) for these tasks were appended to the master service level agreements the SCE established with its suppliers. The segmentation of larger projects into such small components allowed the SCE to more easily capture all associated costs and manage deliverables and milestones closely. While the transactional overhead of this strategy was considerable, the Manager of the SCE claimed the transaction costs were more than recouped by such close monitoring:

"In our first round [the failed attempt at offshore sourcing], projects were allowed to creep and the only people who saw the creep were the accounts payable people on our end and the accounts receivable people at the supplier. Now, each task has an owner and we watch the projects from a functional perspective, not an accounting perspective. By using this strategy, we are seeing much less re-work and the quality has improved considerably!"

The second part of the strategy involves multi-sourcing. The SCE distributed work among three suppliers (two large and one boutique). While maintaining engagements with multiple suppliers did increase transaction costs and management overhead, the benefits included protection of intellectual property and the creation of a competitive environment to keep costs low and quality high.

In summary, the five knowledge transfer practices resulted in success for the US manufacturer. The manager of the SCE concluded:

"Our suppliers are not only providing a lower cost talent pool, but they are helping us strategically. We keep looking for ways to increase the engagements. Our costs are down, productivity is up, and the quality is as good, if not better than what we can do in house."

Conclusion: realizing the benefits of knowledge sharing

To elevate outsourcing from merely tactical (focused solely on costs) to strategic (focused on quality, innovation, speed and cost) effective knowledge transfer is critical. The suppliers need to have domain knowledge in customer-specific domains including product, process and market; not just a particular vertical. Utilizing these five effective practices, companies can achieve strategic outsourcing engagements by creating an environment that supported knowledge transfer while simultaneously protecting both intellectual property and development quality.

Note

1 Because research participants were guaranteed anonymity, a pseudonym was assigned.

10
IT Offshore Outsourcing Practices

Joseph W. Rottman and Mary C. Lacity

Introduction

Offshore outsourcing of IT work has generated quite a controversy, with some saying it is stealing US jobs, others stating that it is improving the US economy, and still others claiming that all the studies are biased, one way or the other. Based on our past research of domestic outsourcing, and the best practices we uncovered, we have now studied offshoring as well (see also Chapter 9). We have found five practices that apply equally to both domestic and offshore, ten practices that are more important to offshore, and five practices unique to offshore sourcing. Together, these 20 practices can help CIOs swiftly move through the learning curve, mitigate risks, work with offshore suppliers, and achieve satisfactory costs and service levels.

What's the real story on offshore outsourcing of IT work?

Few IT management practices have sparked as much controversy in the general public, especially in the USA, as offshore sourcing of IT. Front-page headlines questioned, "Software: Will Outsourcing Hurt America's Supremacy?" and claimed offshore sourcing is stealing American IT jobs and dragging down US IT bonus pay (Hof and Kerttetter, 2004; McGee, 2003)). US companies that source offshore were blacklisted on television shows, such as CNN's "Tonight with Lou Dobbs."

In contrast to the political backlash, research on offshore IT sourcing has found positive effects on US IT jobs, IT productivity, IT costs and IT quality (Griswold, 2004). For example, although Forrester estimates that 360,000 US service jobs went abroad in 2003, these jobs represented only 1/4 of 1% of the US workforce, which is 130 million people strong (Drezner, 2004). The Cato Institute argues that offshoring low-paying IT jobs will create newer and higher-paying IT jobs in the US over the next eight years. Similarly, global production of IT hardware reduced hardware costs by 30%, resulting in an additional $230 billion in US GDP between 1995 and 2002. Similar effects on productivity are anticipated in software (Lindsey, 2004). Finally, an IBM Consulting Services survey found that 82% of IT managers reported cost savings between 10% and 50% from offshore sourcing – and 68% of the respondents claimed some or significant quality improvement (McCarthy, 2002).

While such studies are certainly important bellwethers, most have been generated by consulting firms – IBM, McKinsey, Forrester Research, Gartner and Global Insight – or IT industry consortiums, such as ITAA and NASSCOM. There clearly is a need for objective academic research. Our study, originally published in 2004 (Rottman and Lacity, 2004) was inspired by Carmel and Agarwal (2002) "The Maturation of Offshore Sourcing of Information Technology Work," published in *MIS Quarterly Executive*. Their work, based on 13 case studies, generated a four-stage model of offshore outsourcing: offshore bystander, offshore experimenter, proactive cost focus, and proactive strategic focus. Subsequently Kaiser and Hawk (2004) reported on an eight-year relationship between a US financial insurance company and an Indian-based supplier. That paper provided lessons on evolving an offshore relationship from proactive cost focus to strategic cosourcing. But there is still a need for detailed research on how CIOs can swiftly move their organizations through these four phases. That guidance, in the form of best practices, is the focus of this chapter.

Research approach

Who we interviewed

Our prior research contained over 100 case studies of domestic outsourcing (where customers outsourced to suppliers in their own country). In that work, we identified best practices, management frameworks, and relationship models (see Chapter 1 for full details of relevant publications).[1] Our current research aims to discern whether best practices for offshore sourcing differ from those of domestic sourcing. We therefore replicated our domestic case study research method (Lacity and Willcocks, 1998), selecting large US organizations that use Indian-based suppliers because India continues to rank as a top locale.

As of the Fall of 2005, we interviewed 159 participants from 40 companies, including 21 offshore client organizations (primarily from *Fortune 500* companies), 10 suppliers that provide offshore services, and 9 offshore advisors that helped clients find suppliers, negotiate contracts, and transition IT work offshore. The interviews from the client organizations were face-to-face and occurred on client premises in the US as well as at five offshore sourcing events sponsored by various user groups, a university, and one offshore supplier. The interviews with offshore suppliers were face-to-face and occurred primarily in Bangalore, Hyderabad and Mumbai on

Table 10.1   Research Participants

Company Role in Offshore Outsourcing	Company Pseudonym	Number of Research Participants
Offshore Clients	1. Aerospace	3
	2. Beverage	1
	3. Biotech	45
	4. Electrical Materials	1
	5. Employee Satisfaction	1
	6. Financial Services 1	10
	7. Financial Services 2	1
	8. Financial Services 3	1
	9. Financial Services 4	1
	10. Financial Services 5	1
	11. Financial Services 6	1
	12. Financial Services 7	3
	13. Industrial Equipment	3
	14. Large Insurance Company	2
	15. Manufacturing 1	2
	16. Manufacturing 2	2
	17. Mining	1
	18. Private Insurance Company	3
	19. Retail	7
	20. Telecommunications	1
	21. Transportation	1
Offshore Suppliers	1. Large Global Supplier 1	7
	2. Large Global Supplier 2	11
	3. Large Indian Service Provider 1	16
	4. Large Indian Service Provider 2	11
	5. Small Indian BPO Provider 1	2
	6. Small Indian BPO Provider 2	3
	7. Small Indian Services Provider 1	2
	8. Small Indian Services Provider 2	4
	9. Staff Augmentation Company 1	1
	10. Staff Augmentation Company 2	1
Offshore Advisors	1. Consulting 1	1
	2. Intermediary offshore consulting firm 1	1
	3. Intermediary offshore consulting firm 2	2
	4. Legal Firm 1	1
	5. Legal Firm 2	1
	6. Legal Firm 3	1
	7. Legal Firm 4	1
	8. Legal Firm 5	1
	9. Legal Firm 6	1
Total Number of Participants		159

the suppliers' premises. The interviews with the offshore advisors were also face-to-face and occurred primarily in the US Because of the sensitive nature of offshore outsourcing, we use pseudonyms to protect the identities of the study participants and their companies.

What we asked

We asked about four offshore challenges:
- How can US organizations swiftly move through the offshore learning curve?
- How can US organizations mitigate offshore risks?
- How can US organizations effectively work with offshore suppliers?
- How can US organizations ensure cost savings while protecting quality?

What we found

We uncovered 20 best practices for moving an organization from offshore bystander to offshore experimenter to proactive cost focus (see Table 10.2). We illustrate them below through the experiences of one *Fortune 500* firm, given the pseudonym "Biotech."

Five practices are equally important to domestic and offshore. The good news for CIOs is that some practices for managing domestic outsourcing do indeed apply to offshore sourcing. In particular, five best practices are equally important for both domestic and offshore outsourcing: create a centralized program management office, leverage in-house sourcing expertise, use pilot projects to mitigate business risks, development meaningful career paths for in-house staff, and create balanced scorecard metrics.

Ten practices apply to both, but are more important in offshoring. These ten are more important to offshore because the risks and transaction costs are greater, and the delivery teams are more remote and culturally diverse. Many CIOs may not have used these practices, such as hiring a legal expert to mitigate legal risks. But, while in-house legal staff may routinely draft domestic contracts, they frequently lack sufficient knowledge to draft offshore contracts to address such important items as export restrictions, foreign tax law, intellectual property rights protection, visa difficulties, and offshore labor laws. Other practices become more important in offshoring, such as openly communicating the sourcing strategy to minimize domestic worker backlash, using real-time dashboards to verify synchronize, and manage work flows, and hiring an intermediary consulting firm to serve as broker and guide to foreign countries, cultures, and suppliers.

Five practices are unique to offshoring. One intriguing offshore practice is giving customers a choice between domestic and offshore sourcing. Program management offices can publish rates for sourcing locales and allow business unit managers to assess the trade-offs between lower costs and greater risks. Other practices unique to offshore sourcing address the rigid Capability Maturity Model (CMM) requirements used by offshore suppliers

Table 10.2 IT Offshore Outsourcing Practices

Sourcing Challenge	Practices to Overcome the Challenge	Equally Important for Both Domestic & Offshore	More Important For Offshore	Unique to Offshore
How can we swiftly move through the learning curve?	1. Create a centralized program management office to consolidate management	X		
	2. Hire an intermediary consulting firm to serve as a broker and guide		X	
	3. Select locations, projects, suppliers, and managers to leverage in-house sourcing expertise	X		
How can we mitigate risks?	4. Use pilot projects to mitigate business risks	X		
	5. Give customers a choice of sourcing location to mitigate business risks			X
	6. Hire a legal expert to mitigate legal risks		X	
	7. Openly communicate the sourcing strategy to all stakeholders to mitigate political risks		X	
	8. Use secure information links or redundant lines to mitigate infrastructure risks		X	
	9. Use fixed-priced contracts to mitigate workforce risks		X	

Table 10.2 IT Offshore Outsourcing Practices – *continued*

Sourcing Challenge	Practices to Overcome the Challenge	Equally Important for Both Domestic & Offshore	More Important For Offshore	Unique to Offshore
How can we effectively work with suppliers?	10. Elevate your own organization's CMM/CMMI processes to close the process gap between you and your supplier			X
	11. Negotiate the CMM/CMMI processes you will and will not pay for to not waste money			X
	12. Cross-examine, or replace, the supplier's employees to overcome cultural communication barriers		X	
	13. Let the project team members meet face-to-face to foster camaraderie		X	
	14. Consider innovative techniques, such as real-time dashboards, to improve workflow verification, synchronization, and management		X	
	15. Manage bottlenecks to relieve the substantial time zone differences			X
How can we ensure cost savings while protecting quality?	16. Consider both transaction and production costs to realistically calculate overall savings		X	
	17. Size projects large enough to receive total cost savings		X	
	18. Establish the ideal in-house/onsite/offshore only after the relationship has stabilized			X
	19. Develop meaningful career paths for subject matter experts, project managers, governance experts, and technical experts	X		

bottlenecks caused by time zone differences, and establishing the ideal in-house/onsite/offshore ratio.

Although first journeys to offshore sourcing are met with many challenges, once learning curves are conquered and best practices are institutionalized, we believe offshore sourcing will assume its rightful place in the IT sourcing portfolio. CIOs will continue to "best source," using a mix of in-house IT staff, domestic contractors, domestic suppliers, nearshore suppliers, co-sourcing with strategic partners, and offshore suppliers.

The next section describes "Biotech's" offshoring journey. It provides a rich description of the underlying challenges of offshore and anchors the following discussion of best practices by comparing its experiences with those of others.

One case example: "Biotech"

Biotech is a *Fortune 500* company and a leading provider of biotechnology-based products. The firm has experienced moderate revenue growth for the past four years, earning billions a year in sales but generating significant net losses in 2002. There were several temporary reasons for the loss, including an accounting restructuring and a major litigation. But one of the enduring reasons for the loss was an excessive amount of Sales, General, and Administrative (SG&A) costs. One main company goal, stated explicitly in the annual report, is to significantly reduce the cost of SG&A. Because IT is part of this cost burden, reducing IT costs became a major goal for the CIO, which ultimately led Biotech down the offshore sourcing path.

It needs to cut its costs

At US headquarters, Biotech employs 600 IT personnel and augments this staff with nearly 200 domestic contractors. The Corporate CIO reports to the CFO. IT Directors in each of the strategic business units report directly to the Corporate CIO, who also has a Global Leadership Team of 12 to 15 IT people who serve as liaisons and leaders to the business units.

From 2000 to 2002, the IT budget remained flat. Then it was reduced by 5% to partly subsidize the net losses from that year. "Doing more with less" became the CIO's major challenge. A few members of the Global Leadership Team championed investigating offshore sourcing, to reduce IT costs by replacing some expensive domestic contract labor with cheaper offshore equivalents. Because Biotech did not plan to reduce its in-house IT staff, its offshoring effort did not elicit the political stigma other US companies experienced.

The global leadership team investigates India

Three members of the Global Leadership Team began their offshore investigation by visiting US companies that were currently engaging in offshore outsourcing. Convinced by the cost savings they witnessed, they hired an intermediary to serve as a guide to India and to Indian suppliers. They selected India as the offshore venue because Biotech already had R&D facilities in Bangalore. In that facility, Biotech had full-time IT employees who ultimately played a significant role in managing offshore sourcing.

In August of 2002, two members of the Global Leadership Team made the trip to India and were subsequently convinced that Biotech should pursue offshore sourcing. Upon their return, the Global Leadership Team began to rally senior management support for offshore sourcing. The CIO approved and created a new Offshore Program Management Office (PMO). The PMO signed Master Service Level agreements with 4 Indian suppliers – two large and two small.

Biotech launches 17 offshore pilot projects

Members of the Global Leadership Team started bringing pilot projects to the Offshore Program Management Office. The idea was not to immediately generate cost savings, but rather to gain experience with the types of applications, suppliers, contracts, and work processes needed to ensure offshore sourcing success. In all, 17 pilot projects were undertaken. Biotech purposefully selected very different types of applications including replatforming from PeopleSoft to SAP, back end systems development, and entire end-to-end systems. They tested the suppliers' capabilities with new (wireless) and old (ERP) technologies. They experimented with different sized projects ranging from a 20-person day project to an 800-person day project (four FTEs for eight months). In several instances, Biotech gave small pieces of the same project to two vendors so that the project served as a control group for better supplier comparison.

Statements of Work (SOW) were appended to the Master Service Level Agreements for each specific pilot. Fixed price contracts were used when requirements were clearly defined. Time and materials contracts were used when requirements were still emerging.

Four pilots were launched in March 2003. They exemplify the learning Biotech accrued during their offshore experimenter phase.

Testing one supplier's staff augmentation capabilities for a small sub-project. Jerry, a member of the Global Leadership Team, was in the midst of launching the new Biotech Intranet. He asked his team to find a small sub-project that was both low risk and highly separable to give to one of the Indian suppliers. They estimated the size of the sub-project to be 20 person days if done in-house. However, the learning curve with the offshore supplier was significant, and the sub-project took longer than estimated. The top challenges identified were: working with the supplier's advanced capability maturity model (CMM) processes, time zone differences, language differences, and cultural differences. Because Jerry anticipated the learning curve, he did not pick a sub-project on his critical path. Thus, although the pilot took longer than 20 person days, it did not delay the overall delivery of the New Generation Intranet.

Testing one supplier's development capabilities for an end-to-end system. The pilot required the supplier to do both analysis and development for a new web-based system. This project was riskier than other pilots because Biotech had a mandatory installation date. There were no in-house IT staff or contractors initially working on the project, thus the supplier had to do this system from scratch. Biotech selected one of the larger Indian suppliers for this project. The analysis and design phases took longer than anticipated, again due to challenges with working with the supplier's processes, time zone differences, language differences, and cultural differences. The ultimate project deadline was met by speedier than anticipated coding and testing phases. Overall, our participants rated the project a moderate success.

Testing two suppliers' conversion capabilities. The third pilot was a large conversion from PeopleSoft to SAP. Biotech decided that before they would commit to one supplier, they would have two of the large Indian suppliers do small pieces of the conversion. Biotech experienced much better project leadership from one of the suppliers in terms of onsite coordination, project status reporting, technical fit with Biotech, and superior daily communications. Biotech selected this supplier to complete the entire conversion. Three months later, when Biotech went live with SAP, the Indian supplier was granted an ongoing maintenance contract for seven FTEs. The overall project was rated a great success.

Testing two suppliers' development capabilities. The fourth project entailed new system development for a marketing application. Like the ERP conversion, Biotech initially assigned small, eight-week pieces of work to two Indian suppliers, one large and one small. To further reduce risk, Biotech required delivery of milestones every two weeks. While the large Indian supplier performed well, the small supplier did not. The small supplier missed deadlines and failed to communicate the project status in a timely manner. Biotech selected the large Indian supplier to complete the system.

Learning from pilot projects

While the pilot projects experienced lower hourly wages, overall cost savings were not evident because of the learning curve and risk mitigation practices, such as small project sizes. By accumulating all of the learning from the pilot projects, Biotech's IT management learned which two suppliers they preferred (one large and one small supplier), the types of processes Biotech needs to develop in-house to facilitate offshore sourcing, and the types and size of projects best handled offshore. In order to truly leverage offshore savings, Biotech knew it would need to embark on larger projects in the future.

Practices to overcome offshore challenges

Biotech, like our other case sites, faced four tough challenges when moving IT work offshore: How can we swiftly move through the learning curve? How can we mitigate risks? How can we effectively work with offshore suppliers? How can we ensure cost savings while protecting quality? Participants identified 20 practices that served to meet these challenges (see Table 10.2).

Practices to swiftly move through the learning curve

US and other CIOs who have never sourced IT work offshore are anxious to swiftly move through the learning curve. Participants identified three helpful practices: create a centralized offshore program management office, hire an intermediary, and carefully select locations, projects, suppliers, and managers to leverage in-house sourcing expertise. These practices are important for both domestic and offshore sourcing, but the need for intermediary consulting firms is greater with offshore.

1. Create a centralized program management office to consolidate management. PMOs set up preferred supplier relationships, negotiate contracts, assess overall performance, define best practices, and disseminate learning. This best practice is not unique to offshore sourcing. The issue here is whether CIOs should create a separate program management office for offshore, such as Biotech did, or whether to integrate offshore into an existing PMO. Participants suggest that CIOs should create a separate office if the offshore initiative represents a significant departure from domestic outsourcing practices or they intend to create a captive center or joint partnership that will require dedicated management. CIOs should create an integrated PMO if they want business requirements to drive the supplier selection and if they want the onshore and offshore suppliers to aggressively compete. Retail, a *Fortune 100* company, used competition managed by the integrated PMO to cut the domestic supplier rates by 20% to 50%.

2. Hire an intermediary consulting firm to serve as a broker and guide. The intermediary consulting market is certainly growing fast, with players such as NeoIT, SourceQuest, Soft Access, Cincom, TPI, and Providio Technology Group. Some experts estimated that by 2005, 64% of offshore contracts were brokered by intermediaries.[2] Biotech certainly found value in hiring an intermediary:

I think it absolutely engaged us more quickly with respect to them informing the offshore vendors of our situation and setting up the arrangements. We would have just had to spend a lot more of our own time with all of that. So I think it streamlined the initial process. – Global Leadership Team member

3. Select locations, projects, suppliers, and managers to leverage in-house sourcing expertise. CIOs have many sourcing experiences that will transfer to the offshore domain. Many companies, such as Biotech, choose a location because of the existence of manufacturing, R&D or other subsidiaries. These locations serve as a home base to launch an IT initiative.

Concerning suppliers, some US CIOs move offshore via one of their domestic suppliers such as EDS, IBM, or Accenture because they can leverage the existing relationships. For example, AT&T preferred to move offshore through its existing partnership with IBM, rather than try to build a new relationship with a new supplier in a new country. Other customers, such as Financial Services 3, prefer to select established offshore suppliers such as Wipro because of their maturity. Other customers, including Biotech, look for smaller niche suppliers with domain expertise.

All participants cited the need for veteran project managers as a critical success factor.[3] However, there was some debate as to the type of experience required. Most participants believed the offshore project managers should have successfully managed in-house projects on the same subject matter as the offshore engagement. But one participant found that it was better to select a project manager with domestic supplier management expertise than it was to select a project manager with subject matter expertise. To this participant, the more important skill is vendor relationship management rather than domain knowledge.

Practices to mitigate risks

All CIOs are aware of the risks associated with offshore sourcing including business, legal, political, infrastructure, workforce, social, and logistical risks. While many of these risks are also present in domestic outsourcing, most are greater with offshore sourcing, and 11 risks are unique to offshore sourcing (see Table 10.3). We asked participants to provide specific examples of successful risk mitigation practices. They identified common, but important, best practices such as using pilot projects, hiring legal experts, and openly communicating the offshore initiative to assuage fear. Some identified more unique and intriguing practices such as giving the customer a choice.

4. Use pilot projects to mitigate business risks, but don't make them too small. Biotech brought the concept of piloting to reduce risk to a new level. Biotech chose 17 pilot projects that were mostly small in size, required frequent delivery of milestones, and gave pieces of the same project to two suppliers. In some ways, Biotech may have reduced risk at the expense of some additional learning:

"I am not sure our selection of projects told us as much as it could have. Bad project selection skews your results in both ways. If the pilot was too small, it led the teams to conclude the overhead is too large and we can't be successful, we won't have savings. We had other projects that were not complex that lead us to believe, offshore is wonderful, it's

Table 10.3 Outsourcing Risks[1]

Risk Category	Sample Risks	Equally Risky for Both Domestic & Offshore	More Risky For Offshore	Risk Unique to Offshore
Business	Backlash from external customers damages reputation		X	
	No overall cost savings	X		
	Poor supplier in terms of capability, service, financial stability, or cultural fit	X		
	Wrong types of activities outsourced		X	
	Inability to mange the supplier relationship		X	
Legal	Inefficient or ineffective judicial system at offshore locale			X
	Intellectual property rights infringement		X	
	Export restrictions			X
	Inflexible labor laws			X
	Difficulty obtaining visas			X
	Changes in tax laws could erode savings		X	
	Inflexible contracts	X		
	Breach in security or privacy		X	
Political	Backlash from internal IT staff		X	
	Perceived as unpatriotic			X
	Democrats threaten to punish US companies that source offshore			X
	Political instability within offshore country			X
	Political instability between U.S. and offshore country			X

Table 10.3   Outsourcing Risks[1] – *continued*

Risk Category	Sample Risks	Equally Risky for Both Domestic & Offshore	More Risky For Offshore	Risk Unique to Offshore
Workforce	Supplier employee turnover		X	
	Supplier employee burnout		X	
	Inexperienced supplier employees		X	
	Poor communication skills of supplier employees		X	
Infra-structure	Poor telecommunications		X	
	Poor utilities (electricity, gas, water)			X
Social	Cultural differences		X	
	Holiday and religious calendar differences			X
Logistical	Time zone challenges			X
	Managing remote teams		X	
	Coordinating travel		X	

[1]Sourcing risks were identified by participants from the current research and compared to risks identified by previous participants as documented in Lacity, M. and Willcocks, L., *Global Information Technology Outsourcing: Search for Business Advantage*, Wiley, Chichester, 2001.

wildly successful. But we didn't really test the supplier's capabilities. Neither view is correct." – Global Leadership Team member

A pilot project must be large enough to extract learning and metrics and to attract good suppliers, but small enough to minimize risk. But experts do not agree on the ideal size. According to the Gartner Group, an ideal pilot size is ten to 15 people for six months. According to the CEO of an intermediary consulting firm, pilot projects should be sized at two man-years, representing a project cost between $50,000 and $100,000.

Another issue is trying to attract and motivate suppliers. When planning the role of external suppliers within the sourcing strategy, CIOs need to understand that their ability to attract a great partner largely depends on their "client attractiveness". In our research, the size of the client's contract was really the key to a client's attractiveness. Although it takes time to build a good supplier relationship, suppliers were more motivated to allocate their best resources to clients with large contracts. Like clients, suppliers incur large transaction costs to assemble bids, negotiate contracts, and manage client accounts. Suppliers can only afford to devote their best resources to clients with a large volume of current business or the very real possibility of a large volume of business in the future.

5. Give customers a choice of sourcing location to mitigate business risks. Using an offshore provider for customer–facing activities presents considerable risks. CIOs need look no further than Dell Computer's experiences to see the effects of poorly executed offshore service centers. In a widely publicized move, Dell Computer "re-shored" technical support for its corporate customers (approximately 85% of its customer base) due to customer dissatisfaction with the call center in Bangalore, India.

The CIO of Financial Services 4 allows strategic business units a choice for application development. The SBUs can source IT from three preferred offshore suppliers or from approved domestic suppliers. Rates are lower with the offshore suppliers, but risks are lower with the domestic suppliers. The CIO believes the business unit managers should be the ones assessing the trade-offs.

6. Hire a legal expert to mitigate legal risks. Hiring a legal expert for domestic outsourcing has been a standard best practice for 15 years. Many legal firms specialize in outsourcing, such as Shaw Pittman and Milbank Tweed. The need for legal expertise with offshore sourcing is even more pronounced because customers must abide by different legal systems and more regulatory requirements. Participants hired legal firms to help with tax implications, protection of intellectual property, business continuity, regulatory compliance, visa formalities, governing law, and dispute resolution. For example, lawyers helped participants define arbitration clauses to resolve disputes rather than rely on India's 15-year litigation process.

7. Openly communicate the sourcing strategy to all stakeholders to mitigate political risks. At Financial Services 1, senior management viewed offshore sourcing as a potential way to decrease the immense application backlog caused by the refinancing boom. But senior management chose to keep the pilot project "low key rather than panic the IT staff while we were simply testing the waters." One day, the domestic IT staff showed up for work to find 11 people from India working in cubicles. The domestic IT staff began to panic and question the future of their careers. The Indian workers were isolated and treated with suspicion, if not contempt. The IT staff found frequent reasons for complaining about the offshore sourcing projects. Eventually, the CTO held a town meeting and told the staff that there would be no layoffs caused by offshore sourcing. However, he would replace fewer in-house IT staff caused by natural attrition. In contrast, Biotech was very open about the offshore pilots and told the internal IT staff that offshore sourcing was about "doing more with a flat budget" and that no internal IT workers would be fired as a result of offshore sourcing.

In the previous examples, CIOs had an easy message to sell because offshore outsourcing resulted in no planned layoffs. But some organizations, like a financial services firm, used a sourcing strategy to dramatically reduce costs, partly by reducing internal headcount. The lesson, however, is still the same—announce the sourcing strategy as soon as the organization begins searching offshore. At this company, senior leaders from the finance organization announced the transformation program to the staff as soon after they selected India as the location for their new captive center. The employees were told that the team did not know exactly who would be impacted yet, but that everyone would know within five months. Some employees would be included in the succession and some employees would be given severance packages. Some employees knew 18 months in advance that they would no longer have a job with the company. We call the situation "asking staff to build their own guillotine." Among our case companies, that situation worked if redundant staff were given hefty bonuses to stay during the transition and if their redundancy packages were tied to the successful transition of work to new offshore employees.

8. Use secure information links or redundant lines to mitigate infrastructure risks. Early articles on offshore sourcing focused on poor infrastructure quality in low cost countries as a major risk factor. Our participants reported only minor problems because in India, at least, the infrastructure has improved. First, many participants use secure communications links between the customer and offshore supplier to enable easy and secure access. Second, many US customers opt for redundant lines so that downtime is not an issue. Third, the Indian government has replaced the telecommunications monopoly with competition. According to the former President of MCI, India is in the process of laying fiber optic cables in 100,000 Indian buildings – as compared to 30,000 buildings wired in the US All of these initiatives serve to increase telecommunications service quality and reduce costs.

9. Use fixed-price contracts, when possible, to mitigate workforce risks. Several participants complained that some of the suppliers' employees were inexperienced, overworked, and frequently turned over. The customer is most affected by workforce risks when using a time and materials contract. Because the customer is billed hourly, the customer subsidizes a new supplier employee's learning curve. Also, supplier employees who are unproductive take more hours to complete tasks, again reflected in a higher customer bill. Some customers try to mitigate this risk by demanding to see resumes of supplier employees or by setting minimum years of experience. These practices place the customer in the business of managing the supplier's resources, which can increase transaction costs and create animosity between customer and supplier. A better practice is to incent the supplier by using a fixed price contract with clearly defined deliverables. The supplier can best decide how to staff the project to meet their contractual obligations while maximizing their own profit margin. The supplier is incented to put their most productive people on the project to increase their margin, or the supplier may make a strategic decision to finance their own employees' learning curves.

Practices to effectively work with offshore suppliers

Managing remote teams with project members from different countries, cultures, time zones, and who speak different languages is one of the most difficult challenges of offshore sourcing. While some of these challenges are evident in domestic outsourcing, such as dealing with a supplier that has a different culture, the issues are much more prevalent offshore. Fortunately, there are many practices to help customers work effectively with offshore suppliers.

10. Elevate your own organization's CMM/CMMI processes to close the process gap between you and your supplier. Every participant brought up the need to coordinate work processes, particularly with suppliers who are committed to the Software Engineering Institute's Capability Maturity Model. While Indian suppliers were all assessed at CMM/CMMI level 4 or 5, our US customers were at best a level 2. At higher CMM/CMMI levels, an immense amount of documentation is required. US project managers have never before been through such a rigorous process to define requirements.

At Biotech, requirements definition is an informal process when done onshore. Project managers speak frequently with users who are usually located on site. The user feedback cycle is quick. In contrast, project managers working on the offshore pilots had to engage in many formal and planned communications with suppliers and users to create the required documents. One Biotech Global Team Member said, "the overhead costs of documenting some of the projects exceeded the value of the deliverables."

So what can be done to more effectively coordinate work processes? One Indian supplier places a CMMI expert who is purposefully naïve about the business process at the client site. This person reviews the client's business requirements from a CMMI perspective to raises issues of ambiguity before sending it offshore.

Other participants suggested that the best way to extract value from the supplier's CMMI processes is to adopt CMMI processes yourself:

"A real problem we had was our CMM level 1.5 guys talking to the vendor's level 5 guys. So together, we have worked out a plan with our vendor to help bring our CMM levels up. When we do, it will be a benefit to both of us; our specifications will be better and so they can use them more efficiently." – Director of Application Development, Transportation

The outstanding issue is the CMMI level required to effectively work with suppliers. The Vice President at Financial Services 4 believes that customers only need to reach level 1.8 to extract value. The Officer of IT Services at Financial Services 3 set a more ambitious goal as he pushes hard to bring his own organization up to at least a level 3.

11. Negotiate the CMM/CMMI processes you will and will not pay for to not waste money. The project manager at Financial Services 1 noted, "You ask for one button to be moved and the supplier has to first do a twenty page impact analysis – we are paying for all this documentation we don't need." He is negotiating for exactly which documents Financial Services 1 will and will not pay. This will enable him to only use the CMM processes he perceives to add significant value. While this practice is unique, a customized interface with each customer could serve to increase the supplier's costs, which may eventually result in higher prices.

12. Cross-examine, or even replace, the supplier's employees to overcome cultural communication barriers. We heard from many participants that Indian employees would not challenge the customer, readily deliver bad news, or express incomprehension. One frustrated participant said, "The place could be on fire and they would say, 'Oh it's great, a little warm, but it is great!'"

One American who works for a major offshore supplier says he learned to cross-examine his Indian counterparts to ensure they tell him bad news. Whereas in America he asks, "How is the project going?," in India he asks much more pointed questions, to the point where he worries about being rude. Another participant solved the issue by complaining to the supplier's senior management that the supplier's project manager was evasive about the project status. The supplier replaced that individual with a woman who was much more forthcoming. Although the communication was more open with the woman, the participant had to "go over her head three times" to get answers.

13. Let the protect team members meet face-to-face to foster cama-raderie. As a corollary to the previous lesson, the need for the customer's project manager to visit the supplier site is clearly emerging as a best (and expensive) practice to get past cultural communication barriers. It is much easier to switch to lower cost media such as teleconferences and email after meeting people face-to-face. Biotech bore the cost of the team members meeting face-to-face:

> "Once you get good at specking out what you need face-to-face, then an awful lot of the work happens by e-mail and it's just follow up questions and lots of that happens by e-mail – Jerry, Global Leadership Team member"

14. Consider innovative techniques, such as real-time dashboards, to improve workflow verification, synchronization, and management. Project managers noted difficulties with transferring work, keeping track of programming and database versions, and when and how to verify supplier work. At Biotech, most pilot projects required transfer of work every two weeks. At Financial Services 1, the customer takes possession of programming code every 15 days, but needs to check the database architecture daily. Sometimes there are discrepancies in the database schemas. One possible solution is a real-time dashboard. Dashboards are emerging tools that allow the customer to glimpse at the supplier's work in real-time. Although only one of our participants (Industrial Equipment Manufacturer) has implemented a dashboard, they all saw a need for better work flow management.

15. Manage bottlenecks to relieve the substantial time zone differences. Time zone differences are often marketed as a bonus of offshore sourcing because operations can occur around the clock. While that benefit may be realized for call centers, time zone differences do not typically facilitate IT development projects. For concurrent tasks, like telephone conferences, the US customers have to stay at work very late or the supplier has to get up very early. For sequential tasks, if US customers don't stay late to complete deliverables, the consequence is that the supplier sits idle for an entire day. For example, the project manager at Financial Services 1 said he doesn't have the power to make the database administrator stay late to finish schemas, resulting in a bottleneck as the supplier waits.

Biotech learned that a best practice to minimize bottlenecks was co-located people: have some Indian supplier employees on site in the US and some Biotech staff on site in India. A boutique Indian supplier minimized the problem by setting the work hours in Hyderabad from 1:00pm to 10:00pm to provide a three-hour overlap with US customers.

Practices to ensure cost savings and protect quality

During the experimenter phase, participants' main objective was testing the concept. Substantial cost savings can only be achieved after learning has accumulated and size of projects increase. In this section, we discuss what participants learned about the necessary size of projects and quality assurance practices to ensure cost savings while protecting quality. While some of these practices apply to domestic sourcing as well, we see why they are more difficult to implement in the offshore context.

16. Consider both transaction and production costs to realistically calculate overall savings. For US companies, the initial offshore driver is undoubtedly labor cost savings, a production cost. In the US, average labor cost per year per IT employee is $63,331, compared to less than $6,000 in India (Thibodeau and Hoffman, 2003). The management challenge is extracting overall cost savings when both transaction and production costs are considered.

Transaction costs are considerably higher with offshore sourcing. According to a study by the Meta Group, Gartner Group, and Renedis, transaction costs of offshore sourcing range from 15.2% to 57% of contract value for vendor selection, transitioning the work, layoffs and retention, lost productivity due to cultural issues, improving development processes, and managing the contract (Ambrosio, 2003). In contrast, transaction costs of domestic outsourcing range between 4 and 10% of contract value (Lacity and Willcocks, 2001).

Most CIOs find it very difficult to calculate the total costs of offshore sourcing. At Biotech, the Head of the Offshore Program Management says:

"It is clear that we saved money on a per hour basis, there is no way to argue about that, but did they [offshore provider] save us money overall? Did they do it as fast as we would do it? The other big complaint came from the project managers: "Managing offshore projects is really hard... if I had to count up how hard this is, then we lost money."

17. Size projects large enough to receive total cost savings. Our research did not identify a definitive benchmark for the size of IT project required to achieve significant savings. We asked a senior researcher at the Gartner Group how big an IT software project has to be in order to achieve 15 to 20% overall savings. He quoted us between 80 and 100 FTEs, although he admonished that this number was based on his personal experience. Participants from Biotech agree that larger sized projects are the key to getting overall cost savings:

"We tended to pick what we perceived as low risk projects for the pilots. And in some cases that meant that we picked projects that were so small, the overhead crushed any value. – Patrick, Head of Offshore Program Management Office"

After pilot tests were complete, Biotech launched two very large application development projects. These projects will be two to three years in duration and represent over a million dollars each in IT spend, with significant cost savings anticipated.

18. Establish the ideal in-house/onsite/offshore only after the relation-ship has stabilized. The CEO of an offshore intermediary firm stated that the ideal ratio is 15% of client staff onsite to maintain direction, 15% supplier staff on site to serve as liaisons and project managers, and 70% of the supplier staff offshore. While customers are in the experimental phase, the ratio is likely to be much higher. For example, when Financial Services 3 started offshore sourcing in 2001, the onshore/offshore ration was 50/50. Wipro, the supplier, has a dedicated staff onsite, as well as a dedicated off-shore delivery team. Thus far, the relationship has been successful in that Wipro delivered 115 projects with an above average customer rating. As Financial Services 3 has conquered the learning curve and established a good supplier relationship, the Officer of IT Services aims to shift the ratio to 30/70.

19. Develop meaningful career paths for subject matter experts, project managers, governance experts, and technical experts to help ensure quality. Participants stressed the need for subject matter experts (SMEs) and good project managers to define and deliver business requirements and governance experts to manage external suppliers. But as US organizations increasingly outsource entry-level positions like programmers, how will future generations of SMEs, project managers, and governance experts be groomed?

> "All of the best project managers I have ever worked with all started as coders. If all the hardcore coding is being done offshore, where will we get our good project managers? – Pam Global Leadership Team Member."

This worry prompted the Vice President of Technologies for Financial Services 6 to work with local universities to create a Center of Excellence for the development of skill sets aimed at "priming the pump" to ensure the talent pipeline does not dry up. These centers work with Financial Services 6 to understand the changing landscape of IT work and adapt their curriculum to create graduates with the necessary combination of business, project management, and technical skills.

20. Create balanced scorecard metrics. All participants identified the need for measures that consider costs, quality, timeliness, and risks, but only participants from one company were fully satisfied with current assessment measures. Industrial Equipment Manufacturer, a *Fortune 100* Firm, tracks in-house, domestic and offshore suppliers' costs, quality, and productivity using a standardized activity measure. The data is captured by an in-house dashboard and analyzed monthly by management to monitor real development costs and trends. They learned that real savings from offshore do not occur until after they have invested significant upfront training of every offshore developer and team leader. They also share this data with vendors so that all parties understand the total cost trends.

In contrast, at Biotech, offshore measures are still in the formative stage. Traditionally, Biotech's IT managers conduct subjective audits on the back end of a system implementation. Critical feedback from the customers and the sponsoring SBU is deemed the most important assessment factor. As the CIO notes, "IT cannot make this assessment alone, it has to be done with the sponsoring and user group." The Head of the Offshore Project Management Office is developing more quantitative metrics, but the effort is not complete.

Some participants are pressuring suppliers to develop a set of metrics to serve as industry benchmarks:

"Our vendor must have many customers who are all trying to do the same thing. And maybe some have already done it. If they could just come up with five to seven key measurements to help me, I could better manage the project and explain the process to my boss. But every time I ask for "best of breed" metrics, they tell me, "metrics really need to be company specific and business driven, not vendor provided" That does not help me!"

Conclusion

Despite the media hype predicting the demise of US jobs and the political uncertainties that could affect offshore sourcing, we predict that offshore sourcing will become part of the rich and multi-faceted sourcing of IT work at most large US firms. The best practice has been and will continue to be best sourcing, including a mix of in-house IT staff, domestic contractors, domestic suppliers, near-shore suppliers, co-sourcing with strategic partners, and yes, offshore suppliers. The good news for CIOs just adding offshore sourcing to their IT sourcing portfolios is that many sourcing experiences transfer to the offshore domain. In this paper, we highlighted which best practices are the same or different about domestic and offshore sourcing. These practices can help CIOs swiftly move through the learning curve, mitigate risks, work with offshore suppliers, and achieve satisfactory costs and service levels. But what next?

There will be many shifts in preferred offshore sourcing locales and players. Countries such as the Philippines and China will likely resume the role traditionally held by India – low cost staff augmentation for repetitive or highly defined tasks. India will remain a strong player, but with a different focus. The large Indian suppliers are trying to position themselves higher in the value chain, competing on par with IBM, EDS, CSC, and Accenture. As the large Indian suppliers gain experience and build relationships with US customers, they will be able to demand higher prices to reflect higher value. However, the transition will be tough because Indian suppliers are coping with significant challenges caused by rapid growth. By the same token, IBM, EDS, CSC, and Accenture established captive centers or joint ventures in India to leverage offshore advantages on behalf of their US customers. Smaller Indian firms are also effectively competing on quality of staff, domain expertise, and flexibility. There is still much to be learned in terms of better customer/supplier coordination, types and sizes of projects best suited for offshore, and balanced scorecard metrics to compare internal, domestic, and offshore sourcing alternatives.

Notes

1 Lacity, M. and Willcocks, L. (2001) *Global Information Technology Outsourcing: Search for Business Advantage*, Chichester: Wiley.
Lacity, M., Willcocks, L. and Feeny, D. (1996) "The Value of Selective IT Sourcing," *Sloan Management Review*, Vol. 37, 3, pp. 13–25;
Lacity, M., Willcocks, L. and Feeny, D. (1995) "Information Technology Outsourcing: Maximizing Flexibility and Control," *Harvard Business Review*, Vol. 73, 3, pp. 84–93.
2 Field, T. (2002) "The Man In The Middle," *CIO Magazine*, April.
3 For more on Project Leader Veterans, see Brown, C., and Vessey, I. (2003) "Managing the Next Wave of Enterprise Systems: Leveraging Lessons From ERP," *MIS Quarterly Executive*, Vol. 2, 1, pp. 65–77.

References

Ambrosio, J. (2003) "Experts Reveal Hidden Costs of Offshore IT Outsourcing," *CIO Magazine*, April.
Carmel, E. and Agarwal, R. (2002) "The Maturation of Offshore Sourcing of Information Technology Work," *MIS Quarterly Executive*, Vol. 1, 2, pp. 65–77.
Drezner, D. (2004) "The Outsourcing Bogeyman," *Foreign Affairs*, Vol. 83, 3, pp. 1–7.
Field, T. (2002) "The Man In The Middle," *CIO Magazine*, April.
Griswold, D. (2004) "Outsource: A Boon to the American Economy," *National Review*, May 3, pp. 36–38.
Hof, R. and Kerttetter, J. (2004) "Software: Will Outsourcing Hurt America's Supremacy?," *Business Week*, March 1, pp. 84–95.
Kaiser, K. and Hawk, S. (2004) "Evolution of Offshore Software Development: From Outsourcing to Cosourcing," *MIS Quarterly Executive*, Vol. 3, 2, pp. 69–81.
Lacity, M. and Willcocks, L. (2001) *Global Information Technology Outsourcing: Search for Business Advantage*, Chichester: Wiley.
Lacity, M., Willcocks, L. and Feeny, D. (1996) "The Value of Selective IT Sourcing," *Sloan Management Review*, Vol. 37, 3, pp. 13–25.
Lacity, M. and Willcocks, L. (1998) "Practices in Information Technology Outsourcing: Lessons From Experience," *MIS Quarterly*, September, Vol. 22, 3, pp. 363–408.
Lacity, M. and Willcocks, L (2001) *Global IT Outsourcing: Search For Business Advantage*, Chichester: Wiley.
Lacity, M., Willcocks, L. and Feeny, D. (1995) "Information Technology Outsourcing: Maximizing Flexibility and Control," *Harvard Business Review*, Vol. 73, 3, pp. 84–93.

Lindsey, B. (2004) "Job Losses and Trade: A Reality Check," *Cato Institute Trade Briefing*, No. 19, March, 17.

McCarthy, K. (2002) "Redefining Offshore Outsourcing," *InfoWorld*, Vol. 24, 28, p. 56.

McGee, M. (2003) "Offshore Outsourcing Drags Down U.S. Bonus Pay," *Information Week*, August 25.

Rottman, J. and Lacity, M. (2004) "Twenty Practices for Offshore Sourcing," *MIS Quarterly Executive*, Vol. 3, 3, pp. 117–130.

Thibodeau, P. and Hoffman, T. (2003) "Surviving Offshore Cutbacks," *Computerworld*, Vol. 37, 17, pp. 41–42.

11

Selecting and Leveraging Outsourcing Suppliers

Sara Cullen, Leslie P. Willcocks and Mary C. Lacity

Introduction

Outsourcing – and as part of this, choosing and leveraging suppliers – is most successful when managed as a life-cycle, and not as a one-off transaction. In our version (see Cullen *et al.*, 2006), this outsourcing life-cycle consists of nine building blocks in four phases. The first four blocks comprise the *Architect Phase*, which lays the foundation for the deal. The fifth and sixth blocks make up the *Engage Phase*, when the client selects the supplier and negotiates the deal. The seventh and eighth blocks make up the *Operate Phase*, when the deal is operationalized and managed. *Regenerate*, the final phase, is where the client assesses options and then resumes the cycle. The client's bargaining power fluctuates throughout this life-cycle, as shown in Figure 11.1.

This chapter focuses on the *Engage Phase* shown in Figure 11.1 – the selecting and negotiating tasks during which, client power is at its height. All too often clients can emerge from this phase with unrealistic expectations of what their responsibilities are, what the service provider will actually do for the price, and how the deal will work out in practice. The more a client uses its power well during this phase, the greater will be the eventual chances of success. Organizationally and strategically, especially in

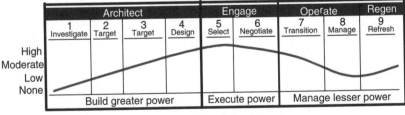

Client Bargaining Power

Figure 11.1   Bargaining Power and the Lifecycle

large-scale deals, the client organization's CEO is the ultimate pivot of bargaining power and must be involved in forming and utilizing this power. As a management process, the constant aim across the outsourcing life-cycle is to build and manage relative bargaining power. Clients entering the *Engage Phase* of the life-cycle without having amassed the best possible bargaining power prior to negotiation, will find it very difficult indeed thereafter to improve their position. One response in the *Operate Phase* is to focus much more on building and bringing to bear the core retained capabilities needed to manage the supplier, in the game of 'catch-up' described in Chapter 15 of this book. Our research demonstrates that a much better practice is to have these capabilities already in place during the *Architect Phase* (Figure 11.1), not least because this enhances bargaining power during the process of supplier engagement. The abiding principle is clear, then, namely that leveraging suppliers is essentially about establishing and maintaining bargaining power.

But how is this done during the *Engage Phase*? Here we point to the need to focus on supplier capabilities and competencies, not resources. We also discuss four types of supplier configuration and the risks and benefits of each. We also describe, and use case studies, to illustrate how local versus global, niche versus broad, and domestic versus offshore decisions about suppliers can be made. The chapter then deals with the key criteria that should be applied for qualifying a candidate supplier, and details effective bid facilitation techniques. Finally, using two case studies, we show the deleterious consequences of using strong bargaining power ineffectively, leaving a supplier with a 'winner's curse deal, from which they stand little chance of making profit. The conclusion summarizes the key lessons of the chapter.

Capabilities and competencies versus resources

When evaluating suppliers clients tend to focus on suppliers' resources because these are highly visible on site tours, balance sheets and resumes. But they should be more interested in suppliers' ability to turn these resources – its physical and human assets such as physical facilities, technologies, tools and workforce – into capabilities that, in turn, can be combined to create high-level customer-facing competencies. Figure 11.2 illustrates the relationship between these three types of asset.

Our research (see Feeny *et al.*, 2005) has identified 12 key supplier capabilities briefly described below:

1. *Leadership* – the capability to identify and deliver overall success throughout the deal.
2. *Business management* – the ability to deliver in line with service agreements and the supplier's and client's business plans.

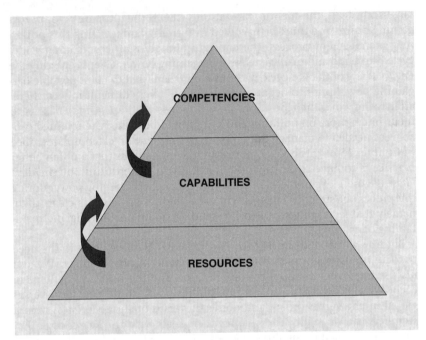

Figure 11.2   The Relationship between Supplier Resources, Capabilities & Competencies

3. *Domain expertise* – the capability to retain and apply professional knowledge, including technical and domain (sectoral and organizational) expertise.
4. *Behavior management* – the ability to motivate and inspire people to deliver high-level service
5. *Sourcing* – the ability to access resources cost-effectively as needed
6. *Process improvement* – the capability to incorporate changes to the service process, to meet dramatic improvement targets.
7. *Technology exploitation* – the capacity to swiftly and effectively deploy new technology for business purpose.
8. *Program management* – the capability to deliver a series of inter-related projects.
9. *Customer development* – the ability to help customers make informed choices about service levels, functionality and costs.
10. *Planning & contracting* – the capability to deliver "win/win" results for customer and supplier.
11. *Organizational design* – the ability to design and implement successful organizational arrangements.
12. *Governance* – the capability to define, track, take responsibility for and measure performance.

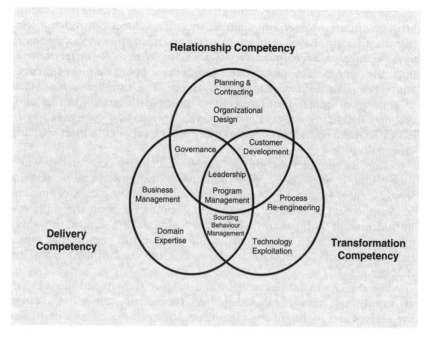

Figure 11.3 Twelve Supplier Capabilities

These 12 capabilities, in turn, can be leveraged into three important competencies (Figure 11.3):

- **Delivery competency** based on the supplier's ability and willingness to respond to a customer's day-to-day operational needs.
- **Transformation competency** based on the supplier's ability to deliver radically improved services in terms of cost and quality.
- **Relationship competency** based on the supplier's capacity and will to align itself with the customer's values, goals and needs. By far, this is the hardest competency to find in a supplier.

The **delivery competency** primarily involves the supplier's leadership, business management, domain expertise, behavior management, sourcing, program management and governance capabilities. The **transformation competency** mainly involves the supplier's leadership, behavior management, sourcing, process improvement, technology exploitation, program management and customer development capabilities. The **relationship competency** primarily relies on the supplier's leadership, customer development, planning and contracting, organizational design, governance and program management capabilities. Amongst these, the planning and contracting capability presents the greatest challenges because it is very difficult to align customer and supplier incentives. Most outsourcing relationships are still based on fee-for-service contracts, in which a customer pays the supplier a fee for delivery of a service. With a fee-for-service contract, the customer is motivated to squeeze the supplier for more resources and services without wanting to pay more. The supplier is motivated to squeeze as much profit margin as possible through contract add-ons and delivering only to service levels agreed. The customer has to ensure that the plans and contracts motivate the supplier to meet sourcing expectations.

Customers should focus on the supplier's delivery competency when they primarily want the supplier to maintain or slightly improve existing services, such as maintaining legacy systems, operating data centres, or servicing a fleet of desktop devices. They should focus on the supplier's transformation competency when they are seeking radical improvements in costs and services and on the relationship competency when they are seeking a substantial and long-term commitment from the supplier.

While the 12 capabilities model was developed to help customers evaluate suppliers, it has other uses. Suppliers, for instance, can use it to assess themselves and highlight the capabilities they will devote to a particular customer account. Customers and suppliers can use it collaboratively to improve their existing relationships. Customers can also use the model to help improve supplier performance. Suppliers cannot deliver the 12 capabilities if they are not significantly enabled to do so by the customer.

Getting the supplier configuration right

There are a number of ways to choose suppliers (Cullen and Willcocks, 2003). The first involves deciding which configuration of suppliers best fits the client's purposes. There are four options: *Sole Supplier, Prime Contractor, Best-of-Breed* and *Panel*.

- *Sole Supplier* is where a single supplier provides the entire portfolio or deal. The benefits include sole accountability and seamless service, but this model can compromise service quality, as no one supplier is outstanding in all areas.
- A *Prime Contractor* arrangement consists of a network, with several suppliers under the control of the head contractor. It is a well recognized form of supply chain contracting. The head supplier is accountable, and contractually liable, for the entirety of the contract but uses any number of subcontractors to deliver all or part of it. Typically, the subcontractors have expertise or operate in regions, that the head contractor does not, or

they are deployed by the client to support its local customers. Alliance networks where two or more suppliers to offer services as a package have identified as a long-term trend in outsourcing. However they require contract provisions that limit what can be sub-contracted, and to which firms, and how the sub-contractors will be monitored and controlled.

- In a *Best-of-Breed* network (also known as multi-vendor, multi-sourcing or selective sourcing) the organization has a number of suppliers and thus is in effect the head contractor itself. It represents a low risk outsourcing option that has been adopted by 75% of UK and 82% of US organizations. The benefits and problems associated with this option relate to competition: although competitive tension leads to continuous improvement and cost effective benchmarking, it is often difficult to constructively manage suppliers working in keen competition with one another.

- In a *Panel* arrangement there is a list of preferred suppliers working in continuous competition. Interactions are many and brief, and work is not guaranteed: each supplier competes on a regular basis for various contracts or work orders over a defined period. This approach is often used in applications development, hardware purchasing, and consulting, as the work tends to be periodic and the requirements vary with each initiative.

Table 11.1 provides a summary of the benefits, risks and issues associated with each configuration.

Another way to choose suppliers relates to the supplier market in which the client wants to operate. It involves three main choices:

- *Domestic Versus Offshore*
  Offshoring is predominately a "best-of-breed" approach, although some organizations have set up a prime contractor to manage offshore suppliers. Typical services for which the overseas labor market has demonstrated superior cost advantages include applications coding, call centre operations, data entry and transaction processing. As a result, the offshore market tends to be very niche-orientated.

- *Local Versus Global*
  Global providers are a common choice if an organization opts for the sole supplier configuration, due to their international reach and broad service offerings. Such large suppliers have access to more resources and are better able to assemble and deploy SWAT teams as needed.

- *Niche Versus Broad*
  The respective advantages of these two types of supplier are described in Table 11.2. In their limited service offerings niche suppliers represent a 'best-of-breed' option and are either contracted directly with the client, or indirectly through a prime contractor.

Table 11.1 Supplier Configuration Options

Option	Benefits	Risks	Management Issues
Sole Supplier	• Sole accountability • Potential to pass on economies • Streamlined contracting costs and processes • End-to-end key performance metrics	• Monopolistic supplier behaviors • Compromise quality where the supplier is not best of breed (in services, industries or geographic locations)	• Extensive contract flexibility rights due to the dependence on supplier • Independent expertise to avoid solution channelling and ensure value for money (quotes are market values)
Prime Contractor	• Single point of accountability • Allows best-of-breed subcontracting • Streamlined, but a bit more complex, contracting costs and processes • End-to-end KPIs	• Prime must be expert at subcontracting (selection, management, disengagement) • Client may desire different subcontractors • Client often required to resolve issues between the prime and subcontractor/s • Primes and subcontractors often encroach "territories"	• Contract ensuring various rights over the subcontracting (access, selection, veto, etc) • Compliance auditing ensuring the prime passes obligations to the subcontractors • Oversight ensuring all parties are operating as an efficient and united front
Best of Breed	• Greater control • Flexibility to chop and change • Promotes competition and prevents complacency	• Attracting the market for small "slices" of work • Keeping suppliers interested, giving management focus, and allocating staff • Interdependent services and contracts • Integration complexity • Tracing accountability	• Designing interdependent contracts between independent suppliers • Multi-party interface and handover management • End-to-end process management is more difficult • Multiple lifecycle management

Table 11.1 Supplier Configuration Options – *continued*

Option	Benefits	Risks	Management Issues
Panel	• Buy services and assets when required • Promotes ongoing competition • Prevents complacency	• Attracting the market when panel is a pre-qualification and does not guarantee work • Adding new panel members or wanting to use suppliers not on the panel	• Panel bidding process for work • Ongoing ranking of panel members based on performance • Managing and evaluating the total program

Table 11.2   Niche Versus Broad

Supplier Capability	Niche Supplier	Broad Supplier
Leadership	Supplier leaders will be well known and there will be easy access to CEO and straightforward deployment of resources	Harder to contact top management
Planning & Contracting	Suppliers have more vested interest in the relationship because they cannot absorb or afford failures	The client should push hard for creative contracts, as suppliers have greater ability to absorb risk than niche players
Organization Design	Less formal design is required and the deal is more based on personal relationships	Formal organizational design is more important.
Process Improvement	Niche suppliers may rely less on processes (like Six Sigma, CMM) but make up for this with domain expertise	Broad suppliers may rigidly use CMM
Domain Expertise	There will be better domain knowledge because of specialization, but specific elements of business knowledge will still need to be transferred to the supplier	Clients need to pay special attention to knowledge transfer. Large suppliers can gain domain knowledge through the transfer of relevant employees

The supplier model: two case studies

Case study 1: domestic versus offshore

This case study shows how customers can compare current domestic suppliers with an offshore supplier by assessing their relative capabilities and competencies. The customer was a large US retailer with an eight-year relationship with a domestic supplier for legacy system maintenance and enhancement. The existing contract was quite large, with the supplier assigning nearly 500 IT workers to the account. The question was whether to award a large re-platforming project (from Visual Basic to Java) to the existing supplier or an Indian supplier. The existing supplier was seen as capable but costly. It charged $100 per hour for programming, while the Indian supplier charged $30 per hour. The Indian supplier had already performed well on some pilot projects, but the retailer had underestimated the extra burden of managing remote teams and the volume of re-work required because the supplier did not understand the business. These issues eroded much of the cost savings.

Table 11.3   The Relative Capabilities of a Domestic and an Offshore Supplier

Supplier Capability	Domestic Supplier	Offshore Supplier
1. Leadership	*Strong* The supplier had named a well-respected manager with a good support team.	*Good* The supplier had named a well-respected manager but is less clear on who will serve in the supporting team.
2. Business Management	*Strong* Given the high cost bid, the supplier should have been able to deliver the project and still earn a profit.	*Strong* Although the bid was low, the supplier cost base was low and should have been able to deliver and still earn a profit.
3. Domain Expertise	N/A	N/A
4. Behavior Management	*Strong* Supplier employees would ask the customer if they needed clarification. Many of supplier staff would have worked with the client before.	*Weak* Supplier employees were eager to please but did not share bad news promptly. The supplier staff were mostly new to the client.
5. Sourcing	*Weak* It was likely that the supplier would assign low level programmers.	*Weak* It was likely that the supplier would primarily use new hires from Indian universities.
6. Process Improvement	N/A	N/A
7. Technology Exploitation	*Strong* The supplier had performed this work in the past and had automated. tools.	*Strong* The supplier had performed this work in the past and had automated tools.
8. Program Management	*Strong* The supplier had demonstrated this capability in the past.	*Weak* The supplier relied heavily on an on-site engagement manager who was expected to fulfil too many roles.
9. Customer Development	N/A	N/A

Table 11.3   The Relative Capabilities of a Domestic and an Offshore Supplier
– continued

Supplier Capability	Domestic Supplier	Offshore Supplier
10. Planning & Contracting	*Weak* The supplier was very expensive.	*Strong* The supplier's bid was 60% lower than the domestic supplier.
11. Organizational Design	*Strong* Supplier staff were primarily on-site.	*Weak* The supplier staff would be offshore, with an on-site engagement manager as the contact.
12. Governance	*Strong* The supplier already had reporting processes in place and reported twice a week.	*Weak* Although the supplier was CMM5, internal supplier reports were not shared, and in the past the client had had to request daily reporting.

Rather than letting the hourly rates dominate the decision, we show how the twelve-point capabilities model can help bring about an informed decision.

In this scenario, the retailer was primarily interested in the following supplier capabilities (see Table 11.3):

- leadership (who will be responsible?)
- business management (can the supplier earn a margin on this bid?)
- program management (can the supplier organize, manage, test, and transfer the large number of program rewrites?)
- sourcing (will we get the supplier's best programmers and project managers?)
- behavior management (will supplier employees be motivated, productive, and easy to work with?)
- organizational design (where will supplier employees be located and how will we interface with the supplier organization?)
- technology exploitation (does the supplier have automated tools to develop and test the new platform?)
- planning and contracting (what is the fixed price?)
- governance (how will the supplier track, report, and fix performance?)

Because the re-platforming project was primarily technical and involved clear requirements, the supplier would not have to interact with end-users, so customer development and domain expertise capabilities were not pertinent. Furthermore, the retailer was not seeking new processes, so the process design capability was also irrelevant.

Looking at the analysis in Table 11.3, it is quite clear that the domestic supplier had superior capabilities to deliver the project compared to the offshore supplier. But the Indian supplier clearly won on contract price. The retailer decided to use the offshore supplier bid to pressure the domestic supplier to reduce its price by 10% to 50%.

'We were paying about $100 for commodity type coding (with domestic suppliers),' commented the Director of Contract Management. 'The domestic suppliers saw the writing on the wall. We put out a bid to the approved list of domestic contractors and the current director of the PMO made it very clear that we were not going to pay those kinds of prices anymore. Our domestic prices dropped from about $100 per hour to $80 and some of the rates even dropped into the $50 range for some services.'

However, by forcing the domestic supplier to reduce their costs the retailer weakened the domestic supplier's business management capability (its ability to earn a profit while delivering the service). Significantly, our research has found that domestic suppliers are increasingly using offshore captive centres to compete with Indian suppliers on costs, while leveraging their domestic presence to keep customer service levels high.

Case study 2: small versus large

The senior managers of a large US company decided that the Applications Development Director should outsource at least a third of new development work offshore. Such senior management decisions are common in the large US organizations that we have studied and are based solely on the lower hourly wages of offshore workers. However, typically they neglect or underestimate the high transaction costs involved in coordinating and managing offshore suppliers.

The context was a new software development for a large intranet that would connect the customer's sales force with a centralized customer ordering, inventory, and logistics centre. This required new technologies (wireless) and a good understanding of the customer's business. The Applications Development Director was considering two Indian suppliers of very different sizes. The larger Indian supplier had over 40,000 employees. The smaller one had only 250 employees, of which 220 resided in Hyderabad and 30 in the US.

Respective analyses of the suppliers' 12 capabilities are summarized in Table 11.4. They indicated that the larger Indian supplier had superior business management., domain expertise, sourcing, and technology exploitation capabilities. However, the smaller supplier had superior leadership, behavior management, customer development, and organizational design capabilities. The Application Development Director finally chose the smaller supplier, mainly because its CEO was hungry for the business and personally committed to the

Table 11.4 The Relative Capabilities of a Large and Small Supplier

Supplier Capability	Smaller Supplier	Larger Supplier
1. Leadership	**Strong** The CEO was personally committed to the customer. He had handpicked the supplier's leaders, and the CEO would personally oversee and help them deploy resources to ensure contract success.	**Weak** The customer knew it would be difficult to get through to the supplier's top team.
2. Business Management	**Weak** The supplier was just starting to build the business and incurring substantial start-up costs. The customer was worried that it would be responsible for the supplier's survival.	**Strong** The supplier had annual revenues of $1 billion and had earned substantial net revenues.
3. Domain Expertise	**Questionable** The supplier's CEO had a good understanding of the business context because he had worked closely with the Application Development Director before. But it was doubtful whether the rest of the supplier's employees had the same understanding.	**Strong** The supplier organization had previously created similar applications for other clients.
4. Behavior Management	**Strong** The supplier had a unique strategy to attract and retain top talent. He had built a compound in Hyderabad that integrated the families of the employees physically and socially. He had only a 7% turnover. His team was highly geared towards customer service and willingly deferred holidays and worked through weekends to deliver.	**Weak** The supplier relied heavily on new hires and people with less than five years' experience. Turnover was nearly 25%. The employees worked rigidly within the confines of the supplier's CMM processes.
5. Sourcing	**Weak** The small supplier did not have much breadth or depth of resources.	**Strong** The large supplier had access to more resources and was better able to assemble and deploy specialist teams as needed.

Table 11.4   The Relative Capabilities of a Large and Small Supplier – *continued*

Supplier Capability	Smaller Supplier	Larger Supplier
6. Process Improvement	**Weak** The supplier would not help re-design business processes but expected the client to articulate requirements clearly.	**Weak** The supplier would not help re-design business processes but expected the client to articulate requirements clearly.
7. Technology Exploitation	**Weak** The customer had expertise with intranets but not in wireless technologies.	**Strong** The supplier had proven wireless and intranet expertise.
8. Program Management	**Weak** The supplier was still finding its way, tailoring work processes to each new customer. While this resulted in higher customer service, it could equally have resulted in cost escalation, scope creep or lower quality.	**Slightly weak** The supplier relied heavily on CMM processes. In the past the customer had complained that the rigidity of these processes had increased costs. One possibility might have been negotiating 'flexible CMM' in which the customer specifies which documents they will or will not pay for.
9. Customer Development	**Strong** Many of the supplier's project managers had lived and worked in the US on similar accounts. They understood US culture and feel comfortable interacting directly with users.	**Weak** The supplier did not generally interact directly with end-users but relied on the customer's project managers to document user requirements.
10. Planning & Contracting	**Strong** The supplier would have more vested interest in the relationship because it could not absorb or afford failure.	**Strong** The customer might have been able to push harder for creative contracts as the supplier had greater ability to accept risk than a smaller supplier.
11. Organizational Design	**Strong** The supplier's US-based project managers nearly all lived within 30 miles of the customer's headquarters. For the customer this was a big plus.	**Weak** The supplier was willing to release 30% of the staff to the customer's site but the customer would be charged on-shore rates plus expenses (hotels, transportation, visas, etc).

success of the project. Furthermore, the supplier's project managers were local, and the supplier's employees seemed highly motivated. He rejected the large supplier because he was afraid that his company would be only a 'small fish in the big supplier's pond.'

Applying appropriate selection criteria

Not every business context requires suppliers to excel in all 12 capabilities and all three competencies. Every supplier does not have to be a partner possessing a strong relationship competency. Some suppliers may be better at delivering commodity services, such as desktop services, for which the typical vendor management practices apply. Customers who want suppliers to maintain legacy systems will focus on the capabilities that enable the delivery competency. Customers should seek a supplier with a strong relationship competency if they are looking for a long-term partner to serve as the primary source of IT services. Customers who want the supplier to transform their IT functions should focus on capabilities that enable the transformation competency.

Clients need to assess a supplier capabilities and competencies in each new business context. A supplier's ability and willingness to deliver the 12 capabilities is not fixed across the supplier organization, nor is it fixed in time. Because supplier organizations can be very large (some suppliers employ more than 100,000 people worldwide) and complex, a single supplier can present many different faces.

Suppliers' willingness to deliver the 12 capabilities also largely depends on their perception of the desirability of the customer. Customers falsely assume that all suppliers are vying to have their business. A supplier's willingness to 'go the extra mile' for a particular customer depends on:

- The prestige of the customer
- The size of the contract
- The potential for additional supplier revenues and good profit margins with this client and with other clients because of this deal
- The opportunity to enter into new markets
- The opportunity for knowledge transfer to supplier
- The perceived risks
- The supplier headquarters' sales targets or other financial considerations like meeting quarterly sales quotas.

There are three main types of criteria that can be used to evaluate suppliers:

1. Mandatory – the first gate in which the bidders must pass
2. Qualitative – the 'value' part of the value for money equation
3. Price – the 'money' part of the value for money equation

Mandatory criteria are 'drop dead' criteria – the first cut that eliminates non-compliant responses and disqualifies providers who cannot meet even the most basic expectations. Typically, mandatory criteria are of such importance that if these criteria are not met it does not matter what else is in the bid or how low the offered price.

Qualitative criteria are the criteria applied to the non-financial attributes and solutions the provider is offering. These criteria (and their importance relative to one another), determines what kind of information clients request from bidders, and it makes most sense to develop the information requirements after deciding what criteria will drive the selection process. The task of evaluation is simplified, and providers do not waste time on low-priority items.

Each evaluation team must construct the most appropriate listing. How each organization judges what attributes are relevant, which are more important, and the manner in which it interprets these attributes can

Table 11.5   Qualitative Criteria List

Criteria	Description
General Capabilities	These relate to the overall character of the provider and include: • Its 12 core capabilities • Its service and product offerings • Its market share, strategies and focus • The geographic areas where it has current operations • Stratification of its client base • Its financial viability
Track Record	These relate to the provider's experience and proven skills and competencies in relevant areas including: • The client's industry • The geographical areas of operation required by the client • Specific services and assets required in the deal • The nature of the proposed arrangement • Prime contracting and managing subcontractors • Customer reference checks
Proposed Approach	This reflects the detailed solutions proposed by the provider such as: • Service delivery • Staffing and staff management • Transition in and out of the deal • Risk management • Account and client relationship management • Compliance with the contract and SLA (Service Level Agreement) • Continuous improvement • Industry development (if applicable) • Price approach and viability

vary tremendously. Nevertheless, there are standard categories of criteria (see Table 11.5).

Bidding effectively – how to avoid the 'winner's curse'

Successful outsourcing is not about getting the lowest price at all costs. It is about getting the lowest price for a sustainable solution under a fair contract from a superior service provider. Outsourcing is not an isolated economic transaction that automatically implements itself after the parties sign an agreement but an ongoing commercial relationship with long-term economic and strategic consequences that depend on the choices the parties make and how they subsequently conduct themselves. If a client chooses unwisely, these consequences can be very bad.

There can be severe repercussions when the provider is saddled with a contract from which it stands to make no money – the so-called 'winner's curse'. The consequences can be devastating, not only for the service provider but also the client. A 2002 study of 85 contracts found the winner's curse came into play in nearly 20% of the cases and that in over 75% of those cases it was also visited on the client (Ken *et al.*, 2002).

Clients should be on their guard. A provider may deliberately offer a very low price to get the organization's brand into its portfolio. Alternatively, it may be so desperate for business that it undercuts other bids in the hope that, once the contract is secured, it can recoup profits by selling additional services to the client – in other words, the provider is prepared to take a hit in one area in order to make it up in others. Under worst-case scenarios providers may even bank on securing a profit through restricted interpretations of the contract and exploiting contract loopholes and ambiguities.

Clients, therefore, should not automatically select the least expensive option. Nor should they leap to the opposite extreme and opt for the service provider that is qualitatively ranked highest. Instead, they should weigh price against quality to get the best value for money. Indeed, choosing service providers on a 'best value for money' basis has become the norm in outsourcing. Organizations have learnt that the lowest bid price does not mean the lowest cost overall. In fact, the opposite is often the case. The costs involved in additional oversight, out-of-scope charges, constant renegotiation, dispute resolution, re-working and back-sourcing, can make the price originally agreed no more than a distant memory.

Most organizations use tendering to select service providers. Such an approach has the advantage of putting pressure on service providers to deliver best value for money against their industry peers and of disclosing a variety of capabilities and potential solutions, thus allowing a well-informed selection decision to take place. The alternative is direct negotiation with appropriately placed organizations. However, this strategy is only likely to be successful if:

- One service provider is so outstanding that there is no benefit in evaluating alternative service providers
- The client is an informed buyer and knows the market prices and industry norms regarding service definitions, technology and key performance indicators
- The organization knows exactly what it wants and can quickly draw up an effective contract, service level agreement and price schedule
- Speed is more important than cost or exploring alternative solutions comparing service providers. But organizations must be careful not to throw away advantages in speed by poor preparation
- The client is an experienced outsourcing manager and can expertly manage the provider and the arrangement
- The client has significantly more bargaining power than the service provider.

In contrast, non-competitive processes such as direct negotiation may seem easier to carry out and faster to put in place. But they may not get the best results. For most organizations tendering is the most appropriate strategy. In addition many organizations, particularly in the public sector, require competitive tendering.

Turning to the detail of the bidding process, paper transactions – issuing documentation and expecting an informed and comprehensive response – is unrealistic. Bidders require interaction to be effective. The more an organization can help potential providers understand its organization, strategies and ways of operating, the better the responses will be. There are a number of techniques to help service providers acquire this kind of knowledge, as shown in Table 11.6:

Conversely, there are a number of interactive techniques by which clients can increase their knowledge of potential suppliers, as shown in Table 11.7.

The winner's curse: two case studies

Case study 1: a global manufacturer

A well-known global equipment manufacturer had a successful outsourcing business in Europe and wanted to enter the Asia-Pacific market. It cut a deal with an industrial manufacturer that wanted to outsource its IT function. The service provider created a new wholly-owned subsidiary for the region. The deal was the first of what were planned to be many.

In order to get the first critical deal with the client, the supplier's sales team bid a price that was below cost. It did not realize that, however, since it was dealing with its first client and had no idea what the actual cost would

Table 11.6 Bid Facilitation Techniques

Facilitation Technique	Description
Bidder Discovery/ Due Diligence	The aim of this is to allow bidders to verify the representations made by the client in its market package and other communications. Due diligence by the provider helps clarify the assumptions on which their proposals are based. This has the benefit of limiting potential caveats, disclaimers, and risk contingencies in bids. It can include:
	• Reviewing existing service agreements, contracts, subcontracts, service provider agreements, lease agreements, supply and equipment sources, maintenance practices and related items for which the service provider will take responsibility
	• Verifying the inventory of all assets to be purchased, or provided by the organization, verifying the ownership, determining the condition and market value
	• Validating service definitions, KPIs, baseline costs, capacities, loads, backlogs
	• Confirming configuration, systems software, documentation, security, change control
	• Reviewing applicable organizational standards, policies and procedures that they will need to comply with
	• Confirming the employment conditions of staff that may be transferred under conditions no less favorable to those they current enjoy
	• Interviewing management, users and other key stakeholders
	• Running integration tests and diagnostics.
Briefings	Most providers welcome opportunities to meet and obtain information from the client. At a market briefing providers are usually presented with:
	• Background information on the organization, its history and its future strategies
	• Reasons for outsourcing, discussion of key requirements and the organization's expectations of the service provider
	• Introductions to key stakeholders and their views
	• an overview of the market package; evaluation criteria, key dates and further stages in the selection process
	• objectives, issues, and other items that are difficult to communicate or emphasize in a voluminous market package.
Data Rooms	When it is not practical to include information or data in the market package, a data room can play a useful role. This is a secure room containing data, bulk information and, if appropriate, a secure terminal to assist prospective providers in formulating bids. All registered prospective bidders are allowed an opportunity to visit the room and view the data but usually are not allowed to copy documents without authorization.

Table 11.6   Bid Facilitation Techniques – *continued*

Facilitation Technique	Description
Questions and Answers	Service providers generally have questions throughout the response period. The best way to handle these is to have a written request/response procedure. Only information clarifying the Market Package is sent out and never any proprietary information relating to other bidders
Site Visits	When documentation cannot adequately convey the full range of information, bidders can be offered the opportunity to visit sites.
Workshops	Workshops can help providers explore options with the organization so that they can tailor responses more sensitively and effectively. These can take a number of forms – brainstorming, problem solving sessions or discussions to increase understanding of how the organization works.

Table 11.7   Interactive Bid Evaluation Techniques

Evaluation Technique	Description
Presentations	It is worthwhile having bidders present their proposals, so that the client can see how they interpret the bid, what they see as important and what their strengths are.
Interviews with key supplier personnel	Interviews with the key individuals in the supplier's account and service delivery teams can help the client better understand what bidders are proposing and how well they understand its needs. They also allow the client to assess the personal capabilities of the individuals concerned and their ability to work with the client.
Site visits	Inspecting the provider's operations is invaluable in gaining understanding of how they conduct their business and manage relationships in practice.
Workshops	Workshops or field experiments provide an opportunity to see how well the parties can work together. Such opportunities to exchange views and problem-solve, whether focused on real or hypothetical issues, are almost always worthwhile. However, government probity rules, which dictate that all bidders must receive exactly the same information, may not permit them in the public sector, given the fluidity of conversations in such workshops.

be. It basically bid the price it thought necessary to win the contract without having a firm grasp of what price was needed to make a reasonable profit. The client knew the service provider could not be making money on the deal but took comfort in the strength of its well-known global brand.

After 18 months the service provider still had not won any further clients. A review of the subsidiary by its parent organization showed that it was making unacceptable losses and there was little possibility of a rapid turnaround. So it had to start making money from its one client. The service provider assigned a new account manager – a lawyer. His mission was to re-interpret the contract and reclaim any possible money he could. This was possible because the contract had no date limitations regarding when work could be billed and reimbursements claimed.

Nine months of intense dispute followed. Invoices were raised for work deemed out of scope, a number of additional charges and reimbursements were claimed which went right back to the start of the contract. Work that the client had been obtaining was stopped if the account manager interpreted the work as out-of-scope. Eventually the two parties reached a settlement through a third-party intermediary. The wholly-owned subsidiary was wound-up, and the client had to find a new service provider.

However, further difficulties followed with the new service provider. The client had developed a deep distrust of service providers, and the new service provider had to invest a lot of time and effort in relationship management – and repair – to regain enough trust to be able to function effectively.

Case study 2: a major retailer

The IT department of a retailing company had recently been transferred to its Corporate Services division. The general manager believed that commodity functions should be outsourced so the division could focus on adding value to the operational business units. She saw IT services as a commodity and put data centre operations to tender. As a commodity market, she believed providers of data centre operations were undifferentiated in their services and approaches, and the contract was awarded solely on the basis of price. The successful bid was 30% lower than the nearest other bid.

Things soon began to go wrong. Scope and price variations became common. Eventually a post had to be dedicated to variation management. Service levels were rarely achieved, because they had been set up as targets, not minimum standards. This was because the client accepted the service provider's 'standard' service level agreement rather than developing one that represented its needs. The service provider capped the amount of resources they would provide for the price and would only provide more if more money was paid. In time, the general manager had to hire specialists to work in the data centre in order to restore service to previous levels and meet peak demands.

Within a year the total cost of contract outstripped the bid and the in-house baseline. Moreover – and most telling – the efforts of the division's remaining IT people had become focused on fighting the contract, not on adding value to the business.

Conclusion – key lessons

Key lessons regarding selecting and leveraging suppliers emerge from our research into over 1,200 organizations. The first is that the selection and negotiation phase is when the client enjoys most bargaining power and, if this power is not used wisely at this point, there can be very negative repercussions. Secondly, customers need to assess suppliers' capabilities and competencies rather than their resources. We have identified 12 key capabilities that in turn can be converted into three competencies of overriding importance to clients – delivery, transformation and relationship competencies.

Choosing the right supplier model or configuration of suppliers is the essential first step. There is no one best way. Sole supplier, best-of-breed, network and panel models all have their own benefits and risks. Moreover, as we demonstrated, in modern outsourcing the selected model must also fit across whether domestic or offshore outsourcing, local or global coverage, and a niche or broad market player are more suitable choices for a specific set of needs and circumstances.

Fourthly, customers should assess a supplier's capabilities and competencies for each new business context: not every business context requires suppliers to excel in all 12 capabilities and all three competencies. In assessing suppliers there are three different sets of criteria – mandatory, qualitative and price. Fifthly, in negotiating, it is vital to avoid the 'winner's curse' – bids which excessively favor the client at the expense of the supplier, as these do not work to the client's advantage in the long run. As two case studies demonstrated, the key is getting the best *value* in return for a fair price. Sixthly, tendering is generally the most common and effective strategy to select suppliers. Direct negotiation without tendering is only for highly experienced clients.

Finally, the more interaction and transparency between client and potential supplier at this stage the better. A range of techniques have been developed to facilitate this on both sides. These include bidder discovery, due diligence, briefings, data rooms, questions and answers, site visits, and interviews with key supplier personnel. We detail these techniques, because while, in our research, we have seen many contracts agreed in principle, and many promises made by both sides, the devil, and delivery is in the detail. Clients (and suppliers) who fail to be diligent may manage to get a quicker deal signed, but are very likely to regret very much in the operationalization stage, their oversights and haste during the selection and negotiation phases.

References

Cullen, S., Seddon, P. and Willcocks, L. (2006) Managing The Sourcing Process: A Life-Cycle Perspective. In Willcocks, L. and Lacity, M., *Global Sourcing of Business and IT Services*. London: Palgrave.

Cullen, S. and Willcocks, L. (2003) *Intelligent IT Outsourcing: Eight Building Blocks To Success*. Oxford: Butterworth/Computer Weekly.

Feeny, D., Lacity, M. and Willcocks, L. (2005) Taking A Measure Of Outsourcing Providers, *Sloan Management Review*, 46, 3, 41–48.

Kern, T. and Willcocks, L. and Van Heck, E. (2002) The Winners Curse In IT Outsourcing: Strategies For Avoiding Relational Trauma. *California Management Review*, 44, 2, 47–69.

12
Managing Relationships across the Life Cycle of an Outsourcing Arrangement

Mary C. Lacity and Leslie P. Willcocks

Introduction

As noted in the Introductory chapter, IT outsourcing research has evolved from a focus upon what firms outsource to successfully managing outsourcing relationships. In this chapter, we aim to contribute to practice by better understanding the underlying nature of the client-supplier relationship. In analyzing our rich research base comprising in-depth interviews with senior executives, CIOs, suppliers, IT staff, IT users, and IT outsourcing consultants, we found that the client-supplier dichotomy fails to capture the complexity of all stakeholder relationships involved in IT outsourcing. The "client" actually includes senior business managers who pay for IT, senior IT managers who manage IT, IT staff who deliver IT, and finally the users who actually receive the IT service. The "supplier" includes senior management who negotiate deals, account managers responsible for earning a profit on the deal, and supplier IT staff charged with delivery. If IT unions, external consultants, lawyers, subcontractors, or multi-sourcing are involved, additional sets of stakeholders are added to the party. By attending to these multiple stakeholders, we have a better understanding of the complex relationships among stakeholders, and operate from a more informed base for improving these relationships.

This chapter summarizes previous research on IT outsourcing, pointing out, as do Kern and Willcocks (2001), a surprising shortage of specific research on the relationship dimension, despite widespread recognition of its importance. It then presents an overall framework for understanding relationships among stakeholders before, during, and after IT outsourcing contracts are signed. The primary contribution of the chapter is an IT outsourcing relationship framework that focuses on three key elements: (1) relationship stakeholders (2) relationship types, and (3) six relationship phases and their related activities. We found IT outsourcing stakeholders behave antagonistically, cooperatively, and also collaboratively, depending on the alignment of goals for the issue at hand. Relationships are quite dynamic, and organizations that face up to the complex realities of shared, complementary, and conflicting goals are much more likely to develop productive outsourcing arrangements over time. Thus our research indicates that the "allies or adversaries" question has to be re-framed, and that relationships are dependent on the particular task facing the stakeholders involved, and the particular phase reached in the outsourcing arrangement.

The research literature on IT outsourcing

As organizations accumulated IT outsourcing experiences in the 1990s, academic research increasingly described and analyzed the phenomenon. Table 12.1 lists major IT outsourcing research, including descriptive case studies, surveys of current outsourcing practices, surveys of practitioners' perceptions of risks and benefits of outsourcing, studies of determinants of outsourcing, and identification of best practices that distinguish success from failure.

There is still considerable debate among the body of research on best practices which distinguish successes from failures, and our primary contribution has been to address this debate by relating actual sourcing outcomes to various managerial practices (Lacity and Willcocks, 1998, 1999, 2000). Most of the empirical research agrees that a detailed formal evaluation process is required and that shorter term contracts, outsourcing commodity IT on a selective basis, and retention of requisite management capabilities, contribute to success (Grover *et al.*, 1996; Klepper, 1995; Lacity and Hirschheim, 1993, 1995; Willcocks and Fitzgerald, 1994; De Looff, 1995). Controversy, however, still surrounds the appropriate governance structure. Some research has found that "strategic alliances" are the best governance structure (McFarlan and Nolan, 1995; Klepper, 1995; and McLellan *et al.*, 1995), while other research has found that detailed contracts and performance measures remain central to any outsourcing arrangement (for example Douglass, 1993; Lacity and Hirschheim, 1993; Lacity and Willcocks, 1998; Willcocks and Fitzgerald, 1994). All these studies also recognize the importance of relationships in determining success or failure, but as Kern (1999) points out in a foundational study on the topic, none really study the complexities of the relationship dimension. Instead, most research either accepts client-supplier assumptions of shared goals or focuses on the dichotomous relationship between them (Kern and Willcocks, 2001). Thus the trading partners are the only relevant stakeholders, the only winners or losers–in short – the only unit of analysis.

In the context of IT outsourcing relationships, we found that the dyadic client-supplier relationship perspective sheds only limited understanding. Instead, we found that a more micro-analysis of multiple stakeholders within the trading partners is required for in-depth understanding. Our own research study also showed that the general notion of phases of relationship

Table 12.1 Empirical Research on IT Outsourcing

Author(s)	Research Method	Scope of the Research	Findings
Ang and Straub (1998))	Survey of 243 US banks	Influence of production, transaction economies and financial slack on outsourcing decisions.	Banks were strongly influenced by production cost advantages in their decisions to outsource. Transaction economies was much less of a determinant while financial slack was not a significant explanator.
Applegate and Montealegre (1991)	Case study	Kodak's IS outsourcing decision	Documented the immediate impact on processes and services of Kodak's decision.
Arnett and Jones (1994)	Survey of 40 CIOs	Description of sourcing practices in US companies	The most commonly outsourced IT functions were contract programming (67%), Software support and training (56%), Workstation/PC maintenance (39%), and systems integration (28%).
Auwers and Deschoolmeester (1993)	Case study	Belgium Chocolate company's outsourcing decision	Found that outsourcing helped leverage resources during a mainframe conversion to SAP.
Clark, Zmud, and McCray (1995)	63 interviews with executives	Analysed the forces driving IS outsourcing and developed a sourcing decision framework.	The perceived benefits identified: 1. Reducing costs and/or infusing cash 2. Developing IT applications more rapidly 3. Improving service quality and productivity 4. Gaining access to leading edge technologies 5. Reducing technological risk and increasing technological flexibility 6. Implementing change more rapidly 7. Assessing current information management capabilities 8. Enhancing the status of senior IS executive 9. Easing the IS management task of senior management

Table 12.1 Empirical Research on IT Outsourcing – *continued*

Author(s)	Research Method	Scope of the Research	Findings
			The perceived risks identified: 1. Increased costs 2. Increased risk 3. Loss of internal technical knowledge 4. Loss of flexibility 5. Increased IS management complexity
Collins and Millen (1995)	Survey of 110 US companies	Description of US outsourcing practices.	They found that 50% outsource education and training, 49% outsource PC support, 33% outsource network services, 33% outsource applications development, 33% outsource application maintenance, and 24% outsource data centers.
Cullen (1997)	120plus survey of Australian organizations	Type, rationale, gains and problems in outsourcing	The study finds 80% of organizations outsourcing, mainly on a selective basis, and mainly hardware support, education and applications support/development. Skills, technology, then costs savings were the main reasons. Substantial cost savings were not achieved, but technological and some service improvements were noted. Cost was the main item benchmarked, and fixed fees the dominant cost structure.
Currie and Willcocks (1998)	53 case studies and a 150 organization survey	Study of success factors in total, selective, in-house and single and multiple supplier sourcing.	They found selective IT outsourcing the most successful set of practices, but delineate effective and ineffective practices in all forms of sourcing, and note generic capabilities required to run any IT sourcing arrangement.
De Looff (1995)	30 interviews with individuals in Dutch organizations	Identified critical factors associated with successful IS outsourcing	Few decisions were formally evaluated.

Table 12.1 Empirical Research on IT Outsourcing – *continued*

Author(s)	Research Method	Scope of the Research	Findings
Earl (1996)	Unspecified methodology, based on discussions with senior executives and IT managers.	Limits to IT Outsourcing	Identifies 11 risks in outsourcing.
Griese (1993)	Survey of 65 Swiss companies	Perceived benefits and risks of outsourcing	The perceived benefits of outsourcing in rank order: 1. cost reductions 2. concentration on core business 3. smaller lead times 4. less overcapacity 5. more flexibility 6. higher innovation The perceived risks: 1. special requirements 2. sensitive data 3. partnership risk 4. contract risk 5. opposition of the IS department
Grover, Cheon and Teng (1994, 1996)	Survey of 63 US companies; Survey of 188 companies	Described the sourcing practices in US companies; correlated perceived success with type of function outsourced.	36% outsource systems operations, 30% outsource applications development and maintenance, 17% outsource telecommunications management, and 16% outsource end user support. (They did not ask respondents about other IT activities such as data entry, training, etc.); IS managers perceive a high success with outsourcing systems operations and telecommunications, but not with outsourcing applications development, end user support, or management.

Table 12.1 Empirical Research on IT Outsourcing – *continued*

Author(s)	Research Method	Scope of the Research	Findings
Heinzl (1993)	Survey of 359 companies in Germany, Europe and the US.	Looked at linkages between company characteristics and outsourcing behavior; analysed motives and effects of outsourcing.	The main motives for outsourcing are: 1. achieve cost improvements 2. increase the poor service mentality 3. ameliorate management & control problems 4. improve rate of innovation German companies are likely to outsource their IS services within the company more often than other European or US corporations.
Hu, Saunders and Gebelt (1997)	Study of 175 firms outsourcing between 1985–95	Assessed the determinants of outsourcing.	The main sources of influence on IT outsourcing adoptions were a mix of external media, vendor pressure and internal communications at a personal level.
Huber (1993)	Case study	Continental Bank	The bank used outsourcing of many services, including IT, to help turnaround poor financial performance due to bad loans.
Klepper (1995)	Two case studies	Proposes that marketing theories can be used to understand IS outsourcing relationships	Found that the most important aspects of good relationships are determined prior to forming the partnership, including vendor screening and pre-partnering exchanges.
Lacity and Hirschheim (1993; 1995)	63 interviews in 21 organizations	Studied total outsourcing and total insourcing decisions, identified myths of IS outsourcing propagated in the trade literature.	Total outsourcing decisions were fraught with problems due to poor contracts. High excess fees for services beyond the base contract and degrading service levels were the main problems; Insourcing may lead to lower costs if internal IT managers replicate cost-reduction tactics.

Table 12.1 Empirical Research on IT Outsourcing – *continued*

Author(s)	Research Method	Scope of the Research	Findings
Lacity, Willcocks and Feeny and (1995; 1996); Lacity and Willcocks (1998)	145 interviews in 40 US and UK organizations	Managerial frameworks for making sourcing decisions.	The authors developed frameworks to assist practitioners with sourcing decisions based on strategic, economic, technical factors. The HBR paper distills the learning points for managers. The 1998 paper re-analyses the data and delineates six success/failure factors in outsourcing. Also analyses 1995–98 outsourcing developments.
Lacity and Willcocks (2001)	101 organization UK/US survey, and 114 case histories 1991–98	Documents current (1998/9) practices and outcomes. Issues revealed by longitudinal analysis.	Dominant form is selective outsourcing (US 83%, US 75%) with multiple suppliers (79% of organizations outsourcing). Good satisfaction rates but array of problems still identified. Cases show a 38% success rate for total outsourcing, and a 76% and 77% success rate for in-house sourcing and selective outsourcing respectively. Identifies reasons for these outcomes.
Loh and Venkatraman (1992a,b)	Secondary sources, including stock market data and annual reports.	Determinants of Information Technology Outsourcing	Identified Kodak's IS outsourcing decision as a critical event in the diffusion of innovation; identified the determinants of IS outsourcing including high IS costs and poor IS performance; demonstrated positive stock market reaction to IS outsourcing announcements.
McFarlan and Nolan (1995)	Case studies of over a dozen outsourcing situations.	Applied strategic grid model to IS outsourcing decision	Found that strategic alliances was the key to successful outsourcing.
McLellan, Marcolin & Beamish (1995)	Case studies of North American banks	Studied the motives of IS outsourcing as well as the relationships	IT was outsourced even though it was considered a core competency.

Table 12.1 Empirical Research on IT Outsourcing – *continued*

Author(s)	Research Method	Scope of the Research	Findings
Pantane and Jurison (1994)	Survey of US companies	Trends in Off-Shore Outsourcing	Strategic applications are not typically outsourced and will not likely be in the future.
Reponen (1993)	Study of six Finnish companies	Looked at the main reasons, difficulties, and consequences of outsourcing	The structure of outsourcing was primarily the setting up of new companies.
Saarinen and Saaksjarvi (1993)	Case studies of two Finnish Woodworking companies	Studied the differences in the sourcing strategies of two companies.	The heavily insourced IS function performed much better than the heavily outsourced IS function.
Sobel and Apte were (1995); Apte, U., Sobol, M., Hanaoka, S., Shimada, T., Saarinen, T., Salmela, T., and Vepsalainen, A. (1997)	Survey of 48 US companies; 86 Japanese companies, and 141 Finnish companies	Description of sourcing practices in the US	The most commonly outsourced functions in the US support operations (47.9%), training and education (47.9%), disaster recovery (39.6%), and data entry (22.9%); The perceived benefits in the US are: 1. allows cost containment 2. reduces need to hire IS professionals 3. improves cost predictability 4. leaves more time to focus on strategic IS use 5. more vendors are available 6. gives access to leading edge technologies 7. reduces need for capital investment in new technology The perceived disadvantages in the US are: 1. monitoring outsourcing vendors is difficult 2. loss of quality and time control 3. difficult to explain business needs to vendors 4. leads to potential loss of secrets and intellectual property 5. limits long-term career prospects of IS staff 6. outsourcing controls are high cost 7. decrease size of IS department

Table 12.1 Empirical Research on IT Outsourcing – *continued*

Author(s)	Research Method	Scope of the Research	Findings
Strassmann (1995, 1997)	Analysis of financial statements of *Fortune* 1000 companies	Determinants of outsourcing	Found that companies with poor financial performance are the most likely to outsource.
Valor, Fonstad and Andreu (1993)	Survey of 63 Spanish CEOs	Perceptions of benefits and risks of outsourcing	The top perceived benefits are 1. allows focusing on own business 2. reduction of IT staff 3. access to experts 4. access to the latest technology The top perceived risks: 1. leakage of confidential information 2. breach of contract by vendors 3. dependence on specific vendors
Willcocks and Fitzgerald (1994), Willcocks, Lacity and Fitzgerald (1995)	In-depth interviews with 75 individuals in 30 UK firms	Studied selective sourcing decisions; identified best practices for sourcing evaluations, contract negotiations, and vendor management.	Identified the need for a thorough evaluation process, including accounting for the full costs of internal services. They found that technically mature activities are easiest to outsource, but success still depends on sound contract.
Willcocks and Kern (1998)	Longitudinal case study of relationships in a total outsourcing single supplier deal	Focused on the development of issues and relationships over time	Found that even in a well prepared outsourcing arrangement the relationship dimension was neglected at first, but that relationships, processes and trust can develop over time if managed pro-actively.

development over time could be transferred across from the inter-organizational research literature, but that a particular model, with its own stakeholders, relationships, phases and activities, grew out of our specific analyses of IT outsourcing arrangements.

Information technology outsourcing stakeholders

An IT stakeholder group consists of people tending to have the same expectations, perceptions, and goals for IT and outsourcing. Rather than merely categorizing people as either "clients" or "suppliers", our research identified eight types of IT stakeholders (see Table 12.2). However, while our stakeholder analysis is richer than previous dichotomous analyses, we still note that stereotypes ignore individual personalities. In the conclusion, we address how personal charisma (or abrasiveness) can sometimes supersede stakeholder stereotypes.

In general, we found four distinct client IT stakeholders and three distinct supplier stakeholders. In cases of multi-sourcing (such as the sourcing options pursued from 1993–8 by British Petroleum Exploration with three suppliers, and DuPont from 1996/7 with two suppliers) the number of supplier stakeholders, and interactions among stakeholders increases. The addi-

Table 12.2   Stakeholder Expectations and Goals

Stakeholder	IT Expectations/Goals
Client senior business managers	Client senior business managers expected demonstrated business value for IT expenditures. Inability to assess the benefits of IT often caused senior business managers to focus on IT costs.
Client senior IT managers	Client senior IT managers balanced service excellence expectations from users with cost containment expectations from senior business managers.
Client IT staff	As technical enthusiasts, Client IT staff focused primarily on service excellence, but within budget and time constraints.
Client IT users	IT users expected service excellence. Cost implications were often not apparent due to centralized accounting and contracting for IT.
Supplier senior managers	Supplier senior managers negotiated deals that would satisfy the clients while maximizing profits.
Supplier account managers	Supplier senior managers balanced customer service and profitability.
Supplier IT staff	As technical enthusiasts, supplier IT staff primarily focused on service excellence, but within budget and time constraints.
Subcontractors	Delivering on their contracts.

tional complexity of multi-sourcing is often deemed worthwhile because of the benefits of best sourcing and eliminating the monopoly power of a sole supplier. In addition, it is quite common for suppliers on large IT outsourcing contracts to hire subcontractors.

Client Senior Business Managers. Though responsible for achieving business results from IT expenditures, in many of our cases, senior business managers did not have the tools to assess whether the IT function was adding value. They often asked senior IT managers for evidence of business value. In cases where senior managers could not assess the value of IT, they focused primarily on the financing and costs of IT. The questions naturally arose: Can IT be delivered more efficiently? Can IT assets (which may represent up to 20% of all capital assets) be removed from the balance sheet? Can large fixed annual IT budgets be transformed into a "pay for use" model? And ultimately, "Can an IT outsourcer save us money?"

Client Senior IT Managers. Typically these are centralized and responsible for balancing the costs of IT with the services provided to ensure value for money. In general, senior IT managers were often frustrated by their charge. Users often demanded service excellence while their bosses often demanded cost containment. One senior IT manager explains:

> "I cannot get any support in how to allocate these resources. And we cannot be the traffic cop in this whole process because it is not right. I'm trying to satisfy everybody and it's not working." – Former Director of IS, US petroleum company

In most of our cases, senior IT managers maintained their focus on balancing IT costs and services throughout an outsourcing process. Senior IT managers are rarely threatened by IT outsourcing, which meant their roles being redefined rather than lost. Indeed, most senior IT managers became valuable contributors to outsourcing evaluations, contract negotiations, and post contract management. Although we discussed the political behavior of a few IT managers biased against outsourcing in Lacity and Willcocks (1998), by far the preponderance of IT managers expressed a goal to balance costs and service delivery.

Client IT Staff are responsible for IT service delivery. Although they are expected to meet budgets and deadlines, we found that IT professionals are generally technology enthusiasts who also seek to please users. The internal IT staff were often the stakeholder groups most profoundly affected by outsourcing evaluations. They felt their senior managers were making life choices for them about transition and retention, and often without their input on careers, salaries, and benefits. In cases where IT staff are unionized, the unions were often very vocal against outsourcing. For example, unions initially opposed the decisions at British Aerospace, Inland Revenue, and Westchester County. Ultimately, we found client IT employees almost always agreeing to transfer to the supplier. Acceptance rates were above 95% in all our cases except at a US public sector organization and at a US metal company.

IT Users. These typically focused throughout all phases on IT service excellence, expecting systems to be up and running, to provide business functionality, and to facilitate the execution of their business responsibilities. IT users rarely resisted outsourcing, although they frequently had questions about confidentiality and integrity of data.

In most instances, IT users were supportive of outsourcing because they perceived that the supplier would radically improve IT service. But IT users' expectations for service excellence were often unrealistic, believing that an infusion of new IT and better service would be provided by the supplier virtually free of charge. The gap in expectations and reality often dampened their initial enthusiasm.

Supplier Senior Managers. These stakeholders are responsible for sales and negotiations. They must balance the need to satisfy their clients with the need to generate a profit for their organization. A tremendous amount of judgment, typically based on years of experience, is often needed to assess what can be delivered at what price while still generating a profit.

According to one supplier senior manager, suppliers "never knowingly sell a deal by reducing IT cost" because the margins are too small. For his company, IT cost reduction deals typically require 50% overhead (25% for supplier corporate headquarters; 25% for profit on the account) while still being able to reduce client's costs by 10 to 20%. Few IT cost reduction deals qualify. Instead, supplier senior managers typically focus on the value they can add to a client in terms of improving service, re-designing business processes, providing scarce IT skills, helping clients re-finance IT, and developing new added-value systems.

Supplier Account Managers. Supplier account managers are responsible for profitability and client satisfaction on a given IT contract. Again, supplier account managers must strike a delicate balance between the often conflicting goals of service excellence and cost containment. Because the supplier account manager is so critical to the success of an outsourcing relationship, many clients include approval clauses in the contract for this role.

Supplier IT Staff. A primary concern of supplier IT staff is with providing good client service. Like client IT staff, supplier IT staff are generally technology enthusiasts who are anxious to please users. Sometimes their enthusiasm for client service had to be harnessed by their management to protect profit margins. Most IT staff, however, are well aware of budget and time requirements. Although they aim to please their clients, their organizations must earn a profit:

> "We are an IT company, so we can transfuse current IT, state of the art IT, future IT, conceptual IT. But of course that transfusion as far as we

are concerned is not free. The big problem is these people think that transfusion is free." – Quality Manager, IT Supplier

Subcontractors. Subcontractors are hired by prime suppliers to deliver part of the service to clients. According to International Data Corporation (IDC), 36% of IT outsourcing contracts involve subcontractors. An Information Week survey found an even higher frequency of subcontractors: 50% of IT suppliers hire contractors. Clients often have limited or no interaction with subcontractors. Over 15% of 55 IT managers surveyed by IDC stated that their IT suppliers do not notify them when they hire subcontractors. Half of the suppliers in the InformationWeek survey admitted that subcontractors sometimes cause problems, including service quality (67%), costs (30%), viruses (17%) and security (10%).

According to surveys, prime contractors hire subcontractors to access scarce technical skills. Ironically, clients often outsourced for the same reason: to gain access to scarce IT skills of the prime contractor. But prime contractors face the same global shortage of IT skills as everyone else (Caldwell *et al.*, 1997). Clearly, the widespread usage of sub-contracting brings additional dimensions and issues to outsourcing; our research experience is that these are all too often overlooked by client organizations (Lacity and Willcocks, 2001).

In summary, the eight types of stakeholders generally held different IT expectations and goals. Some stakeholders primarily focus on IT costs because they are the ones paying for IT. Other stakeholders focus on service excellence because they are the ones using the IT service. Other stakeholders must strike a delicate balance between service excellence and cost containment. Clearly such diverse goals and orientations amongst typical stakeholders can have a profound impact on types of relationships that can develop.

Types of stakeholder relationships

As previously noted, stakeholder relationships are quite dynamic. The same two people can fight one minute and collaborate the next, and we found stakeholders regularly operating at different points along the relationship continuum. In general, at least four types of relationships were evident (see Figure 12.1).

Tentative Relationships. These were quite common when stakeholders had no shared history. Thus, stakeholders were unsure whether goals were shared, complementary or conflicting. Most of the time behavior manifested itself in polite caution, but sometimes a predisposition towards enthusiasm was evident. For example, *client* and *supplier senior managers* were often quite enthusiastic – albeit tentative – when exploring the possibility for a "partnership." At this stage, there was no commitment, and

Relationship Type	Tentative	Cooperative	Adversarial	Collaborative
Goal Alignment	Unknown	Complementary	Conflicting	Shared

Figure 12.1   Relationship Types

thus no motivation to behave aggressively or antagonistically. One informant described senior management talks as a "peacock dance" because each party was anxious to impress the other with their organizations' assets and capabilities.

Another common example of tentative relationships was the first few meetings between *supplier stakeholders* and *client IT staff* identified for transfer. The tentativeness mostly occurred on the part of the IT staff, who were quite naturally concerned about their new careers, salaries, and benefits. Most supplier stakeholders immediately began to build confidence by guaranteeing equivalent salaries and benefits and by allowing potential transfers to speak with previously transferred employees.

Collaborative Relationships. These occurred when stakeholders' goals were shared. In many cases, shared goals were fostered by being part of the same organization. Client stakeholder goals were often aligned for a number of negotiation activities:

- *Client senior business* managers and *client senior IT managers* typically both wanted to negotiate the best service at the lowest cost.
- *Client senior managers* and *client IT staff* typically both wanted to negotiate the best salaries and benefits for employees targeted for transfer to the supplier.
- *Client senior managers* and *client IT users* typically both wanted to negotiate the best possible service level agreements with the supplier.

Similarly, *supplier senior managers* and future *supplier account managers* had the shared goal of negotiating a deal with enough leeway to ensure profit margins, even assuming unforeseen events.

Cooperative Relationships. These manifested themselves when goals were complementary. Each party needs something from the other party to succeed. Many IT outsourcing activities are based on the notion of an exchange – a client pays a fee in exchange for a service. Client and supplier goals are therefore complementary: the client needs the supplier to provide the service; the supplier needs the client to pay the fee. While it is clear these goals are not shared, each party has a vested interest in the other's success. Indeed, client stakeholders never wanted suppliers to lose money on the account because if the supplier suffers, the client suffers:

> "Suppliers have to make a reasonable margin to stay in business. You don't want them to lose money because the worse their business gets, the worse your business gets. At the same time you don't want them to make outrageous profits at your expense." – Contract Administrator, South Australian Government

Adversarial Relationships. These occurred when stakeholder goals were in *conflict*. Stakeholders were adversarial when the conflict entailed millions of dollars, such as a conflict over an interpretation of financial responsibility in a contact clause. In particular, three activities are inherently adversarial:

- negotiating the original contract
- establishing precedents for contract interpretation during the transition phase
- renegotiating or realigning the contract midway through the contract

The key here was for the client and supplier to have equal power to achieve an equitable outcome. When one party had more power than the other, the stronger party clearly dominated the weaker. In the early mega-deals, suppliers clearly had more power due to information impactedness. Oliver Williamson defines information impactedness as follows:

> "It exists in circumstances in which one of the parties to an exchange is much better informed than is the other regarding underlying conditions germane to the trade, and the second party cannot achieve information parity except at great cost–because he cannot rely on the first party to disclose the information in a fully candid manner (Williamson, 1975, p. 14)."

Clients were often inexperienced with negotiating IT outsourcing contracts. To balance the power during contract negotiations, clients are hiring more outside experts to represent their interests. In fact, few new IT outsourcing deals were signed without the client's extensive reliance on outside technical and legal consultants. Clients employed a number of other strategies to balance the power:

- Established non-exclusivity clauses which enables the client to competitively bid beyond-baseline services
- Multi-source rather than give monopoly power to a sole supplier
- Selective source to limit the power of a supplier to a targeted subset of IT activities

The objective of these strategies, again, is not to necessarily dominate the other party, but to have enough power to favorably and fairly resolve adversarial tasks. Indeed, client empowerment contributes to our understanding why recent contracts have higher success rates than older contracts (Lacity and Willcocks, 1998).

In summary, the dynamic nature of stakeholder relationships was clearly evident in case study organizations. The same stakeholders can have tentative, collaborative, cooperative, and adversarial relationships depending on the task at hand. By understanding relationship complexities, clients and suppliers can abandon the naive quest for continual harmony. Instead, stakeholders should accept the ebbs and flows of the evolution of relationships. Stakeholders can occasionally fight, yet still have an effective relationship overall.

Relationship phases and activities

We identified six outsourcing phases, each comprising multiple activities (see Table 12.3). Stakeholder relationships vary during activities within phases, depending on goal alignment. For each of the phases, we describe the major stakeholder goals, interactions, and outcomes witnessed in our cases.

Phase 1: scoping

Client goal: "Create a strategic vision of IT sourcing".

The two main activities in this phase were identifying core IT capabilities and identifying IT activities for potential outsourcing. Typically, the *client senior business managers* and *client senior IT managers* were the primary stakeholders involved during this initial phase. Senior business managers had agendas prompted by financial pressures. Such pressures often led to a "core competency" strategy where the organization focused on the "core", and downsized or outsourced the rest. Because senior business managers viewed much of IT as a non-core competency, they regularly questioned if some or all of the IT function could be potentially outsourced.

Senior IT managers had typically coped with a legacy of trying to balance service excellence demands from the user population with IT cost containment pressures from their senior managers. In the past, there was often

Table 12.3 I.T. Outsourcing Phases and Activities

	Scoping Phase	Evaluation Phase	Negotiation Phase	Transition Phase	Middle Phase	Mature Phase
Activities:	• Identify core IT capabilities • Identify IT activities for potential outsourcing using business, economic, and technical criteria	• Measure baseline services • Measure baseline costs • Create RFP • Develop evaluation criteria • Invite external and internal bids	• Conduct due diligence to verify RFP baseline claims • Negotiate service level agreements • Create responsibility matrixes • Price work units • Negotiate terms for employee transfer • Negotiate mechanisms for contractual change, including benchmarking, open book accounting, non-exclusivity clauses, and pricing schedules.	• Distribute contract to IT users • Interpret the contract • Establish post-contract management infrastructure and processes • Implement consolidation, rationalization, standardization • Validate service scope, costs, levels and responsibilities for baseline services • Manage additional service requests • Foster realistic expectations of supplier performance • Publicly promote the contract	• Benchmark performance to (theoretically) reset prices • Realign the contract to reflect changes in technology and business • Involve the supplier on more value-added areas	• Re-calibrate investment criteria to reflect shorter time horizon for recouping investments • Determine if the relationship will be terminated or extended
Objective:	Identify flexible IT organization, including IT activities for potential outsourcing	Select best and final offer	Sign contract(s)	Establish operational performance	Achieve value-added above operational performance	No lapses in operational performance during final transition

tension between CEOs and senior IT managers because the latter often struggled to demonstrate value for IT expenditures to their bosses (see Feeny *et al.*, 1992, Willcocks *et al.*, 1997).

A full-blown investigation of IT sourcing options, however, often served to align goals between senior business and IT managers. As previously noted, because senior IT managers rarely lose their jobs as a consequence of outsourcing, they usually welcomed a reasoned approach to sourcing the IT function. With the support of their bosses, senior IT managers could overcome user resistance and implement cost reduction and outsourcing strategies (see Lacity and Hirschheim, 1995 for case studies on IT empowerment as a consequence of outsourcing evaluations).

Supplier stakeholders were not typically involved until the evaluation phase. However, in a few cases, *supplier senior managers* actually prompted the decision to consider outsourcing by wooing client senior executives in this phase. For example, the vice-president of IS at one petroleum company told us that EDS prompted a sourcing decision by offering cash during a major court battle at his company:

> "The Chairman of the Board of EDS wrote a letter to our chief executive officer saying that they would be most interested in paying substantial cash for our whole IS organization. That includes all the people, and they would be very happy to meet him, and discuss that with him." – VP of IS, US petroleum company

Client and supplier senior executive interactions were typically characterized by tentative enthusiasm and optimism during the scoping phase. But one lesson that clearly emerged from our body of research is that client and supplier senior executives should not make outsourcing decisions without IT managements' input. The "CEO handshake deals" typically failed because of inattention to detail. Two CEOs can get very excited about an alliance, but the success of IT outsourcing deals rely on the details of the cost and service to be delivered.

Phase 2: evaluation

Client goal: "Identify the best source for IT activities".
The major activities during this phase were:

- Measuring baseline services and costs
- Creating an RFP (Request for Proposal)
- Developing evaluation criteria
- Inviting internal and external bids

Lacity and Willcocks (1998) discussed the need for joint senior management and IT management participation in sourcing evaluations. We also discussed the evaluation process that most frequently led to success: create an RFP, and invite both external and internal bids. We showed how this practice ensures that a supplier's bid is not merely compared with current IT performance, but with IT performance that could be achieved if internal managers were empowered to behave like suppliers.[1]

Supplier stakeholders became much more active during this phase. In addition to the ***supplier senior management*** team, a host of supplier experts attended bid presentations. In some cases, like British Aerospace (BAe), suppliers helped to win the bid by talking to many client stakeholders. While CSC obviously talked to senior business managers about finances, they also talked to BAe users about service, to the IT staff about career paths/benefits, and to IT managers about baseline service level agreements. Several BAe and CSC informants indicated that CSC was successful in winning the bid, in large part because of their expertise in aerospace and their ability to talk business language:

> "The senior managers within BAe and even more the managers within the business wanted to hear people talking their language, the language of making airplanes. And we were able to do that, we were able to produce these people who talked their language." – CSC Quality Manager (Transferred from BAe)

Like the previous phase, the client/supplier interactions – although tentative – were typically characterized by enthusiasm and optimism at the senior management level during the evaluation phase.

The ***client IT users*** were primarily concerned with service excellence during the entire outsourcing evaluation. As previously noted, IT users sometimes questioned confidentiality and privacy of data with IT outsourcing. But in general, IT users typically supported outsourcing because they perceived that suppliers – with their IT expertise – would increase service and provide new IT to the user community.

At the ***client IT staff level***, however, IT professionals were frequently threatened by the impending decision. Some organizations, particularly those with an IT labor union, experienced significant resistance from this stakeholder group. Indeed, British Aerospace and Inland Revenue's unionized IT staff both held strikes in opposition to outsourcing.

In cases in which IT staff were invited to submit an alternative bid, the internal bid process often served as a galvanizing force. In some cases, senior management granted a request for an internal bid more as a "morale-preserver" than as a serious contender against external bidders. Once given free rein to compete based on cost efficiency, internal IT managers from eight of our cases surprised senior management by submitting the winning bid. Sourcing evaluations which led to continued insourcing of the IT function, proceeded to a transition phase. The primary activity of the insourcing transition phase is the implementation of consolidation, rationalization, and standardization of the internal bid proposal (see Lacity and Hirschheim, 1995 for details of implementing insourcing proposals).

Sourcing evaluations that result in outsourcing were found to proceed through four further phases (see below). Unlike insourcing, IT outsourcing requires significant changes in duties and responsibilities of IT management, staff, and users (Currie and Willcocks, 1998; Feeny and Willcocks, 1998). Also, more stakeholders must adapt and learn to interact with each other to deliver a cost effective IT service.

Phase 3: negotiation

Client Goal: "Negotiate a contract to ensure sourcing expectations are realized".

Lacity and Willcocks (1998) discussed some of the principles of negotiating deals, including the proven practices of negotiating short-term contracts and detailed contracts. The South Australia Government, DuPont, British Aerospace, and Inland Revenue spent more than a year negotiating contract details. These contract details included:

- conducting due diligence to verify RFP baseline claims
- negotiating service level agreements for 500 or more IT services,
- creating client/supplier responsibility matrixes for more than 700 responsibilities,
- pricing 20 to 30 units of work, such as CPU minutes, number of UNIX boxes, man-hour of analyst time, etc.
- negotiating terms for transfer of employees at equivalent or better benefits
- agreeing on mechanisms for contractual change, including benchmarking, open book accounting, non-exclusivity clauses, and pricing schedules.

It is quite clear that contract negotiations are antagonistic, as the client stakeholders and supplier stakeholders are each accountable to protecting the interests of their respective organizations. Participants have used the nouns "war", "blood bath", and "battle" to describe negotiations. No parties, however, seemed to expect a different type of relationship during contract negotiations. Each side expected the other to be a tough negotiator. Indeed, even one CSC account executive complimented BAe on their negotiating skills:

> "BAe, say for Military Aircraft, 70% of the cost of that Eurofighter is brought in from somewhere else. So they are used to, and their whole culture is around one of deal-making and negotiating and hard-bargaining. And they are brought up in that and they play hard ball extremely well." – CSC Account Executive

During outsourcing negotiations, ***client IT managers*** were typically tough negotiators. They fought very hard to represent the interests of their organzations. At a US bank, for example, the VP of IS was adamant that she was not going to pay a $500,000 software license transfer fee. The supplier threatened to shut down the data center (and thus the bank) unless the bill was paid. Here is how the VP of IS and the financial manager responded:

"We called our attorneys. Our attorneys called their attorneys. Ours said, 'How dare you threaten to shut down a national bank. You think you can shut down a national bank?' But that was a very difficult period, after they sent us that shut down letter. Finally, they said, 'I think we better go see these people.' Thursday morning they came in and it was a shouting match back and forth. And they said, 'We don't have to put up with this.' And they got up and left. Their attorneys called me the next day and apologized for their marketers. The next week we negotiated from $500,000 down to $110,000."

Despite tough negotiations, the bank's deal ended up being a success. We found similar situations in many organizations: tough battles during contract negotiations between client and supplier constituents often led to successful arrangements. After a contract is signed, however, the clients and suppliers sought a more harmonious relationship. The South Australian (SA) government even hosted a session between SA IT managers and EDS managers to quickly transition from the adversarial posturing of contract negotiations to the more cooperative delivery of the contract.

IT users are another stakeholder group that are involved in contract negotiations. Because IT outsourcing contracts typically rely on a baseline measure of services, users became involved in documenting current service levels and volumes. IT users were generally motivated to actually inflate current service levels. In essence, this would enable them to get the supplier to increase service levels under a fixed-fee baseline price. But suppliers were keenly aware of the motivation, and thus suppliers required a documented and detailed due diligence process to verify baseline claims.

During the negotiation phase, potential *supplier account managers* are often interviewed by the client stakeholders. Initial meetings were often characterized by tentativeness as each party explored the other's motivations and values. Client stakeholders were motivated to select a person who would primarily focus on client service. Supplier stakeholders – who are accountable to their shareholders – needed a person who would protect their profit margins. In many of our cases, clients did not select a person who was part of the supplier negotiating team. When clients experienced a supplier's tough negotiating skills firsthand, they naturally retreated from the individual. Instead, a fresh face often helped the transition from antagonism during the negotiation phase to cooperation during the transition phase.

In general, all parties agree that even though contract negotiations are antagonistic, the process is worthwhile for both sides. Detailed contracts document expectations and are therefore a pre-requisite for a successful relationship:

> "It is important to have a sound base contract. It is important because that's how operating trust is built." – CSC Vice President

> "There should be no ambiguity in the contract as to what is baseline or fixed price or essentially free, in scope. What is actually there to be done and who is paying for it. It should be totally crystal-clear." – CSC Account Manager on BAe Contract

Phase 4: transition

Client Goal: "Establish precedents for operational performance".

On large contracts, transition activities may last from 18 months to over two years. Our research shows eight main areas of activity here, as we now detail.

1. Distributing the contract. Many actual IT outsourcing contracts are impossible to execute from because they are typically massive documents written in obscure legal terminology. Mega- contracts may contain 30,000 lines and require several legal-sized boxes for a single copy. In the early days of a mega-contract, one of the major tasks of the centralized contract management team is to develop user guides to the contract. The guides are designed to describe what the supplier is obligated to provide under the fixed-fee structure in user terms.

The major stakeholders involved in this activity are the *client IT managers* and the *IT users*. Often the stakeholders goals were in conflict. IT users, particularly division managers, wanted to see the entire contract. IT managers wanted only to distribute summaries of the contract because they felt every IT user would interpret the contract differ-ently:

> "We find anything you write down and distribute to a group of people, those people interpret it differently and they try to execute against their interpretation." – DuPont, Global Alliance Manager

Indeed, on many contracts, *IT users* fought with *supplier IT staff* over the contract. At DuPont, for example, work on 150 major projects was halted due to lack of project pricing. Lower level employees were not sure how to behave – how can we do this work when it has not been properly priced and approved? Once the DuPont IT managers and CSC account managers were aware of the problem, they sent clear messages to lower level employees: do the work and we'll worry about the price:

> "But just last week, they had a client that was doing design work for them on the network connection. CSC quoted a price they felt too high. And I looked at it and said, "We'll just do it, we'll worry about the quote later." – Duel British Aerospace/CSC Account Executive

2. Interpreting the contract. No matter how well the negotiating teams believe they nailed down the details, the contract was always open for interpretation. Typically, the *client IT managers* and *supplier account managers* were in charge of resolving contract interpretation issues. Clearly stakeholder goals are conflicting because each side is charged with protecting their own organization's interests. Each side sought a fair resolution, but financial pressures fueled the tension; A precedent resolved during the transition phase could have millions of dollars worth of consequences during the remainder of the contract:

> What may be only £6000 today might set a precedent worth £10 million. – IT Services Manager, British Aerospace

Some examples serve to illustrate the ambiguity typically found in contracts:

- If the client needs system maintenance that requires the supplier to bring the data center down over the weekend, who pays supplier overtime?
- What is included in the fixed price of a standard hardware upgrade? Is analyst time spent identifying requirements billable or included in the fixed price? Are installation, wiring, and shipping and handling costs included or billable?

DuPont, like other clients, realized that more staff should have been retained to address these issues:

> "Had we known that was coming, we would have saved more resources, or kept more resource to help with both the continuing negotiation, definition of the deal, as well as I would say it has taken more resources than anticipated to put in place all these managing processes that are required as part of the transition or start-up of the deal." – DuPont, Global Alliance Manager

3. Establishing post-contract management infrastructure and processes. Here, clients typically established centralized teams to facilitate the contract monitoring and vendor development roles. Centralized teams focused on financial and strategic management of the contract. Contract facilitation roles were typically decentralized (see Feeny and Willcocks, 1998 and Willcocks *et al.*, 1997 for details on these roles). Decentralized teams focused on daily operations.

For problem resolution, many clients and suppliers sought cooperative processes rather than unproductive adversarial processes. At DuPont and Inland Revenue in 1999, joint client-supplier teams are delegated responsibility for solving operational problems. The teams are typically comprised of *client IT users, client IT staff,* and *supplier IT staff.* The goal is for the joint teams to resolve the problem before escalating the issue to their superiors:

> "If we think that there are any stand-offs that are occurring, any differences of opinion we can't get to the bottom of, we attempt to try and sort it as joint teams... we apply it at the contract level and the two contract management teams ... have active discussions about particular issues and they consider positions from both sides. And... where they can't come to some agreement, it comes up the management hierarchy and will come to myself and an equivalent within EDS to see if we can mediate on these things." – Inland Revenue, Account Manager.

Although clients are expected to represent client interests, and suppliers are expected to represent supplier interests, the joint teams create an environment of compromise. The operating principle of joint teams is to be fair and not to exploit any contract inefficiencies. At DuPont, by late 1998, 120 operational problems had been successfully resolved in this manner.

4. Implementing consolidation, rationalization, and standardization. Client stakeholders were well aware that suppliers' bids were based, in part, on projected savings from implementing cost reduction practices after the contract was signed. Cost reduction tactics included consolidating data centers, standardizing software and hardware platforms, creating stringent service request approval processes, centralizing IT staff, implementing chargeback systems, etc. These practices were often unpopular with IT users because they perceived that such practices would reduce service levels. In fact, insourcing proposals were often rejected because senior executives perceived that internal IT managers lacked the political clout to overcome user resistance to cost reduction tactics. Once a supplier takes over a client's assets, however, they clearly had the power to manage resources in a more efficient manner.

Client IT managers supported *supplier account managers* in their cost reduction practices. They realized that the supplier needed the savings to earn a profit on the account. Indeed, many clients complimented suppliers on their ability to consolidate, rationalize, and standardize:

"EDS did in 12 months what we couldn't do in four years" – Contract Administrator, South Australia Government

"I was so impressed with the preparation activities and the actual execution of the migration to their data center. There were few interruptions in service to the users. (The vendor) made this very detailed, complex move look like it wasn't difficult at all." – Manager of IS, US metal company

5. Validating baseline service scope, costs, levels and responsibilities. A major transition challenge for all relationships was validating the baseline. Supplier bids were based on the RFP and discoveries made during due diligence. Any undiscovered items were typically subject to excess fees. After the Inland Revenue/EDS contract went into effect, for example, IR had to pay for the following items that surfaced:

- £100,000 for software license fees
- £5 million per year caused by inaccuracies in the original tender offers
- £15 million per year for hardware maintenance.

As far as validating baseline service levels, typically **client IT staff** and **supplier IT staff** are charged with the task. At DuPont, for example, baseline service levels are verified by joint teams distributed around the globe. Because failure to meet service levels can result in financial penalties, the stakeholder goals were typically in conflict. Each is motivated to blame the other for service lapses. To avoid disputes during the transition phase, DuPont agreed to suspend cash penalties for non-performance for the first year of the contract. As one DuPont employee noted, "90% of the service lapses were inherited from us." Because the financial consequence was removed, parties at DuPont are working together to improve service lapses, rather than merely trying to blame one another.

   6. Managing additional service requests beyond baseline. Services beyond baseline–and thus subject to excess fees – can be triggered by:

(1)   exceeding projected volumes on existing services,
(2)   changing the composition of baseline services, and/or
(3)   demanding entirely new services.

Nearly every outsourcing client we studied experienced all three sources of change. Indeed, a common lament among **client IT managers** and **supplier account managers** was, "we completely underestimated user demand." During an often two-year outsourcing decision process, many organizations instituted a buying freeze. Once the contract went into effect, user demands were no longer constrained:

> "The whole process until we had a contract in place was about two and a half years. During that period of time, the government pretty much put a freeze on buying equipment, things like that. So there was a pent-up demand that we all under-estimated. The number of change requests overwhelmed us. The number of change requests so far has been something like 2,000. And this is new servers, new LANs, those kind of things. We went for example, and these are approximate numbers, at the time of taking over the baseline, they had about 1,000 LAN servers out there. And there are now about 1,800. So that's an example."
> – Vendor VP of Operations in major central government deal.

Supplier account managers typically have the resources and financial motivation to meet any volume of demand. *Client IT managers* were typically charged with keeping excess fees to a minimum. Thus, stakeholder goals were often in conflict during this task. At the very least, client IT managers tried to ensure that users only requested beyond baseline items if the benefits generated covered the excess costs. For example, one business unit manager at British Aerospace requested a shop control system that would save him £250,000. But the BAe Contract Manager pointed out that it would cost £500,000 to build!

7. **Fostering realistic expectations of supplier performance.** We have noted several times that *IT users* often have misperceptions about what the supplier is obligated to provide the client. Although contract summaries are distributed to IT users, the user community can comprise thousands of individuals.

IT users often expected a step-change in service, but contracts typically required maintenance of current service levels at a reduced cost. Both *client IT managers* and *supplier account managers* shared the goal of communicating contractual obligations to the IT user community. Client IT managers wanted users to have realistic expectations for several reasons:

- not wanting IT users to demand a higher level of service that could trigger excess fees
- not wanting IT users to be disappointed in their management of the contract
- not wanting IT users to complain unfairly to the supplier because it causes tension and requires management intervention.

Suppliers also wanted users to understand the contractual obligations because client satisfaction is obviously a goal of all suppliers – and client satisfaction requires realistic expectations of supplier performance.

Because goals are shared, client IT managers were generally very support-ive of the supplier for this activity. Internal IT managers have historically been in the same position of trying to balance user expectations for service excellence with cost constraints. The contract administrator at the South Australian government, for example, expressed his support of the supplier in achieving realistic IT user expectations:

> "I've actually been an outsourcer before.... There is generally an expect-ation of management on the user side that here is this knight in shining armor, I'll get three times better service at half the price. And also what happens, that expectation grows as you get closer to contract, so you have this large gap in expectations from the start." – Contract Administrator, South Australian Government

8. Publicly promoting the IT contract. Another common activity in which client and supplier stakeholders had shared goals was promoting the IT contract to the general public. Particularly in public sector outsourcing, taxpayers and opposing elected officials were often critical of outsourcing, and thus the *client senior managers* and *supplier senior managers* would often jointly hold press conferences to explain the benefits of the relation-ship to the public. Although both sides admit relationships are not always easy, clients and suppliers stress the overall value to taxpayers.

At UK Inland Revenue, the status of the contract is actually reported to Parliament. Both Inland Revenue contract managers and EDS supplier account managers collaborate on parliamentary and strategic planning committees:

> "It's a Committee chaired by the Deputy Chairman, and actually we have representation from EDS on that committee. So we have joint representation on that committee and of course when we are providing estimates of what certain policy changes would cost, estimates are coming from the EDS camp. We've got [EDS and IR] people collaborat-ing with our feasibility appraisal team in what those estimates would be and what the costs would be." – Inland Revenue, Account Manager

Phase 5: middle phase

Goal: 'Achieve value-added above and beyond operational performance'
Here, clients seek to adapt and to improve the contract beyond the base-line. Cost reduction, service improvement and more strategic views of IT service delivery are sought. The major activities in this phase included bench-marking performance, realigning the contract, and involving the supplier in value-added areas. Because of the history of working with the supplier, parties during the middle phase were typically comfortable changing hats from adversaries to cooperators to collaborators, depending on the task at

hand. By the middle phase, the complexity of relationships had become second nature, though the relational climate much depended on how the overall outsourcing arrangement was turning out.

1. Benchmarking performance. Benchmarking is the practice of comparing a client's IT performance against a reference group of similar organizations. In this phase, benchmarking is used as a tool to ensure that the supplier's cost and services are among the best-of-breed. Clients view benchmarking as a powerful tool to leverage their bargaining position with the supplier.

The major stakeholders involved in this activity were the *client IT managers* and the *supplier account managers*. Clients wanted to use benchmarking to reduce prices or increase service levels under the fixed-fee umbrella. Suppliers wanted to use benchmarking to demonstrate that their performance is already superior, and therefore prices need not be reduced. Thus, it is quite clear that stakeholder goals are in conflict. In addition, because benchmarks could reset prices, the financial consequences of this activity could again result in millions of dollars, serving to add to the tension.

In general, benchmarking firms competently measure the cost and service of technical platforms, such as IBM mainframe data centers, UNIX midrange computing, or LAN performance. But client and supplier participants both agree that the benchmarking industry is immature in a number of areas, particularly desktop computing and applications development and support. A few clients, for example, used function points to measure application productivity and quality. But benchmarking results were contested by the supplier. Application productivity depends not only on the supplier's performance, but on the quality of the systems inherited from the client. Over-customized and jury-rigged legacy systems required a significant amount of supplier support. Is it fair to compare their performance against the productivity of application packages?

> "Our experience being honest is that I haven't been terribly happy with the benchmarking process. This is not happy for CSC nor BAe. It's just the process seems to be a little bit naive." – BAe Contract Manager

Despite the limitations of benchmarking, clients believe it is still a valuable tool because it provides at least some rational data on performance (see Lacity and Hirschheim, 1995 for a detailed analysis).

2. Realigning the contract. Clients frequently found that the original contract became obsolete as technology advanced, business requirements changed, and false assumptions became illuminated. Technology changes included a shift from mainframe computing to client/server, deregulation of the telecommunications industry, and the emergence of new technologies such as the Internet and enterprise-wide systems (such as SAP). Business requirement changes were prompted by government regulations – such as the self-assessment project at Inland Revenue – acquisitions, mergers, and divestitures. Illuminated false assumptions included poor estimates of baseline services, volumes and costs. In addition, original contract mechanisms designed for one purpose may be operationalized in unintended ways. Some clients capped supplier margins which actually motivated supplier underperformance in practice, such as awarding the supplier a set mark-up on new capital IT investments; The more the technology cost, the more the supplier earned.

A number of participants claimed that contracts could not be valid for a period of more than three years. After that, contracts had to be renegotiated:

"The nature of this technology is volatile, that it was extremely difficult to predict for even two or three years, much less ten, with any degree of confidence...And whether it's two years, three years, five years, you're increasingly going to see involvement in renegotiating to cover the kinds of technology situations that were unforeseeable when you struck the deal." – Director of IS Planning, energy company

During a contract realignment, *client IT managers* and *supplier account managers* were the most active stakeholders. Stakeholder goals were in conflict because each side is motivated to protect the interests of their own organizations. By this stage in the relationship, however, relationships have progressed beyond the tentativeness of original contract negotiations. The client and supplier constituents had a history of working together, and both were committed to perpetuating the relationship. At British Aerospace and Inland Revenue, both sides wanted to realign the contract to help set realistic expectations. Indeed parties expect to go through a realignment exercise every few years:

"We've come to the conclusion that actually what we have is, and what we need to do intellectually, is come to terms with the contract itself. [It] has to be a much more dynamic, moving, changing thing, rather than a set-in-stone thing. And without wishing to change the past, we've jointly been working to realign the mechanisms so that they produce results which are more in keeping with what we went after. But the important factor is that we anticipate to do the same thing again in two to three years time. And then two to three years after that, we will do the same thing again. Not because we got it wrong, but because the change in technologies and changing user requirements." – BAe, General Contract Manager

3. Involving the supplier in value-added areas. The primary focus of the transition phase was to establish operational performance. From the number of transition activities discussed in the previous phase, it was quite apparent that clients and suppliers devote all their time and resources to making the IT service work. Once transition tasks have been accomplished, client and supplier stakeholders alike sought ways to extend the relationship into more value-added areas. Indeed, one of the nine core IT capabilities discussed in Willcocks *et al.* (1997) is this "vendor development" role. Here, the "value-added" may include cooperative relationships or collaborative relationships, depending on whether goals are complementary or shared. Value-added areas included:

- Supplier participation on steering committees. The idea was to include an IT perspective on business initiatives and strategies.
- Selling client IT assets and jointly sharing profits. We only have a few limited examples of this activity, such as a supplier selling a client's data models at a UK retailer.
- Supplier participation on business processing re-engineering projects. Again, we only have a few examples of this value-added, such as re-engineering the invoicing process at UK Inland Revenue.

The search for value-added continues to be a goal – albeit an elusive one – among participants. While everyone was talking about "value-added", few had actually achieved it. The following quotations express these sentiments:

> "Value-added, it's one of the goals. It's value adding but has to be done on both sides. CSC has to turn a profit and has to allow BAe to turn a profit. If you were signing up a partner, you wouldn't want your partner to lose money. You want your partner to be successful. So I think the value-added term is used with the implicit understanding that that implies that CSC is also prospering to some level." – CSC Account Executive

> "One of the things that the clients seem most disappointed in is that they looked at these kind of suppliers as "you understand the future of IT and what its capabilities are and harnessing IT for the business value." And from that perspective, they seem to be disappointed that now everything is very technical–how many LANs, WANs, desktops, etc.... They complain that the contract is getting in the way. And I think the contract is getting in the way of that kind of vision. We took IT strategy right out of the contract." – Consultant, South Australia Government

Phase 6: the mature phase

Client Goal: 'Determine and plan for the fate of current sourcing options'
During the mature phase, the client's goal is to first ensure continued operational performance if the relationship is not to be renewed. In cases where relationships are extended, the mature phase provides an oppor-

tunity to learn from past experiences as well as to explore creative options when constructing a new deal. Assessment of these options will depend as much on business strategic concerns and the nature of the current and future competitive climate as on the strength of relationships and past value of the outsourcing arrangement. Although only a few of our long-term deals have researched this stage, two activities were apparent.

1. Recalibrate investment criteria. When suppliers make IT investments on behalf of a client, the supplier needs time to recoup the investment. As the contract reaches the expiration date, reinvestment becomes a major issue. The suppliers will not want to invest in new capital assets if the client decides not to extend the relationship. At Inland Revenue, for example, both sides must make sure that EDS has an opportunity to gain a return on investment as the contract matures:

> "Unless we can some way manage a revenue stream for them beyond the contract, that's going to be increasingly difficult if we are asking them for investment. We are both jointly aware that that's a real difficulty for us. We've got to re-explore how we are going to cope with that. Otherwise we are going to stultify entirely as we get closer and closer to the end of the contract." – IR, Account Manager

2. Determine if relationship will be extended or terminated. Some participants were so concerned about what happens at the end of contracts, that they avoided outsourcing altogether:

> "Another concern that we had was that if we did a five-year deal say, what happens at the end of the five years? If we don't get along well, or we want it back and we had transferred the people, then we are in a real bad situation." – Corporate manager of planning and administration, petroleum company

But are clients in a bad position? In general, three options are possible: (1) extend the contract with current supplier(s) (2) switch supplier(s), or (3) bring the IT activity back in-house. our CIO survey data also shows that all three options are commonly practiced in the US and UK markets: 51% switched supplier, 34% brought the activity back in-house, and 11% renewed the original contract (according to other 1999 surveys mainland European organizations show much less propensity to change supplier or bring IT back in-house at the end of contracts). On termination of agreements in 1998 BP Exploration successfully renewed some contracts, reduced others and also brought in a new supplier. We have examples of all three options from our case studies. In no situation were the consequences devastating – indeed all three options can be executed without serious disruption in service as long as clients plan for events well in advance.

Directions for research

This chapter has provided an overview of research findings, within an organizing framework of relationships and their management across six phases of any IT outsourcing arrangement. It is clear that we already know a great deal about certain aspects of the outsourcing phenomenon. Research has been particularly strong in applying, and assessing the usefulness of transaction cost analyses to various IT sourcing options (see for example Ang and Straub, 1998; Lacity and Willcocks, 1996). Less work has been done on the applicability of other theoretical frameworks, such as contingency theories, game theory, investment option theory, and the role of knowledge sourcing, whose importance is implied by the chapter in this volume by Alavi, and is discussed in detail by Scarbrough (1998). The need for further theoretical development, and its testing empirically, remain as significant academic tasks, especially in the light of our own findings on the limited usefulness of Transaction Cost Economics to understanding and explaining IT sourcing phenomena.

The urgency of this agenda for theory building is underlined by the fact that IT outsourcing has outlived the five-year lifetime of a management fad. Many organizations are working through into permanent changes in the ways in which they are organized and managed. In the light of these developments continued empirical analyses and longitudinal case study research remain imperative. Much research has already been conducted on making IT sourcing decisions, what can be outsourced, and what cannot, how vendor bids are assessed, contracts constructed, assessment regimes operated and needed before and after contracts are signed, and what practices make for success and failure. However, in changing circumstances, ongoing research on a case and survey basis needs to continue to be conducted in different sectors and economies on these already established themes, not least because cultural factors in different countries and organizations have been underrated as influencing factors.

But past research has neglected several other themes that we see emerging as critical. One theme is greater exploration of suppliers, their strategies, capabilities and the changing nature of the vendor marketplace. An early paper here, by Michell and Fitzgerald (1997) leads the way, but much more needs to be understood as the IT service marketplace and its players dynamically evolve. A second, strangely neglected area has been in-depth theorizing and analysis of relationship dimensions in IT outsourcing, despite the fact that students and stakeholders of outsourcing invariably assign key importance to relationship characteristics and issues, and despite the existence of extensive work on these themes in marketing, organizational theory, strategy and economics, for example. Kern (1999) has done the lead research so far in this area in developing and convincingly applying a relationship framework to illuminate issues in total and selective IT outsourcing arrangements. The work is further developed in Kern and Willcocks (2001), but much more still needs to be done in this area.

From about 1995 there has been an on-going debate, fed by many emerging practices, that focuses on effective ways of utilizing external IT services. Some, like McFarlan and Nolan (1995), have argued for strategic alliances through long-term deals, usually with single suppliers while recognizing the risks of such an approach, and the need for devices such as equity shares in each other, selling jointly developed products/services on the external market, and/or payment on business results, to secure the relationship. In 1995 many such deals and emerging practices were in their early phases. Further longitudinal research can now be carried out to find out whether such arrangements, or indeed more selective approaches did prove effective, and how they could be improved upon. As one example, Davis (1996) found the Xerox-EDS deal almost an exemplar of how strategic partnering can be achieved. However the deal was only signed in 1994. Kern (1999) revisited the deal and found that it had been radically restructured subsequently, on the basis of some significant issues and disappointments, and that there was much less certainty, in retrospect, that a single supplier, long-term total outsourcing arrangement was the most effective option. The use of our six phase model, or a variant thereon, may well prove a useful tool for pursuing such longitudinal research.

In IT outsourcing, there is a perennial judgment that has to be made, and revisited, as to which IT assets, activities and skills are core, critical and differentiating, and which are commodity (Lacity *et al.*, 1995, 1996). We have found organizations running regularly into a number of difficulties in making such assessments, not least because much depends on circumstances, the business an organization is in, the technologies being used and newly adopted, and how dynamic these factors reveal themselves to be. In our view, the continuing study of these circumstances and decisions will produce dividends for academics and practitioners alike. The additional study of what might be called "backsourcing" will add another intriguing dimension to, and illumination of such a judgment area. Why would organizations "backsource", that is take back in-house assets, activities and skills previously outsourced? And should backsourcing be total or selective? What criteria could be used for making such judgments? Our own studies have already provided examples of both total back sourcing – for example the cancellation in late 1997 by UK-based retailer Sears of a 1996 344 million pound ten-year deal with a single supplier. More frequent has been incremental backsourcing. For example, when Australian-based financial services giant MLC renegotiated its outsourcing deal with a single supplier in 1998 it also arranged to bring back in-house the management of its application development and maintenance. In such examples organizations reveal that circumstances have changed and that what was previously commodity is now differentiating in character, or that the outsourcing experience has shown that their original assessment was flawed in some ways, and that some degree of corrective backsourcing needs to take place. Feeny and Willcocks (1998) found this phenomenon particularly prevalent in the IS human resource capabilities and skills area, where organizations in practice have found it difficult to make accurate assessments of the requisite in-house capabilities needed to identify and deliver on business requirements, retain control of IT destiny while managing external supply. In our estimation future research needs to be conducted in these important and neglected areas.

At the same time the degree to which changes in technology, and the speed of such changes, impact on choices in, and the conduct of, IT sourcing has emerged as both significant and underestimated. John Cross, IT director of BP in 1998, said that in the course of the 1993–98 deals with three suppliers the organization went through two generations of technology. How organizations can source for such dynamic technological trajectories, and how they can contract effectively with the IT services market are increasingly important academic and practitioner questions deserving in-depth research distinctive to the IT field.

Changes in technology can also be tied to a number of emerging practices that are increasingly worth studying. On some estimates business process outsourcing, with IT embodied in the process – already current in areas like billing, accounting and cheque processing – will be the leading growth market, set to reach US$16 billion in 2002. Increasingly, application service providers like Oracle, SAP and Baan are offering web-based remotely hosted enterprise software services that can stretch from provision to software management, while companies like Compaq offer "future sourcing" – installing and running new systems, while not straying into the strategy and policy areas of the client. Other suppliers, such as IBM and EDS have picked up on the staff shortages and rapid speed needed to build e-business capability, and offer to source e-business projects, both in technology and sometimes business planning areas. For similar reasons some organizations have also moved into technology partnering with suppliers, in order to source IT development and provision. One example is the joint venture by Bank of Scotland and FI Group in the United Kingdom. Here a separate entity – First Banking Systems – has 310 bank staff and 120 FI staff, and with a US$220 million budget over five years, will provide commercial software development, IT systems planning and architecture for the bank. Conversely, in some cases IT services have become, over time, such a standardized commodity in a specific sector that, for example, a company like Andersen Consulting can provide accounting services on a shared service basis to seven oil companies – an example of client companies cooperating over aspects of IT supply in order to compete more effectively in other, less commodified areas. Such new developments, or in some cases re-applications of old practices, are innovative ways of attempting to leverage the uses of the external services market for business advantage in the face of changes in technology, or in their business value. In our view, as such developments and their accompanying practices grow, they too will increasingly repay further study.

Conclusions

Many inter-organizational relationship perspectives consider the "client" and "supplier" as the only relevant stakeholders. Our research has found this duality to be very over-simplified. To fill the gap in the literature, this chapter focused on the dynamic relationships among at least eight distinct types of stakeholders. Furthermore, while much prior research has focused on making sourcing decisions, little academic work has addressed in detail post-contract management transition, middle and mature phases – in our opinion, still a potentially highly productive research area. By understanding the common post-contract management activities and the inherent stakeholder goals and relationships during these activities, clients and suppliers can better plan and manage their contracts.

By attending to the expectations and goals of many IT outsourcing stakeholders, apparent anomalies in relationships are understood. Why, for example, do client contract managers and supplier account managers *collaborate* to mediate IT user expectations, then feel perfectly comfortable *fighting* over a monthly bill? Quite simply, **the dynamics of stakeholder relationships vary with the task.** We do, however, note one caveat about stereotyping stakeholders. Our stakeholder analysis described the general goals and perceptions of stakeholder members. While generalizations are an effective tool for summarizing common experiences, they ignore the role of individual personalities in the success of client/supplier relationships. In several instances, stakeholder relationships improved when the person was replaced. Client and supplier account managers, in particular, had a high turnover rate in several of the mega deals studied. The following participant quotes testify to the effectiveness of new faces:

"I think the major thing that's driven change in the relationship is the fact that there has been a change in the head of IT and there's been a change of CSC account executive. It just so happened that [the CSC Account Executive] and myself worked in another British Aerospace industry together which was much smaller with less problems so that we were able you develop a good working relationship and we've brought that relationship to MAD" – BAe Contract Manager, MAD Division

At the beginning of this contract, we actually had to change both of the contract managers three months into the contract to get a more reasonable basis for the relationship because the two of them over the opening three months had continued the negotiations. They were locking horns day-in-day-out. We had to take both of those individuals out and try to recover that relationship. i think that's been successful. – account manager, public sector organization

"I think it's unhealthy in any case to perpetuate the same relationships for too long, because you then know each other so well that you very rarely bring a new perspective onto things, a fresh pair of eyes with a new set of ideas." – BAe, General Contract Manager

Thus, relationship management not only requires an understanding of stakeholder goals and expectations, but also a human resource sensitivity as to the individuals who fill these roles.

Note

1 For a comprehensive review, including evaluation in IT outsourcing arrangements, see Willcocks and Lester, 1999.

References

Ang, S. and Straub, D. (1998) "Production and Transaction Economies and Information Systems Outsourcing – A Study of The US Banking Industry," *MIS Quarterly*, Vol. 22, 4, pp. 535–552.

Applegate, L. and Montealegre, R. (1991) "Eastman Kodak Organization: Managing Information Systems Through Strategic Alliances," *Harvard Business School Case 9–192–030*, Boston, Massachusetts.

Apte, U., Sobel, M., Hanaoka, S., Shimada, T., Saarinen, T., Salmela, T. and Vepsalainen, A. (1997) "IS Outsourcing Practices in the USA, Japan and Finland: A Comparative Study," *Journal of Information Technology*, Vol. 12, 4, pp. 289–304.

Arnett, K. and Jones, M. (1994) "Firms that Choose Outsourcing: A Profile," *Information & Management*, Vol. 26, pp. 179–188.

Auwers, T. and Deschoolmeester, D. (1993) "The Dynamics of an Outsourcing Relationship: A Case in the Belgium Food Industry," paper presented at *The International Conference of Outsourcing of Information Services,* University of Twente, The Netherlands.

Caldwell, B., Violino, B. and McGee, M. (1997) "Hidden Partners, Hidden Dangers: Security and Service Quality may be at risk when your outsourcing vendors use subcontractors," *InformationWeek*, Issue 614.

Clark, T., Zmud, R. and McCray, G. (1995) "The outsourcing of information services: transforming the nature of the business in the information industry," *Journal of Information Technology*, Vol. 10, 4, pp. 221–237.

Collins, J. and Millen, R. (1995) "Information Systems Outsourcing by Large American Industrial Firms: Choices and Impacts," *Information Resources Management Journal*, Vol. 8, 1, pp. 5–13.

Cullen, S. (1997) *Information Technology Survey: A Comprehensive Analysis of IT Outsourcing In Australia.* Deloitte & Touche, Melbourne.

Currie, W. and Willcocks, L. (1998) *New Strategies In IT Outsourcing.* Business Intelligence, London.

Davis, K. (1996) "IT Outsourcing Relationships: An Exploratory Study of Interorganizational Control Mechanisms". *Unpublished DBA Thesis*, Harvard University, Boston.

Douglass, D. (1993) "New Wrinkles in IS Outsourcing," *I/S Analyzer*, Vol. 31, 9.

De Looff, L. (1995) "Information Systems Outsourcing Decision-making: A Framework, organizational theories, and case studies," the *Journal of Information Technology*, Vol. 10, 4, pp. 281–297.

Earl, M. (1996) "The Risks of IT Outsourcing," *Sloan Management Review*, Vol. 37, 3, pp. 26–32.

Feeny, D., Edwards, B. and Simpson, K (1992) "Understanding the CEO/CIO Relationship," *MIS Quarterly*, Vol. 16, 4, pp. 435–448.

Feeny, D. and Willcocks, L. (1998) "Core IS Capabilities For Exploiting Information Technology". *Sloan Management Review*, Vol. 39, 3, pp. 9–21.

Griese, J. (1993) "Outsourcing of Information Systems in Switzerland: A Status Report," paper presented at *The International Conference of Outsourcing of Information Services*, University of Twente, The Netherlands.

Grover, V., Cheon, M. and Teng, J. (1994) "A Descriptive Study on the Outsourcing of Information Systems Functions," *Information & Management*, Vol. 27, pp. 33–44.

Grover, V., Cheon, M. and Teng, J. (1996) "The Effect of Service Quality and Partnership on the Outsourcing of Information Systems Functions," *Journal of Management Information Systems*, Vol. 12, 4, pp. 89–116.

Heinzl, A. (1993) "Outsourcing the Information Systems Function Within the Company: An Empirical Survey", paper presented at *The International Conference of Outsourcing of Information Services*, University of Twente, The Netherlands.

Hu, Q., Saunders, C. and Gebelt, M. (1997) "Research Report: Diffusion Of IS Outsourcing: A Reevaluation of Diffusion Sources," *Information Systems Research*, Vol. 8, 3, pp. 288–301.

Hu, Q., Gebelt, M. and Saunders, C. (1997) "Achieving Success in Information Systems Outsourcing," *California Management Review*, Vol. 39, 2, pp. 63–79.

Huber, R. (1993) "How Continental Bank Outsourced Its 'Crown Jewels,'" *Harvard Business Review*, Vol. 71, 1, pp. 121–129.

Kern, T. (1999) *A Framework For Analyzing IT Outsourcing Relationships*. Unpublished DPhil thesis, Oxford: Oxford University.

Kern, T. and Willcocks, L. (2001) *The Relationship Advantage: IT, Outsourcing and Management*, Oxford: Oxford University Press.

Klepper, R. (1995) "The Management of Partnering Development in I/S Outsourcing," *The Journal of Information Technology*, Vol. 10, 4, pp. 249–258.

Lacity, M. and Hirschheim, R. (1993) *Information Systems Outsourcing: Metaphors, Myths and Realities*. Chichester: Wiley.

Lacity, M. and Hirschheim, R. (1995) *Beyond the Information Systems Outsourcing Bandwagon: The Insourcing Response*, Chichester: Wiley.

Lacity, M. and Willcocks, L. (1996) "Interpreting Information Technology Sourcing Decisions From A Transaction Cost Perspective: Findings and Critique". *Accounting, Management and Information Technologies*, Vol. 5, 3, pp. 203–244.

Lacity, M. and Willcocks, L. (1998) "An Empirical Investigation of Information Technology Sourcing Practices: Lessons from Experience," *MIS Quarterly*, September pp. 363–408.

Lacity, M. and Willcocks, L. (1999) A Survey of IT Outsourcing Experiences in US and UK Organizations. *Journal Of Global Information Management*.

Lacity, M. and Willcocks, L. (2001) *Global Information Technology Outsourcing: In Search of Business Advantage*, Chichester: Wiley.

Lacity, M., Willcocks, L. and Olsen, T. (1996) "Information Technology Outsourcing Experiences in Scandinavia, United Kingdom and United States," *Oxford Institute of Information Management Working Paper*, Templeton College, Oxford.

Lacity, M., Willcocks, L. and Feeny, D. (1996) The Value Of Selective IT Sourcing. *Sloan Management Review*, 37, 3, pp. 13–25.

Lacity, M. Willcocks, L. and Feeny, D. (1995) IT Outsourcing: Maximize Flexibility and Control. *Harvard Business Review* article reprinted in *Business Value From IT*. Harvard Business Press, Boston, 1999.

Loh, L. and Venkatraman, N. (1992a) "Diffusion of Information Technology Outsourcing: Influence Sources and the Kodak Effect," *Information Systems Research*, pp. 334–358.

Loh, L. and Venkatraman, N. (1992b) "Stock Market Reaction to Information nology Outsourcing: An Event Study," *Working Paper 3499–92BPS*, Alfred P. Sloan School of Management, MIT.

McFarlan, F.W. and Nolan, R. (1995) "How to Manage an IT Outsourcing Alliance," *Sloan Management Review*, Winter, pp. 9–23.

McLellan, K., Marcolin, B. and Beamish, P. (1995) "Financial and Strategic Motivations Behind IS Outsourcing, *Journal of Information Technology*, Vol. 10, 4, December, pp. 299–321.

Michell, V. and Fitzgerald, G. (1997) "The IT Outsourcing Marketplace: Vendors and Their Selection". *Journal Of Information Technology*, 12, 3, pp. 130–148.

Pantane, J. and Jurison, J. (1994) "Is Global Outsourcing Diminishing the Prospects for American Programmers?" *Journal of Systems Management*, Vol. 45, 6, pp. 6–10.

Reponen, T. (1993) "Outsourcing or Insourcing," *Proceedings of the Fourteenth International Conference on Information Systems*, Orlando, Florida, pp. 103–116.

Saarinen, T. and Saaksjarvi, M. (1993) "Empirical Evaluation of Two Different I.S. Outsourcing Strategies in Finnish Wood Working Industry, paper presented at *The International Conference of Outsourcing of Information Services*, University of Twente, The Netherlands, May 20–22.

Scarbrough, H. (1998) "The External Acquisition of Information Systems Knowledge" in Willcocks, L. and Lacity, M. (eds) *Strategic Sourcing of Information Systems*, Wiley, Chichester.

Sobel, M. and Apte, U. (1995) "Domestic and Global Outsourcing Practices of America's Most Effective IS users," The *Journal of Information Technology*, Vol. 10, 4, December, pp. 269–280.

Strassmann, P. (1995) "Outsourcing, A Game for Losers," *ComputerWorld*, Vol. 29, 34, August 21, p. 75.

Valor, J., Fonstad, D. and Andreu, R. (1993) "Outsourcing in Spain: An Empirical Study of Top Management's Perspective", paper presented *at The International Conference of Outsourcing of Information Services*, University of Twente, The Netherlands, May 20–22.

Willcocks, L., Feeny, D. and Islei, G. (eds) (1997) *Managing IT As A Strategic Resource*. McGraw Hill, Maidenhead.

Willcocks, L. and Fitzgerald, G. (1994) *A Business Guide To IT Outsourcing*. Business Intelligence, London.

Willcocks, L., Fitzgerald and Lacity, M. (1995) "IT Outsourcing in Europe and The USA: Assessment Issues". *International Journal Of Information Management*. 15, 5, pp. 333–351.

Willcocks, L. and Kern, T. (1998) "IT Outsourcing As Strategic Partnering: The Case Of The UK Inland Revenue". *European Journal Of Information Systems*, 7, pp. 29–45.

Willcocks, L. and Lester, S. (eds) (1999) *Beyond The IT Productivity Paradox*. Wiley, Chichester.

Williamson, O. (1975) *Markes and Hierarchies: Analysis and Antitrust Implications. A Study in the Economics of Internal Organization*, New York: The Free Press.

13

IT Sourcing: Reflections on Practice

Mary C. Lacity and Leslie P. Willcocks

Introduction

For more than 15 years, the authors have studied the best, worst, and emerging sourcing practices in 543 large and small organizations world-wide. In this chapter we present the major lessons customers have learned, in order to successfully exploit the global IT outsourcing market. Major supplier lessons are also identified, which call for superior supplier integrity in selling, negotiating, and delivering IT services. Customers now expect many business advantages from IT outsourcing, including lower costs, better service, infusion of new technology, transformation of fixed IT budgets to variable IT budgets, improved business processes, and even increased revenues (Lacity and Willcocks, 2001; Willcocks and Lacity, 2006). In short, customers expect IT outsourcing to transform IT functions into lean, dynamic groups that respond quickly to business needs and opportunities. But how do customers actually achieve such business advantage? Our research shows that customers must become adept at managing four continual processes to successfully exploit IT outsourcing:

- Assess the in-house IT portfolio to determine which activities are best outsourced
- Evaluate market options for the best sourcing models and best suppliers to achieve customer objectives
- Craft contracts to align customer and supplier expectations and incentives
- Continually manage supplier relationships

Although many people view these activities as sequential, we found that these are continual and concurrent processes. Even within the same customer-supplier relationship, customers frequently revisit the scope of the deal and re-craft contracts several times. This iterative learning process is reflected in Figure 13.1.

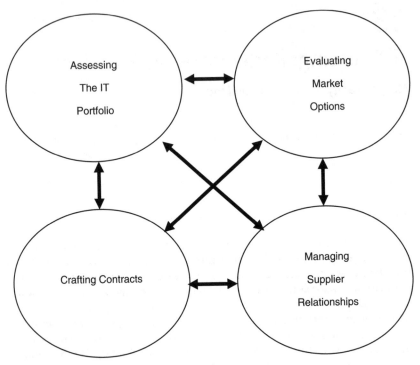

Figure 13.1 Learning and Feedback in Effective IT Sourcing Processes

In this chapter, we extract 14 customer lessons most frequently associated with success for these fours processes. We identify two additional lessons to help customers stay abreast of evolving IT sourcing practices. Furthermore, we identify four lessons aimed at suppliers to help them educate, inform, and attract good customers.[1] Our overall message is that customers can successfully exploit the IT outsourcing market, but that it requires a tremendous amount of in-house management. Some of our research participants expressed this sentiment as follows:

"[Outsourcing] requires a massive hands-on effort every day. You must manage suppliers daily or outsourcing will either fail, or the customer will incur higher costs." – Global Alliance Manager for DuPont's $4 billion IT contracts

"I think mega-deals can work, but they take a lot of hard work." – BAE SYSTEMS IT outsourcing report on a £900 million contract

"How do we manage the relationship at the operational level?...We've got a relationship where there's interfaces taking place between our business and the supplier account managers, every hour, every day. And any one of those can be taking a wrong turn." – Inland Revenue Account Manager for a £1 billion contract

Research method

We and a range of co-authors (principally David Feeny, Thomas Kern, and Rudy Hirschheim) have studied IT sourcing practices in 543 organizations world-wide (see Table 13.1). We have done in-depth case studies based on interviews with over 300 senior executives, IT managers, supplier account managers, business users, and outsourcing advisors in the United States, United Kingdom, Australia, Europe, and Japan. We have surveyed over 400 CIOs in the United States, United Kingdom, and Europe.

As the Introduction to this book makes clear (see Chapter 1), one key feature of our case studies and samples is that we measured actual outcomes compared to expected outcomes. For the surveys, this included perceptual assessments of expected and actual outcomes for costs, service levels, access to scarce IT skills, infusion of new IT, IT flexibility, financial restructuring, control of IT resources, and ability to refocus in-house staff (Lacity and Willcocks, 2000; Kern *et al.*, 2001). For the case studies, we used the triangulation of stakeholders' perceptions as well as secondary documentation to compare expected and actual outcomes (Lacity and Willcocks, 2001). We then created an indicator of success with four possible outcomes:

Table 13.1 Major IT Sourcing Research Projects

Research Method	Sample Size	Data Collection Dates
Exchange-based, traditional IT outsourcing and insourcing case studies (Lacity and Hirschheim, 1995; Lacity and Willcocks, 2001; Willcocks and Lacity, 2006; Also chapter 6)	111 in US, Europe, Australia	1989 to 2005
Exchange-based, traditional IT outsourcing and insourcing survey (Lacity and Willcocks, 2000)	141 in US, UK, Scandinavia	1998
Joint venture case studies (Feeny *et al.*, 2002abcd)	7 in US, Australia and Europe	1994 to 2002
Netsourcing case studies (Kern *et al.*, 2002a)	10 in US and Europe	2001 to 2002
Netsourcing survey (Kern *et al.*, 2001)	274 in 28 countries	2001

- YES, customers achieved most of their expectations
- NO, customers did not achieve most of their expectations
- MIXED results, customers achieved some major expectations but other major expectations were not achieved
- TOO EARLY TO TELL whether expectations were achieved

By correlating these outcomes against sourcing practices, we were able to assess the practices which were most frequently associated with success.[2] Let us now look at the customer lessons emerging from our work.

Assessing the IT portfolio

Lesson 1: Treat IT as a portfolio. Sound sourcing strategies begin with the assumption that IT should be treated as a portfolio of activities and capabilities. Some of these activities must be insourced to ensure current and future business advantage and flexibility, while others may be safely outsourced. This portfolio perspective is empirically supported by our case study findings that selective outsourcing decisions had a higher relative frequency of success than total outsourcing decisions (see Table 13.2; also Chapter 7).

We defined the scope of sourcing options as:

Total Outsourcing: the decision to transfer the equivalent of more than 80% of the IT operating budget for IT assets, leases, staff, and management responsibility to an external IT provider.

Total Insourcing: the decision to retain the management and provision of more than 80% of the IT operating budget internally after evaluating the IT services market.

Selective Outsourcing: the decision to source selected IT functions from external provider(s) while still providing between 20% and 80% of

Table 13.2   Sourcing Decision Scope

Sourcing Decision	YES, most expectations met	NO, most expectations not met	MIXED results	Total
Total Outsourcing	11 (38%)	10 (35%)	8 (27%)	29
Total Insourcing	13 (76%)	4 (24%)	0 (0%)	17
Selective Outsourcing	43 (77%)	11 (20%)	2 (4%)	56
Total Number of Decisions	67	25	10	102

(n = 102 sourcing decisions with discernible outcomes)

the IT operating budget internally. This strategy may include single or multiple suppliers.

Selective outsourcing decisions have been generally successful during the past ten years, with a 77% success rate. This is good news given that selective outsourcing is also the most common sourcing practice according to sample surveys (Apte *et al.*, 1997; Grover *et al.*, 1996). With selective outsourcing, organizations select the most capable and efficient source – a practice some participants referred to as "best-of-breed" sourcing. The most commonly outsourced functions were mainframe data centers, software development and support services, telecommunications/networks, and support of existing systems. In most cases, suppliers were judged to have an ability to deliver these IT products and services less expensively than internal IT managers. The ability to focus in-house resources to higher-value work also justified selective outsourcing.

In general, total outsourcing decisions achieved their expectations less frequently than selective outsourcing decisions or total insourcing decisions. With total outsourcing, only 11 of 29 companies achieved expectations. An example of a total outsourcing success was the South Australian Government's economic development package with EDS. The supplier (EDS) has exceeded yearly targets for delivering $200 million in economic development during the nine-year contract. Note, however, that other aspects of the deal were less successful. (See Chapter 3 in Lacity and Willcocks, 2001 for a full case on the South Australian Government and Cross *et al.*, 1997 for an example of successful outsourcing at British Petroleum).

Ten of the 29 total outsourcing cases (35%) with discernible outcomes, expectations were not realized. Participants encountered one or more of the following problems:

- excess fees for services beyond the contract due to increase in user demand,
- excess fees for services participants assumed were in the contract,
- "hidden costs" such as software license transfer fees,
- fixed-prices that exceeded market prices two to three years into the contract,
- inability to adapt the contract to even minor changes in business or technology without triggering additional costs,
- lack of innovation from the supplier, and
- deteriorating service in the face of patchy supplier staffing of the contract.

For total outsourcing, about 27% of total outsourcing decisions achieved such mixed results. The biggest difficulty was not achieving expected cost savings. Other expectations were more readily achieved such as Year 2000 compliance, switch to the Euro, and accessing enterprise resource planning expertise from suppliers' global workforce.

Exclusive sourcing by an internal IT department has remained generally successful (76%). We found, however, that such success stems from a potential threat of outsourcing (Lesson 9 below explores this further).

Given that IT should be treated as a portfolio, the next question is how to assess which parts of the portfolio should be outsourced or insourced? While common wisdom tells customers to insource core capabilities and to outsource non-core capabilities (Saunders *et al.*, 1997), the distinction is not very useful. More thorough assessment tools are needed to identify exactly what is core and non-core, as Chapter 7 makes clear. The following two lessons therefore explore the theoretical and practitioner tools to make core/non-core assessments.

Lesson 2: Identify core capabilities for insourcing. There is a rich theoretical foundation for make-or-buy decisions that have been applied to IT outsourcing, including resource dependency theory, agency theory, auction theory, game theory, institutional theory, and, by far the two dominant theories: Transaction Cost Economics (TCE) and the resource-based view (RBV).

In many ways, TCE is the ideal theoretical foundation because it specifically addresses make-or-buy decisions based on generic attributes of assets and describes appropriate ways to govern customer-supplier relationships (see Chapters 2 and 3 for more detail). Transaction Cost Economics posits that transactions with high asset specificity (the degree to which assets can be redeployed elsewhere without losing value), high uncertainty, and/or occur frequently are managed less expensively in-house, while the rest should be more efficiently outsourced (Williamson, 1991ab). Specifically, the theory posits that when asset specificity is high, the activities are so idiosyncratic and customized, that insourcing is less costly than outsourcing. When uncertainty is high, contracts cannot be clearly defined for effective outsourcing, thus increasing the threat of supplier opportunism. A number of IT outsourcing empirical studies have found that asset specificity has been a significant factor (Ang and Straub, 1998; Lacity and Willcocks, 1996; Nam *et al.*, 1996; Poppo and Zenger, 1998), although uncertainty has not been a significant factor. The TCE view guides customers to focus on the most cost efficient sourcing option.

The resource-based view (RBV) has been the second most widely-applied theory to IT outsourcing context (Straub *et al.*, 2002; Teng *et al.*, 1995). RBV suggests that managers keep valuable, rare, non-imitable, and non-substitutable resources in-house because they contribute to a firm's competitive positioning and profitability (Barney, 1991). Other resources may be outsourced. *Valuable* resources can be used to exploit strategic opportunities or ward off threats, allow the customer to charge premium prices, attract top human resource talent, and attract investors. Resources are *rare* if few competitors have them. *Non-imitable* resources are difficult or costly for competitors to imitate. *Non-substitutable* resources have no immediate equivalents. RBV guides customers to focus on the strategic potential of resources when making sourcing decisions.

TCE and RBV are both valuable perspectives because they guide managers to treat the entire IT function as a portfolio of transactions/capabilities – some which must be insourced, some which may be outsourced.

The most direct assessment of IT as a portfolio was first articulated by Feeny and Willcocks (1998). They defined four broad core IT categories (CITC) which customers must keep in-house, even if they intend to outsource nearly all of IT:

- *IT governance*: IT strategy, mission, and coordination
- *Business requirements:* understanding business needs as they relate to IT, and relationship building among management, users, and IT
- *Technical ability:* The architecture operation may be outsourced, but the customer maintains control over architecture design and keeps some in-house technical workers to help assess supplier claims and performance.
- *External supplier management:* Customers must make informed buying decisions, monitor and facilitate contacts, and seek added-value opportunities from suppliers.

These four categories are covered in more detail in Chapter 15 of the present volume. To illustrate how these three different assessment perspectives might yield different prescriptions, consider the example of an enterprise resource planning (ERP) implementation in a global manufacturing company. Based on the resource-based view, the ERP project would not likely pass any of the core capability tests as ERP systems are widely used by competitors, thus outsourcing would be prescribed. But Transaction Cost Economics suggests insourcing the ERP project if:

(a) The ERP system had to be highly customized to meet a specific business context (high asset specificity) or
(b) The customer's unique requirements could not be fully articulated in a sound contract (high uncertainty).

The Feeny and Willcocks model would suggest a mixed model. Their model would insource parts of the ERP project associated with governing the project, articulating business requirements, and managing the political terrain among users. But their model would suggest outsourcing certain aspects of the project, such as programming, testing, and systems integration to access market expertise.

Lesson 3: Best source non-core capabilities. Once core IT assets or capabilities are identified, it does not automatically mean that the remaining non-core capabilities should be outsourced. As Chapter 7 makes clear, we found that customers who considered additional business, economic, and technical factors of non-core capabilities were most frequently satisfied with their sourcing decisions (see also Lacity *et al.*, 1996).

From a business perspective, some IT capabilities which are non-core today, could become core in the future. Outsourcing this non-core function now may impede strategic exploitation in the future. For example, one of our case studies outsourced their web site design and hosting in 1995, which initially served as a marketing tool. As the web became increasingly important to their strategy, including online sales and customer service, the customer found their outsourcing relationship impeded the strategic exploitation of the web. It subsequently terminated the supplier at a significant switching cost and brought the function back in-house.

From an economic perspective, some non-core IT activities can be more efficiently insourced. For example, several of our case study participants were willing to outsource their large data centers but could not find suppliers who could do it cheaper (see Chapter 6 for further examples).

From a technical perspective, some non-core IT capabilities are highly integrated with other core activities. This makes outsourcing extremely difficult. For example, one case study participant outsourced factory automation but found the supplier could not adapt to the rapid redirections from the sales department, let alone manage the supply chain implications. The system was eventually brought back in-house after paying a significant early termination fee.

Assuming non-core capabilities pass these Litmus tests, the customer must still evaluate the market options to further validate an outsourcing model and to identify viable suppliers, as discussed in the next section.

Evaluating market options

An important and ongoing IT sourcing process is to keep abreast of market options, even if the organization is exclusively insourcing at present. At a high level, managers should track current supplier capabilities and practices in four general IT outsourcing models: time and materials, exchange-based or traditional IT outsourcing, netsourcing, and joint ventures (see Table 13.3.) Keep in mind that these models are often blended, such as having a joint venture component to structure a shared risk and reward and a traditional IT outsourcing component for operational delivery. In general, these models are most suited for particular types of IT activities, as expressed in the following lessons.

Lesson 4: Consider time and materials contracts when business or technical requirements are uncertain. In the time and materials model, supplier capabilities are bought-in to supplement in-house capabilities under in-house management. Typical examples include project work, such as hiring consultants to help in-house teams implement customer relationship management (CRM) systems. In these cases, customers are able to learn

Table 13.3 Four Outsourcing Models

Model	Resource Owner-ship (Infrastructure & People)	Resource Manage-ment	Customer/Supplier Relationship	Typical Location of Supplier Staff	Typical Customer/Supplier Contract	IT Activities Most Suited for this Model
Time & Materials	Supplier	Customer	One-to-one	Supplier staff on customer site	Time & Materials	Core or non-core capabilities; Customized products & services; Uncertain business or technical requirements
Exchange-based (traditional IT outsourcing)	Supplier	Supplier	One-to-one or one-to-some	Mixed (some supplier staff on customer site, some staff centralized at supplier site)	Highly customized contract defining costs and service levels for that particular customer	Non-core capabilities; Customized products or services; Stable business & technical requirements
Netsourcing	Supplier	Varies	One-to-many	Supplier staff not on customer site	Generic contract specifying rental costs and very minimal service guarantees	Non-core capabilities; Standard products or services; Stable business & technical requirements
Joint Ventures	Venture	Supplier Investor	One-to-one: Customer is both investor and first major customer	Mixed (some supplier staff on customer site, some staff centralized at venture)	Highly customized for operations delivery; broadly defined for revenue sharing	Customer non-core, supplier core capabilities; Significant market for venture's product & services

from suppliers during project development, such as learning to support the CRM system after implementation. Because requirements are uncertain, the customer cannot negotiate a detailed contract, and thus the variable price based on time and materials is appropriate.

The time and materials model is the most common, and indeed poses the least risk to customers. Because the scope of such work is often short term, many people do not consider this true outsourcing. The most common model that is considered truly outsourcing, is the exchange-based – or traditional – IT outsourcing (see Chapter 11 for further discussion of this issue).

Lesson 5: Consider exchange-based contracts for stable, non-core activities requiring some customization. In the exchange-based, or traditional IT outsourcing model, the customer pays a fee to the supplier in exchange for a customized product or service. In this model, the customer typically transfers its IT assets, leases, licenses, and personnel to the external supplier. The supplier manages the resources and provides back to the customer a set of products and services governed by a one-to-one contract.

In our early studies of IT outsourcing, we found that customers often had naive expectations about this model. For example, many customers expected to save 25% on IT costs by signing ten-year, fixed-price contracts for a set of baseline services they assumed would remain stable for the duration of the contract. Many customers subsequently re-negotiated, terminated, or switched suppliers mid-stream. For example, our survey found that 32% of respondents had terminated at least one IT outsourcing contract. Of those, 51% switched suppliers, 34% brought the function back in-house, and the remainder eventually reinstated their initial suppliers due to prohibitively high switching costs (Lacity and Willcocks, 2000).

But the good news is that customers have learned to effectively use the exchange-based model by better identifying which activities, suppliers, and contracts suit this model (Willcocks and Lacity, 2006). Examples of successful outsourcing of stable, non-core activities requiring some customization include:

- Data center operations,
- Telecommunications management,
- Network monitoring,
- Application hosting, and
- Application support

Lesson 6: Consider netsourcing for highly standardized, non-core activities. In the netsourcing model, the customer pays a fee to the supplier in exchange for a standard product or service delivered over the Internet or other networks. Netsourcing promises to deliver best-of-breed, scalable, and flexible business applications to customer desktops for a low monthly fee based on number of users or number of transactions at the customer site.

Customers can rent nearly all popular independent software vendor (ISV) products from netsourcing providers, including ERP packages from SAP, Oracle, Peoplesoft, Great Plains, and JD Edwards; CRM packages from Siebel and Convergys; personal productivity and communications packages from Microsoft, Netscape, and Lotus; and all types of e-commerce and e-business software from CommerceOne, E.Piphany, Requistite Technology, and many others. This model is suited for customers wanting lower costs at the expense of accepting standardized solutions.

"Through our (netsourcing) relationship, we have been able to gain the maximum level of services from the hosting model and thus ensuring a high return on investment." – Operations Director, Insurance Company

The revenues generated in this space – depending on which research firm's report you read – were still modest, between $1 and $2 billion in 2003. Our preliminary research on this space found that early adopters were primarily small to mid-sized enterprises. Most worrying, these early adopters were not following proven sourcing practices. For example, contracts in the netsourcing space were flimsy and leaving customers completely vulnerable. Thus there has been an immense opportunity for netsourcing adopters to learn proven practices from more experienced outsourcing customers. When we revisited this space in 2006, it became apparent that stronger business models had become available, and netsourcing looked a much more promising proposition to customers and suppliers alike (see Willcocks and Lacity, 2006).

Lesson 7: Consider customer-supplier joint ventures only if there is a proven market for the partners' complementary capabilities. In the joint venture model, the supplier and customer create a new company. Deals are typically structured so that the customer investor provides personnel, becomes the venture's first major customer, and shares in future profits if the venture can attract external customers.

Customer-supplier joint ventures, although not a very common model in IT, have received significant attention (McFarlan and Nolan, 1995; Kanter, 1994; Klepper and Jones, 1997). More recently, joint ventures for business process outsourcing (BPO) were making headlines. For example, the UK-based IT start-up company Xchanging has a joint venture with British Aerospace Systems (BAE SYSTEMS) called Xchanging HR Services for BPO of human resource management (Feeny *et al.*, 2002c). Becoming the venture's first customer, BAE SYSTEMS signed a ten-year contract worth £250 million and transferred 430 HR employees to the venture. Ultimate success would depend, in part, on the venture's ability to attract customers besides BAE SYSTEMS (something that had not materialized by 2008 – see Willcocks and Lacity, 2009). In the USA, Exult's equity relationship's with British Petroleum and Bank of America warranted significant attention. These major investors transferred over 1,000 employees to Exult in exchange for signing 10-year contracts in excess of $2 billion, guaranteed costs savings, and a share in Exult's profits. By 2004, Exult had won significant contracts beyond British Petroleum and Bank of America, including a $700 million contract with Prudential Financial and a $600 million contract with International Paper (subsequently it was bought by Hewett).

In the 1990s, joint ventures between customers and IT suppliers often failed to attract external customers and the relationships were redefined as exchange-based. Examples include Delta Airlines and AT&T, Xerox and EDS, and Swiss Bank and Perot Systems. Problems arose among such deals because the parties thought they could sell home-grown customer IT assets and capabilities to external customers. But the reality of delivering daily IT services devoured resources and customer IT assets and capabilities turned out to be too idiosyncratic for commercial delivery in highly-competitive markets like ERP (Lacity and Willcocks, 2001).

What became new, in the new century, with Xchanging and Exult was web-enabled software designed for one-to-many delivery combining with a clear demand in the market for BPO. (For example, Gartner estimated that the BPO was $119 billion in 2000 and that this would swell to $234 billion by 2005. In retrospect this was over-optimistic. Our own estimate of the BPO global revenues in 2007 was US$146 billion – see Willcocks and Lacity, 2006).

Lesson 8: Ensure all layers of the service stack are adequately provided. As previously noted, the sourcing options in Table 13.3 are actually simplified archetypes. Even the characteristic one-to-many business model of the initial netsourcing concept is becoming blended with one-to-one customization of some aspects of the supplier's products and services.

In reality, the business models are often blended and customer-supplier relationships can be quite complex. A supplier may have primary accountability to a customer, but the customer may not be aware that their hardware, monitoring, billing, help desk, and support services may actually be subcontracted to many players.

A good way for customers to manage the complexity is to consider outsourcing as a stack of services (see Table 13.4). At the bottom of the stack is IT connectivity, progressing through increasing levels of functionality. Suppose for example a customer selects traditional outsourcing for a business process such as accounting (level 7 in the service stack). The customer needs to understand how the supplier will manage themselves or alternatively, subcontract, the other six layers of the model. Such a diagnosis might even lead the customer to a different decision, such as outsourcing directly with the subcontractor to maintain more accountability and control or to reduce costs by eliminating the prime contractor's margin (Kern *et al.*, 2002b).

Table 13.4   The Service Stack

Stack Level:	Service Provided:
7. Business Process Delivery	Complete end-to-end business process delivery for functions such as human resources, accounting, or finance.
6. Customized Applications	Access and support of customers' home-grown applications
5. Standard Applications	Access and support of Independent Software Vendor applications
4. Application Operating Infrastructure	Middleware layer for accessing applications on remote servers, such as MS Terminal or Citrix products.
3. Hosting Infrastructure	Data center facilities, leasing of servers, server performance management.
2. Network Services	Monitoring and security services
1. Network Connectivity	Internet service providers and telecom companies offer an extensive array of connectivity options which are matched to customers' bandwidth and data throughput rates.

Merely identifying a sourcing model does not mean that there are suppliers worthy or willing to engage in a relationship. There are many ways to woo suppliers, but the most proven method is:

Lesson 9: Compare request-for-proposal to internal bids. During the last ten years, organizations that invited both internal and external bids had a higher relative frequency of success than organizations that merely compared a few external bids to current IT performance. Based on 85 case studies, we found that when customers allowed internal IT bid teams to compete with external suppliers, 83% of those decisions were successful. When no in-house bid was invited and existing costs were compared with 1 or 2 supplier bids, only 42% of those decisions were successful.

We believe that this was because formal external supplier bids were often based on efficient managerial practices that could be replicated by internal IT managers. The question was: If IT managers could reduce costs, why didn't they? In some cases, IT managers could not implement cost reduction tactics because the internal politics of user departments often resisted cost reduction tactics such as consolidating data centers, standardizing software packages, and implementing full-cost chargeback schemes. For example, users in two divisions at a US food manufacturer did not want to consolidate their data centers into the corporate data center:

"[The two divisions] didn't want to come to corporate IS in the first place. They didn't want to close their data centers, a control thing, 'my car is faster than your car' thing." – Data Center Director

Senior executives at this company felt that IT costs had become too expensive and decided to outsource its large corporate data center. The Data Center Director lobbied to submit an internal bid. Once granted permission, he prepared an internal bid that beat an external bid on cost. Within three years, the internal IT department cut costs by 45% by consolidating and standardizing (see chapter 6 and Hirschheim and Lacity, 2000 for more in-depth examples of the empowerment fuelled by internal bids).

Internal bids, however, might be infeasible in some circumstances. For example, rather than use its own capital to invest in much needed IT renewal, DuPont wanted a supplier(s) to make the investment up-front in exchange for variable fees based on usage. Clearly an internal bid team could not compete with the $4 billion deal DuPont subsequently signed with CSC and Accenture.

Lesson 10: Involve senior management and IT management in sourcing decisions. Concerning *who* should be making these assessments, our case study and survey data both suggest that multiple stakeholders need to be involved. In our survey data, 68% of respondents had at least two stakeholders driving the decision, most frequently the IT Director and lawyers or the IT director and senior executives. Our case study data shows that joint senior executive/IT manager decisions or IT managers acting alone had higher relative frequencies of success than senior executives acting alone (see Table 13.5).

We defined decision sponsor as the person who initiated or championed the sourcing decision and who made or authorized the final decision (Beath, 1996). In our study, sourcing decisions made jointly with both senior executive and IT input had the highest success rate (76%). It appears that successful sourcing decisions – like most large-scale IT endeavors – require a

Table 13.5   Decision Sponsor for Sourcing Decisions

Decision Sponsor	YES, most expectations met	NO, most expectations not met	MIXED results	Total
Senior Executive	12 (43%)	10 (36%)	6 (21%)	28
IT Manager	20 (71%)	6 (21%)	2 (7%)	28
Joint Executive/IT	35 (76%)	9 (20%)	2 (4%)	46
Total Number of Decisions	67	25	10	102

(n = 102 sourcing decisions with discernible outcomes)

mix of political power and technical skills. Political power helped to enforce the larger business perspective – such as the need for organization-wide cost cuts – as well as the "muscle" to implement such business initiatives. Technical expertise on IT services, service levels, measures of performance, rates of technical obsolescence, rates of service growth, price/performance improvements, and a host of other technical topics were needed to develop requests-for-proposals, evaluate supplier bids, and negotiate and manage sound contracts. In some cases, this mix of political power and technical knowledge was encompassed in one stakeholder group, as evident by 12 successful decisions sponsored solely by senior executives and 20 successful decisions sponsored solely by senior IT managers.

Crafting deals

Assuming an appropriate sourcing model (see Chapter 7) and viable supplier (see Chapter 11) has been identified, the parties must still negotiate a contract. The two most important proven practices for crafting contracts are discussed below.

Lesson 11: Detail contracts, including responsibilities of both parties and mechanisms of change. Many different types of contracts are used to govern exchange-based relationships:

Standard Contracts: the customer signed the supplier's standard, off-the-shelf contract.

Detailed Contracts: the contract included special contractual clauses for service scope, service levels, measures of performance, and penalties for non-performance.

Loose Contracts: the contract did not provide comprehensive performance measures or contingencies but specified that the suppliers perform "whatever the customer was doing in the baseline year" for the duration of the contract at 10–30% less than the customer's baseline budget.

Mixed Contracts: For the first few years of the contract, requirements were fully specified, connoting a "detailed" contract. However, participants could not define technology and business requirements in the long run, and subsequent requirements were only loosely defined, connoting a "loose" contract.

Detailed contracts achieved expectations with greater relative frequency than other types of contracts (75%) (see Table 13.6). These organizations understood their own IT functions very well, and could therefore define

Table 13.6   **Types of Exchange-based Contracts**

Contract Type	YES, most expectations met	NO, most expectations not met	MIXED results	Total
Detailed	45 (75%)	9 (15%)	6 (10%)	60
Loose	0 (0%)	7 (100%)	0 (0%)	7
Mixed	6 (55%)	1 (9%)	4 (36%)	11
Standard	2 (50%)	2 (50%)	0 (0%)	4
Total Number of Decisions	53	19	10	82

(n = 82 outsourcing decisions with discernible outcomes)

their precise requirements in a contract. They also spent significant time negotiating the details of contracts (up to 18 months in some cases), often with the help of outside experts. For example, the Financial Manager at a US bank spent three months negotiating the data center contract, assisted by the VP of IS, internal attorneys, and two hired experts:

> "And that's when [the VP of IS] and I and the attorneys sat down every-day for three solid months of drafting up the agreement, negotiating the terms, conditions, and services." – Financial Manager

From our survey, customers included the following clauses in their detailed contracts:

- costs (100%),
- confidentiality (95%),
- service level agreements (88%),
- early termination (84%),
- liability & indemnity (82%),
- change contingency (65%), and
- supplier non-performance penalty (62%).

Increasingly, contracts also include responsibility matrices, which outline the responsibilities for both customers and suppliers. This innovation recognizes that suppliers sometimes missed service levels because of their customers. For example, in one of our cases, the supplier did not connect new customer employees to the network within the contractual time limit because the customer systematically failed to properly authorize new accounts.

No matter how detailed contracts become, changes in requirements will occur. Many detailed contracts now have mechanisms of change, including:

- planned contract realignment points to adapt the contract every few years,
- contingency prices for fluctuation in volume of demand,
- negotiated price and service level improvements over time, or even
- external benchmarking of best-of-breed suppliers to reset prices and service levels.

In contrast to the success of the detailed contract, all seven of the loose contracts were disasters in terms of costs and services. Two of these companies, actually terminated their outsourcing contracts early and rebuilt their internal IT departments. Another company threatened to sue the supplier. Senior executives in these companies had signed flimsy contracts under the rhetoric of a "strategic alliance." However, the essential elements of a strategic alliance were absent from these deals. There were no shared risks, no shared rewards, and no synergies from complementary competencies nor any other of the critical success factors identified by researchers (Kanter, 1994). Instead, these loose contracts created conflicting goals. Specifically, the customers were motivated to demand as many IT services as possible for the fixed-fee price by arguing "you are our partners". Supplier account managers countered that their fixed-fee price only included services outlined in the contract. The additional services triggered supplier costs which were passed to the customer in terms of excess fees. Because the customers failed to fully specify baseline services in the contract, the customers were charged excess fees for items they assumed were included in the fixed-price.

Six of the 11 "mixed" contracts with discernible outcomes achieved expectations. The contracts contained either shared risks and rewards or significant performance incentives. A Dutch electronics company spun-off of the IT department to a wholly-owned subsidiary. Because the newly-formed company's only source of revenue was from the electronics company, the venture was highly motivated to satisfy their only client's needs.

Lesson 12: Keep contracts short enough to retain relevancy and control, but long enough for suppliers to generate a profit margin. From the customer perspective, there is clear evidence that short-term contracts have higher frequencies of success than long-term contracts (see Table 13.7). From our 85 case studies, 87% of outsourcing decisions with contracts of three years or less were successful, compared to a 38% success rate for contracts eight years or longer.

Short-term contracts involved less uncertainty, motivated supplier performance, allowed participants to recover from mistakes quicker, and helped to

Table 13.7   Contract Duration

Contract Duration	YES, most expectations met	NO, most expectations not met	MIXED Results	Total
0 to 3 year contracts	28 (87.5%)	4 (12.5%)	0 (0%)	32
4 to 7 year contracts	19 (59%)	10 (31%)	3 (9%)	32
8 to 25 year contracts	8 (38%)	6 (29%)	7 (33%)	21
Total Number of Decisions	55	20	10	85

(n = 85 outsourcing decisions with discernible outcomes)

ensure that participants were getting a fair market price. Another reason for the success of short-term contracts is that participants only outsourced for the duration in which requirements were stable, thus participants could articulate adequately their cost and service needs. Some participants noted that short-term contracts motivated supplier performance because suppliers realized customers could opt to switch suppliers when the contract expired. As the IS director of a UK aviation authority commented, "It's no surprise to me that the closer we get towards contract renewal, it's amazing what service we can get."

In contrast, long-term contracts have remained troublesome, with failure to achieve cost savings as the primary reason. Few total IT outsourcing mega-deals reach maturity without a major stumbling block. Conflicts are increasingly being resolved through contract re-negotiations. In 1997, the Gartner Group, based on a survey of 250 CIOs, estimated that 75% of all IT outsourcing customers would renegotiate their deals (Caldwell, 1997; Caldwell and McGee, 1997).

Suppliers, however, have a clear preference for long-term relationships to recoup excessive transition and investment costs. Returning to DuPont's ten-year deal, the transition activities lasted over 18 months as the contract was operationalized in 22 countries to a population of nearly 100,000 users. The transition also included massive investments by one supplier in IT infrastructure, which the supplier could only recoup in a long-term deal (see Lacity and Willcocks, 2001 for full details of the Dupont case. See also Chapter 8). Clearly, the customer's incentives for short-term deals must be balanced with the supplier's incentives for long-term deals.

Managing external suppliers

For all the sourcing models, there is an inherent adversarial nature in the contracts in that a dollar out of the customer's pocket is a dollar in the supplier's pocket. (This is even true for joint ventures because the customer investor is also the venture's primary or even sole paying customer.) If the customer followed best practices up to the point of signing the contract, they should be sufficiently protected from the devastatingly negative consequences experienced in the early days. If the supplier negotiated a favorable deal, they should be able to deliver on the contract and still earn a profit margin. But even under the most favorable circumstances, relationship management is difficult:

> "Really our challenge is relationship management...I know, I certainly haven't found the answer yet, but not too many other people have found the answer either," – Customer of a AU$600 million contract

Lesson 13: Put core customer capabilities in place to protect the customer interests as well as to foster supplier success. These capabilities, as defined by Feeny and Willcocks are detailed in chapter 15. They include Informed Buying capability as an overall supply-facing ability to understand the market, supplier strategies and capabilities, and what a good deal with a specific supplier entails. In addition we briefly describe here, for convenience, the three other major capabilities we are referring to:

Contract Monitoring capability to ensure that the supplier delivers on the contract. This capability also monitors best-of-breed cost and services emerging in the market to motivate and negotiate improved supplier performance over time.

Contract Facilitation capability to provide a vital liaison role between the supplier and the customer's user and business communities to ensure supplier success. For example, the contract facilitator role makes sure the user community understands what the supplier is contractually obligated to deliver to prevent unrealistic expectations of the supplier. Contract facilitation helps suppliers implement vast change programs such as consolidation, standardization, and rationalization. The role also evaluates user demand to harness spending beyond baseline.

Supplier development capability explores ways the customers and suppliers can engage in win-win activities beyond the legal requirements of a contract. The parties may question: Can the supplier sell any of the customers assets externally? Can the customer serve as a test site for a new supplier offering? This capability is usually not evident until the transition period is over and operations are stabilized.

Lesson 14: Embrace the dynamics of the relationship. Even with these capabilities in place, customer and supplier relationships will sometimes be adversarial. For example it is quite natural that customers and suppliers will fight over a monthly bill or an interpretation of the contract, but still have a good relationship overall. Rather than seek to extinguish such fights, the best relationships embrace the dynamics. This subject is covered in more detail in Chapter 12 but is touched on briefly here, again for convenience.

We identified three other common types of customer-supplier interactions besides adversarial: tentative, cooperative, and collaborative. These are based on the extent of goal alignment for the task at hand:

- Tentative interactions occur when goal alignments are unknown, such as during the bidding process. At such times, each side tends to exaggerate their strengths and hide their weaknesses.
- Cooperative interactions occur when goals are complementary, such as the customer wants the service, the supplier wants the payment.
- Collaborative interactions occur when both sides have shared goals, such as educating the user community on what they can expect from the contract or presenting a positive face to the press.

The important lesson emerging from Chapter 12 is that each side must have equal power so that they can achieve equitable outcomes. The aims of each party should be fairness, not domination or exploitation. Again, this common playing field can only occur if the customer has successfully executed the IT assessment, supplier evaluation, and contracting processes.

Other sources for customer learning

Customers have learned many lessons about evaluating their IT portfolios, evaluating market options, crafting contracts, and managing suppliers. But learning is never stagnant, and customers must find ways to keep abreast of emerging sourcing practices. Two proven ways are discussed below.

Lesson 15: Consider incremental outsourcing to develop experience with outsourcing. Just as someone cannot learn to drive from reading a manual, someone cannot learn to successfully outsource merely by reading about other people's experiences. We found that the best way to accumulate learning is through incremental outsourcing, in which customers adopt this outsourcing strategy precisely to develop an in-house knowledge about outsourcing. With incremental outsourcing, organizations outsourced a small and discrete part of its IT activities, such as third-party maintenance or shared processing services. The experience gained from this first incremental approach was then fed back into further outsourcing. In two cases we researched, a petrochemical company and an electric utility, the organizations found themselves ultimately engaging in total outsourcing.

Lesson 16: Hire help. Another very important factor in customer learning is the widespread use of key IT outsourcing consultants and IT outsourcing legal firms. We are witnessing an institutional isomorphic effect where outside experts, such as Technology Partners International (TPI), Gartner Group, Corbett & Associates, Equaterra, Shaw Pittman, Millbank Tweed, the Everest Group and many others seed client organizations with similar standards and methods. The overall effect of these external constituents is the dissemination of 'best' practices. In particular, mega-deal contracts are now templated, with all the customer costs, service levels, performance measures, mechanisms of change, and other clauses nearly identical. Although each organization participating in the research regards these practices as "competitive secrets", practices are nearly identical across mega-contracts. By 2007, a typical mega-deal contract contained 30,000 lines, over 600 service level agreements, and over 50 different pricing mechanisms.

Outside experts have also standardized many post-contract management practices, such as external benchmarking of data centers, networks, desktops, and applications; color-coded problem resolution systems, joint supplier/customer teams to resolve disputes; and responsibility matrices to clearly define customer responsibilities and supplier responsibilities. For example, we found BAE SYSTEMS, DuPont, Inland Revenue, Government of South Australia using these practices.

In addition to hiring external experts, customers may also access external expertise through outsourcing interest groups, such as ITTUG or the Sourcing Interest Group. Groups provide an opportunity for both customers and suppliers to share and disseminate data. For example, the Outsourcing World Summit has regularly drawn over 300 outsourcing customers and suppliers each year and has featured prominent speakers, panels, Q&A sessions and many opportunities for informal exchanges.

Lessons for suppliers

Nearly all of our exchange-based cases studies in which the deals were worth in excess of $500 million or more, the suppliers were EDS, IBM, CSC, and/or Accenture. These suppliers are among the few organizations which have had a significant global presence to service such large deals (This may well change over the next few years as Indian suppliers become more global – see also Chapters 9 and 10). We found significant variability in the success of such deals. Given the suppliers are the same, it is logical to assume the differentiating factor is the customer. Put simply from the supplier perspective: *good customers make for good relationships*. The ideal customer has significant experience with outsourcing the right activities, crafting the right types of contracts, and ensuring supplier success through the previously discussed roles and practices. The following lessons stand out as viable ways to educate, inform, and attract good customers, primarily through superior supplier integrity.

Lesson 17: Educate your customer during the earliest possible phase. Increasingly, we advise suppliers to help educate naive customers on the issues discussed in this chapter. For example, after presenting the core IT capabilities framework to one supplier bidding on a significant US government contract, the supplier went back to the US government agency and told them to reduce the scope of their RFP and to retain more supplier management capability. The agency was quite taken back with this approach, revised its RFP, and subsequently selected the aforementioned supplier because they trusted them. Such education is likely also to help strengthen relationships (see Chapter 12; also Willcocks and Cullen, 2006).

Lesson 18: Briddle your public relations staff, unbriddle your account managers. Increasingly, we talk to outsourcing shoppers who are shying away from some suppliers because they simply don't believe them. The potential customers complain that the supplier oversells with polished PR and salespeople. Legitimate concerns about possible escalating costs and service lapses are readily dismissed with appeals to their "world class expertise." Client reference lists often include only new customers, where expectations are still high and supplier delivery is still unproven. Customers are not naive – they know that outsourcing relationships will encounter roadblocks and problems. They want to hear stories of past disasters and how the supplier responded to them, what the supplier learned from them.

Consider one of our case study from a multi-billion dollar company. Senior managers rejected bids from big suppliers and instead signed a ten-year, $1 billion dollar contract with a small start-up company. The big players sent their slickest salespeople to present. The start-up sent the unpolished, but enthusiastic team of people who would actually be doing the work:

> "The early presentations were really quite crap, lots of feeling, lots of passion, lots of drive, lots of enthusiasm. There is a certain pleasure in the naivety...it's like looking at a Lowry painting, it's still beautiful but is naïve, rather than a Gauguin or something like that. I would hate to lose the touch that's in here for the sake of being slick." – Practice Director from the winning supplier

Lesson 19: Submit realistic, open bids. Some suppliers underbid in order the secure the contract. Such a strategy was often fruitful in the past because suppliers knew that the customer's needs would change, and opportunities for upsell would more than compensate for the loss on the baseline contract. But customers are increasingly aware of such strategies and intentionally select other suppliers for add-ons to keep a competitive playing field. It serves the supplier far better to offer a realistic bid and to disclose how they can deliver on the bid and still earn a profit. Such disclosure might entail their non-imitiable costs in IT infrastructure and capabilities due to economies of scope and scale. For example, Xchanging can boast that one of their process experts previously implemented General Electric's Six Sigma program which saved GE $54 million. (Disclosures also makes customers question the unrealistic bids of competitors.)

Lesson 20: Propose and price value-added options. Once transition periods are complete, customers generally find that suppliers can deliver on operational objectives of IT contracts. But customers increasingly expect more innovations and opportunities for generating revenues, even if the deals are essentially exchange-based (see Chapter 11). Customers express continued disappointment on this front:

> "Sure, the supplier delivers the contract...but trying to get them to iden-tify the added-value we both talked about at the beginning, let alone deliver on it, is very difficult." – IT Contract Manager, US Bank

> "Yes, the supplier can achieve all the things that were proposed – but where is this famous added-value service? We are not getting anything over and above what any old outsourcer could provide." – IT Services Director, Aerospace Company

The value-added supplier proposes and prices options which signifi-cantly benefit the customer. Examples from our case studies include significant cost savings and service improvement by web-enabling human resource management, creating wireless connections for sales force support, and helping customers use online auctions to reduce procurement costs.

Conclusion

Once dominated by a few big players (EDS, IBM, CSC), the IT outsourcing market has fragmented into many niche services. Moreover, other sup-pliers are gaining size, either through revenue growth, acquisitions or a combination of these. From the customer perspective, this increased competition affords them more power to bargain for shorter contracts, more select services, and better financial packages. But to harness this market opportunity, customers need to learn how to continually monitor market options, assess the contribution of their IT portfolio for current and future business value, decide what type of relationships suite their needs, craft optimal contracts, and successfully manage supplier relationships. The overall message for customers is clear: ***all outsourcing requires continual and significant in-house management***. This point is pursued in Chapter 15 of this volume.

For suppliers, they must be able to select educated customers with clear goals, and have the ability to execute such deals while still generating a profit. At the end of the day, success is measured by the operational delivery of the contract, ability to fairly adapt to change, and the ability to identify added-value services. These points are discussed in much more detail in 11, 12, and 14 of this book.

Notes

1 A shorter version based on 12 customer lessons was initially published in Lacity, M. (2002) "Global Information Technology Sourcing: More Than A Decade of Learning". In *IEEE Computer* 35 8, pp. 26–32.
2 Further details on the research methods may be found online at www.umsl.edu/ ~lacity/guide.html and www.umsl.edu/~lacity/cases.htm.

References

Ang, S. and Straub, D. (1998) "Production and Transaction Economies and Information Systems Outsourcing – A Study Of The US Banking Industry," in *MIS Quarterly* 22, 4, pp. 535–552.
Apte, U., Sobel, M., Hanaoka, S., Shimada, T., Saarinen, T., Salmela, T. and Vepsalainen, A. (1997) "IS Outsourcing Practices in the USA, Japan, and Finland: A Comparative Study," in *Journal of Information Technology* 12, 4, pp. 289–304.
Barney, J. (1991) "Firm Resources and Sustained Competitive Advantage," in *Journal of Management* 17, 1, pp. 99–121.
Beath, C. (1996) The Project Champion, in Earl, M. (ed.): *Information Management: The Organizational Dimension*. Oxford: Oxford University Press.
Caldwell, B. (1997) Outsourcing Deals Often Renegotiated, in *InformationWeek*, Issue 628, http://www.informationweek.com/628/28mtout.htm [1997–04–28; as of 2002–10–26]
Caldwell, B. and McGee, M. (1997) No Big Savings – Too Many outsourcing deals don't pay off as expected. In *InformationWeek*, Issue 621, http://www.information-week.com/621/21mtout.htm [1997–03–10; as of 2002–10–26]
Cross, J., Earl, M. and Sampler, J. (1997) "Transformation of the IT Function at British Petroleum," in *MIS Quarterly* 21, 4, pp. 401–420.
Feeny, D. and Willcocks, L. (1998) "Core IT Capabilities For Exploiting Information Technology," in *Sloan Management Review* 39, 3, pp. 9–21.
Feeny, D., Willcocks, L. and Lacity, M. (2002a) The Enterprise Partnership as Vehicle for Transforming Back Office to Front Office: The Story of Lloyd's of London and Xchanging's Claims Administration Transformation. *Oxford Institute of Information Management Working Paper,* Templeton College, Oxford University.
Feeny, D., Willcocks, L. and Lacity, M. (2002b) The Enterprise Partnership as Vehicle for Transforming Back Office to Front Office: The Story of Lloyd's of London and Xchanging's Policy Administration Transformation. *Oxford Institute of Information Management Working Paper*, Templeton College, Oxford.
Feeny, D., Willcocks, L. and Lacity, M. (2002c) The Enterprise Partnership as Vehicle for Transforming Back Office to Front Office: The Story of BAE SYSTEMS and Xchanging's Human Resource Management Transformation. *Oxford Institute of Information Management Working Paper*, Templeton College, Oxford.
Feeny, D., Willcocks, L. and Lacity, M. (2002d) The Enterprise Partnership as Vehicle for Transforming Back Office to Front Office: The Story of BAE SYSTEMS and Xchanging's Indirect Procurement Transformation. *Oxford Institute of Information Management Working Paper*, Templeton College, Oxford.
Grover, V., Cheon, M. and Teng, J. (1996) "The Effect of Service Quality and Partnership on the Outsourcing of Information Systems Functions," in *Journal of Management Information Systems* 12, 4, pp. 89–116.

Hirschheim, R. and Lacity, M. (2000) "Information Technology Insourcing: Myths and Realities," in *Communications of the ACM* 43, 2, pp. 99–107.

Kanter, R. (1994) "Collaborative Advantage, The Art of Alliances," in *Harvard Business Review* 72, 4, pp. 96–108.

Kern, T., Lacity, M. and Willcocks, L. (2002a) *Netsourcing: Renting Business Applications & Services Over a Network.* New York: Prentice Hall.

Kern, T., Willcocks, L. and Lacity, M. (2002b) "Application Service Provision: Risk Assessment and Risk Mitigation," in *MIS Quarterly Executive* 1, 2, pp. 113–126.

Klepper, R. and Jones, W. (1997) *Outsourcing Information Technology, Systems, and Services.* New York: Prentice Hall.

Kern, T., Lacity, M., Willcocks, L., Zuiderwijk, R. and Teunissen, W. (2001) *ASP Market-Space Report 2000: Mastering the Customer's Expectations.* CMG, Netherlands.

Lacity, M. (2002) "Global Information Technology Sourcing: More Than A Decade of Learning," in *IEEE Computer* 35, 8, pp. 26–32.

Lacity, M. and Hirschheim, R. (1995) *Beyond the Information Systems Bandwagon: The Insourcing Response.* Wiley, Chichester.

Lacity, M., Willcocks, L. and Feeny, D. (1996) "The Value Of Selective IT Sourcing," in *Sloan Management Review* 37, 3, pp. 13–25.

Lacity, M. and Willcocks, L. (1996) "Interpreting Information Technology Sourcing Decisions From A Transaction Cost Perspective: Findings and Critique," in *Accounting, Management and Information Technology* 5, 3/4, pp. 203–244.

Lacity, M. and Willcocks, L. (2000) Inside IT Outsourcing: A State-of the-art Report. Templeton Executive Briefing, Templeto College, Oxford.

Lacity, M. and Willcocks, L. (2001) *Global IT Outsourcing: Search for Business Advantage.* Wiley, Chichester.

McFarlan, F.W. and Nolan, R. (1995) "How to Manage an IT Outsourcing Alliance," in *Sloan Management Review* 36, 2, pp. 9–23.

Nam, K., Rajagopalan, S., Rao, H. and Chaudhury, A. (1996) "A Two-level investigation of Information Systems Outsourcing," in *Communications of the ACM* 39 (1996) 7, pp. 36–44.

Poppo, L. and Zenger, T. (1998) "Testing alternative theories of the firm: Transaction cost, knowledge-based, and measurement explanations for make-or-buy decisions in information services," in *Strategic Management Journal* 19, 9, pp. 853–877.

Saunders, C., Gebelt, M. and Hu, Q. (1997) "Achieving Success in Information Systems Outsourcing," in *California Management Review* 39, 2, pp. 63–79.

Straub, D., Weill, P. and Stewart, K. (2002) Strategic Control of IT Resources: A Test of Resource-Based Theory in the Context of Selective IT Outsourcing. Working paper, Georgia State University and MIT. Sloan School of Management, Boston.

Teng, J., Cheon, M. and Grover, V. (1995) "Decisions to Outsource IT Functions: Testing a Strategy-Theoretic Discrepancy Model," in *Decision Sciences* 26,1, pp. 75–103.

Willcocks, L. and Cullen, S. (2006) *The Outsourcing Enterprise 2: The Power of Relationships.* LogicaCMG, London.

Willcocks, L. and Lacity, M. (2006) *Global Sourcing of Business and IT Services.* Palgrave, London.

Willcocks, L. and Lacity, M. (2009) *Outsourcing: From ITO to BPO and Offshoring.* Palgrave, London.

Williamson, O. (1991a) "Strategizing, economizing, and economic organization," in *Strategic Management Journal* 12, pp. 75–94.

Williamson, O. (1991b) "Comparative economic organization: The analysis of discrete structural alternatives," in *Administrative Science Quarterly* 36, pp. 269–296.

14
IT Offshore Outsourcing: Supplier Lessons on the Management of Expertise

Ilan Oshri, Julia Kotlarsky and Leslie P. Willcocks

Introduction

On our figures, revenues from offshore outsourcing of information technologies exceeded US$25 billion by 2008, and will experience compound annual growth averaging 20% over the next five years (Willcocks and Lacity, 2006; Willcocks and Cullen, 2005). For IT executives this means offshoring, either directly, through a captive, or indirectly through a domestic supplier, has become a serious option; indeed many have already embarked down this path. For outsourcing vendors this means a growing number of clients will offshore outsource their IT systems expecting the vendors to maintain and in some cases to continue developing their IT applications from remote locations. But client executives already ponder a major question: where do you draw the line on outsourcing knowledge and expertise? How can a selected vendor develop knowledge and expertise of the client's domain, systems and practices, not only to maintain continuity of service, but also to achieve the much vaunted targets of innovation and transformation? At the same time, we find executives of IT outsourcing vendors themselves asking: how can expertise be quickly developed around new areas, particularly where teams are remote and dispersed? How can we retain knowledge when people, in which it resides, move on? This chapter describes ongoing research into how one IT outsourcing vendor built expertise management systems in order to ensure the diffusion of client knowledge and the sharing of learning across the entire organization.[1] Our research experiences point to major lessons for client and supplier organizations. At a big picture level, we show how, in order to compete and deliver on client expectations, over the next five years a supplier will need to make operational a transactive memory system for managing knowledge and expertise – in several ways something clients themselves could learn from.

Towards the management of dispersed expertise

Throughout this chapter expertise refers to the ability to act knowledgeably within a specific domain of application. The word expertise relates to the ability to achieve skillful performance, not least in applying knowledge to develop and improve products and processes. Expertise is a specific type of knowledge that is dynamic and evolving in nature, and consists of embodied knowledge and skills possessed by individuals. For our purposes it refers to knowing in practice (Orlikowski, 2002). How expertise is created, maintained and leveraged is of critical importance to outsourcing suppliers and clients alike.

To understand the complexity faced by an offshore supplier in developing expertise to support client services across several geographical locations dotted around the world, we first introduce Tata Consultancy Services. We then discuss the challenges the company faced in a particular offshore outsourcing project, then draw lessons from the expertise management systems developed to address these challenges.

Background: Tata Consultancy Services (TCS)

As part of the Tata Group, TCS was founded in 1968 as a consulting service firm for the emerging IT industry. Since then, TCS has expanded to become a global player with revenues of over US$2 billion in 2006 (TCS Annual Report and internal documents) With over 74,000 associates and 50 service delivery centers, TCS has established presence in 34 countries providing various services including business process outsourcing (BPO) and IT maintenance and development, to hundreds of clients across the globe. The company has developed a global delivery model in which the execution of projects has been achieved mainly through the support of teams located remotely from the client. In particular, projects are often executed in a manner that the onsite and offshore teams transfer work packages back and forth until the task is completed. Furthermore, project teams based onsite, onshore and nearshore depend upon expertise and knowledge that reside within the company either offshore or in a remote location. This means that TCS has had to invest in developing expertise management systems to leverage local expertise globally regardless of the physical location of either the expert or the expertise seeker. Let us start by first illustrating the challenges TCS faced on managing expertise in a particular large-scale project.

Challenges in developing and managing expertise

The ABN AMRO bank – TCS outsourcing deal was announced in late 2005. In this US$1.2 billion contract, The Netherlands-based bank contracted five vendors, among them Tata Consultancy Services (TCS) to provide support and application enhancement services. TCS will provide these services in cooperation with another Indian company, Patni Computers, with Accenture as the preferred partner for application development. The other partners are IBM for infrastructure, and Infosys, focusing particularly on North America, where the company had been retained previously for offshore services. The outsourcing project organization of the ABN AMRO-TCS deal consists of several arrangements across three continents. There are *onsite* teams at the customer locations in Amsterdam and corresponding offshore teams in Mumbai. Similarly, in Brazil, onsite teams from Sao Paulo correspond with onshore teams from the delivery center located about 100 kilometers away in the Campinas. Lastly, an onsite team in Luxembourg communicates with a nearshore delivery center in Hungary. Typically, team members reside in one location throughout the project, either onsite or offshore, while only a small number of individuals travel between remote locations for short visits. The entire onsite team comprises project members, project leaders, portfolio managers, program managers, a transition head, a relationship manager and other functions – mainly quality assurance, human resource and organization development personnel.

The offshore outsourcing project was divided into two phases; Transition and Steady State. In the Transition phase, the onsite team learns about the client's systems and transfers this knowledge to the offshore team. In the Steady State phase, mainly the offshore team, but also the onsite team, supports the client systems and services as well as engaging in application development activities. This mode of work requires the onsite and offshore/onshore teams to overcome expertise development challenges. For example, one key challenge is to ensure there are no expertise gaps between onsite and offshore, nearshore and onshore teams. This requires expertise developed by the onsite team to be shared and developed to the same proficiency by the offshore team. Eliminating expertise gaps between onsite and offshore teams is particularly important to offshore service companies like TCS. IT vendors need to demonstrate to their clients that offshoring application maintenance and development will not affect the quality of the service provided, and their ability to further develop new applications offshore. As one Delivery Manager from the offshore team in Mumbai recalled:

"When I had my initial discussion with the bank's portfolio managers, … they asked – how are we going to take care of the knowledge base, because they were wondering that they're having 10, 15, 30 years experience in the bank and we [TCS] are going to join afresh: you are just going to have a knowledge transfer for a small duration, they asked: and how do you ensure that you have this knowledge with you? And how you're going to retain the knowledge?"

A second challenge that was expressed by TCS concerned the approaches and methods through which local learning and expertise could become global assets. Put simply, TCS, and other vendors, are exposed to vast knowledge through numerous outsourcing relationships; however this knowledge often becomes a single project asset only, and is hardly shared with other projects that will be confronting similar challenges. The Head of the Learning and Development Department of TCS explained this challenge:

> So how do I create a kind of customer-focused experiences; how do you share this knowledge. How can we enhance our learning about banking and insurance so we not only say that we only know technology but we also know about the banking industry. Basically, I need to develop this domain knowledge and harness that knowledge to other value activities, share it with the entire workforce so our employees can talk to the customer in their [client] own language, in their own [client] domain of expertise as an expert. And that is a challenge for me to create this kind of an expertise.

In summary there were two key challenges TCS had to address:

1. The Client challenge – How can the client's knowledge be captured and retained at both onsite and offshore locations to ensure uninterrupted service and to further develop a client's service? This challenge is about the vendor developing absorptive capacity to quickly and effectively assimilate client's knowledge.
2. The Supplier challenge – How can local supplier expertise be captured, refined and reused by global supplier teams? This challenge is about the vendor developing expertise coordination competences to ensure that assimilated knowledge is effectively re-applied across the organization.

Below we describe the practices developed by TCS to address these two key challenges. We describe these practices through a close examination of the outsourcing relationship with ABN AMRO. However, we have observed that the approach to address such challenges has been applied in other outsourcing relationships (e.g. the Quartz Financial Platform for several clients), and is, in fact, a systematic approach to managing global expertise at TCS.

Practices to develop and leverage local expertise

We have identified eight effective practices at TCS that addressed the two key challenges described above and in particular ensured the absorption of knowledge from clients to offshore, and the coordination of expertise across the organization. After illustrating these practices, we will show how these can be combined into an expertise management system. We will also discuss how such a system becomes more powerful if, as we found in our research, it is treated as part of a much bigger vision for client-supplier knowledge flow, through the creation and renewal of a transactive memory system.

1. Design and implement an organizational structure that is a mirror picture of your client

One key challenge that onsite and offshore teams were facing was to identify their corresponding expert with whom they would engage in knowledge transfer and expertise development activities from the client side but also between the onsite and offshore teams. TCS introduced an organizational structure ensuring that onsite and offshore experts easily identified their counterparts between them and the client's. Fundamental to this solution was the idea that the offshore organizational structure should be a mirror of the onsite organizational structure (see Figure 14.1) and the onsite structure will be the mirror picture of the client.

In this relationship, TCS has gone as far as modifying its knowledge transfer methodology to correspond with the organizational structure of ABN AMRO. Apparently, the organizational structure at ABN AMRO included a number of portfolio managers, something that TCS methodology did not

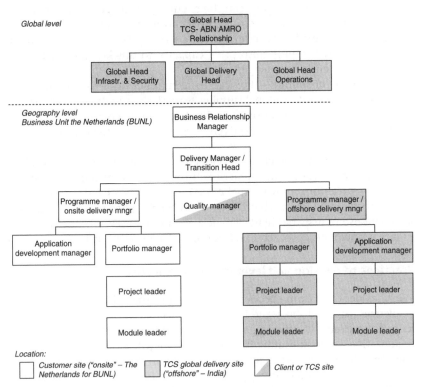

Figure 14.1   The Organizational Structure of one ABN AMRO-TCS Project Team (schematic)

consider. One Portfolio Manager from offshore in Mumbai explained how TCS dealt with this challenge

"The way we have segregated these teams here is added to the way they work at ABN AMRO. So that we wanted a synchronism in the sense that the way business teams are divided there [ABN AMRO] we'd have a similar structure here also. Portfolio Manager is a term that ABN AMRO uses there. We said okay we will also have similar Portfolio Managers so that they can interact one to one and these portfolio names are similar to the way they are using them onsite."

Our wider research into offshore outsourcing arrangements found three major types of organization structure, namely funnel, network and mirror. The first relied on a single point of contact and control, the second multiple, diverse points of contact, and the third multiple contacts through structure replication. Each had its advantages and disadvantages, but the mirror structure proved the most effective for organized knowledge assimilation and transfer (Rottman and Lacity, 2006; Willcocks *et al.*, 2006).

2. Design and carefully implement a knowledge transfer methodology

The transfer of knowledge from the client to onsite, and then offshore teams is often perceived as an activity that the vendor carries out in order to "get a grip" of the outsourced system. Treating this process as such puts the emphasis on the documentation of the knowledge relating to the outsourced applications, the expectation being that when service cannot be properly provided, the vendor can either go back to the documents to look for information, or consult with the client about the specific issue.

However, such an approach may miss a great opportunity to leverage expertise by learning about client's systems with the idea in mind that such knowledge may first contribute for the development of the client's existing systems, but also can leverage the pool of expertise of the vendor and serve the vendor when engaging in contracts with other clients or markets. It is the opportunity to leverage existing expertise that led TCS to a knowledge transition methodology. TCS developed such a methodology to ensure that the teams involved would be able to define, capture, transfer and absorb the critical knowledge required for application maintenance and development. More importantly, TCS knowledge transfer methodology was designed to ensure that it can be replicated across numerous relationships to allow the sharing of the knowledge captured and retained by local outsourcing teams. The Delivery Head in Amsterdam Explained this philosophy:

"[...] the TCS methodology, the activities within that would be the same where I'm working in the Netherlands, as also as I would be undertaking in Brazil....At the end of the day when I look at my organization from a high level, we should not find differences in the approach used any-where else. Hence the overall organization picture is... that a single framework helps us achieve what we want to achieve."

Knowledge was mainly transferred from onsite to offshore teams through the use of standardized templates and forms and based on a glossary of terms agreed between the client, onsite and offshore teams. Responsibility for codifying and documenting the knowledge on standardized templates resided with the onsite team with the support of the Digitization Group based in Mumbai. By the end of each knowledge codification phase, the onsite team would have transferred the codified knowledge to the offshore/onshore team.

The documentation containing the codified knowledge would then be carefully studied by the offshore team to ensure that the knowledge of the application is clear to the team but also to identify areas in which such knowledge is missing. To ensure that expertise had been properly developed and absorbed and that the knowledge acquired can be appropriately (re)applied in problem solving scenarios, the offshore team "played back" the know-how acquired to the onsite team as well as solved problems generated by the client.

The methodology proved vital for the acquisition of both personal knowledge feeding immediately into job performance by TCS staff, but also for developing codified knowledge available for reuse by other and new operatives. At the same time it has to be recognized that codified knowledge can only take performance so far and that building experience and tacit knowledge in the job is necessary to close any knowing-doing gap (see Polanyi, 1983; Willcocks *et al.*, 2004; Pfeffer and Sutton, 2000 and Chapter 8 of the present volume).

3. Develop and implement a knowledge retention methodology

By 2007 a major challenge that IT vendors were facing, particularly in India, was a relatively high employee turnover in their offshore locations, anything from 12% to 35% in fact. These figures come from our on-going research into offshore cases involving diverse suppliers and companies throughout 2006 and 2007. The danger from high levels of employee turnover is a possible loss of the knowledge transferred from onsite to offshore. TCS realized they needed to ensure that knowledge transferred and captured offshore would still be retained with as little dependency as possible on subject matter experts (SME).

The knowledge retention methodology is based on a succession plan that combines both the process and people dimensions of expertise. There is a process in place through which managers select their successors by identifying the individuals who can replace them in case they need to leave the project or decide to leave the company. Such an approach ensures that successors are trained to replace their managers and are prepared for their future roles. Furthermore, these successors back up the manager's knowledge in their respective area of expertise.

Consider any major IT project. One of the hidden, though serious, reasons for project delay is in fact the need to replace the experience and knowledge that walks out of the door when a key player leaves. This is one reason, as well as flexibility, why both researchers and practitioners argue for breaking down large-scale IT projects into smaller ones with short time lines and business outcomes (see for example Willcocks *et al.*, 2003) As we found in our own research, in any major IT outsourcing arrangement whether three, five, seven or ten years in length such losses are, in practice inevitable. When the knowledge implications of such losses are not legislated for, the results can be damaging to service speed and quality, and the supplier's ability to innovate and add value (Lacity *et al.*, 2009).

4. Monitor expertise development and retention at the project and organizational level

The challenge associated with the monitoring of expertise mainly concerns the link between project and organizational levels. In most companies, expertise is managed and monitored at the project level. This means that project managers are responsible for identifying which expertise is required to accomplish a project's objective. Therefore they become responsible for requesting any upgrade of a particular set of expertise, for example through training. While such an approach may satisfy local project needs, its limitations are clear. For example, the organization may have little exposure to the pool of expertise at its disposal across the firm. The advantages of central resources and opportunities for economies of scale will not be obvious. For such reasons, the TCS approach focused on linking project and organizational levels.

Centers of Excellences (CoEs) at TCS played a role in monitoring, and indicating which expertise should be upgraded when there was a gap between existing and required expertise within a project. CoEs are known to be networks of experts who have advanced know-how and experience in a particular market or technological domain. TCS introduced CoEs in several domains, related to technologies (e.g. Windows-based technologies, Java-based technologies) and specific industries (Financial CoE) and services (e.g. Service Practice CoE,). A member of the Oracle CoE describes how he monitored expertise:

"Every month, I do a technical health check review of some projects.... Our quality reviews are done against the quality check lists and quality guidelines. But these (additional COE) reviews are done from a technology perspective, for example if I am doing a project review, I try to find out whether the project is using most advanced solutions."

In cases where projects do not apply best practices, members of CoEs make sure that the know-how required for the proper execution of an offshore outsourcing project, according to TCS best practices, will be shared with the project team. In this regard, CoEs were responsible for acquiring know-how from internal or external sources, and share it with project teams. The member of the Oracle CoE added:

"All those aspects might lead to a risk from a technical perspective[...][we are] also looking at the skill sets which are required for the project and the right set of skills and if there are any gaps there, we bridge those gaps, either through training or through consultation or by inviting over an alliance partner."

Another member of CoE described the expertise development process:

"We have internally a learning and development group who are conducting various training programs depending on the need associated with the project's requirements and to support that we have our individual learning plan [...] we assess the people on the basis of the knowledge that particular resource has and the knowledge that is required for the project and we do a gap analysis about the areas that need further development. Once we do the gap analysis the system tells us, "Okay he needs to do this, this and this to reach the appropriate level." At this stage the person has to undergo the training. We give him/her a particular timeframe in which (s)he can do all these knowledge acquisition activities so (s)he builds up personal knowledge."

The CoEs developed an overview at the organizational level about the pool of expertise existing within each community and mapped out the location of expertise. In a way, CoEs acted as repositories of knowledge concerning a particular technology or market, as well as a directory that could point to the location of an expert when needed.

5. Make expertise development a key organizational value

The values that matter the most for TCS are five: integrity, respect for the individual, excellence, learning and knowledge sharing. Clearly, TCS has considered expertise development high on its value list. To ensure that learning and knowledge sharing takes place across TCS, the Learning and Development Department at TCS oversees various training and knowledge sharing activities. The Head of the Learning and Development Department, which is based in Mumbai, explained:

"The six enablers [to success] that we continuously invest in are: competency enhancement, leadership enhancement, being the custodian of the cultural climate of the company, strategic alignment, motivation of the employees and lastly team integration. Because in our kind of com-

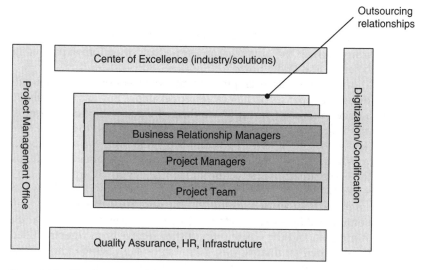

Figure 14.2   The Structure of Outsourcing Relationships and Supporting Groups

pany we all work in teams; individual excellence is fine but we look at the cumulative excellence when people collaboratively work in teams."

To support learning within and across teams, TCS has introduced an organizational structure that places the relationship (i.e. outsourcing project) at the center of knowledge sharing activities (see Figure 14.2).

Each relationship project, which is the box in the middle of Figure 14.2, is supported by several groups. From learning and expertise development viewpoint, the following groups contribute to the continuous development of know-how and skills:

- Center of Excellences: Contribute by providing technical and business solutions. The CoEs are organized around technical solutions (i.e. technologies) and business silos (i.e. industries).
- Quality Assurance: Provides standard templates based on the best practices available within TCS. QA also harvests best practices from each relationship project.
- Digitization and codification: This group, which is based in Mumbai, is responsible for codifying knowledge developed within the relationship and for making this knowledge available to the rest of the organization.

This structure is replicated for any relationship and the support provided is similar regardless of the geographical location or the size of the outsourcing deal.

But expertise development activities have been much wider than just the support provided by specialist groups. The constant improvement of methodologies and processes has been perceived by interviewees as a mechanism through which the organization learned and therefore expanded its pool of expertise and know-how.

In addition, training has been provided to employees on various subjects and during different phases of their career. For example, any employee undergoes an induction training during which this individual will be introduced to the organization, learn about the resources available and how to access expertise and know-how. In our visit to TCS in Sao Paolo, we have asked several employees who recently joined TCS from the local market about their familiarity with TCS organizational structure and online portals. By and large, most employees knew who to contact in Mumbai in case they needed support either from the technology or market side. They were also familiar with portals available online and how to access them. These employees indicated that the induction program and the onsite support they receive from veteran TCSers have enhanced their familiarity with TCS despite them being remote from, and yet dependent, on the headquarters. In addition, TCS developed a portal for the ABN AMRO relationship in order to capture and share learning with any newcomer but also with the client. The portal offers material such as induction manuals, welcome kit, and cultural awareness programs. Such investment in multiple sources of information and the usage of these sources helps TCS develop expertise at all levels.

6. Offer search mechanisms for expertise at the project and organizational level

Bringing expertise to bear in a timely manner has always been a key challenge for organizations. One offshore specialist from Amsterdam explained that this was a real challenge and, in the ABN AMRO deal, has led TCS to adopt similar management processes and systems for Amsterdam, Mumbai and Sao Paulo.

Most organizations, either IT vendors or firms in other industrial sectors, tend to offer search mechanisms through which expertise and solutions can be sought and found within the organization. Such search mechanisms can be in the form of a search engine that provides pointers to either experts of a particular area within the organization (e.g. Yellow Pages systems) or to documentation that provides information about a particular design or domain (e.g. knowledge-bases). While such search mechanisms can be useful in solving problems, they still pose a challenge to IT teams in terms of the management of expertise within an organization that is global and subject to change. In particular, as the pool of expertise within an organization constantly evolves and changes, either through the acquisition of new knowledge or when some expertise become obsolete, search mechanisms do not necessarily take notice of these changes and, therefore, may not represent the breath and depth of the expertise available in-house.

Acknowledging this challenge, TCS has sought to link the search process through which needed expertise can be located and brought to bear in a timely manner with the vehicles through which expertise was developed and diffused. This process was carried out at two levels; project (i.e. onsite and offshore) and the organizational level.

At the project level, the onsite and offshore teams followed a process that created a directory of pointers to where knowledge resides and through which most individuals developed awareness of "who knows what" and "who does what". At the organizational level, a much broader memory system was developed and updated regularly to ensure that expertise could be brought to bear in a timely manner beyond the boundaries of an outsourcing project. We now elaborate on these two memory systems and other mechanisms supporting this practice.

The knowledge transfer and knowledge retention methodology and the organizational structure of both onsite and offshore teams created an expertise directory that contained pointers to "who knows what" and "who does what" within these teams. The pointers to "who knows what" were created and constantly updated during the Transition and Steady State phases, as remote counterparts continuously interacted with each other to ensure the transfer of knowledge and the development of expertise. Furthermore, in collaboration with ABM AMRO, a dedicated TCS team created a Project Portal (internally called Knowledge Base) that contained links to project and system documents stored during the knowledge transfer phase. Furthermore, this Knowledge Base contains information about experts involved in the project, their contact details and other relevant information. At the time of data collection in Mumbai (June 2006), two TCS associates worked full time on development and maintenance of this system. Through a tightly managed knowledge transfer methodology, TCS not only ensured the transfer of knowledge between onsite and offshore teams but have also developed and updated a directory of expertise in which remote counterparts identified subject matter experts and their locations.

At the organizational level, in addition to their role as monitoring the level of expertise, CoEs played a role in bringing together information seekers and subject matter experts. Clearly, the exposure CoEs gained through the monitoring of expertise levels made them an excellent candidate to support the search of expertise. One manager from Mumbai described the role of one technological CoE:

"These are the people who can solve the problems in certain areas so we have a team of certain virtual members, anywhere between 30 and 50 [...]. These are the people who try to address [the problem] if the technical support team cannot address those things."

CoEs also facilitated the re-application of existing solutions from almost the beginning until the end of a project, by connecting experts with project teams to ensure that project teams are aware of and apply best practices and approaches available within TCS. One project leader from Mumbai offshore team provided an example in the context of the ABN AMRO deal:

"I'm also part of a center of excellence for ABN AMRO where we identify kinds of training and what the different environments for various technology requirements at ABN AMRO are. We trained our people before they started their transition, and adopted a "best practice" of ensuring that the knowledge that we gained in the first six months was passed on to the people coming into this ABN AMRO engagement, or who are supposed to work on different technologies."

Members of CoEs who are based within a project act as a linking unit between the project level and the organizational level either on technology, practice or market knowledge. Through this web of connections, experts are becoming aware of "who knows what" within other projects or within other CoEs.

But relying on the organizational structure and information systems to support the web of connections between experts has been seen by TCS as incomplete. Some knowledge-exchange events and seminars organized on a regular basis at different geographical locations were offered to CoEs and other experts to ensure that remote counterparts stay in touch. For example, we found technological fairs being organized several times a year at major TCS development sites (e.g. May 2006 in Mumbai). In this case, experts from different technological domains offered information about different aspects relating to the use and implementation of their technologies. This knowledge exchange event was organized in the form of a traditional trade fair in which TCS employees walked from stand to stand to learn about the applicability of existing solutions to their project.

The importance of these processes becomes apparent when you look at where they are not in place. For example, we found considerable disappointment in two major Customer Relationship Management projects involving clients and suppliers (Finnegan and Willcocks (2007). In neither project was expertise and knowledge managed well. The result was that knowledge did not flow easily between or within the organizations, knowledge silos developed, knowledge was shared on a limited basis, usually between people who were knowledgeable and so had something to trade ("gurus" only talked to "gurus"), while knowledge failed to be accumulated and leveraged to the benefit of the overall project, while none of the organizations could claim major learning as a result of the project implementations.

7. Implement a re-use methodology at the global level

Search mechanisms are only a start on the route to systematic re-use not just of information and knowledge, but of whole practices and components.

Increasingly firms are urged, and strive, to reuse best practices, components and templates. Given the 1990's history of the major Indian IT suppliers' interest in North American methodologies standards and processes, it was not surprising to find re-use high on the TCS managerial agenda. A key requirement to achieve this is a firm's ability to harvest and thereafter disseminate practices which were originated in various contexts and often tailored according to specific client's requirements. Acknowledging this, some firms have promoted standard solutions in the form of templates and tools across global teams. One such approach is the component-based design methodology. Component-based development involves (i) the development of software components and (ii) the building of software systems through the integration of pre-existing software components. *Components* are units of independent production, acquisition and deployment that interact with each other to form a functioning system. Being self-contained and replaceable units, components can be reused across a number of products, and be replaced by more recent and advanced versions of components in a "plug-and-play" manner, as long as the interfaces across the components comprising the products are compatible. (For a detailed discussion about component re-use see Kotlarsky *et al.*, 2007). TCS implemented this methodology at the global level, which meant that often a component was developed and tested by utilizing expertise located in different sites. This required a high degree of coordination between the different sites in order to manage the software development process as well as the inter-dependencies between components. At the same time, the pursuit of a globally distributed component-based design approach at TCS has ramped up expertise across the sites involved. This is because experts from the different sites involved in the development and testing of the component needed to constantly interact and exchange component, product and market knowledge.

The process through which components were reused at TCS was based on a technical database of reusable components (code) from various projects, stripped of confidential client data. A dedicated team checked entries of individual team members submitted to this database, filtered these entries, and made sure that the most appropriate keywords were assigned to each entry. Individual team members, regardless of their geographical location and project association, but who sought solutions to a particular technological problem, could access this database through the TCS intranet, and thus search for reusable components.

While a reusable solution was mainly the outcome of this activity, information about who would be the expert of that particular technology was also provided. In a way, the implementation of Component-Based Design has supported the search mechanisms reported in practice number 6. Through this tool, remote counterparts could contact the expert for consultation prior to implementing the reusable component. Similarly, TCS developed a database that contained business history, i.e. a brief overview and lessons learned from past projects, accessible through the TCS intranet. Through this system team members could find information about projects and contact individuals involved in these projects for advice.

Clearly, re-use is highly dependent on systematic and accurate collection activities at the project, ground level. In TCS we found that such practices had become part of the culture, in the sense of "how things are done around here". However, this culture was the outcome of systematic training from induction onwards, and through the imbedding of collection practices in the methodologies and processes applied routinely throughout the organization. All too often we have found organizations falling at the hurdle of designing knowledge management systems, being over-dependent on software, but failing to shape the culture and routine ways of operating so that staff understand, own, are motivated and capable of contributing to the knowledge creation, collection and re-use process (Finnegan and Willcocks, 2007; Kotlarsky *et al.*, 2007).

8. Continuously measure the contribution of reusable assets

Our research on component re-use has shown that many companies that reuse components do not necessarily assess and measure the contribution of their reusable assets to project and product success (Oshri and Newell, 2007). According to a Gartner report (2007), firms that have achieved a high maturity level are more likely to reap the benefits from building a pool of reusable components. Continuous improvements in methodologies and processes often mean that companies that have achieved capability maturity model level 5 have in fact optimized their processes, often through the application of metrics. TCS, which operates at CMM level 5, have introduced metrics to assess the contribution of reuse and reusable assets to project and product success. Metrics in general, and for reuse in particular, are defined by the Quality Assurance group. In practice, reusable components are assessed in terms of the usage rate, nature of the application and the destination project. This way, TCS is collecting information about the contribution of the reusable asset as well as about the applicability of the asset to particular markets. As one Quality Assurance specialist from Mumbai described it:

> "We have something called Mighty which is accessible to all where associates can go and check for a useable competence. We [Quality Assurance Group] are tracking the competence shared, how often it has been used, and which of our teams has used it. We are now encouraging teams to start using it [Mighty] to make it a single repository for all reusable competence."

Clearly, by operating at CMM level 5 TCS has developed capabilities to measure internal processes such as reuse. Furthermore, the company continues to seek ways to improve the reuse process by centralizing the competence and component repository through the introduction of the Mighty system.

IT offshoring: how expertise is managed

We believe that Figure 14.3 captures the essence of managing expertise from the vendor viewpoint. There are two levels of expertise management described in this figure; the relationship/project level and the organizational level. The inner circle consists of processes vital for expertise management at the relationship level and represents the firm's ability to develop an absorptive capacity. The outer circle comprises processes at the organizational level and supports the coordination of expertise. The two circles interact and, in fact, depend upon each other in terms of the assimilation of new knowledge from clients and the re-application of existing organizational expertise. Furthermore, we have noticed that the management of expertise at TCS (and other IT vendors that operate onshore and offshore) is very much dependent on the organization's ability to develop a system that captures and updates directories of "who knows what" and "who does what". Through the interviews, discussions and observations we have

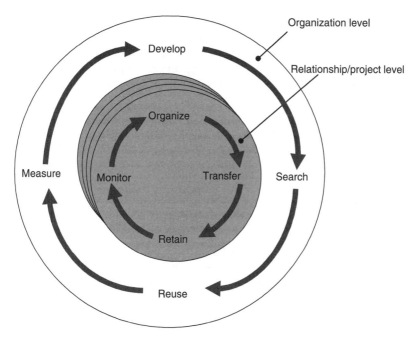

Figure 14.3 Expertise Management Processes at Relationship and Organizational Level

made, it became clear that TCS focused on developing an expertise system that excels in bringing solutions to teams in a timely manner as opposed to other approaches in which individuals and teams are expected to research and develop their own solutions, often bearing higher costs. We also learned that you need to go far beyond just mapping out the pool of expertise available in-house (e.g. the traditional approach of Yellow Pages). In fact, it takes the entire organization to think and act through the lens of expertise. So, Figure 14.3 should be seen as two processes through which TCS has built and maintained a system that not only supported the continuous development and absorption of knowledge and expertise but also, and perhaps more importantly, dynamically updated the location of expertise and knowledge within and across relationships to ensure the coordination of expertise in a timely manner. Let us look at Figure 14.3 more closely.

At the relationship level, the vendor should seek introducing "boundary spanning" mechanisms that will enhance the onsite and offshore teams' ability to absorb new knowledge. As first stage, i.e. the *organize* stage, the organizational structure and the organization of onsite and offshore teams is critical in putting in place such "boundary spanning" mechanisms. Selecting individuals who have previous know-how of the market and technologies will significantly enhance the onsite team's capacity to assimilate client's knowledge. But the absorption of knowledge is also required between the onsite and the offshore teams. For this, the *transfer* stage is critical in establishing a clear methodology through which communication protocols and channels ensure the successful transfer of client's knowledge to offshore teams. For example, most IT vendors, such as TCS, heavily rely on the codification of knowledge captured onsite. This activity is in itself a "boundary spanning" as through codification, standardized templates and glossary of terms, a shared language between onsite and offshore teams is created. Furthermore, the transfer of knowledge from onsite to offshore also renews the directory of "who knows what". Through the exchange of documents, onsite and offshore team members become familiar with who is working on which application or portfolio. And through the use of shared databases the team members also create entries to directories that are pointers to expertise. The *retain* stage is about ensuring that the expertise is indeed assimilated in the teams. This can mainly be achieved by implementing a succession plan at onsite and offshore locations. Devising a succession plan requires the involvement of all levels within the relationship from the vendor side. Basically, as we have observed at TCS, any team member, either onsite or offshore, is part of the succession plan. And lastly, the *monitor* stage concerns with the continuous examination of the expertise within the relationship with two aspects in mind: (i) does the expertise available within the team meet the industry standards, and (ii) which expertise should be enhanced. From absorptive capacity viewpoint, the vendor should monitor its ability to absorb knowledge and following this assessment, the vendor should consider closing on a knowledge gap between the client, onsite and offshore teams but also improving its own knowledge absorption capacity as an organizational process.

At the organizational level, the process of managing expertise involves four key activities; develop, search, reuse and measure. These processes are about developing expertise coordination competences. In TCS and other organizations we have researched Kotlarsky *et al.*, 2008), in addition to the acquisition of know-how, the *development* stage of expertise was again about creating entries to directories of "who knows what" and "who does what". For this to happen, the process of developing expertise (e.g. class training or on the job training) consisted of additional processes such as the codification and storage of this knowledge as well as processes that made this know-how available to the entire organization. The *search* stage required the entries to the organizational directory of "who knows what" in order to locate solutions in a timely manner. Seeking solutions were conducted through both interpersonal networks and databases. Though TCS engaged in a massive codification of know-how, CoEs have also proven to be no less efficient in locating experts and bringing solutions to relationships than the use of database. The *reuse* stage involved the re-application of solutions and know-how originated in one relationship in other relationships. In most cases, we noticed that adjustment and modification in the original solution were needed. Therefore, locating the expert as part of the reuse is as critical as locating the solution (e.g. a component or a template). Last but not least, the *measure* stage concerned the application of metrics that assess the effectiveness of expertise utilization by measuring the degree to which a component has been reused and in what contexts.

We have persistently claimed in this article that expertise management in companies such as TCS is mainly about creating, maintaining and renewing a directory through which each and every individual within an organization can locate, access and bring to bear needed expertise. This can take you a long way but our parallel research leads us to the conclusion that a broader vision is needed if clients and suppliers are going to manage expertise and knowledge in a relational way. Therefore we finally turn to the concept of Transactive Memory to explain how companies can leverage and improve the utilization of their expertise.

Shaping the future: towards Transactive Memory Systems

In the heart of our study, there is the idea of Transactive Memory Systems. This is diagramatically represented in Figure 14.4.

A Transactive Memory System (TMS) is the combination of individual memory systems and communications between individuals. Consider this system as if transactions between individuals link their memory systems and through a series of processes (i.e. encoding, storing, and retrieving) knowledge is exchanged. So, individuals encode information for storing and retrieval, similar to a librarian entering details of a new book in the particular library

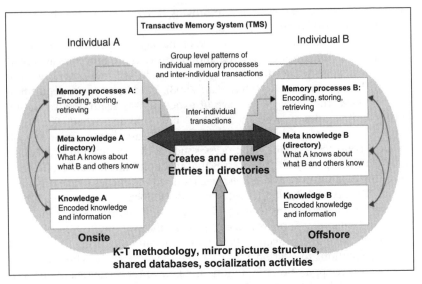

Figure 14.4   Supplier Transactive Memory System

system before putting it on the shelves. Through encoding, knowledge is categorized (i.e. assigned labels that reflect the subjects of the knowledge) for systematically storing the location of the knowledge, but not the knowledge itself. Then, individuals store this information internally (building their own memory), or externally (storing it in databases or indirectly in other people's memories). And lastly, information about the location of the knowledge or expertise is retrieved when someone else asks for it. Retrieval thus consists of two interconnected sub-processes: person A asks person B for information; person B retrieves the information.

A key issue is how a TMS can be made to work effectively so that expertise and solutions can be brought to bear in a timely manner. From our research we can identify three processes to follow:

1) Directory should be updated: this is where actors keep information about "who knows what" up-to-date
2) Information should be allocated: this is where actors decide in whose memory to store new information that arrives in the transactive memory system, and
3) The retrieval of the information about where expertise lies should be coordinated: where actors use a set of guidelines to determine in which order other actors should be consulted for the missing information.

A TMS may offer various benefits to both outsourcing relationship teams and individuals. Through the development of a TMS and the awareness of "who knows what", the performance of a team can be improved (Faraj and Sproull, 2000). More specifically, a TMS may enhance specialization and division of labor. Teams and individuals can develop expertise in their own areas while being aware of the existence of expertise elsewhere. There is already substantial evidence about the positive association of a TMS with team learning, speed to market, new product success, and an efficient coordination of expertise in teams through the development of similar labels and categories for encoding and retrieving information (Oshri *et al.*, 2007).

The development of a TMS can be facilitated through various activities. In fact the early studies about TMS focused on studying close relationships between human couples (Wegner *et al.*, 1991) More recently, research has proposed that training activities contribute to the development of a TMS. In co-located teams, the development of a TMS within a team seems achievable through sporadic training sessions and continuous problem-solving activities but in distributed teams, such as at TCS, this approach may be rather limited.

The challenges that such organizations may face are about:

- Changes in membership that negatively affect the long-term development of a TMS
- Team members do not have any prior experience of working together. Their distributed mode of operation decreases communications and increases the possibilities for conflict, misunderstanding and breakdowns in communication
- The development of shared understanding can be rather challenging because members of such teams do not stand on "common ground".
- Dispersed teams adopt different routines and methodologies
- Difficulties to standardize work practices across remote locations

In Table 14.1 we offer a list of practices by which organizations with distributed teams can improve the management of expertise. The key is building a TMS that spreads beyond the boundaries of a single team. This is particularly important for IT vendors involved in outsourcing relationship with onsite and offshore teams that, necessarily, collaborate constantly throughout the relationship.

Conclusions

This chapter has presented a detailed account of practices that one IT vendor has implemented in order to mange expertise across multiple outsourcing relationships. It is one of the few studies on expertise management in the outsourcing literature. While the vast majority of the outsourcing literature has focused on client strategies and operations, this study highlights knowledge processes at the vendor level and therefore contributes to understanding

Table 14.1 Activities Supporting the Development of a TMS for Expertise Management

TMS processes	Directories and pointers to 'where knowledge lies'	Activities through which such directories can be created and renewed
Directory Update Having a shared 'cataloging' system	– Creating a shared system to categorize information. This can 'cataloging' system be effectively achieved by developing a set of rules of how to label the subject and location of the expertise. – Creating a shared understanding of context and work-related processes, terminology and language.	– Standard document templates (e.g. codification practices onsite and offshore at TCS in practice 2) – 'Glossary of terms' to include unique and clear terminology (practice 2) – Organizational structure (e.g. mirror picture in practice 1, and succession plan in practice 3) – Networks of excellence monitoring expertise in practice 4 – Social/professional gathering (e.g. trade fairs in practice 6)
Information Allocation The way in which the information is organized in physical locations and in the memories of dispersed team members	– Storing information about the subject and location of the knowledge. This can be achieved by creating pointers to the location of knowledge in an expertise directory. – Information allocation includes up-to-date records of available documents and expertise. – Storing information about 'who knows what' and 'who is doing what' in individuals' memories	– Central project repository (e.g. Project Portal at TCS in practice 6) – Standardization of tools and methods across locations (e.g. knowledge transfer methodology at TCS in practice 2) – Centralization of tools (e.g. Digitization group at TCS in practice 5) – Dividing work in a way that increases collaboration between sites (e.g. globally distributed component-based design at TCS in practice 7)
Information Retrieval – Knowing where and in what form information is stored in the dispersed team – Being able to find required information through determining the location of information, and, sometimes, the combination or interplay of items coming from multiple locations	– Developing capabilities to find information necessary to coordinate expertise. – Include search capabilities (e.g. keyword-based) for effective and efficient search and retrieval processes. – Developing interpersonal channels through which individuals can search for information about who has expertise and in which areas, and where this expertise resides	– Standard process procedures that include pointers to the location of information (part of knowledge codification procedures at TCS, practice 2) – Networks of excellence that bring expertise to bear (in practice 6) – Keywords-based search capabilities (practice 6) – An ICT strategy & infrastructure that supports using email, tele- and video-conferencing and other application sharing tools (in line with practice 5)

vendor's operations. Lastly, our observations are based on the in depth study of one IT vendor, TCS, across multiple sites during over a six-year period.

Our conclusions start with a simple recommendation that developing and managing expertise by the vendor takes more than just managing a knowledge transfer between the client, onsite team and offshore teams. It in fact requires investment in the eight practices described above. At this juncture, IT vendors might wonder: which practice should we prioritize and invest most in to ensure the successful management of expertise?

The answer is that success in managing expertise requires IT vendors to think in terms of knowledge absorption and expertise coordination. Knowledge absorption is about the ability to quickly and effectively absorb and integrate knowledge from the client into the vendor's knowledge base. Expertise coordination is about being aware of the existence of expertise within the organization and the ability to bring these expertises to bear in a timely manner. Developing absorptive capacity requires among other factors the development of prior knowledge of the subject matter while coordinating expertise needs the development of a transactive memory system. These two competences, in fact, interlink. In other words, to successfully manage expertise requires the careful update of where expertise resides when the know-how is acquired. IT vendors focusing only on acquiring knowledge are doomed to fail in successfully reapplying this knowledge. On the other hand, IT vendors that invest in creating pointers to where knowledge and expertise reside during the knowledge acquisition and assimilation process are more likely to be successful in reapplying this knowledge and expertise.

We therefore conclude that IT vendors should look for any opportunity to create new entries to their memory systems. Table 14.1 lists the many activities that IT vendors can pursue to create and renew the directories of expertise. From our research we have learned that the investment should be in social, information system and organizational structure aspects. IT vendors, such as TCS, that considered socializing members of the onsite with the offshore teams through various activities and mediums have improved the effectiveness of expertise coordination activities. In a similar vein, expertise can be brought to bear in a timely manner through the support of CoEs. But solutions can also be found through a simple search on a component database (e.g. Mighty at TCS) that not only produces the solution but also provides information about the expertise in question. Having these three channels constantly updated as the pool of expertise of the organization is ever growing is still the challenge that many firms face. Delivering on the vision of a Transactive Memory System will become a key for effective offshoring and outsourcing supply over the next few years. And one unanticipated but significant benefit from outsourcing may well be that client organizations learn much more about how to manage their own expertise and knowledge. But pursuing expertise management in these ways raises a number of future challenges for clients and suppliers:

1. To manage expertise successfully requires the careful update of where expertise resides when the know-how is acquired. IT vendors focusing only on acquiring knowledge are doomed to fail in successfully re-using and developing this knowledge. On the other hand, IT vendors that invest in creating pointers to where knowledge and expertise reside during the knowledge acquisition and assimilation process are more likely to be successful in reapplying this knowledge and expertise.

2. IT vendors should look for any opportunity to create new entries to their memory systems. Table 14.1 lists the many activities that IT vendors can pursue to create and renew the directories of expertise. From our research we have learned that the investment should be in social, information system and organizational structure aspects. IT vendors, such as TCS, that considered socializing members of the onsite with the offshore teams through various activities and mediums have improved the effectiveness of expertise coordination activities. In a similar vein, expertise can be brought to bear in a timely manner through the support of CoEs. But solutions can also be found through a simple search on a component database (e.g. Mighty at TCS) that not only produces the solution but also provides information about the expertise in question. Having these three channels constantly updated is still the challenge that many firms face. Delivering on the vision of a Transactive Memory System will become a key for effective offshoring and outsourcing supply over the next five years.

3. Supplier expertise management systems may well become the norm, but along that path, at least three challenges will arise for the client to address. Firstly, since the client is to be one beneficiary, how far should the client be involved in what can be an expensive activity? Secondly, knowledge and expertise are soft issues but they raise serious intellectual property issues. As one example, to retain intellectual property rights, the client may look to fund client-specific expertise management activity in exchange for ownership of the consequent expertise management systems. As another, how is the client to monitor and deal with misappropriation? Thirdly, what should the active role of the client be in making all this knowledge sharing possible? And what kind of contractual arrangements will commit client staff to such activity?

4. Assuming major suppliers like TCS go down these expertise management routes, one unanticipated but significant benefit from outsourcing may well be that client organizations learn much more about how to manage their own expertise and knowledge. This will be particularly attractive to those with mature enterprise architectures that expect to share enterprise knowledge. How far will clients step up to this challenge? Further, how far will they consider expertise management as a potentially rich area for collaboration with their outsourcing suppliers for mutual gain?

Note

1 The article is based on an ongoing research at TCS between 2001 and 2007. During this period we carried out over 150 interviews with senior executives and operatives at several levels in Mumbai, Gurgaon, Bangalore, Amsterdam, Sao Paulo, Campinas (Brazil), Zurich, and Luxemburg. We also held phone interviews with employees from San Francisco. Interviews ranged between 45 minutes and 90 minutes in length. Each was transcribed, and subject to software coding and analysis. We also collected a range of documents, including presentations, annual reports, and internal management papers.

References

Faraj, S. and Sproull, L. (2000) "Coordinating Expertise in Software Development Teams," *Management Science* 46(12), pp. 1554–1568.

Finnegan, D. and Willcocks, L. (2007) *Implementing CRM: From Technology to Knowledge.* Chichester: Wiley.

Gartner report (2007) *The Benefits of the Capability Maturity Model for Application Development.* London: Gartner.

Kotlarsky, J., Oshri, I. and van Fenema, P. (2008) *Knowledge Processes in Globally Distributed Contexts.* London: Palgrave.

Kotlarsky, J., Oshri, I., van Hillegerberg, J. and Kumar, K. (2007) "Globally Distributed Component-Based Software Development: An Exploratory Study of Knowledge Management and Work Division," *Journal of Information Technology.*, 22. pp. 161–173.

Lacity, M., Willcocks, L. and Cullen, S. (2009) *Global IT Outsourcing: 21st Century Search For Business Advantage.* Chichester: Wiley.

Oshri, I., van Fenema, P. and Kotlarsky, J. (2007) "Knowledge Transfer in Globally Distributed Teams: The Role of Transactive Memory", *Information Systems Journal* (DOI: 10.111/j1365-2575.2007.00243.x)

Oshri, I. and Newell, S. (2007) "Component Sharing in Complex Products and Systems: Challenges, Solutions and Practical Implications," *IEEE Transactions on Engineering Management,* 52(4) pp. 509–521.

Orlikowski, W. (2002) "Knowing In Practice: Enacting a Collective Capability in Distributed Organizing," *Organization Science,* 13, 3, pp. 249–273.

Pfeffer, J. and Sutton, R. (2000) *The Knowing-Doing Gap: How Smart Companies Turn Knowledge into Action.* Boston: Harvard Business Press.

Polanyi, M. (1983) *The Tacit Dimension.* Peter Smith, Gloucester, Mass..

Rottman, J. and Lacity, M. (2006) Chapter 9 in Willcocks and Lacity (2006) *Global Sourcing of Business and IT Services.* Palgrave, London.

Wegner, D.M., Raymond, P. and Erber, R. (1991) "Transactive Memory in Close Relationships" *Journal of Personality and Social Psychology,* pp. 923–920.

Willcocks, L. and Cullen, S. (2005) *The Outsourcing Enterprise: How the CEO Should Be Engaged* LogicaCMG, London.

Willcocks, L., Hindle, J., Feeny, D. and Lacity, M. (2004). IT and Business Process Outsourcing: The Knowledge Potential. *Information Systems Management Journal,* Summer.

Willcocks, L. and Lacity, M. (2006) *Global Sourcing of Business and IT Services.* Palgrave, London.

Willcocks, L., Cullen, S. and Lacity, M. (2006) *The Outsourcing Enterprise 3: How to Select and Leverage Effective Suppliers.* LogicaCMG, London.

Willcocks, L., Petherbridge, P. and Olson, N. (2003) *Making IT Count: Strategy, Delivery and Infrastructure.* Butterworth, Oxford.

15
Playing "Catch-Up" with Core IS Capabilities: The Secrets of Success

Leslie P. Willcocks, Peter Reynolds and David Feeny

Introduction

When making Information Technology (IT) outsourcing decisions, organizations are faced with not only the decision of what to outsource, but also what to keep in-house. A robust stream of research has developed to provide guidelines on **what** Information Systems (IS) human resource capabilities are core to the business's future capacity to exploit IT successfully. Here we make the crucial step of detailing **how** these IS capabilities can be evolved over time. We examine three organizations that used the same framework to develop their internal IS capabilities. Two already had large infrastructure and applications outsourcing deals in place; the third was preparing itself to be in a position leverage outsourcing in the future. Several learnings emerge: 1) Organizations are invariably playing "catch-up" on IS capabilities. Business contexts move too fast for it to be otherwise. But creative and flexible management using ideas from experience can speed the evolution of capabilities and produce superior business results 2) Process, culture and structure mechanisms can be used to develop, nurture, and maintain these capabilities; 3) Internal IS capabilities can be developed through plotting the "where is" on three stages of evolution and moving the organization forward; and 4) The state of IS and organizational context determine how and when to use the external IT services market.

IT outsourcing offers opportunities to acquire new capabilities from outside the organization. These capabilities can be used to reduce the cost and improve IT service levels, provide access to new skills, improve capital management and, indeed, offer a range of other benefits (Cullen *et al.*, 2008).[1] In today's competitive landscape, organizations need to be in a position to successfully exploit the IT outsourcing market. But IT outsourcing is not without risks. How to deal with these? A critical, all too often neglected, risk mitigating practice for organizations is retaining key internal IS capabilities that underpin the business's future capacity to exploit IT. Thus Feeny and Willcocks (1998) suggest that the future IT function has four tasks – *eliciting and delivering on business requirements; ensuring technical capability; managing external supply; and governance, coordination and leadership.* They also find that organizations need to build nine core IS capabilities in order to fulfil these tasks. In practice our research indicates that few organizations, even those that have outsourced for several years, have in place such capabilities. The consequent problems lead to organizations having to play "catch-up", often on a large scale. In this chapter, we first describe the framework, then our key contribution is to describe *how* firms in this era of extensive outsourcing can develop these core IS capabilities through utilizing three organizational mechanisms to transition through three phases of evolution. The chapter distills the lessons from the experiences of three firms – Commonwealth Bank Australia, DuPont and State Super State Financial Services, all of whom successfully evolved their ability to exploit IT for business advantage.

Revisiting the Feeny-Willcocks core IS capabilities framework

This framework identifies nine internal core IS capabilities required for high performing IT functions, along with associated skills and inter-relationships.[2] A capability is a distinctive set of human-based skills, orientations, attitudes, motivations and behaviors that, when applied, can transform resources into specific business activities. Collections of capabilities, in turn, create high-level strategic competencies that positively influence business performance (Hamel and Heene, 1994; Quinn, 1992).[3] We found the skills supporting each capability to be a distinctive mix of interpersonal, technical and business skills. A "core IS capability" is needed to facilitate the exploitation of IT; its application is measurable in terms of IT activities supported, and resulting business performance. Throughout we use the word "role" to refer to a person formally enacting a capability. For example in the role of CIO a person enacts the leadership capability, while in the role of say procurement manager the role holder will enact informed buying.

Nine capabilities populate seven spaces in Figure 15.1. Three spaces are essentially business, technology or external supply facing. A fourth is a lynchpin governance position covered by two capabilities (see Figure 1 – Leadership and Informed Buying). Finally, there are three spaces that represent interfaces between tasks. The capabilities in these spaces – Relationship Building, Contract Facilitation and Making Technology Work – are crucial for facilitating the integration of effort between specific tasks The nine capabilities are described in Table 15.1.

An additional challenge relates to project management capability (not in Figure 15.1). In dynamic business environments, the emphasis has shifted from hierarchical, functionally based organizations toward task and project-based ways of operating. In such organizations, project management must be a core *organizational* capability, and not the preserve of one function or department. However, our research into ITO and BPO arrangements frequently

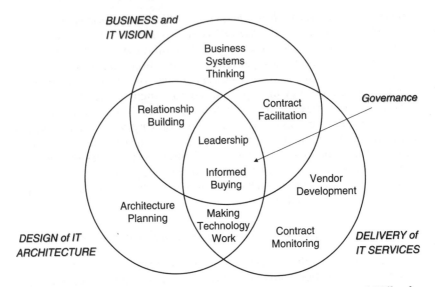

Figure 15.1 The core IS Capabilities Framework (adapted from Feeny and Willcocks, 1998)

Table 15.1 **Nine Core IS Capabilities**

Capability	Description
Leadership (L)	Integrates the IT effort with business purpose and activity
Informed Buying (IB)	Manages the IT sourcing strategy to meet the needs of the business
Business Systems Thinking (BST)	Ensures that IT capabilities are envisioned in every business process
Relationship Building (RB)	Gets the business constructively engaged in operational IT issues
Contract Facilitation (CF)	Ensures the success of existing contracts for external IT services
Architecture Planning and Design (AP)	Creates the coherent blueprint for a technical platform that responds to present and future needs
Vendor Development (VD)	Identifies the potential added value from IT service suppliers
Contract Monitoring (CM)	Protects the business's contractual position present and future
Making Technology Work (MTW)	Rapidly trouble-shoots problems which are being disowned by others across the technical supply chain

reveal organizational project management capability as patchy at best, even though, as we shall see in the CBA and DuPont cases, outsourcing can involve immense organizational, human resource and technological changes that require strong project management skills. In the cases, we investigate whether these should rest in the retained IS function or the IT supplier, where they are not available from the wider client organization.

Our capabilities research has continued since 1998, not least by extending it to IT-enabled Business Process Outsourcing, IT offshoring, and examining the equivalent capabilities for high performance supplier organizations (Feeny *et al.*, 2005; Lacity *et al.*, 2009; Willcocks and Feeny, 2006; Willcocks and Lacity, 2006).[4] This chapter builds on this extensive research by extending the analysis into *how* the organizations developed and evolved their core IS capabilities. Specifically, we examine organizational mechanisms used, and the sequencing of these capabilities over time.

Implementing the core IS capabilities framework: case studies

The cases were selected because they demonstrate the building of the *same* nine core IS capabilities, but also show *different* approaches to how an organization can build its core IS capabilities over time. In examining the dynamics of capabilities over time, we use an evolutionary growth model developed from research by David Feeny.[5] Figure 15.2 shows how an organization may start with very questionable ability to manage IT. Feeny found that such organizations typically need to evolve to a "Delivery" stage, marked by a CIO with the skills to focus the IT group on developing technical service capability and delivering on IT promises to the business. Once technical and service competences are in place, a "Reorientation" phase becomes possible. This will see a CIO and the IT team become more business-focused, while the business executives and units will need to become more pro-active in managing IT for strategic business purpose. Once "Reorientation" has been accomplished, the new challenge is "Reorganization" – devolving IT responsibility to the business units, integrating CIO effort with business strategy and the top team, and streamlining the IT function further into a core IS capabilities high performance model. Figure 15.2 shows the path an organization can take to evolving its IS capabilities and maturing its overall ability to manage and source IT strategically.

In the context of this three phase evolution, we discover within each phase three systems that organizations can use to allow capabilities to be identified and developed (see Table 15.2). Each system represents one lever that can be deployed to develop core IS capabilities. As we shall see, organizations will choose to pull one, two, or all three "levers" or sequence their use depending on the context, and the outcomes required.

We will use later the frameworks in Figures 15.1 and 15.2 and Table 15.2, to drive out the secrets of success in the cases. We select three outsourcing

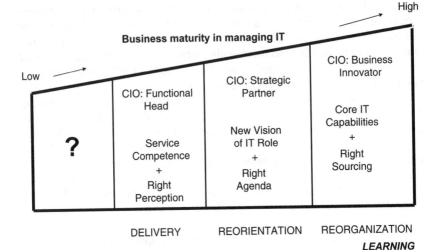

Figure 15.2 Growth Stages for the CIO, IT Function and Sourcing Approach

Table 15.2   Organizational Mechanisms for Building Capabilities[6]

Mechanism	Definition	Source
Processes	Capabilities emerge from problem-defining and problem-solving routines interwoven with individual skills. At a higher level, these become combined formally into organizational processes	Sanchez (2004); Oliver (1997); Dosi *et al.* (2000); Collis (1994)
Culture	Capabilities emerge from links across a mosaic of organizational elements, such as incentive and operating systems, corporate culture elements or behavior-shaping practices such as encouraging 'mistakes'.	Lewing and Volberda (1999); Collis 1994; Helfat and Lieberman (2002); Henderson (1994); Orlikowski (2002);
Structure	Capabilities emerge as a key 'product of the organization as an entire system',the interactions of cultural and structural elements – but begin from formal definitions of changes in structure and role.	Collis (1994); Grant (1996) Peppard and Ward (2004)

cases for this chapter. Two adopted the framework three years *after* entering their respective ten-year IT outsourcing deals, which were amongst the largest in the world at the time of signing. Our third case examines an organization that restructures and re-skills around the core IS capabilities framework *before* outsourcing, allowing it to build the necessary IS capabilities to build a new IT platform and exploit the outsourcing market. Notwithstanding the similarities, the cases are drawn from different industries across finance and manufacturing. In addition, the cases are of different sizes, have different geographic profiles and affect different number of customers and staff. As such they provide different testing contexts in which to apply the core IS capabilities framework, and valuable comparisons and contrasts for learning:

- *Commonwealth Bank of Australia (CBA)* – **a large bank**. CBA is rated as one of the top 25 banks in the world by market capitalization, totaling US$36bn.[7] It provides a full range of banking services to more than nine million clients across retail, commercial, corporate and institutional sectors with 33,000 employees. In 1997, CBA entered into a ten-year US$3.8bn single-source equity joint venture deal for all IT services. The CBA explicitly adopted the core IS capabilities framework in 2000 and successfully delivered a US$1.2bn business transformation in 2005.
- *DuPont* – **a global manufacturer**. DuPont is a diversified chemicals, health care, materials and energy multinational with revenues of $27.3bn and 55,000 staff.[8] It has in excess of 20 business units operating in more than 70 countries. In 1997, DuPont entered into a series of ten-year contracts worth US$4bn with CSC and Accenture (then Anderson Consulting). DuPont explicitly adopted the core IS capabilities framework in 1999. By 2003, it had implemented an IT career model based on IS competencies and was able to fill 90% of its key leadership positions internally, and 90% of the business unit CIO's reporting to the business unit VP/General Manager.
- *State Super Financial Services Australia Limited (SSFS)* – **a medium-sized enterprise**. SSFS provides financial planning and fund management services to over 33,000 current and former public sector employees and their family members. It is a national business with over 400 employees and funds under management in excess of US$3.5bn. SSFS explicitly adopted the core capabilities framework in 2000. By 2005 its IT function had moved from primarily an internal "support function" for all existing systems to a "business-oriented" function. SSFS retained and further developed the internal capabilities to support strategic or "core" IT services but also developed the internal capabilities to manage IT outsourcing for tactical or "non-core" services.[9]

Case Study 1: Commonwealth Bank Australia – capabilities for business transformation

History and context: On 10 October 1997, CBA entered into a ten-year US$3.8bn single-source joint venture with EDS. Internally, it retained a group of 35 IT staff, called Group Technology to manage the contract and maintain control of its strategic IT direction. By mid-2000, good progress had been made on the outsourcing objectives of controlling costs and improving service levels.[10] After nearly three years, however, significant relationship pressures had developed between and within the individual business units, IT function and vendors. There was poor coordination between business units of IT needs, poor relationships with the vendors and a lack of governance across the IT functions of CBA – in particular new IT functions acquired through a merger.

Towards the end of 2000, the need to strengthen CBA's internal IS capabilities led to a conscious adoption of a core IS capabilities framework. The authors' initial assessment was conducted in January 2001 (see Figure 15.3 – in the scoring system, ++ is "very satisfactory" while – – is "very inadequate". (–) relates to serious IT problems being experienced. (– –) indicates these escalating to being serious business problems as well.). Our assessment shows that the outsourcing relationship was being driven from a contractual standpoint (rather than delivery of IT services) and CBA did not have the necessary staff to work on business and IT vision and the design of IT architecture.

Stage 1: Group Technology capabilities. CBA's first step was to strengthen control over the outsourced services – initially ensuring the effective and efficient delivery of IT services from the vendors, then improving the coordination of business demands made to the vendor. The CIO focused efforts within the Central IT group around two IS capabilities – Service Delivery

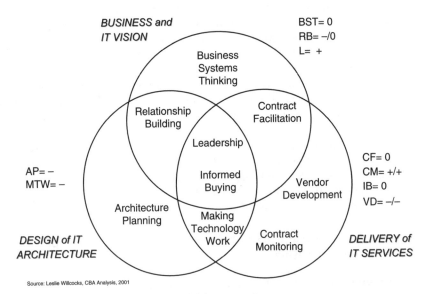

Source: Leslie Willcocks, CBA Analysis, 2001

Figure 15.3 CBA January 2001: Initial Assessment

(encompassing contract monitoring and contract facilitation) and Architecture Planning. Additional resources were recruited to strengthen group technology, including a new head of service delivery.

The head of service delivery quickly recognized the need to work with the service provider to have oversight and input to fundamental IT management *processes* on a daily basis. Service delivery managers were recruited that had a depth of commercial and technology experience. They provided an internal capability to understand the long-term design implications of what was being done, the commercial consequences of the technologies that were being deployed, the potential behavioral implications of the commercial contracts put in place, and to run benchmarking to provide a clear understanding of value. Further, an ex-partner from a "top five" consultancy firm was appointed, to head relationship management and build a demand management capability – working with the business units to help them articulate what they wanted, understand what else was being done and how to get best business value from IT.

The Head of Architecture Planning/Chief Technology Officer built the architecture planning team up to around a dozen people mostly from external recruits. An exception was the head of IT Security, who was recruited from the internal audit team. The team was organized into Enterprise Architecture, Business Systems Planning and Security. Processes were established to review all major IT investments from the business for technology risk, opportunities for scale and leverage, and consistency with the Bank's technical architecture.

In parallel, new roles and responsibilities were defined across Group Technology based on the capability area and *processes* they were responsible for. Responsibilities were assigned in such a way that no individual was expected to have to more than two core IS capabilities in performing their role. The final *structure* focused resources around three functions: architecture planning (to define what the Bank needed), Service Delivery (how services were delivered) and Informed Buying (who they were obtained from). Business systems thinking remained as a function that was seen to be the primary responsibility of the business units, liaising with the architecture planning and Service Delivery teams. The CIO espoused the desired high performance *culture,* including being a small team of high caliber people, a center of IT excellence and leadership that attracted and retained the right people.[11]

Stage 2: Group-wide strategic positioning. The CIO's focus then turned to extending the core capabilities framework across all IT functions within CBA, including the business units, and began building Business Systems Thinking and Relationship Building skills. This required the effective management of IT across the group, including some 400–500 people in IT functions acquired from the merger with Colonial bank in addition to those that emerged in existing business units, or subsidiaries, to fill capability gaps.

Three cornerstone strategies were developed to achieve Reorientation and address the capabilities required by CBA to support its corporate strategy.

An IT&T Strategy was facilitated by Group Technology across each of the business units. All business unit heads were engaged to agree a consistent view of customer requirements in 3–5 years and defined the enterprise IT architecture,[12] with the supporting IT policies, processes and standards to guide the way systems were built. An IT sourcing strategy integrated much of the learning from the first three years of managing the IT agreements to present a staged plan of activities in preparation for contract renewal due to commence in 2005/6. The IT management model provided a framework for decision-making and *processes* for managing IT across the Bank.

Under the IT management model, the central IT group was responsible for decisions on strategy, architecture and policy as well as recommendations related to all service elements for core infrastructure. Business units IT functions were made responsible for consolidating their business systems functionality requirements, implementation planning, design, vendor selection and delivery management of IT-based business projects.

At this stage the CIO was reporting into one of the business unit heads.[13] Managing IT across the group from within one of the business units was not without its challenges and in July 2002, the CIO was appointed as a direct report of the CEO.

By the second review conducted by the authors in August 2003, headcount had risen from 37 two years earlier to 116. In addition, Group Technology was being entrusted with the management of enterprise-wide systems, such as Group data warehouse and PeopleSoft ERP systems. This had rapidly added another 200 plus people to the team. CBA had a clearer business/IT vision, improved management of suppliers, and better the control through the new IT governance processes.

The review highlighted the influx of new IT resources into Group Technology, which were noted as "capabilities by recruitment". It identified that there was yet to be a framework embedded in the key HR processes of appraisal and targeted development for nurturing internal capabilities once inside the bank. The review also noted the need for broader educational processes across the business units linked to specific business/IT problems as they arise. While the business unit IT functions were aware of the framework, how the capabilities could be harnessed to resolve problems was less clear.

Stage 3: IT-based business transformation. In September 2003, the CEO decided to accelerate the business change and announced a US$1.2bn cultural transformation program over $2\frac{1}{2}$ years, called "Which new Bank" (WnB).[14] The program focused on "excelling in customer service through engaged people who are supported by simple processes". A coordinated set of some 120 projects were assembled which incorporated over US$500m IT investment.

Delivery of so many business projects required CBA to rapidly extend its internal capabilities of Business Systems Thinking, project management and change management in the business units. These business projects would deliver major components of the enterprise architecture by integrating all of the different channels (e.g. branch, call center, and internet), providing a consistent Service Oriented Architecture access to back-end systems, and providing role-based access to applications:

> "Getting the architecture capabilities and through that process putting in place an IT strategy that people can buy into and start building towards was a really important breakthrough. That really helped the articulation of what, in an IT sense' needed to happen in order to get the "Which new Bank' process going" – Group CIO

The cornerstone of WNB was a new customer management platform, CommSee,[15] to provide consistent customer information and processes to customer-facing staff in any location. Faced with an ambitious timetable[16] and the need to have the CommSee platform in place to support the implementation of other WnB components, the CEO made the decision to leverage the capabilities from CBA's innovative online stockbroking subsidiary, Commonwealth Securities. This internal team consisted of approximately 60 people and had a track record of rapid delivery using a combination of decoupling projects into independent components, prototyping, and iterative development. With the strong support of the CEO, the CommSee team rapidly demonstrated its capability in a pilot in Tasmania by February 2004 and scaled up its team to over 500 IT staff by mid-2004, culminating in approximately 800 IT staff by the end of the project.

The central IT team moved to strengthen its governance role around IT project delivery. This included IT portfolio, program and project management. Portfolio management looked at all the asset classes of IT, trying to understand how collectively they added value to the organization but also understanding the individual capability of those asset classes to contribute. The program office coordinated IT projects across the Bank to defined appropriate project standards.

> "We created a project office in Group Technology under the portfolio management area as well... So we have to define end to end how any project with an IT&T component should be managed in the Bank and how that must interface with what we do from an enterprise perspective when it comes to project management." – Executive manager

Our final assessment in January 2005 highlighted the massive dual task of managing US$1bn. per annum IT expenditure and an additional US$500m expenditure on the WnB program over $2\frac{1}{2}$ years. The Service Delivery function was stable, with its focus moving to the implementation of the new sourcing strategy. The role of Group Technology had been expanded to consolidate demand, and deliver some of the key infrastructure projects. The architecture planning team had ensured a set of enterprise-wide architectures, policies and standards to ensure project alignment to the IT&T blueprint. The WnB program had delivered the opportunity to introduce new IT capabilities, which in turn created new business opportunities.

> "If you line up [all of the priorities of the executive committee] with what's actually happening.. you make this huge correlation between the priorities of the IT strategy of 18 months ago and what's actually happening" – BM05

The external review, however, highlighted the need for more internal capabilities to focus on a revised sourcing strategy to reflect the changing market and internal arrangements. This presented new challenges to extend the internal capabilities to design and integrate solutions delivered from multiple internal and external parties:

> "There is a need for a layer that can put all that together, recognizing that we've probably got two or three commercial contracts in place to support [an] outcome. That's the kind of integration that needs to bring all that to life in a way that delivers the business outcome we need" – Service Delivery Executive

By August 2005, the CEO was able to announce that the WnB program was making significant progress. He then retired from CBA. By the end of the year a new CEO had been appointed and the CIO had also changed. The new CIO observed that the technology teams had a great deal to be proud of and his belief that the bank had effective investment in technology and also proven their capability to deliver. He announced a new business unit-led structure with all IT functions reporting to the central IT group, renamed, Enterprise Services. This structure focused on its alignment to business units, with the primary focus on each of the business unit CIOs and business systems thinking capabilities. A new set of challenges faced the new CIO as he focused on "getting the best value from technology investments by leveraging the capabilities and standardizing our technology offerings".

CBA summary. In Table 15.3 we provide a summary of how CBA built core IS capabilities in a way that matured its ability to manage IT for increasingly strategic business purposes. Referring to Figures 15.2 and 15.3, CBA should have been at the Reorganization stage in 1997. By 2001 it had gained limited benefits, mainly cost reduction, from large-scale outsourcing, but experienced rising problems on a range of fronts. By 2001 CBA needed to start delivering on major IT-enabled business improvements, without having evolved properly even through the Delivery stage (see Figures 15.2 and 15.3). Table 15.3 indicates the process of "catch-up" that went into operation to evolve the IT organization through the three phases, and also address new business

Table 15.3   Building Capabilities – CBA

Stage of growth	Characteristics
Starting Point 1997–2000	• Business focus on cost and service levels. • Single-source 10-year joint-equity IS outsourcing deal, later separated telecoms. • Team of 35 people, Group Technology, retained to oversee the contract. • CIO as 'functional head'. • Despite early success, poor relationships between and within business units, IT and vendors – dominated by CM capability. • new CIO adopts CISC framework.
Delivery 2001–23	• Processes in place to manage the vendors and business IT investment. • *Resources* added – 'capabilities-by-appointment'. • Central IT roles and responsibilities established around each capability area. • Espouses a high performance *culture*.
Reorientation 2002–5	• Capabilities defined to extend the framework to emerging business unit IT functions. • Focus on BST, RB and CF, reorienting capabilities within business units. • Three strategies agreed: IT architecture, IT management and Sourcing. • Supporting IT governance *processes* agreed across the group to build towards a consistent outcome (enterprise architecture). • CIO appointed to report to CEO in a 'Federal' IT model. • 117 people in central IT with over 600 people in enterprise services and business unit IT functions.
Reorganization 2003–7	• WnB business transformation announced. • Focus on BST, project management and change management. • Capabilities acquired from subsidiary for CommSee (60 grown to 800). • Multiple other internal delivery teams and sourcing from external vendors. • Central IT team focuses on project governance, managing suppliers and IT infrastructure. • CIO integrated into the business Executive Team, all IT reports to CIO, over 1,700 people. • Positioned to leverage existing relationships and renegotiate relationships into the future. EDS contract renegotiated by 2006.

challenges as they arose. A combination of culture, process and structure mechanisms were used creatively and flexibly to facilitate this evolution (Table 15.3).

The Commonwealth Bank's implementation of the core IS capabilities framework represented an evolution, providing good results for managing the vendor to the necessary service levels, and ensuring delivery in accordance with the IT strategy. Distributing different capabilities across IT functions presented governance challenges, yet provided a coherent framework to establish an agreed business and IT vision. The main challenges experienced by CBA were the integration of different capabilities required to solve to an individual problem (rather than assigning to a functional group with certain capabilities) and the integration of IS capabilities with the organizational core capabilities of project management and change management. Indeed, an argument was made that components of these business capabilities around the delivery of IT-based business projects are IS specific and should be formally retained as part of then Bank's internal IT team. Finally, we observed capabilities at CBA continuing to evolve into high-order capabilities, such as that of designing and integrating multiple internal and external functions to deliver IT-based business outcomes.

Case Study 2: DuPont – building capabilities to re-position IT within the organization

History and context: In 1997, DuPont signed a series of long-term contracts, worth US$4 billion, with CSC and Accenture (then Andersen Consulting). By 2002, 80% of its IT spending (total: $600 million a year) and 75% (3,000) of its IT staff had been transferred to its alliance partners. CSC was responsible for shared infrastructure worldwide, and corporate, regional and business specific applications, while Accenture managed the Chemical division's business enterprise applications. DuPont initially retained 100 (later reduced to 60), central staff to manage the contracts, and over 1,000 distributed technical and business people to provide IT leadership and management in the business units, together with process control computing in manufacturing, and R&D computing.

For new project work, DuPont retained the right to source from anywhere as well as from one or both sitting suppliers. As one example, by the late 1990s DuPont had identified a new $400 million worldwide SAP/Y2K project. One supplier brought 400 SAP people on to the project. To supplement the other supplier's SAP skills, DuPont transferred 300 people from the divisions over to the supplier. The supplier then bore the costs of their SAP training. DuPont also adopted a balanced scorecard approach for benchmarking the health of its IT service silos. By 2001, DuPont had reduced its 90% fixed IT costs to 50% fixed, was getting quicker injections of skills from suppliers than it had before outsourcing, was achieving increases in some service speeds and flexibility, was probably achieving modest cost reductions on a pro rata basis (though the overall IT budget actually increased due to greater demand), and had given a range of its ex-employees real career development opportunities. However, even by 1999, it was questioning whether it had given away too much IT technical and management expertise.

Stage 1: Rethinking IT organization and core capabilities. By this date, the CIO headed two organizational units – Global Services and Alliance Operations. Global Services had 70 people providing leadership of strategic planning, architecture, security, emerging technologies, and enterprise-wide projects. Oversight of regional and specialized services was delegated to 350 people across five regions responsible for country-specific IT architecture and administration and management of regional suppliers. Global Services also had a Business Unit Support group made up of 500 employees across 20 divisions. These looked after manufacturing process and production controls, business-specific applications, and IT for central R&D. Alliance Operations consisted of 47 people who managed business unit demand for supplier services, monitored supplier service delivery, developed SLA metrics and achieved continuous performance improvement. Of the 47, 10 dealt with Infrastructure, including oversight of the CSC deal and service responsibility for desktop, telecom, midrange and mainframe. Another five dealt with Applications, including oversight of Accenture/CSC and liaison with four business divisions. Three employees looked after contract management, including performance scorecards and contract dispute resolution. A further 20 people managed IT Finance, including invoices, charges to business units, audit billing accuracy and timeliness.

While this seemed sufficient, by early 1999 DuPont began to question whether its internal capabilities were strong enough. IT were often excluded from critical business discussions and decisions; succession planning for IT leaders and core staff needed attention; employees were looking for guidance on changing skills and career paths. About this time DuPont adopted the Feeny-Willcocks framework to begin formalizing competencies, job families, personal development opportunities, and career paths. DuPont defined Relationship Building, Leadership, Contract Facilitation, Informed Buying and Making Technology Work as "general competencies", and pointed to three career paths: (1) Business and IT Vision (needing Business Systems Thinking) (2) Design of IT Architecture (requiring Architecture Planning) and (3) Delivery of IT Services (including Vendor Development and Contract Monitoring). In December 2000, DuPont launched an intranet-accessible career management site, enabling employees to identify required competencies – business, interpersonal and technical – for each of its DuPont's 55 existing and prospective IT roles.

Our own analysis of DuPont's retained IS capabilities took place in July 2001. The overall finding of weaknesses in retained core capability some four years into a large-scale outsourcing arrangement was not, in fact, untypical of what we have found elsewhere.[7] On Business and IT Vision, we found the following. With limited local resources, business unit IS Leaders tended to be driven to operate also in Relationship Building and Contract Facilitation modes. The focus on service delivery, automation and fire-fighting diluted focus on strategy and value creation. Business unit executives themselves commonly positioned IT as an agent of cost reduction, rather than of business value creation. Business Systems Thinking was being squeezed out of the IT frame. Suppliers were not filling the gap in stimulating innovation for business value.

On IT Service Delivery, we saw the Informed Buying and Vendor Development roles needing considerable enhancement. Many Business Unit IT leaders needed to move from fire-fighting to a more strategic focus. Making Technology Work was often underpowered, given the IT demands and the variable strengths of the suppliers operating in different parts of DuPont. Neglect of the Vendor Development capability contributed to a number of adverse supplier behaviors and practices. The type of relationship had not moved on, and this was inhibiting DuPont's ability to tap into the suppliers' intellectual capital. Weakness in Informed Buying limited sourcing vision, intra-DuPont learning, and future sourcing flexibility. As a result, the issue of how to anticipate and cope with sourcing changes over the next four to ten years was not being addressed sufficiently.

On Designing IT Architecture, DuPont's position on this capability fitted fairly well with our findings elsewhere. DuPont had already noted its weaknesses here and was rebuilding this capability. It needed to develop career paths and more staff for this core area. One weakness of our own framework, identified in work in 2001 on building e-business infrastructure, is that technical architecture needs to be more closely aligned with business strategy. Our conclusion in our 2001 study was that infrastructure and architecture planning were now Boardroom issues because the technology platform now influenced greatly what was and was not possible as a business (Willcocks and Sauer, 2001). The implication for DuPont was to ensure that architecture planning became closely co-located with business planning. Here we recommended development of career paths for this core retained capability, with the possible quick hiring of experienced staff to fill the vital gap.

On a regional basis, we found Asia Pacific quite well adapted and leveraging the core IS capabilities concept. Europe and South America had not yet tailored the capabilities to their environments and resource levels. Some core IS capabilities definitely needed enhancement in terms of making local resources available. In particular, Contract Facilitation, Making Technology Work, Business Systems Thinking and Contract Monitoring capabilities were lacking. In terms of DuPont's overall objectives, we felt it could only move from cost reduction to business value if business executives were educated into the transformational possibilities of IT. Increased delivery speed needed more in-house project management capability and a rapid application development approach, risk-reward contracts with suppliers, a change

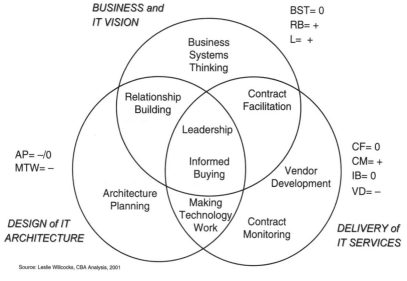

Figure 15.4 DuPont 2001: Assessment

in the bureaucratic process by which work was contracted for and assigned, Architecture Planning linked to business vision, and strengthened Making Technology Work and Contract Facilitation capabilities in order to leverage the operational service. Innovation could be delivered through enhanced Business Systems Thinking, Informed Buying and Vendor Development capabilities to unlock supplier potential and greater internal and external networking. To facilitate these moves, the core IS capabilities framework was correctly positioned for career development, but needed to be further imbedded in human resource processes, including selection, appraisal and reward systems.

Stage 2: Moving through delivery, reorientation and reorganization. By early 2003, the competency modelling and career development self-service efforts had generated several positive results. Eighty percent of staff accessed the site in 2002 and 30% created career plans. Employees and managers focused on competencies rather than administrative tasks. By 2003, the company was able to fill 90% of key IT Leadership positions internally, despite the fact that it had reduced the pool of potential successors from 4,000 to 1,200 as a result of outsourcing. The projected short-fall of in-demand employees was reduced from 30 in 1999 to two in 2004. The strength of emerging IT leaders was recognized by business management, with 90% of business unit CIOs reporting to a business unit VP/General Manager as opposed to 50% previously. Even more importantly, DuPont felt that it had wrested back control of its IT destiny and put itself in a much better position to leverage its relationships with suppliers, and renegotiate sourcing arrangements into the future, as it began to do from 2003 onward.

DuPont summary. As at CBA, in 1997 DuPont considered that it had sufficient resources to manage its outsourcing arrangements. But, experiencing problems, from 1999 it was looking to rebuild its internal capability, fol-

Table 15.4 Building Capabilities – DuPont

Stage of growth	Characteristics
Starting Point 1997–9	• Business focus on reduction of overhead costs and increased capital efficiency; including IS outsourcing. • Series of 10-year IS outsourcing contracts for infrastructure and applications. • CIO managed two functional areas – alliance operations (60 people) to oversee the contract and global operations (over 1,000 people) within business units. • Capabilities established in CF and CM: continuous service level improvements. • Focus on service delivery, automation and 'firefighting' diminished value creation. • CIO adopts CC framework as a basis for staff development and career succession.
Delivery 2000–3	• *Culture and Process*: formal competencies, job families and personal development plans. • *Culture and Process*: defined career paths: Business and IT vision, design of IT architecture and delivery of IT services. • Reduced 'firefighting' with vendor by enhancing CF, RB and MTW. • *Structure*: Bolstered senior technical and architecture planning capability to control 'IT destiny'.
Reorientation 2001–4	• *Culture*: Strengthened BST and Leadership – focus on leadership and business systems capability to manage IT strategically. • *Culture*: Innovation to be delivered through enhanced business systems thinking, informed buying and vendor development capabilities. • Closely aligned architecture planning with business planning. • Built IB capabilities for future contract renewal.
Reorganization 2002–6	• *Structure*: 90% of business unit CIO's reporting to VP/ General manager. • Strong local alliance management teams. • *Process*: Focus on core IS capabilities model applied globally. • *Process*: Variable take-up in different global regions – good in Asia-Pac, weaker in Europe/ South Americas – ed to provision of further local resources in BST, CF and CM. • Positioned to leverage existing relationships and renegotiate outsourcing deals and relationships into the future.

lowing the core IS capabilities model. In 2001 we found a number of cultural change initiatives, coupled with processes were operating to build such capabilities over several years, but more pro-active management interventions were needed. In practice, like CBA, DuPont should have been at the Reorganization stage in 1997, but by 2000 had to revisit all three stages in order to get up to speed on managing business changes from 2000–6 and trying to get much much more out of its existing and renegotiated outsourcing deals (see Table 15.4).

By 2001, after four years of outsourcing, and like CBA, they found that they had to revisit and strengthen their Delivery focus with CF, MTW and RB skills, and reduce the firefighting done by IT managers in the business units. In fact DuPont's adoption (in 2000) of the core IS capabilities framework led to development programs being offered to IT employees, encouraging them to Reorient themselves and so eventually the IT function in order to reposition IT as more strategic and value creating for the business units. This led to the business units and IT Group shifting their focus Reorientation – that is, developing the more strategic capabilities, including Architecture Planning, Business Systems Thinking, Leadership, Informed Buying and Vendor Development. Between 2001 and 2006 DuPont also moved itself forward to be in a stronger position to renegotiate its outsourcing agreements as they came up for renewal. Having addressed Reorganization during 2002–6, DuPont found it could then better manage its re-negotiated outsourcing arrangements while keeping control of its IT destiny and ensuring IT aligned with strategic business purpose.

Case Study 3: State Super Financial Services (SSFS) – building capabilities to create a new IT platform and exploit the outsourcing market

History and context. SSFS Australia Limited's strategic plan during 2002–5 identified three core competencies: attraction, conversion and retention of clients. It established key mission success indicators needed to achieve its goal of becoming "one of Australia's leading financial planning and funds management organisations" (in-house strategy document).

Stage 1: Redefining and delivering on IT strategy. In 2000, the IT function was staffed by 17 people including the CIO, a developer, and 15 support staff. Historically, IT had provided a purely support role for IT infrastructure and externally-sourced business applications. From 2000, IT developed an enabling capability as the company sought to gain competitive advantage from its IT investment. By 2002, a number of IT issues had been identified. SSFS had a strength in its unique in-house financial planning and marketing software. However, there was under-utilization of IT in SSFS's work processes, and the threat of loss of clients due to an inability to readily match competitors' in the provision of e-commerce capabilities.

The 2002 IT action plan consisted of three broad activities:

1. exploit competitive advantage of the in-house developed software
2. achieve productivity improvements through business process automation by integrating disparate IT systems, and
3. deliver IT services to meet existing and future business needs.

An analysis of the external IT environment found four major forces to which SSFS needed to respond. First, there was an increasing focus on integration of existing IT services. This required a shift in emphasis from development to systems integration. It required sourcing appropriate skills sets and buying/building the appropriate IT infrastructure. Second, there was a greater move to outsourcing. SSFS identified a need to selectively source more external IT services once it had identified core in-house capabilities and ways of benchmarking service provision. Third, SSFS assigned itself a watching brief on the evolution of web services for information exchange, believing this to be two to three years away from commercial adoption. Lastly, business units were looking outside the company for the information sharing vital to value creation. Therefore, SSFS needed to extend IT service delivery outside the organization, with 24 ¥ 7 availability. This implied expanding the skills in relationship management and negotiation with business partners, and the need to increase the collaboration between employees with skills sets in legacy systems and those operating with newer technologies.

Technically, the 2002 IT strategy involved integration of the company website, its virtual private network, its financial planning, registry and customer relationship management (CRM) systems, together with a Business-to-business (B2B) capability through its Pillar and Master Custodian/Fund Manager software and systems. SSFS intended to develop in-house any system/software that gave it competitive advantage, but eventually to outsource the rest. While IT network and service availability compared favorably against competitors, there was a noticeable gap in e-commerce offerings. By 2003 much progress had been made on the new security, systems and network architectures, and work on the information architecture had commenced.

On infrastructure, a number of weaknesses needed to be addressed. The network contained numerous single points of failure. A single failure could result in all central IT services being unavailable to a regional office. Disparate servers and business applications made information storage fragmented across a large number of servers. The data back-up strategy was complex and time-consuming, while disaster recovery was complicated. The centralized management of systems and networks was limited. All these problems would only be exacerbated by the future planned growth of the company. The new proposed infrastructure was to be scalable and modular, capable of supporting 24 × 7 applications, provide levels of redundancy, and improve back-up, recovery and disaster recovery. The infrastructure program of work carried out from 2003–5 involved enterprise database consolidation, disaster recovery upgrade, replacement of the Unix operating system on which Registry and CRM applications ran, a move to centralized storage and back-up, upgrading from Windows NT to Windows 2000, and improvement of the messaging infrastructure.

On business applications, 2002–5 saw the in-house upgrading of Financial Planning systems. The Registry system was a third-party package with limited functionality that, as a core system, needed in-house work to achieve integration with other applications. The core customer relationship management (CRM) system was a third party package not being further supported by the supplier, was costly, and needed to be replaced. In effect, 2003–5 saw 12 business application programs of work operationalized to remedy the situation.

Stage 2: Reorientating IT organization and capabilities. SSFS, under the CIO's advice, adopted a centralized IT organization structure. This was because of the small size of the company and the fact that much of the business structure itself was centralized. This allowed close scrutiny and control of IT costs, and also facilitated the task of building an IT infrastructure that adhered to a single set of architectures. By 2003, the CIO reported directly to the SSFS Managing Director. The CIO had under him four departments: Application Development had nine staff, IT Systems Network eight, Technology Architecture two and Project Office two. This structure, evolved in the course of 2002–3, represented a significant shift from the inherited situation of 2000, and was designed to facilitate the 2003–5 programs of IT work.

In its forward strategy, SSFS had also explicitly adopted the Feeny-Willcocks core IS capabilities framework. A piece of thinking in 2002 saw SSFS IT competencies classified into:

1. Nine core IS capabilities – enabling the company to exploit IT successfully, however the IT services were provided (Feeny-Willcocks framework)
2. Strategic IT services – supporting business differentiation and competitive advantage
3. Tactical IT services – supporting the provision of business services necessary for ongoing operations.

Both (1) and (2), as "core", would be internally sourced. In the case of (2), the IT function would provide development and support for two applications (MTW capability). The PSP/Profile systems clearly differentiated the SSFS provision of financial planning advice from that of competitors. Meanwhile, SPIRS (superannuation payments information reporting systems) gave SSFS competitive advantage through the information and analysis of information provided under agreements with clients. This enabled the company to manage a more targeted and effective marketing effort.

Tactical IT services, on the other hand, would be reviewed regularly, externally benchmarked, and provided through the most cost-effective means possible. This covered all non-core work in environment management, systems and network management, IT help desk, application support, project management, and applications development. In 2002, SSFS already used external suppliers for a range of IT services, including web-site hosting and management, security assessment, infrastructure design, web-site development, and graphical design. The updated strategy pointed to even greater outsourcing of non-core IT services.

In May 2000, the in-house core IS capabilities were as shown in Figure 15.5. Remembering the relatively small size of SSFS and the support role of IT at that time, the CIO's assessment was that, on the business face, SSFS were "doing okay." Having said that, the CIO was responsible for both Leadership and Business Systems Thinking, and there was no Relationship Building capability. Given the plans by 2002, all three capabilities would need significant bolstering if progress was to be made. The gaps on Architecture Planning and Making Technology Work were all too obvious, with a legacy of 15 IT support staff and only one developer in-house. Implementation of the IT strategy, on SSFS's own evidence, needed significantly more capability in these areas. Likewise, in May 2000, SSFS was not at all set up to manage external IT supply, with, in fact, the CIO carrying out the Informed Buying role, limited Contract Facilitation competence, and very little Contract Monitoring and Vendor Development capability.

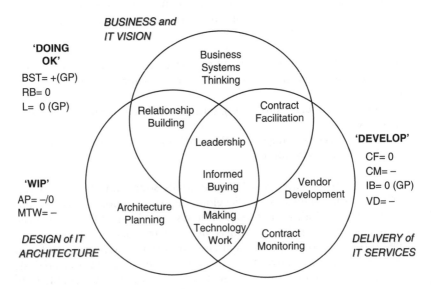

Figure 15.5 SSFS May 2000: Initial Assessment

Stage 3: Restructuring IT. Not surprisingly, the 2002/3 IT strategy took explicit note of these gaps and presented a modified structure that had been developing over the previous 18 months, and which embodied the core IS capabilities more obviously. The Systems and Networks team was to be the first "port of call" for any business users with IT issues. It also planned, selected and deployed IT infrastructure (along with the Technology and Architecture team). It also (with the Applications Development team) provided support specific to any key application utilized. This embodied aspects of the Technology Fixing, Relationship Building and Contract Facilitation roles from the Feeny-Willcocks framework.

The Applications Development team was made responsible for developing applications in-house, selecting applications packages supplied by suppliers, and second-level application support. This covered the Making Technology Work and Contract Facilitation roles. The Technology Architecture team was made custodian of the technical architecture. It was responsible for the review and approval of all new technology within the company, thus covering the Feeny-Willcocks's Architecture Planning role. In 2003 SSFS also recruited a new Project Office team to work in the IT function, reflecting the large number of new IT projects (see also the CBA experience). The CIO continued to carry out the Leadership, Informed Buying and Vendor Development roles. Operational contract monitoring was pushed into the Systems and Network and Project Office teams.

SSFS summary. SSFS presents a case where the core IS capabilities model is implemented *prior* to large-scale outsourcing, to improve internal delivery capability and business relationships while positioning the organization to take advantage of the external services market. Whilst resources were not increased substantially, there is a restructuring of capabilities and a repositioning of IT within the business. By 2000 IT was recognized as vital to business strategic advantage. The IT work needed to build the IT applications and infrastructure began then and continued through to 2006 (see Table 15.5). By 2002, with a clearer idea of IT strategy, the CIO embarked on reorientating the IT organization and its capabilities to match the IT strategy. The CIO used restructuring to move the IT function through Delivery and Reorientation, thus pushing it closer to the business, while positioning it for Reorganization and large scale outsourcing at a later stage.

From 2000, SSFS developed an enabling IT capability as the company sought to gain competitive advantage from its investment in IT. SSFS could be seen, in its forward planning, to move from enhancing its Delivery capability, to Reorientating its IT function in order to be much more business and strategy focused. The end point of the plan was to Reorientate and Reorganize from a traditional IT function to one based on the core IS capabilities model, able to source extensively and effectively from the external IT service market while aligning IT usage much more closely with the business's strategic imperatives. But as a medium-sized enterprise with financial

Table 15.5   Building Capabilities – SSFS

Stage of growth	Characteristics
Starting Point 2000	• In-house IT function supporting IT infrastructure & externally-sourced business systems. • 15 IT staff, centralized as per the business structure. • Under-utilization of IT in SFSS work practices. • CIO adopts the CC framework to enable IT competitive advantage.
Delivery 2000–5	• New IT strategy developed, which identifies the need for the nine core IS capabilities, the need for greater business and strategic focus, and separates 'strategic' and 'tactical' IT. • Large infrastructure program underway, delivering to a single set of architectures – *Process* focus on starting to train/build MTW, RB and CF capability. Need for AP capability identified. • 12 business applications programs initiated, performing upgrades and integration in-house – *Process* focus on MTW and CF. • 'Buy-in' of IT services on a resource basis. Ad hoc outsourcing.
Reorientation 2002–4	• *Structure* – restructure around four teams: systems and networks, applications development, technology architecture, and project office. • CIO reports directly to MD. • *Culture*: Small team defined with CIO performing key roles – Leadership and Business Systems Thinking. • Strengthen Relationship Building capability further. • Greater outsourcing of 'tactical' IT services – developed IB role further by recruitment.
Reorganization 2002–6	• Focus on coping with business growth. • Reinforce capability to manage external suppliers to rebuild the IT infrastructure and deliver 'tactical' IT services. • Enhanced IT infrastructure put in place (2005) (scalability, modularity and 24 × 7 operation). • 'Strategic' applications' put in place (2003–6) as a source of competitive differentiation.

constraints and limited human resources, SSFS had to be pragmatic and creative in how it developed and spread IS capabilities around legacy and new IT staff.

Adopting the core IS capabilities framework: the secrets of success

The core IS capabilities framework was developed to identify the enduring IS capabilities required to successfully exploit IT. Our three cases provide examples of organizations with different profiles and different challenges adopting all nine capabilities of the framework. What secrets of success emerge?

1. Three organizational systems are available for developing capabilities. The organizational mechanisms used to develop the capabilities differ in each case. Starting from different places, each organization has a different resource-base (in both number and mix) from which to develop IS capabilities. For those organizations requiring additional resources, we see executives recruiting, developing and/or acquiring from other parts of the organization. To transform the resources into IS capabilities we see in each case, to differing levels, executives implementing 1) *Processes* to define the governance, in particular the decision-rights across the organization, and how capabilities can be applied to solve individual problems; 2) *Culture*, which provides a powerful tool to focus the efforts and development of the IT function as well as repositioning the role of IT within the organization; and finally 3) *Structure*, along with supporting roles and responsibilities, that enable focusing these resources to group specific capabilities and address specific organizational challenges. In practice all three levers were used by the three organizations, though each chose and illustrates different starting points, emphases, and reliances (see Figure 15.6).

CBA adopted a more ***process-led*** approach, first focusing on the control of the vendors and the business IT investment, which was then extended to business units around business systems capabilities. Initially, resources were appointed from outside the organization to strengthen the central

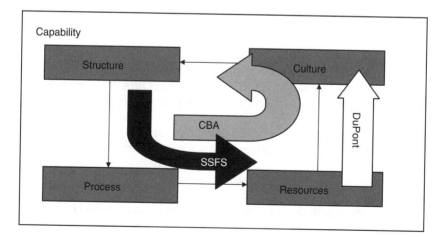

Framework Source: Bitar and Hafsi, 2007

Figure 15.6   Organizational Systems for Building Capabilities

team's core IS capabilities. Later, resources were leveraged from mergers, or subsidiaries, before finally being centralized. Governance processes are put in place at each stage to define roles, responsibilities and decision rights.

In **DuPont**, we see a voluntaristic *culture-led* approach with formalized competencies, job families and personal development plans to evolve the capabilities. Some additional resources were acquired to bolster technical and architecture planning skills. The establishment of three career paths oriented around the three "faces" of the Core IS Capabilities framework provided a creative way of ensuring capabilities were developed on an ongoing basis.

In **SSFS**, we see a *structure-led* approach to developing capabilities – the implementation of a new structure as a new IT infrastructure was built and the organizations started to take advantage of the sourcing market. As the capabilities emerged, in concert with new IS capabilities (infrastructure and business applications), new processes were implemented (e.g. regular review of non-core services), and the need for strengthening of specific capabilities emerged (e.g. stronger informed buying capability in 2005, greater RB capability from 2003).

2. When to use the process-led approach

Where the CIO does not have direct control of all IT resources in the organization, then a process-led approach provides a useful starting point. New governance mechanisms are required to ensure vendors are managed effectively, demand is coordinated and IT investment is fully leveraged. This can then be followed by cultural and structural approaches – as we saw in the CBA case where the structure was implemented across all of IT in the final stage.

3. When to choose a culture-led approach

Where sufficient resources are available but there needs to be orientation towards developing the individual capabilities, a culture-led approach may be preferable. As we see in DuPont, culture can be used to focus the existing resources and provide career progression. Later as the culture changes, new processes and structure may be implemented, such as the business unit IT managers reporting to the business unit VP/general managers.

4. When the structure-led approach is powerful

Where the CIO does have direct control of resources across the organization, controls both the structure and career progression of the IT resources, consideration must be made whether there are the sufficient skills in the right places across the organization to fill each of the nine capabilities. Where there are not the necessary resources, a *structure-led* approach is powerful, as we saw in the SSFS case – to establish new positions, reallocate resources and recruit new skills. Within the context of the structure-led change, process and culture approaches were also used as the need arose.

5. How to prioritize the development of core IS capabilities.

In each case, we see the organization start at a different stage in capability development, and adopt the core IS capabilities framework for different business objectives. But behind the cases we can discern a common pattern and timing to the building and usage of specific capabilities (see Figure 15.7).

In the first stage – Delivery – organizations need to focus on Contract Facilitation, Making Technology Work and Architecture Planning. The CIO, as Leader, will have a strong technical and service track record. These capabilities ensure effective delivery of services in accordance with the contract, and that "firefighting" does not impede the development of the longer-term capabilities. At the same time Architecture Planning ensures the development of a coherent blue print for the present and future technical platform. In the SSFS case we see these capabilities being developed in order to take advantage of the sourcing market to rebuild its infrastructure and delivery of "tactical" services. At this stage the CIO will be focusing on building the reality of technical and service competence, while ensuring that business managers gain a correct perception of improving IT performance.

With the Delivery phase accomplished and providing a reliable platform, a Reorientation phase will see the business units needing to become more pro-active in leveraging IT strategically for business purpose while the IT

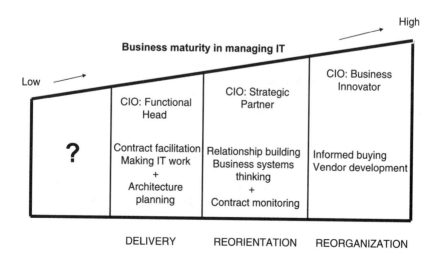

Figure 15.7   Evolving Core IS Capabilities

staff need to become more business-focused. To accomplish this objective, priority will be given to developing Business Systems Thinking and Relationship Building capabilities, while the CIO will be more focused on, and need the skills for, working with senior executives and the Board. At this stage, we often see the CIO repositioned as a direct report to the CEO. Reorientation is a crucial phase. Once an organization has the right IT and business capabilities in place and orientated towards leveraging IT strategically for business purpose, then effective IT-enabled business transformation (see CBA and DuPont cases) becomes feasible. But only providing the business has also developed and can apply core organizational capabilities in program, project and change management (even if these are first developed within the IT function).

With Delivery and Reorientation accomplished, the organization can now embark on Reorganization. With IT and business strategy closely aligned, and business managers mature in their ability to fulfil their roles in leveraging IT for strategic purpose, many IT responsibilities can be devolved to the business units (see DuPont). Meanwhile the IT function can complete its move to a high performing, core capabilities model by focusing on strengthening considerably its Contract Monitoring, Informed Buying and Vendor Development capabilities. This allows it to leverage the external services market more extensively and on a more long-term, collaborative basis. The CIO could well assume the role of business innovator at Board level, able to focus on how IT can be used for business innovation and strategic business purpose.

6. How and when to use the external services market

The evolution of core IS capabilities shown in Figure 15.7 has strong implications for how to mitigate the risks inherent in using the external IT services market. At the Delivery stage the IT function will not be good at managing outsourcing; and its main priority should be building up internal technical and service capability. Where external resources are needed, they should be contracted for on a "buy-in" basis, whereby the organization pays for external resources that remain under internal management control. To assist this approach, typically some Contract Monitoring capability is needed.

At the Reorientation phase selective outsourcing – typically 15–35% of the IT budget's handed over to third party service provider management becomes a low risk option. There is an IT strategy in place, technical service is understood and being measured, and low value IT work can be passed on so that new development and work of higher business value can be prioritized by the internal IT workforce. However, apposite Informed Buying must be built to match the degree of outsourcing to be undertaken.

In our experience large-scale outsourcing is highly risky unless an organization has moved its IT function and its business management practices well into the Reorganization phase. Thus both CBA and DuPont only fully came to terms with their capability problems some three years into their respective large-scale outsourcing deals. They then had to play catch-up – implementing core IS capabilities that really needed to have been in place before contract signing.

7. The key role of creative and flexible management

Managers operate in conditions of uncertainty, complexity, dynamic contexts and ever changing business requirements. In such circumstances rational planning can only get you so far. But how do you respond to short-term crises and needs while preserving future business direction and differentiation? In our research we found managers able to grab diagnostic tools and apply them to solve specific problems in distinctive contexts, while preserving the future IT platform and how it could be leveraged for business advantage. Senior managers demonstrated such creativity and flexibility in developing core IS capabilities in CBA, DuPont and SSFS. In terms of Figure 15.6, they all started at different points, but creatively went about pushing their IS capabilities forward, within the resource constraints pertaining, dealing with urgent issues, while always having in mind the end point of the evolutionary process. Such characteristics helped them play and deliver on the vital game of "catch-up", and endorse why applying the core IS capabilities approach will continue to be perennially powerful in contemporary organizations.

Notes

1 Cullen *et al.* (2008) identified 25 possible goals organizations pursue with outsourcing; typically they choose between three and seven major goals.

2 Since then over 35 organizations across the globe have used this framework, and its extensions, to build their internal IS capabilities. A version of the framework developed to cover also business process outsourcing appears in Willcocks, L. and Lacity, M. (2006) *Global Sourcing of Business and IT Services*, Palgrave, London.

3 The importance of such capabilities is established in the resource-based view of the firm (RBV), which argues that firm performance depends on the organization's ability to acquire, deploy and maintain a set of advantageous "resources" (or "assets"); see, for example Penrose E. (1995) *The Theory of the Growth of the Firm*, third edition, Oxford University Press, Oxford. Extending RBV, the capability-based perspective focuses on intangible resources, suggesting that a firm is a learning organization that builds and deploys assets, capabilities and skills in order to achieve strategic goals – popularized through Prahalad, C.K. & Hamel, G. (1990) The Core Competence of the Corporation. *Harvard Business Review.*

4 See Willcocks, L. and Feeny, D. (2006) Implementing Core IS Capabilities at DuPont. *Information Systems Management Journal,* December. The BPO research can be pursued in Feeny, D., Willcocks, L. and Lacity, M. (2005) "Taking the Measure of Outsourcing Providers," *Sloan Management Review*, Vol. 46, 3, Spring, pp. 41–48. Also Hindle, J., Willcocks, L., Feeny, D. and Lacity, M. (2003) "Value-added Outsourcing at Lloyds and BAE Systems," *Knowledge Management Review*, Vol. 6, 4, pp. 28–31. Also Lacity, M., Willcocks, L. and Feeny, D. (2003) "Transforming a Back

Office Function: Lessons from BAE Systems' Enterprise Partnership," *MISQ Executive*, Vol. 2, 2, pp. 86–103.

5 Originally detailed in Feeny, D. "The Five Year Learning of Ten IT Directors". In Willcocks, L., Feeny, D. and Islei, G. (eds) (1997) *Managing IT As A Strategic Resource*. McGraw Hill, Maidenhead. It is further elaborated in Willcocks and Lacity (2006) *op. cit.*, p. 94

6 Adapted from Bitar and Hafsi (2007). "Strategizing through the capability lens: sources and outcomes of integration", *Management Decision* 45(3), pp. 180–192. Bitar and Hafsi formulated the three mechanisms from the range of academic sources abbreviated in the Table, and we have customized their work in order to locate it in the IS arena. We also draw on Grant, R. (1996) "Towards a knowledge-based theory of the firm". *Strategic Management Journal*, 17, pp. 109–122, and Peppard, J. and Ward, J. (2004) "Beyond strategic information systems: towards and IS capability". *Journal of Strategic Information Systems*, 13, pp. 167–194.

7 Baker-Self, T., Partridge, A., and Ghavimi, B. (2005) "TOP 1000 World Banks," in *The Banker*, p. 143.

8 Note: these are 2004 figures

9 The CBA case is based on over 50 interviews conducted from 2000, participating as the Bank implemented its capabilities, and the analysis of in-house and public documents. The DuPont case is based on 26 interviews conducted in August 2001 to discover how the framework was being utilized, the challenges it presented, and the outcomes of its use, and we have tracked progress since that time. The SSFS case is based on four interviews over the 2000–4 period and analysis of in-house documents relating to the function, its in-house capabilities, the progress of outsourcing and the development and success of the IT function. An earlier analysis of the DuPont case appears in Willcocks, L., and Feeny, D. (2006) Implementing Core IS Capabilities at DuPont. *Information Systems Management Journal*, December

10 Source: Russell Scrimshaw (2002) CBA Head of Technology, Operations & Procurement, "Strategic Considerations for IT outsourcing", Salomon Smith Barney, *The 2002 Australian Banking Conference.*

11 McKinnon, R. (2001) *Restructure of Group Technology*, CBA staff memorandum.

12 Similar to most financial services organizations, the Bank's systems had evolved separately for different products, channels (e.g. branch, call center, and internet), and business units – Define enterprise architecture – to include the IT-based capabilities (versus IS capabilities)

13 Technology Operations and Property/Procurement (TOP)

14 The CBA is one of Australia's most recognized brands, incorporating its "Which Bank?" slogan

15 Commonwealth Bank Services Excellence Every Day (CommSee)

16 Under the outsourcing arrangements, applications development was non-exclusive. Business units would generally define their requirements up-front, conduct an extensive product and vendor selection and negotiate a compatible contract with the existing agreements. For major projects, this often took over a year.

References

Baker-Self, T., Partridge, A. and Ghavini, B. (2005) "TOP 1000 World Banks," in: *The Banker*, p. 143.

Bitar and Hafsi (2007) "Strategizing through the capability lens: sources and outcomes of integration," *Management Decision* 45(3), pp. 180–192.

Cullen, S., Seddon, P. and Willcocks, L. (2008) ITO Success: A Multi-Dimensional, Contextual Perspective on Outsourcing Outcomes. Paper in *Proceedings of the Second Global Sourcing Conference,* Val d'Isere, France, March 10th–13th.

Feeny, D. (1997) "The Five Year Learning of Ten IT Directors," in Willcocks, L., Feeny, D. and Islei, G. (eds) *Managing IT As A Strategic Resource.* Maidenhead: McGraw Hill.

Feeny, D. and Willcocks, L. (1998) "Core IS Capabilities For Exploiting Information Technology," *Sloan Management Review,* 39, 3, pp. 9–21.

Feeny, D., Willcocks, L. and Lacity, M. (2005) "Taking the Measure of Outsourcing Providers," Sloan Management Review, Vol. 46, 3, Spring, pp. 41–48.

Grant, R. (1996) "Towards a knowledge-based theory of the firm," *Strategic Management Journal,* 17, pp. 109–122.

Hamel, G. and Heene, A. (eds) (1994), *Competence-Based Competition,* Chichester: Wiley.

Hindle, J., Willcocks, L., Feeny, D. and Lacity, M. (2003) "Value-added Outsourcing at Lloyds and BAE Systems," Knowledge Management Review, Vol. 6, 4, pp. 28–31.

Lacity, M., Willcocks, L. and Cullen, S. (2009) *Global IT Outsourcing: 21st Century Search of Business Advantage,* Chichester: Wiley.

Lacity, M., Willcocks, L. and Feeny, D. (2003) "Transforming a Back office Function: Lessons from BAE Systems' Enterprise Partnership," MISQ Executive, Vol. 2, 2, pp. 86–103.

Penrose, E. (1995) *The Theory of the Growth of the Firm.* Third Edition, Oxford: Oxford University Press.

Peppard, J. and Ward, J. (2004) "Beyond strategic information systems: towards and IS capability," *Journal of Strategic Information Systems,* 13, pp. 167–194.

Prahalad, C.K. and Hamel, G. (1990) "The Core Competence of the Corporation," *Harvard Business Review.*

Quinn, J. (1992) "The Intelligent Enterprise: A New Paradigm," *Academy of Management Executive,* 6, 4, pp. 44–63.

Russell Scrimshaw (2002) CBA Head of Technology, Operations & Procurements, "Strategic Considerations for IT Outsourcing," Salomon Smith Barney, *The 2002 Australian Banking Conference.*

Willcocks, L. and Feeny, D. (2006) "Implementing Core IS Capabilities at DuPont," *Information Systems Management Journal,* Winter, pp. 49–56.

Willcocks, L., Feeny, D. and Islei, G. (eds) (1997) *Managing IT As a Strategic Resource.* Maidenhead: McGraw Hill.

Willcocks, L. and Lacity, M. (2006) *Global Sourcing of Business and IT Services.* London: Palgrave.

Willcocks, L. and Sauer, C. (2001) *Building The E-Business Infrastructure.* London: Business Intelligence.

Index